EDUCATION
IN THE
UNITED STATES

EDUCATION
IN THE
UNITED STATES

An Historical Perspective

Gerald L. Gutek
Loyola University

Prentice-Hall, Englewood Cliffs, New Jersey 07632

Library of Congress Cataloging-in-Publication Data

Gutek, Gerald Lee.
    Education in the United States.

    Includes bibliographies and index.
        1. Education   United States   History.
2. Educational sociology—United States—History.
I. Title.
LA205.G87   1986   370'.973   85-20991
ISBN 0-13-235680-5

Editorial/production supervision and
    interior design: Debbie Ford
Cover design: Ben Santora
Manufacturing buyer: Barbara Kelly Kittle

© 1986 by Prentice-Hall
A Division of Simon & Schuster, Inc.
Englewood Cliffs, New Jersey 07632

Printed in the United States of America

10   9   8   7   6   5   4   3   2   1

ISBN 0-13-235680-5 01

Prentice-Hall International (UK) Limited, *London*
Prentice-Hall of Australia Pty. Limited, *Sydney*
Prentice-Hall of Canada Inc., *Toronto*
Prentice-Hall Hispanoamericana, S.A., *Mexico*
Prentice-Hall of India Private Limited, *New Delhi*
Prentice-Hall of Japan, Inc., *Tokyo*
Prentice-Hall of Southeast Asia Pte. Ltd., *Singapore*
Editora Prentice-Hall do Brasil, Ltda., *Rio de Janeiro*
Whitehall Books Limited, *Wellington, New Zealand*

This book is dedicated to my grandparents, Joseph and Susan Gutek,
who as immigrants left the old world,
and to A. J. and Anna Novotney,
who helped to create a new world.

CONTENTS

PREFACE

Education in the United States: An Historical Perspective seeks to place the history of American education in it broad cultural, political, social, and economic contexts. Chapters one through three examine the transference of European educational ideas and styles to North America, where they were transformed by both the frontier environment and the impulses of revolutionary republican ideology. Chapters four through six describe the historical development of such basic American educational institutions, as the common school, high school, college and university. The remaining chapters—seven through fourteen—examine the evolution of American education during such crucial historical events as the Civil War and Reconstruction, the era of emergent industrialism, the progressive period, the economic depression of the 1930s and the post-World War II decades. The concluding chapters examine the 1960s, 1970s, and 1980s.

In writing the book, I have sought to relate American education to its significant political context. Special attention has been given to areas of interpretation that have been neglected in recent writing in American educational history. For example, the role of civic education is examined, particularly in the context of the ideology of the American Revolution. Comparisons of the American common school movement with contemporaneous efforts to create elementary school systems in Europe are made. In particular, I have sought to internationalize the treatment of the history of American education by examining the impact of world affairs on the shaping of American educational policies.

The book is a product of my teaching of the history of American education at Loyola University of Chicago for the past twenty-three years. I hope that it will be useful to students and teachers who wish to examine and explore our country's educational past.

Gerald L. Gutek
Chicago, Illinois

EDUCATION
IN THE
UNITED STATES

1
EDUCATION IN COLONIAL AMERICA

From the time of settlement until the winning of political independence, the colonies established on the Atlantic Coast of North America were claimed as possessions of Great Britain. Initially, the colonies were outposts of the expansive. British Empire. But as time elapsed, these new lands became more than outposts of the empire to those who lived in them. They became a homeland that had its own meaning and purpose.

As outposts, the colonies were viewed at first as extensions of British culture, politics, and power. The transplanted Englishmen who lived in them brought along the educational philosophies, institutions, and instructional methods with which they were familiar. In many ways, these colonies—a narrow fringe of English culture along the Atlantic Coast—formed the embryo of a developing nation. Over time, the institution imported from Europe were transformed into agencies that suited a new people in a new land.

EDUCATION IN BRITISH NORTH AMERICA

The history of American education begins with the study of educational developments in the New England colonies, the Middle Atlantic colonies, and the Southern colonies. The New England colonies included Massachusetts, Connecticut, New

Hampshire, Vermont, and Rhode Island. The Middle Atlantic colonies were comprised of New York, Pennsylvania, Delaware, and New Jersey. The Southern colonies included Maryland, Virginia, Georgia, North Carolina, and South Carolina. These three regions exhibited important cultural similarities and diversities. Although their cultural and educational differences have often been exaggerated, important distinctions did exist between them.

Common Elements in Colonial Education

Although important non-English-speaking groups, such as Germans, Dutch, French, and others, lived in the British colonies, the major linking language between the colonies was English. The colonists were, for the most part, Englishmen who had been transported to the New World. As such, they shared the common language and loyalties that made them British subjects.[1] They shared a common conception of education that was shaped by the classical humanism of the Renaissance and the sectarian denominationalism of the Protestant Reformation. The English colonists, regardless of their region of settlement, were strongly imbued with a sense of religious commitment. Although their religious observances varied, they shared a general orientation to Protestantism that shaped their views of life and education. They divided education into two discontinuous sets of schools. For the children of the common people, there was the vernacular school, an elementary or primary school where basic religious doctrines were learned, along with the essential skills of reading, writing, spelling, and arithmetic. Although some children progressed upward from the vernacular schools, they were rare. After completing a few years of study at the primary level, children ended their formal study to enter the world of work.

The Latin grammar schools and colleges, the upper education track, were designed for the sons of the privileged social classes, who were destined for leadership positions in the church, state, and courts. In these institutions, the classical humanism of the Renaissance, especially the study of Latin and Greek and their literatures, was blended with the religious denominationalism coming from the heritage of the Protestant Reformation. After learning the rudiments of their own language, boys of the upper classes entered the Latin grammar school, a college preparatory school, that prepared them for entry into either the colonial colleges or the prestigious colleges of England. It is important to note that the languages of educated men, particularly professionals, were Latin and Greek.

Although the social exclusiveness of the two-track European system has often been exaggerated by historians of education, the dual structure was nonetheless real as well as formal. In the colonial era, the notion of consecutive, upward movement through interconnected schools was largely absent. The contact between the inherited institutional structures and the leveling influence of the western frontier produced a sense of educational and social mobility. But in the early days, the frontier influence had not yet eroded the inherited European structures.

[1] The definitive work on colonial education is Lawrence A. Cremin, *American Education: The Colonial Experience, 1607-1783* (New York: Harper & Row, Pub., 1970).

Distinctive Elements in Colonial Education

The three regional groups of colonies bore not only the imprint of being settled by particular groups of Englishmen but also of the shaping influences of various topographies and climates.[2] Perhaps, the most obvious difference was in the governance and support that schooling received in these colonies. With the exception of Maryland's Roman Catholic settlement, the British colonies were settled by Protestants. Even among those who shared Protestantism's general tenets, there were important differences in attitude and outlook that influenced views of education and schooling. The New England colonists, particularly in Massachusetts and Connecticut, were Calvinists who believed that school establishment and support were necessary elements in their life in the New World. The importance they gave to organized education and their consensus about the knowledge and values that should be imparted to their children made schools a part of the political as well as religious community.

Residents of the Middle Atlantic colonies lacked the uniformity of belief that existed among the New England colonists to the north. Anglicans in New York, Quakers in Pennsylvania, and Presbyterians on the frontier were of different persuasions not only about theology but about the state's role in education. It also was in the Middle Atlantic colonies that the largest non-English population lived. Although surrounded by English groups, Dutch, Jewish, German, and Swedish settlers struggled to preserve their linguistic and cultural identities. In the absence of a general agreement, each ethnic and denominational group tended to go its own separate way in educational matters and establish its own parochial schools; there was no network of town and district schools that emerged as in New England.

In the Southern colonies, geographical and climatic conditions helped to create a particular economic and social system based on slavery, the South's "peculiar institution." During the colonial era, a sparse population, dispersed over a wide land expanse, inhibited the growth of schools in the South. Also, the dominant social class in the southern colonies, who were members of the Church of England, regarded education as a private undertaking to be paid for by parents or guardians and not the public.

While the English colonists of North America shared a common language and cultural heritage, the regions in which they settled gave rise to varying conceptions of society and education. Indeed, much of American history, including the American educational experience, is the record of the interaction between westward-moving people and a series of changing environments. As they moved from seacoast to forest lands, to mountains, to prairies, the pioneers carried with them their institutions, including their schools. Their concepts of formal education, transported initially from Europe, were transformed by this interaction. The European vernacular school, in time, was transformed into the American common school. Egalitarianism, nurtured on the frontier, eroded the dual-track European school

[2] For a readable and accurate treatment of education in the three colonial regions, see Sheldon S. Cohen, *A History of Colonial Education, 1607-1776* (New York: John Wiley, 1974).

system. In its place was created the American educational ladder of related and consecutive elementary, secondary and higher institutions. The American frontier shaped both the character and the institutions of American life.

EDUCATION AND SOCIETY IN NEW ENGLAND

The New England colonies included Massachusetts, Connecticut, New Hampshire, Vermont, and Rhode Island. Of these colonies, Massachusetts was settled by Puritans, who followed John Calvin's religious theology; as such it can serve as a representative model for examining education in New England. As is true of education in any place at any time, education in Massachusetts was shaped by the culture of its people. The culture was a product of two major factors: (1) the heritage of the English Puritans who established the Massachusetts Bay Colony; and (2) the impact and transformation of an Old World culture in a New World environment. To describe education in New England, particularly Massachusetts, we shall focus on the various cultural elements that had an impact on the inhabitants of that colony.

Very important in Massachusetts was the element of religion. The religious perspective that the Puritans brought with them to the New World was based on the theology of John Calvin, a French religious reformer who had moved to Switzerland. Rebelling against Roman Catholicism's elaborate ceremonial liturgy and sacramental system, Calvin developed a religious orientation both intellectually sophisticated and ritually simplified, or purified, of what he regarded as "popish pomp and practices." Like many theologians before him, Calvin wrestled with the problems of free will, an all-powerful benevolent God, and the existence of evil in the world. If God created all existence, how was it possible for evil to exist and for human beings to choose evil over good? Calvin's solution to the problem of good and evil was rooted in his doctrine of Predestination. In brief outline, the Calvinist answer to the question of good and evil was: (1) God was a Supreme Being who created all creatures; (2) of His human creations, God predestined some to eternal salvation and others to ever-lasting damnation; (3) those destined to salvation, the elect, were God's chosen people; (4) the elect were destined to salvation, not because of their merits or good works, but because God identified them as the elect; (5) the elect followed a rigorously righteous code of behavior characterized by frugality, earnestness diligence, good conduct, and hard work.

As a religion, Calvinism appealed to Europe's entrepreneurs, merchants, and professionals who at the time of the Protestant Reformation were outside of the general theological framework of both Roman Catholicism and Anglicanism, which appealed to the landed aristocracy, gentry, and peasantry rather than to the middle classes. In fact, the medieval Church had strong injunctions against money lending, which was condemned as usury.

Calvinism seemed to justify and sanction the existence of the middle classes. In regions where the middle classes were large, such as the Netherlands, England, and Scotland, the various Calvinist churches attracted many members. Like all religious creeds, Calvinism had social, economic, and educational implications. An examination of these implications is useful in illuminating the social and educational orientation of the Puritans. This orientation was important not only for the Puritans of colonial New England but also for the shape that education would take later on in the United States. In a generalized sense, Puritanism was the basis of the Protestant ethic—a religious pattern of values. Around the Puritan ethic clustered an entire set of values and attitudes, primarily economic, that influenced the American style of life.

The concept of property was of great importance in the Puritan value structure. The acquisition of property was held to be a good act, and a good man was recognized by his property. God entrusted property to His elect, who in turn, were to act as stewards of the wealth. By hard work, prudence, and effort, the elect built up their earthly wealth. If guided by right conduct, there was no conflict between material possessions and spirituality. Right conduct meant that wealth was not to be squandered on idle pursuits or luxurious comforts, but rather was to be invested wisely so that it earned more wealth. The gaining of property was related to the concept of work. Work gave meaning to a person's life. Idleness was the source of evil. If the diligent life and the acquiring of property were signs of goodness, then idleness and poverty signified evil. In the Puritan world view, education, both informal and formal schooling, had a definite role. Education was a means of learning the principles of true religion, the way to live, and the way to earn a living. Education combined, for the Puritans, a religious as well as an economic and social significance.

Calvinism was a book-centered religion. For Calvin, the Bible was the "Good Book" by which God had revealed Himself to humankind. Good Calvinists therefore had to be literate; illiterate and uneducated people, on the other hand, had to be idle, ignorant, and evil. Illiteracy and poverty went hand-in-hand. Illiterates were not likely to be producers or stewards of wealth. As Calvinist theology carried over into education, it emphasized literacy, reading, writing, arithmetic, and religion. In their simply designed, undecorated churches, the Puritans worshipped a stern God. The purified Calvinist liturgy was a highly verbal mode of worship that focused on Scripture reading, sermons, and preaching. The elaborate ceremonies of Catholicism and Anglicanism, with their music, choirs, and candles, were "purified" by the Calvinists. What was needed to participate in Calvinist religious worship were literate individuals who were conversant with Biblical references and who heard the word of God as preached by their ministers.

Despite the fact they had been dissenters in England, the Puritans—upon settling in New England—became intolerant of and persecuted dissenters from their religion. Their intolerance was founded on the premise that they were the only true believers. Their religious values penetrated to the heart of their social, political, and economic institutions; and they saw dissent as carrying the seeds of anarchy and disorder. For them, it was important that the lessons learned in schools created in the young a commitment to preserve Puritanism as it had been taught to them by their elders.

Calvinism carried with it a definite social design. The City of God that the Puritans tried to create in New England was an orderly city, a city governed by divine laws and administered by educated men. While the idea of an absolute monarchy ruled by an earthly king did not appeal to the Calvinists, neither did a democracy of equals. What appealed to them was the concept of a trustee and rule by trusteeship. According to the consent of the trustee, certain of the elect assumed the civil responsibility of governing the earthly city. Acting as stewards, they administered the government, courts, and schools of the earthly kingdom. As the church had its boards of trustees, so did other agencies, including schools. The concept of an elected board of trustees, or selectmen, shaped the governance of organized education in the New England colonies. After the colonial period had ended, the concept of a board of trustees developed into the elected school board, or board of education.

In short, this was the legacy, influenced by Calvinism, that the English Puritans brought to Massachusetts and to the other colonies of New England. In the New World environment, the social, religious, and educational concepts of Puritanism became transformed and reshaped. But in this reshaping, there was a continuity between the old world and the new. New England seemed to the Puritans to be the place where a New Jerusalem could be created. England with its established church and landed aristocracy was not governed by the elect, but New England could become a City of God governed by a Puritan elect. It was a wilderness to be cleared and made fertile. The Puritans, who left England for religious reasons, developed farms and businesses in New England through toil, effort, and diligent work.

SCHOOLING IN NEW ENGLAND

Shortly upon arriving in the New World, the Puritans of Massachusetts Bay began to look to the education of their children.[3] Through organized and deliberate schooling, the adult members of any society recreate themselves as they shape their children into their own image. The New England schools were designed to create educated Puritans who would perpetuate the religious, social, political, and economic beliefs of the adults.

What kind of education to impart to the young is always a sensitive issue in any society. In societies where there are divisions of opinion about what knowledge and values are of most worth, there is also controversy over education. In societies where the adults, especially the dominant groups, agree, a particular kind of education can be imparted more easily. In Massachusetts Bay, the ruling groups, believing that their efforts were divinely sanctioned, proceeded directly to the task of educating the young. The New England Puritans agreed on the aims of education: For them, schooling should be deliberate and should leave little to chance. The

[3] Edmund S. Morgan, *The Puritan Family: Religion and Domestic Relations in Seventeenth-Century New England* (New York: Harper & Row, Pub., 1966), pp. 87-108.

A school scene in colonial New England. *(From Leroy V. Goodman, ed.,* **A Nation of Learners.** *Washington, D.C.: G.P.O., 1976, p. 13. Library of Congress Collection.)*

basic aim of education was to prepare an educated ministry and a literate, God-fearing, productive citizenry. It was to create a community united by a core of common religious beliefs.

Upon arriving in Massachusetts Bay, the Puritans moved to fulfill the aim of preparing an educated ministry by founding Harvard College. An educated ministry would be prepared in the classical languages of Latin and Greek, which were the marks of educated people and regarded as tools for Biblical scholarship. Educated ministers were also to be orthodox believers who were knowledgeable in the doctrines enunciated by Calvin.

The aim of preparing an educated citizenry was fulfilled in Puritan Massachusetts by a system of town and Latin grammar schools. In these schools, children were taught reading, writing, arithmetic, and the principles of faith as stated in the catechism.

In order to prepare an educated laity, the General Court of Massachusetts enacted legislation to make certain that all children met certain minimal educational standards. The members of the General Court were motivated by their zeal for religious orthodoxy and hegemony. Following the Puritan emphasis on the importance of property, the members of the General Court also wanted to prevent the rise of a class of dependent poor. Education was therefore regarded as a form of social insurance.

In 1642, the General Court of Massachusetts enacted a law that required the selectmen of towns of fifty or more families to oversee the "calling and employment of children." The selectmen were to make certain that all the children in their towns were able to read and to understand their religion and the laws of the commonwealth. Children who were not receiving instruction were to be apprenticed to masters, who in turn would be responsible for teaching them a trade, reading, writing, and religious principles. The Law of 1642 demonstrated the importance that the Puritans gave to organized schooling. The apprenticeship provision of the law was based on the English Poor Law of 1601, which required apprenticeship for the children of the indigent poor.

The Law of 1642 was followed by that of 1647, called the "Old Deluder Satan Act." Seen as a law designed to outwit Satan, the Law of 1647 gave evidence of the relationship that the Puritans saw between ignorance and evil. Based upon the premise that ignorant people were prone to evil, the Law of 1647 sought to train up a literate population sufficiently schooled to resist the temptations of the devil. The law required every town of fifty or more families to provide its children with elementary education; every town of one hundred families or more was to provide a Latin master to prepare its boys for college.

The Town as a Civil and Educational Unit

The Laws of 1642 and 1647 and later legislation emphasized the educational role of the civil government, as well as the local unit, the town.[4] In Massachusetts, the pattern of settlement was based on the town, a geographical and political unit that ranged in size from twenty to forty square miles. The towns, settled by members of particular congregations, were also corporations. When a congregation had occupied an area of land, it petitioned the colony government, the General Court, for recognition. The school organization in Massachusetts evolved through several stages: the town school, the moving school, and the district school.

After the removal of the Indians in 1675, the population began to disperse from the town centers. As the population moved to more remote areas of the town, a moving school, more aptly called a "moving teacher," became the agency to educate the town's children. An itinerant teacher would be engaged by the town selectmen and would travel from one settlement to another within the town. He would provide instruction for part of a term and then move on to the various settlements in the town. In time, the various settlements were given the right to form school districts, with their own board of selectmen or trustees.

Types of New England Elementary Schools

The town school, educating the children of the town and governed by its selectmen, was New England's basic unit of elementary education. In addition to the town school, there were also other elementary education arrangements. Apprenticeship was a form of elementary education that had originated in the medieval period when children were bound to masters in order to learn a trade. In

[4]Michael Zuckerman, *Peaceable Kingdoms: New England Towns in the Eighteenth Century* (New York: Knopf, 1970).

New England, children might be apprenticed to masters to learn trades such as navigation, surveying, and printing.

Very young children might attend a dame school, which was a simple primary school where little children learned their ABC's in a sing-song fashion from a woman teaching in her home. Wealthy families might employ tutors who lived in the family home and instructed the children.

Puritan Child Psychology

Like most of the educational concepts in New England, child psychology was based heavily on Calvinist theology.[5] Conceived in sin and born in corruption, children were regarded as having a propensity to idleness and evil. Childish behavior was frowned upon. The "childlike" child was not highly regarded. Children were to be seen and not heard. Schooling was regarded as a form of societal exorcism by which childish inclinations were bridled and tamed by hard work, discipline, and often corporal punishment. The good child was one who behaved like a miniature adult. Puritan ministers such as Jonathan Edwards preached sermons to parents in which children were portrayed as being born "with a corrupted nature" and then "perverted by sinful examples."

Children in New England were impressed with admonitions that even they too could suffer damnation. Children, like adults, were preoccupied with thoughts of death.

Although New England children played like all children throughout the ages, there was little or no provision for play in schools. Indeed, play was seen as contributing to wasted time and childish idleness. Children were expected to imitate their parents and other adults in performing religious, social, and work activities.[6]

Children in New England were also economic assets who were expected to earn their keep by augmenting the family income. On a New England farm, family members were expected to contribute to the unit's economic self-sufficiency. The performance of chores, such as carrying in firewood, milking cows, and working in the fields was a kind of informal learning. Since children were already engaged in meaningful economic activities, the school's formal curriculum did not need to include vocational instruction. School was a place to learn the basics of religion and literacy; work was to be done at home and on the farm.

Methods and Materials of Elementary Instruction

The schools of Puritan New England were places where literacy was cultivated. Like most Protestant educational agencies, New England's town schools stressed reading. The initial reading material was usually the hornbook, a paddle

[5] Sanford Fleming, *Children and Puritanism: The Place of Children in the Life and Thought of New England Churches, 1630-1847* (New Haven: Yale University Press, 1933), remains the classic study on the subject.

[6] Ross W. Beales, Jr., "In search of the Historical Child: Miniature Adulthood and Youth in Colonial New England," *American Quarterly*, 27 (October 1975): 379-98, thoroughly examines this issue.

containing a single sheet of parchment, covered by flattened, transparent cow's horn. The hornbook contained the alphabet, vowels, syllables, numbers, the Lord's Prayer, and other verses.

One of the most widely used books in New England was the *New England Primer*, which first appeared in 1690. The *New England Primer* contained the twenty-four letters of the alphabet, each letter being illustrated with a drawing and a verse to impress it on the child's mind. The primer also contained various lessons and admonitions for youth, the Lord's Prayer, and the Ten Commandments. During a time of sectarian conflict, children were taught to be loyal to their faith, even to death. To build commitment, heroic figures such as that of the Protestant martyr John Rogers were used. The primer had a large picture entitled "The Burning of Mr. John Rogers," with a caption that read "The first martyr in Queen Mary's reign; and was burnt at Smithfield, February the fourteenth, 1554. His wife, with nine small children, and one at her breast, followed him to the stake; with which sorrowful sight he was not in the least daunted, but, with wonderful patience, died courageously for the gospel of Jesus Christ."[7] The most important part of the *New England Primer* was an outline of Puritan theology based on John Cotton's *Spiritual Milk for Babes.*

In any school system, the reading material conveys the values of the society supporting the school. The vocabulary and the narratives introduce the young to what is prized by the adult society. Colonial New England was no exception to this generalization. Reading materials stressed Biblical themes and conveyed to the child the concept of the righteous life that should be lived by a good Puritan. The methodology used to teach reading was based on the sing-song approach and the recitation. A group of children would sing out or recite the letters of the alphabet in unison. Words would be spelled out syllable by syllable. After mastering the letters of the alphabet and simple phrases, students would stand before the master and recite a piece that had been assigned as homework. In these days before uniform textbook adoptions, children used books owned by their families. In one-room town schools, the wide variety of books forced teachers to make individual assignments and hear individual recitations.

Along with reading, writing was an important subject. Writing on slates or using ink and quill pens, students learned by imitation as they copied the teacher's handwriting. Spelling was also stressed. Puritan children, like children in American schools at a later time, learned to spell long lists of difficult words by memorizing them. A number of spelling books were used, such as George Fox's *Instructions for Right Spelling and Plain Directions for Reading and Writing True English* and Thomas Dilworth's *A New Guide to the English Tongue.*

Arithmetic, or ciphering as it was then called, was another basic skill taught in the schools of New England. This subject included basic addition, subtraction, multiplication, and division. After learning the basics of computation, children went on to decimals, fractions, weights, and measures.

[7]Paul L. Ford, ed., *The New England Primer* (New York: Teachers College Press, Columbia University, 1962).

The New England School Master

The New England Puritans, who highly valued education, did not always place an equal value on the teacher who educated their children. Schoolmasters possessed a wide range of qualifications and occupied a broad range of social statuses. There was a distinction between elementary and Latin grammar masters. Teachers in the town and district schools were often employed on the basis of their doctrinal orthodoxy rather than on their knowledge of subject matter or teaching competence. At times, a schoolmaster was a young man who used teaching as a temporary career to earn money to support later study for the ministry or the law. Also, some teachers were indentured servants who taught to pay off the passage money that they owed.

EDUCATION AND SCHOOLING
IN THE MIDDLE ATLANTIC COLONIES

The Middle Atlantic colonies provided an interesting social, economic, political, and educational contrast to the New England and Southern colonies. Perhaps, the greatest contrast lay in their social, cultural, and religious diversity. In New England, cultural consensus rested on Calvinism's religious doctrines and the linguistic uniformity arising from the common use of the English. The Middle Atlantic colonies possessed neither religious nor linguistic uniformity. In fact, the Middle Atlantic colonies exhibited an ethnic, linguistic, and religious pluralism that resulted in cultural diversity with very little cultural assimilation.

Before examining the nature of pluralism in the Middle Atlantic colonies, let us look briefly at the impact of cultural homogeneity and diversity on education and schooling. In a society where the great majority of people speak a common language, share the same religious beliefs, and embrace the same social, economic, and political doctrines, there is a cultural consensus about the social order and the role of organized education. In New England, the English language, the Puritan church, and the shared social, political, and economic beliefs resulted in a general agreement about what knowledge and values should be transmitted by the schools to the young. There was a general certainty about how life should be lived and how youngsters should learn to live that life.

In the Middle Atlantic colonies, there was wide cultural diversity because of ethnic, linguistic, and religious differences among the people who settled in that region. In many respects, the origins of American cultural pluralism can be traced to the Middle Atlantic colonies and not to New England or the South. At the same time that this cultural diversity existed, the Middle Atlantic colonies lacked a cultural consensus that could create a system of uniform schools. Along with being the cradle of cultural pluralism, the Middle Atlantic colonies were also the cradle of parochial and private schooling; each religious and language group sought to perpetuate its style of life by transmitting it to its children. Recall that the non-English-speaking groups in the Middle Atlantic colonies were surrounded by English-speaking colonies to the North and South. Often, the non-English-speaking groups were minorities within the Middle Atlantic colonies as well.

Throughout its history, from the colonial period to the present, American society has experienced tension between a tendency to cultural homogeneity and uniformity and a countervailing tendency to cultural diversity and pluralism. For institutions and agencies to function in any society, there needs to be a generalized agreement by the majority of people on the role and functions of social institutions. In the absence of such an agreement, the subgroups in a society will establish their own institutions according to their own outlook on the world and not on a perspective shared by the whole society.

In addition to this cultural consensus, some generalizations can be applied to the colonial educational experience. First, the settlement of the Middle Atlantic colonies initiated the erosion of cultural particularities and the onset of a different and more homogenized style of life. The frontier experience of groups moving westward continued that homogenization process. However, during the colonial era, the frontier had not had sufficient time to stimulate cultural borrowing and reorganization. For many years, peoples of different languages, religions, and lifestyles sought mutual protection by living, working, and learning together.

While cultural consensus facilitates the creation of common institutions, including educational ones, if the consensus is dogmatic, closed, and rigid, then the resulting institutions and the people who attend them will be intolerant to divergent views. Such was the case in Puritan New England, where dissent was considered to be dangerous to the common welfare. At the same time, if there is insufficient agreement on important beliefs and values, then it is difficult to build a common culture.

Middle Atlantic Pluralisms

The pluralisms that had the greatest impact on education in the Middle Atlantic colonies were those of religion, ethnicity, and language. As was true in New England, religious denominationalism was an important factor in the Middle Atlantic colonies because religious belief established the basic moral codes and outlook on life. Among the religious denominations was the Dutch Reformed Church, centered in New Amsterdam (later New York). The Dutch Reformed Church, a Calvinist denomination, stressed a literate clergy and laity, as did the Massachusetts Puritans, but in the style of Dutch culture. There were Anglicans living throughout the Middle Atlantic colonies, especially in New York and New Jersey, where the Church of England was the established church in these proprietary colonies. Pennsylvania was a refuge for Quakers, who had been persecuted in England and in other colonies, especially in New England. There were settlements of Germans, both Lutherans and members of small Pietist groups such as Moravians, Dunkers and Anabaptists. Scotch-Irish Presbyterians, French Huguenots, Irish and German Roman Catholics, and Jews also lived in the Middle Atlantic colonies. Members of each of these denominations strove to preserve their particular religious doctrines, beliefs, and practices and to transmit them to their children, not only at home, but also in school. Given the strong religious orientation of the colonists, members of various denominations established their own schools, which were often located near their churches.

If religious denominationalism promoted parochial schooling, ethnicity and language were also strong factors. The list of ethnic groups that located in the Middle Atlantic colonies was a long one that numbered Dutch, English, Swedish, French, Walloon, Norwegian, Danish, Irish, German, Scotch, and Scotch-Irish settlers. Members of these ethnic groups tended to make the dangerous passage across the Atlantic as groups, not as individuals. Upon arriving in the New World, their very understandable reaction was to associate with those who spoke their language and practiced their customs. Thus, their languages and cultural beliefs were perpetuated by a self-isolation that kept them from being assimilated by the dominant English-speaking group.

Intimately related to education (in the general and informal sense) and schooling (in the formal sense of organized education) is language. Language carries with it not only the means of verbal and written communication but also the linguistic group's values and world views. The transmission of a language from adults to children is the means by which a group maintains its identity. With the language also comes the group's literature and history. In many respects, the establishment of church-related schools by the various ethnic groups in the Middle Atlantic colonies was a means of preserving linguistic and cultural identity.

New Netherlands and New York

New Netherlands was founded as a commercial outpost of the Dutch West India Company. In the late sixteenth and early seventeenth centuries, the Netherlands—like Great Britain—had assembled a far-flung world empire. New Netherlands, fated to be conquered by the English and renamed New York, was at that time part of the Dutch colonial empire that included parts of Brazil, islands in the West Indies, and the East Indies. New Netherlands was ruled jointly by the government of the Netherlands and the Dutch West India Company, which attempted to create a rather feudalistic economic and social order in the New World at a time when it no longer existed in Holland. The result was the patroon system, in which large hereditary estates were owned by a few wealthy landlords. The Dutch governors ruled autocratically and encouraged little or no popular representation. The priorities of the colonial government were given over to commercial and military affairs rather than to encouraging extensive settlement.

When the Dutch government realized that the isolated colony of New Netherlands faced encirclement and possible absorption by the surrounding English colonies, it began to encourage greater immigration and settlement by other ethnic groups. It also tolerated other religious denominations to increase the colony's population. The Dutch Reformed Church was recognized by the colonial government as the official religion, although other denominations were tolerated. Since it was a Calvinist church, it believed that education should be closely related to its religious mission. The governance and support of the schools in New Netherlands was based upon an unusual contractual arrangement in which the Dutch West India Company supported the schools financially, the Dutch Reformed Church exercised curricular control, and the colonial governor approved and certified the teachers. In these schools, the curriculum consisted of reading, writing, arithmetic, and the principles of the Dutch Reformed creed. After the colony was absorbed by the English, many of the Dutch schools survived and were maintained by the congregations of the Dutch Reformed Church to preserve the Dutch language, customs, and religious beliefs.[8]

In 1664, New Netherlands was occupied by English forces and renamed New York, after the Duke of York, the king's brother. New York, a royal colony ruled directly by the king's representative, the colonial governor, did not develop representative institutions. An elite of large landowners and merchants dominated politics and society. The Church of England was established as the official church, although the Dutch Reformed and other churches were tolerated. Although important, religion did not dominate New York's educational life.

Formal educational arrangements in New York did not develop extensively in the colonial period. The Anglicans regarded schooling as a private matter to be handled by parents, guardians, and families rather than state authorities. The church and state did attempt to provide limited schooling for poor children, however, through the auspices of the Anglican missionary society, the Society for the Propagation of the Gospel in Foreign Parts. These English charity schools offered a primary curriculum of reading, writing, arithmetic, and religion. These schools, supported, organized, and inspected by officials of the society, were under the protection of the royal governor, who licensed the teachers. Members of other religious denominations, such as Dutch Reformed, Quakers, Presbyterians, Baptists, Jews, and Catholics, maintained their own schools. New York, especially the port of New York, was beginning to be a commercial and trading center. In response to the diversified and somewhat specialized occupations in New York, a number of private teachers operated schools as profit-making ventures. In these private-venture schools, teachers were paid tuition fees by students who enrolled to learn specific trades. New York was not unique in having such private-venture schools; they existed throughout the colonies, especially in commercial areas or in regions where other forms of schooling were underdeveloped. In many respects, such private-venture arrangements were an educational response to the utilitarian needs of the merchant and commercial classes. Private-venture teachers offered courses in surveying, navigation, bookkeeping, French, Spanish, Italian, Portuguese, music, and other subjects not taught in the schools.

Pennsylvania

Pennsylvania was established as a refuge for Quakers under the proprietorship of William Penn (1644-1718), its first governor. The Society of Friends, known as

[8]William H. Kilpatrick, *The Dutch Schools of New Netherland and Colonial New York* (Washington, D.C.: GPO, 1912).

the Quakers, was founded in 1652 by George Fox (1624-1691). Fox and his followers, dissatisfied with the dogmatism and formalism of the Church of England, believed that religious experience should be as introspective, personalized, and unritualized as possible. For them, all persons should follow the inner light that comes from the divine illumination of God's presence in all human beings. They were called Quakers because some members experienced physical trembling and shaking during prayer meetings.

Unlike Roman Catholics, Anglicans, Puritans, and most other denominations, the Society of Friends did not believe in specially trained and ordained ministers or priests. Theirs was a ministry of all believers. In addition to the absence of a trained ministry, another feature of the Quaker religion that differed from conventional Protestantism was their adherence to pacifism and nonviolence, which led them to refuse to bear arms or to pay taxes in support of war. Unusual for a time of religious contention, the Quakers also were dedicated to the ideals of tolerance, brotherhood, and the equality of all persons.

In their religious observances, the Quakers held meetings in which those who were so moved testified, preached, or bore witness to the Spirit within them. In their daily live, they were known for their plainness of speech, dress, and behavior. While their social and religious beliefs were meant to be nonthreatening to their neighbors, members of other religious denominations, particularly the Puritans, regarded the Quakers as revolutionary dissenters whose beliefs threatened religious and social stability.

Members of other religions feared Quaker beliefs as a form of socioreligious anarchy. Because of such fears, the Quakers were persecuted in England and, outside of their haven in Pennsylvania, in the British colonies in North America.

The Quaker theology, which was liberal for the times, had strong implications for education as well as society. Despite their rejection of a specially trained ministry, the Quakers advocated literacy. Their view of the child was also enlightened. Children, as well as adults, were treated with respect since the light of Christ was present in all people regardless of their age, sex, or race. Abhoring violence in social life, the Quakers did not inflict corporal punishment on their children. Since they rejected all creedal prescriptions and indoctrination, instruction in the Quaker schools was not oriented to the memorization of catechism questions and answers and religious admonitions. Freed from such doctrinal requirements, the Quaker child was encouraged to learn from direct experience.

Unlike the other royal or proprietary colonies, Pennsylvania under William Penn's leadership enjoyed more representative political institutions. The colony had a two-chamber legislature, elected by its taxpayers. Also, unlike the other colonies, religious liberty was guaranteed to all who confessed and acknowledged one almighty and eternal God. In theory, the government of Pennsylvania encouraged education, following the rationale that: (1) government should encourage good and suppress evil; (2) a good social order depends on wise and virtuous citizens; (3) virtue and wisdom are encouraged by education.

Motivated by these principles, several educational provisions were enacted by

Pennsylvania's government during the colonial era. The governor and council were to establish and control all schools. All twelve-year-old children were to be "instructed in reading and writing" and were to learn "some useful trade or skill" so that "the poor may work to live, and the rich if they become poor may not want." The governor and council were also to "encourage and reward the authors of useful sciences and laudable inventions." The provision for rewarding scientists and inventors was an unusual and far-reaching one. Philadelphia became a leading intellectual and scientific center in this country's early decades. It was here that the American Philosophical Society and the American Academy of Sciences were founded and flourished.

Although the colonial government's intentions were commendable for encouraging education, their implementation was limited by two factors, one external to the colony, the other internal. Externally, the English government, which held ultimate authority, vetoed the enactments of 1683 that required compulsory school instruction in reading and writing. Internally, the non-Quaker elements in the colony's population opposed the compulsory establishment of schools, which they feared would be controlled solely by Quakers. For example, German Lutherans and Pietists in southern and central Pennsylvania preferred to establish their own schools, taught in the German language. Scotch-Irish settlers scattered along Pennsylvania's western frontier feared that compulsory schools would increase the domination of the Quaker establishment. Facing such internal opposition, the colonial government reversed its plan to establish compulsory public schools and instead allowed the various denominations to build and maintain their own schools.

Despite their difficulties in establishing public schools throughout the colony, the Quakers had some success in setting up and maintaining their own schools. William Penn, the colony's first governor, was deeply interested in education. According to Penn, in his *Reflections and Maxims*: (1) children should use their senses to study nature rather than merely memorizing words that they did not understand; (2) teachers should use children's interests to motivate them; (3) the useful applications of subjects should be emphasized (for example, mathematics should be taught as it applies to carpentry, shipbuilding, surveying, and navigation and not as an isolated set of abstractions); (4) the curriculum should include utilitarian and practical subjects such as farming, animal husbandry, science, and invention.

The Quaker schools were controlled and supported financially by the Quaker congregations. The schools were to provide education that was free to the individual child and open to all, including blacks and Indians, who were excluded from schools in other colonies. Quaker schools were also coeducational.

The Quaker educational efforts in Pennsylvania were noteworthy for emphasizing the practical and utilitarian and for stressing children's own interests as the means to motivate learning rather than external discipline and corporal punishment. Unlike other colonial schools, which emphasized the memorization of religious doctrines and classical studies, the Quaker schools provided a more utilitarian education.

Pietism and Education

The Middle Atlantic colonies, as well as some of the Southern colonies especially North Carolina, became home to several Pietist groups, primarily German, which had come to the New World to escape religious persecution. The name "Pietist" loosely applies to religious denominations that practiced what was called the "religion of the heart" rather than following an intellectual theological framework. German-speaking groups of Moravians, Mennonites, Amish, Dunkers, Seventh-day Adventists, River Brethren, and Rappites came to the New World because they were largely outside of the religious settlements that protected Lutherans, Calvinists, and Catholics. In addition, English-speaking Shakers began to arrive and were to have a long history in North America.

Pietist groups established many agricultural communal societies and practiced their religious beliefs in isolation from other groups. Conscious of their minority status, they sought to preserve their identity as a "special people." Many German Pietist communities prospered because of their social organization and superior knowledge of agriculture.

As a religious reaction against the formalism of Catholicism and Lutheranism and the intellectualism of Calvinism, Pietists subordinated theological and doctrinal controversy to the "religion of the heart." Living in self-contained and self-supporting agricultural communities, Pietists opposed movements to create established church and school systems and preferred to go their own way.

Some Pietist groups were millennialist and expected the Second Coming of Jesus Christ to occur at any moment. In the thousand-year apocalypse that was to come, certain Pietist groups saw themselves as God's chosen people. In addition, several Pietist denominations, such as the German Rappites and the English Shakers, practiced celibacy. Following the admonition to live each day as their last day, Rappites and Shakers developed a style of life that emphasized simplicity and utility. Because their educational programs focused on handicraft and agricultural skills, these communities became centers of industriousness and prosperity.

The educational efforts of the Moravians deserve special notice.[9] The Moravians sought to Christianize the Indians. They were influenced by the pedagogical principles of the great European educator and Moravian bishop, John Amos Comenius, who developed one of the first picture books to teach Latin and the vernacular languages. Moravians worked among Indian tribes in North Carolina, Pennsylvania, and in the Ohio territory. Moravian educators devised a written script for several Indian languages and translated the Bible and other religious materials into these languages.

One of the first pedagogical books in North America was written by Christopher Dock, a Pietist schoolteacher.[10] His book *Schul-Ordnung* contained

---

[9] Kenneth O. Gangel and Warren S. Benson, *Christian Education: Its History and Philosophy* (Chicago: Moody Press, 1983), pp. 171-87.

[10] Martin G. Brumbaugh, *The Life and Works of Christopher Dock, American Pioneer Writer on Education* (Philadelphia: Lippincott, 1908).

a precise set of instructions for schoolteachers to follow. He emphasized a system of rewards rather than punishments to motivate learning.

EDUCATION AND SCHOOLING IN THE COLONIAL SOUTH

The Southern colonies differed in a great many ways from the New England and Middle Atlantic colonies. Climate and topography produced cultural variations in Virginia, North and South Carolina, and Georgia. Maryland, a border colony, showed characteristics of both the Southern and the Middle Atlantic colonies. The Southern colonies enjoyed a climate that was much more temperate than that of the northern colonies. In fact, the subtropical climate of some regions permitted only certain kinds of agriculture.

Although the Southern region was first a place of small farms like the other colonies, plantation agriculture came to dominate the area. Large agricultural units, frequently economically self-sufficient and owned by single families, occupied the best and most fertile lands. The mode of cultivation was the single staple crop, rather than diversified farming. The staple crops raised were tobacco, indigo, rice, and cotton. Although other colonial regions had African slaves, the Southern colonies—with their large plantations—made extensive use of slave labor. The result was a flourishing slave trade and slave-supported economy that set the region sharply apart from the northern colonies.

The planation and slave systems produced significant cultural variations in the Southern colonies. Outside of the Tidewater coastal area around Chesapeake Bay, the Southern colonies had a relatively small population that was diffused over a large expanse of land. This factor inhibited the establishment of schools on any extensive basis. Since the most fertile and productive land was possessed by the plantation owners, other less prosperous whites were pushed into the infertile scrublands of the back country. Even when the line of settlement moved westward, isolated areas behind this line retained their frontierlike social arrangements.

While social and economic class distinctions were relatively fixed throughout the colonies, those in the Southern colonies were more rigid than in the North. The plantation-owning whites became economic competitors with the disadvantaged "poor whites." The real economic divisions between these classes were often obscured by their mutual desire that the black slave population be kept in bondage. On self-sufficient plantations, skilled work such as carpentry, millwrighting, blacksmithing, as well as field work was done by black slaves. The use of blacks as skilled laborers and as craftsmen discouraged the growth of such skills among the poor whites.

While in New England, the sense of community and social values grew out of the Puritanism, Southern attitudes and values—indeed, the way of life—were determined by white superiority and supremacy. From an economic foundation in the slave system, social and moral relationships developed that governed society in the South.

The Slaveholder's Ideology

The political, social, and educational attitudes—the generalized world view of a class of people—is referred to as an *ideology*. While it may or may not be accurate, ideology gives people their particular sense of history. Often the historical perspective that comes from ideology is largely mythic. While the Puritans of New England saw their historic destiny to be that of creating a New Jerusalem in the New World, the plantation owners subscribed to a myth that proclaimed them to be descendents of noble English Cavaliers. From the Cavaliers came a code of conduct that sought to replicate a version of chivalry. According to this code, the plantation owners were "gentlemen" who were to a form a leisure class in an agricultural setting. Like the Athenians in ancient Greece, apologists for slavery claimed that the slave system would lead to the rise of a class that deserved to enjoy the finer things in life.

While ideologies such as the Cavalier myth encourage certain kinds of formal school arrangements, the most effective ingraining of ideology occurs informally, through imitation and association. In this way, life on the planation was a kind of informal school. Young men would learn to become gentlemen-managers of large plantations and young women would become the mistresses of plantation households.[11]

Poor White Education

Although the disadvantaged white farmers were not included in the Cavalier myth, they believed that they were superior to the black slaves by virtue of the pigmentation of their skin rather than their economic and social situation. Their fear of black slaves was actually a sublimation of their economic hostility to the plantation-owning class. On the small farms in the Southern back country, white farmers often earned a living at the subsistence level. Maintaining the farm was a family enterprise that involved the entire family in tilling fields and hunting. Here education was direct, with the boy learning farming, hunting, and trapping from the father and the girl learning domestic chores, such as cooking, sewing, spinning, and weaving, from the mother.

Black Education

The Africans who provided the slave labor for the plantation system were captives and victims of the slave trade. The sources of slaves were varied. At times, slaving parties would raid West African villages to take slaves; at other times, tribes defeated in war would be sold into slavery by other Africans. Regardless of how they were enslaved, the journey of the captives across the Atlantic was a cruel passage; countless thousands were tightly packed into slave ships for transport from Africa to the New World. Many perished during the long voyage. Usually, the

---

[11] Catherine Clinton, "Equally Their Due: The Education of the Planter Daughter in the Early Republic," *Journal of the Early Republic*, 2 (April 1982): 39-60.

captives were brought to the West Indies to be sorted out and sold at auction. Some remained in the Caribbean, while others were brought to the colonies in the American South for sale as plantation slaves.

While all immigrants from Europe to North America experienced culture shock, the transporting of blacks from Africa to slavery in North America was the most depressing experience. Most, but not all, Europeans were voluntary immigrants; virtually all blacks were unwilling immigrants. Since European immigrants were able to preserve their religious beliefs and languages, they enjoyed the psychological and social security that comes from mutual association with one's own kind. In order to minimize the possibilities of slave insurrection, the slave traders and dealers deliberately isolated their captives from their families, kin group members, and tribal groups. Most African slaves found themselves isolated from others who came from the same region, were of the same ethnic group, or spoke the same language.

Once in the New World, African slaves had to learn a new way of life and work. Forbidden to learn to read and write, the slaves were trained in the vocational and agricultural skills needed by the plantation system. Slave occupations and slave society were specialized. At the top of the slave occupational hierarchy were the household servants—the maids, butlers, valets, and coachmen. Next came the skilled craftsmen—the carpenters, millers, cooks, and blacksmiths. At the bottom of slave society were the fieldhands.

Schooling in the Colonial South

As indicated, the growth of formal educational institutions, or schools, was not as extensive in the Southern colonies as it was in the New England and Middle Atlantic colonies. While the plantation owning gentry were generally well educated in the formal sense, the poor whites did not enjoy extensive opportunities to attend school. Formal education for the black slave population was prohibited.

At the primary and elementary levels of schooling, apprenticehip and charity schools were available for a minority of youth. Modeled after English patterns, youth in the Tidewater region had some apprenticeship situations available to them. For example, young men in the coastal cities might learn navigation, surveying, and other occupations from masters skilled in these areas. Reflecting the English Poor Law of 1601, laws were enacted in Virginia and North Carolina that required the compulsory apprenticeship of children of the dependent poor.

The Tidewater region, like the more populated coastal areas throughout the colonies, had private-venture arrangements to serve people whose educational needs were not met by formal schooling. Private-venture schools offered instruction in modern languages like French, Spanish, and Portuguese that were useful for commerce; in navigation, which was useful for piloting ships that plied the Atlantic; and in surveying, which was useful in determining plots of land on the frontier. There were also schools in which girls could learn music, drawing, and needlework.

The Southern colonies were royal colonies and were administered by governors directly responsible to the king. The Church of England was the established church. According to the Anglican view, it was the primary responsibility of parents and guardians to educate their children, not the civil government. The church did assume a limited responsibility for educating orphans and the children of paupers. Although its initial mission in the New World was to convert the Indians, the Anglican missionary society, the Society for the Propagation of the Gospel in Foreign Parts, maintained some charity, or endowed schools that offered instruction in reading, writing, arithmetic, and religion. Some charity schools were called *old field schools*, since they were sometimes located on donated land that was no longer under cultivation.

Although wealthy families throughout the colonies sometimes employed tutors for their children, the Southern plantation owners made an extensive use of them. Several factors contributed to tutorial education: (1) the tutorial relationship was often used by wealthy families in England, and the Southern gentry were imitating an arrangement with which they were familiar; (2) the planters had pretentions of becoming the Cavaliers of the New World, and tutorial education was well suited to this aristocratic conception of life; (3) since the distances between plantations were large and the number of children small, it was not practical to congregate children in rural areas into schools, as was done in New England.

The tutor, often a young man studying for a career in law or the ministry, was usually versed in Latin, Greek, and the classics. Children of plantation owners learned these subjects and often had access to the family library, a featured part of the manor house.

Preparatory and higher education in the Southern colonies followed a pattern similar to that in the other colonies. Boys of the upper classes, scions of commercial families in the Tidewater cities or the planter class, might be prepared for college by tutors or might attend Latin grammar schools, the preparatory school of the colonial era. For their higher education, they might attend the College of William and Mary, which was established originally to prepare ministers for the Church of England. Initially, William and Mary was organized into three schools, or departments: grammar, philosophy, and theology. In 1779, the college was reorganized to offer courses in the departments of natural philosophy (science) and mathematics, law and politics, anatomy and medicine, moral philosophy, law of nature and nations, fine arts, and modern languages.

CONCLUSION

Education in colonial America is the story of the efforts of people who sought to recreate European educational institutions and processes in North America. Among the forces shaping education in the colonial period, religion had the greatest impact, especially in New England. Concepts derived from Puritanism shaped educational attitudes and practices in Massachusetts and the other New England colonies. The cultural diversity of the Middle Atlantic colonies encouraged a greater parochialism in that region. The planation system and slavery had diffeent educational consequences in the Southern colonies. Despite regional variations, the colonists in North America shared many cultural elements that resulted in certain educational commonalities. Foremost of these commonalities was the transplanting of a class-centered, dual system of schools.

DISCUSSION QUESTIONS

1. Compare and contrast education in the New England, Middle Atlantic, and Southern colonies.
2. Examine the impact of the westward-moving frontier on the reshaping of transplanted European educational concepts and institutions.
3. How did religious doctrines influence educational philosophies and school practices?
4. Examine the significance of the concept of the trustee or the steward in American education.
5. Distinguish between education and schooling. Apply your distinctions and relationships to colonial America.
6. Examine the significance of the town in colonial New England and in later American educational history.
7. Compare and contrast the Puritan concept of child psychology with later concepts.
8. Describe the academic preparation and socioeconomic status of the colonial teacher.
9. Examine the educational consequences of cultural diversity and pluralism in the Middle Atlantic colonies.
10. Examine the impact of slavery on society and education in the Southern colonies.

RESEARCH TOPICS

1. Become familiar with the following historical journals: *History of Education Quarterly, Educational Studies: A Journal in the Foundations of Education, Vitae Scholasticae: The Bulletin of Educational Biography. Journal of American History, Journal of the Early Republic, American Historical Review,* and your state historical society journal. Survey these journals for the past year. Identify articles that are relevant to the course.
2. Select one colony and write an overview of its education program.
3. In an interpretive essay, examine the impact of the Protestant ethic on American culture and education.
4. Read a carefully selected book on general colonial history or on the history of colonial education; isolate and analyze the social and cultural characteristics of colonial society.

5. Select one of the Middle Atlantic colonies and examine the educational implications of cultural diversity and pluralism in that colony.

6. Select one of the Southern colonies and examine education in that colony.

7. Write an overview essay on black slavery in the colonial South.

REFERENCES AND READINGS

Bailyn, Bernard. *Education in the Forming of American Society:* New York: Random House, 1960.

Benes, Peter, and Benes, Jane Montague, eds. *New England Meeting House and Church, 1630-1850.* Boston: Boston University, 1979.

Bridenbaugh, Carl. *Early Americans.* New York: Oxford University Press, 1981.

Brumbaugh, Martin G. *The Life and Works of Christopher Dock, American Pioneer Writer on Education.* Philadelphia: Lippincott, 1908.

Cremin, Lawrence A. *American Education: The Colonial Experience, 1607-1783.* New York: Harper & Row, Pub., 1970.

Cohen, Sheldon S. *A History of Colonial Education, 1607-1776.* New York: John Wiley, 1974.

Fleming, Sandford. *Children and Puritanism: The Place of Children in the Life and Thought of New England Churches, 1630-1847.* New Haven: Yale University Press, 1933.

Ford, Paul L., ed. *The New England Primer.* New York: Teachers College Press, Columbia University, 1962.

Gangel, Kenneth O., and Benson, Warren S. *Christian Education: Its History and Philosophy.* Chicago: Moody Press, 1983.

Greene, Jack P., and Pole, J. R., eds. *Colonial British America: Essays in the New History of the Early Modern Era.* Baltimore: Johns Hopkins University Press, 1984.

Hofstadter, Richard. *America at 1750: A Social Portrait.* New York: Random House, 1973.

Kilpatrick, William H. *The Dutch Schools of New Netherland and Colonial New York.* Washington, D.C.: GPO, 1912.

Lucas, Paul R. *American Odyssey, 1607-1789.* Englewood Cliffs, N.J.: Prentice-Hall, 1984.

Morgan, Edmund S. *The Puritan Family: Religion and Domestic Relations in Seventeenth-Century New England.* New York: Harper & Row, Pub., 1966.

Silverman, Kenneth. *The Life and Times of Cotton Mather.* New York: Harper & Row, Pub., 1984.

Zuckerman, Michael. *Peaceable Kingdoms: New England Towns in the Eighteenth Century.* New York: Knopf, 1970.

2

EDUCATION IN A REVOLUTIONARY SOCIETY

Today, many Americans no longer think of the United States as a revolutionary society. In history's retrospect however, this nation was born out of the discontent of a colonial people who yearned for self-government. In this chapter we shall examine the American republic's revolutionary origins and their educational consequences. In particular, we shall look at the impact of the concepts generated by the eighteenth-century Enlightenment as a source of republican ideology. We then analyze the educational ideas of four leading figures of the early republic: Benjamin Franklin, Thomas Jefferson, Benjamin Rush, and Noah Webster. While the social, political, and ideological ferment of the revolutionary era generated many plans for education in the new republic, the ideas of these four statesmen and educators are representative of the thought of the period.

The political designs for the new republic and their educational corollaries represented a search for order. Monarchial and aristocratic social and political structures and mercantilist economic policies and the educational patterns derived from them were ill-suited to the needs of a republican society. Franklin, Jefferson, Rush, Webster, and others were embarking on a search for a new social and educational order.

The revolution that erupted in Great Britain's thirteen colonies in North America in 1776 was precipitated by many forces—economic, political, and ideological. To understand the impact of these forces, we must look at the general nature of that revolution and its particular effect on society in North America. The movement toward revolution in Britain's thirteen colonies followed the states of discontent, the organization of prerevolutionary elements in the population, and of revolutionary action. The development of the revolutionary impulse in North America was shaped by the ideas of the Age of Reason, or Enlightenment, and a sequence of events that was particular to the American situation.

THE IDEOLOGICAL IMPULSES OF THE ENLIGHTENMENT

The ideas and impulses emanating from the eighteenth-century Enlightenment were generalized currents that shaped the intellectual world view of the time; these ideas operated in informal education rather than in formal schooling. The impact of Enlightenment ideology was first felt in society and only later in schools. Although the degree to which schools reflect or change society is often debated, the general tendency is for formal educational institutions to reflect the knowledge, values, and attitudes of the society's dominant groups. Also, institutions are slow to change and often lag behind the social, economic, and cultural events occurring in the society.

As for the Enlightenment's impact on North America, these concepts became part of an ideology that stimulated political revolution and social change.[1] It was not until well after the American Revolution that schools embodied principles of republican ideology in their instructional programs.

The Contract Theory of Government

One of the most significant Enlightenment concepts was the contract theory of government developed by John Locke, the English philosopher. While Jean-Jacques Rousseau also developed a contract theory in his *Du contrat social*, Locke's version stirred the greatest response among North America's revolutionary generation.[2] In his theoretical justification for the Glorious Revolution of 1688 in England, Locke proclaimed the sanctity of the individual's natural rights.[3] According to Locke, individuals living in a state of nature, with neither an organized social order nor a civil government, possessed inherent and intrinsic natural rights of "life,

---

[1] For well-written and succinct discussions of the liberal Enlightenment ideology's stimulus to revolution, see Frederick M. Watkins, *The Age of Ideology: Political Thought from 1750 to the Present* (Englewood Cliffs, N.J.: Prentice-Hall, 1964), pp. 2-18; and W. Warren Wagar, *World Views: A Study in Comparative History* (Hinsdale, Ill.: Dryden Press, 1977), pp. 24-51.

[2] For treatments of Rousseau's social contract theory, see Lester G. Crocker, *Rousseau's Social Contract: An Interpretive Essay* (Cleveland: Case Western Reserve University Press, 1968).

[3] For Locke's view of the contract theory of government, see John Locke, *Two Treatises of Government,* ed. Peter Laslett (New York: NAL, 1965). Also recommended is J. W. Yolton, *John Locke and the Way of Ideas* (Oxford, Eng.: Oxford University Press, 1956).

liberty, and property." The *social contract* emerged as these individuals joined in groups to protect these natural rights against aggressors. The leaders became the government that arose from the group itself, the governed. In the Lockean version, the natural rights of the individual exist in the person and are not given by the government. Government, whose origin is secondary to the intrinsic natural rights of the individual, has as its primary purpose the protection of these natural rights.

In Locke's theory, government arises from the consent of the governed, who initiate a social contract between themselves and the government, the political agency created to govern. Governments originate to secure or protect the individual's inherent natural rights. The rulers, or the governors, govern by consent and remain in office only if they abide by the social contract. Whenever any government violates these natural rights, then the members of the political body have the right to overturn that government, to revolt, and to establish a new government in its place. Thus, Locke justified the right of Englishmen to revolt against James II, the Stuart king, and to replace him with William and Mary in the Glorious Revolution of 1688. The political lessons of Locke's *Treatise on Government* were not lost on the leaders of the revolutionary generation in the colonies. Washington, Franklin, Adams, and particularly Thomas Jefferson, eagerly used Locke's rationale to justify their rebellion against Great Britain and King George III.

Locke's contract theory of government contrasted sharply with the divine right theory, which asserted that a monarch was born to be king, was accountable only to God, and reigned by the grace of God and not the consent of his subjects. Government came not from the governed but from those ministers appointed by the king to administer the kingdom, keep order, and collect taxes. Locke's rationale and the American revolutionists who implemented his contract theory in the New World not only dethroned George III as sovereign of the thirteen colonies but also dethroned the divine right theory. Monarchs could even be dethroned if they violated the natural rights of individuals who were protected by the social contract.

When the American colonies revolted, they declared their independence from Great Britain in Thomas Jefferson's Declaration of Independence. Jefferson accused George III of violating the social contract and of depriving the American colonists of their natural rights of life, liberty, and the pursuit of happiness. Using the natural rights theory of the Enlightenment, Jefferson argued that it was a "self-evident" truth that "all men are created equal" and are endowed "by their Creator with certain unalienable rights, and that among these are life, liberty, and the pursuit of happiness." In the Declaration of Independence Jefferson asserted further:

> That whenever any form of government becomes destructive to these ends, it is the right of the people to deter or abolish it, and to institute a new government, laying its foundation on such principles and organizing its powers in such form as to them shall seem most likely to effect their safety and happiness.

While the social contract theory had its greatest impact in the political realm, it also had important implications for education as well as for society. In the divine right theory, the flow of political authority, as well as social position, is based on birth. The king who gets his authority from God, in turn, delegates authority to his nobles, judges, and officers, often members of the aristocracy. In such an ascribed social and political order, the education one receives is "appropriate" to one's rank in the social hierarchy. For example, a crown prince receives an education in the arts of kingship that will prepare him to be a ruler. The same rule applies to the sons of the aristocracy, who receive an education appropriate to their future social and political roles. Appropriate formal and informal education based on an ascribed role to be performed in the future is relatively simple and direct.

In the republican society that flows from Locke's and Jefferson's contract theory, political roles are based on election by the governed rather than on birth. In fact, no one knows whose children are going to become political leaders.

In a republic, the governors come from the ranks of the governed; and after performing their responsibilities of office for a time they return to the governed from which they came. Education, both formal and informal, becomes immensely more complicated in a republic for the following reasons: (1) since no one knows who is destined to govern, all potential rulers—literally all future citizens—need to be prepared to govern; (2) since all citizens choose their governors by election, they, too, need to develop a general civic competency; (3) participants in a republic need a generalized civic or citizenship education. While in a republic other forms of appropriate education, such as those relating to social and economic roles and occupations, remain, education for citizenship becomes more generalized and diffuse. (Women's education in the early republic was based on considerations of what was regarded as appropriate to their gender, not to citizenship.) In the year after the American Revolution, American social and educational theorists grappled with the problem of creating a generalized civic or citizenship education suited to the requirements of life in a republic. Later sections of this chapter examine the educational plans of representative theorists of the revolutionary era. Later chapters, especially Chapter 4 on the common school, will treat the implementation of plans for civic education in formal education or schooling.

Progress

In addition to the contract theory, Enlightenment ideology also brought forth the concept of *Progress*, which was of great significance for American society and education.[4] The philosophers of the Enlightenment believed the universe to be a huge mechanism, operating according to built-in laws or patterns. Through science, they reasoned, it was possible to discover these operational laws and

[4]Of the many excellent works on the doctrine of Progress in the Enlightenment, the following are particularly valuable: Carl Becker, *The Heavenly City of the Eighteenth-Century Philosophers* (New York: Yale University Press, 1932); Charles Frankel, *The Faith of Reason: The Idea of Progress in the French Enlightenment* (Oxford, Eng.: Oxford University Press, 1948); Peter Gay, *The Enlightenment: The Science of Freedom* (New York: W. W. Norton & Co., Inc., 1977); Sidney Pollard, *The Idea of Progress: History and Society* (Baltimore: Penguin, 1971).

patterns. Once the natural laws that governed the physical universe were discovered, then human social organizations—societies and governments—could be reorganized according to these universal laws. Nature could be harnessed to serve human purposes and governments, and societies could be organized to permit humankind to reach perfection.

An important corollary of the doctrine of Progress was that of the perfectibility of human nature. Unlike the Calvinist theologians, the Enlightenment philosophers no longer viewed human beings as the willful victims of an inherently corrupt human nature. The Enlightenment theorists saw human beings as inherently good and capable of being perfected. Societies, too, were seen as being capable of perfection. What was needed to achieve this individual and social perfection was the discovery of universal natural laws and their application to social organization, government, and education. To reach human and social perfection, an enlightened education would liberate human reason from the chains of ignorance and superstition that imprisoned it. Philosophers and action-oriented politicians attacked inherited governmental institutions such as the divine right of kings, religious institutions such as established churches, and educational institutions devoted to religious indoctrination and the learning of "dead" classical languages. They sought a thoroughgoing revolution that would implement the doctrine of Progress. The doctrine influenced education not only during the American Revolution but also during the nineteenth and twentieth centuries. It produced a radically different perspective on human nature, a devotion to science and an effort to bring scientific thinking into all realms of human experience, and an optimism about the course of human history. While the Puritan divines had preached humankind's total depravity, the Enlightenment theorists proclaimed that human beings were inherently good. If given the right education and the right environment, humanity's natural goodness could flourish and grow. In pedagogical practice, the emphasis on repressing children's evil nature yielded to Rousseau's and Pestalozzi's glorification of children's freedom. The application of the scientific method of life had a great impact on education and dethroned philosophy and theology as the authoritative basis for educational theory and practice. Educators, imbued with the spirit of the Enlightenment, sought to incorporate the scientific method into teaching and learning. Finally, the doctrine of Progress manifested a view that the future would be better than the past, if human beings used their intelligence to make it so. From this orientation was born the attitude that contributed to the Progressive Movement in politics and education in the early twentieth century.

Deism

The Enlightenment worked to change the way many human beings thought about the universe and their relationship to it. The theism of the Puritans and other religious groups held that the universe was the handiwork of a personal God who created the world and human beings within that world and then directed the course of human destiny. The deism of the Enlightenment thinkers held the creator to be an impersonal first cause, a rational principle, not a personal God. In such a universe, humankind was to shape its own destiny. A favorite analogy used by the deists was that God resembled a clockmaker who had made the world a clock-like mechanism; once it was put into operation, it continued to function on its own according to its built-in patterns. These patterns were the laws of nature, which were discoverable by using the scientific method.

The deist orientation held many political and educational implications. Fore-most was the view that organized religion, particularly established churches, impeded freedom to examine and to reorganize political and educational institutions. The deist perspective was secular and sought to disestablish religion. In the colonies, church, state, and school were closely related and often governed by the same authorities. In the attitude of republicanism that flowed from Enlighten-ment ideology could be found the beginnings of separation of church and state.

The Liberal Impulse

The American and French revolutions were stimulated by the liberal impulse in society, politics, and economics.[5] For economic historians, the American Revolution resulted from a middle-class protest against commercial restrictions imposed by Great Britain's mercantilist policies. At the close of the eighteenth century, merchants, manufacturers, and other men of commerce wanted the power and status that had been reserved to aristocrats of blood and birth. While the new middle classes were making money, the old aristocracy still held political power. The Enlightenment, with its concepts of a meritocracy based on effort, initiated the political challenge that would dislodge the old aristocracy, especially in North America and in France.

The colonists in British North America were an economically exploited people. According to mercantilist policy, colonies were to supply raw materials for the mother country and were to purchase English manufactured products. The liberalism of the Enlightenment sought to curb government's powers and inaugurate "negative freedoms." To bring about free trade, liberals wanted government to erect no restrictive barriers to the "natural laws" of supply and demand. To ensure free speech, press, and assembly, government was not to restrict these rights.

Enlightenment Ideology and Education

The republican ideology, stimulated by the ideas of the Enlightenment, reshaped the American experience gradually and unevenly. While the political con-sequences of the contract theory and of economic liberalism had a rather rapid impact on American life, the currents unleashed by Progressivism and deism worked more slowly. While many of the leading republican theorists were deists, other revolutionary leaders and the majority of Americans were members of churches,

[5] For discussions of the rise of liberalism, see Robert Anchor, *The Enlightenment Tradition* (New York:Harper & Row, Pub., 1967); and D. J. Manning, *Liberalism* (New York: St. Martin's, 1976).

who, while they accepted political republicanism, also continued their commitment to their denominational religious beliefs and creeds. For them, education and schooling remained closely tied to religious doctrines and values. While many theorists argued for a scientific education suited to the needs of republican society, the educational institutions of the early republic, particularly those of higher learning, remained tied to Latin, Greek, philosophy, and theology. While the birth of the American republic was in many respects the logical consequence of the Enlightenment in politics, strong inherited beliefs continued to exist and cause tension between religion and secularism in American life and education.

EDUCATION AND THE U.S. CONSTITUTION

While Enlightenment ideology contributed to the American Revolution, the ratification of the United States Constitution created the government that formalized and incorporated this ideology into the law of the land. Let us examine the provisions of the Constitution that had a particular relevance to education and to schooling in the United States.

The Articles of Confederation

In the years of the Revolution and those immediately following it, institutionalized education continued much as it had in the colonial era. In some areas, war had disrupted schooling; in areas largely untouched by battle, schooling continued to follow prewar patterns. Prior to the adoption and ratification of the Constitution, the national government under the Articles of Confederation enacted two ordinances pertinent to education. The Land Ordinance of 1785 set aside the sixteenth section of government land in each township for school support. Article Three of the Northwest Ordinance of 1787 expressed a generalized commitment to education by the national government in that "Religion, morality, and knowledge being necessary to good government and the happiness of mankind, schools and the means of education shall forever be encouraged."

In 1788, American leaders, after a rather uncertain political period under the Articles of Confederation, ratified the Constitution as the supreme law of the land. The Constitution represented a combination of Enlightenment political theory, British law, and practical politics. Reflecting a distrust of strong centralized government, the Constitution separated powers by a system of checks and balances between the executive branch (the presidency), the legislative branch (the Congress), and the judicial branch (the federal courts). The tripartite division of governmental powers would in the future affect not only laws pertaining to education but all laws in the republic.

Adhering to general precedents of English common law, the new Constitution borrowed from British precedent in guaranteeing the right of trial by a jury of peers, the right of habeas corpus, and in denying ex post facto laws. In addition to incorporating elements of both Enlightenment theory and British common law, the

Constitution—especially the first ten amendments, or Bill of Rights—affirmed such liberal principles as the separation of church and state; freedom of religion, press, speech, and assembly; the right of petition; and the right to due process of law.

Although several of its provisions and amendments carried implications for education, the Constitution did not address the subject specifically. Under the "reserved powers" clause of the Tenth Amendment, control over education was reserved to each state of the union. Unlike other nations, the United States did not create a central system of education. Education, especially schooling, became a state prerogative. For most of the nation's educational history, education remained exclusively a state function. In turn, most states delegated responsibilities for providing education to local units of government. In their constitutions, most states acknowledged the importance of education to public health and well-being but did very little to create and support schools.

While the federal government did not assume a direct relationship with educational institutions in the early republic, the provisions and amendments of the Constitution were interpreted in later years to bear on education. For example, the First Amendment's provision that "Congress shall make no establishment of religion" was used to support the doctrine of separation of church and state and publicly financed schooling. The injunction "to promote the general welfare" was interpreted to mean that the federal government should try to promote the general welfare by various means, including schooling.

Nationalism

Perhaps the greatest force unleashed by the American Revolution was nationalism. When the revolution had been accomplished, the transplanted Englishmen were no longer the king's subjects but a new people, Americans. The Declaration of Independence proclaimed the country's political independence from Great Britain. To accompany political independence, the revolutionary generation began to proclaim a cultural as well as a political nationalism. Americans needed to develop a language, a literature, and an experience that would be uniquely American. Benjamin Franklin, Thomas Jefferson, Benjamin Rush, and Noah Webster sought to develop an education that was suited to the needs of the new republic.

BENJAMIN FRANKLIN

The revolutionary and the early national periods were a time of nation-building. The founders of the American republic developed political and educational theories to ensure that their newly created nation would establish itself successfully and endure over time. One of the Founding Fathers of the new republic was Benjamin Franklin, who was respected as a scientist, philosopher, and diplomat not only in his own country but in Europe as well. Franklin had already proposed a plan for an English grammar school in Philadelphia in 1749, a proposal that was important because it revealed the stimulus for a new education to accompany the new republic. To understand this new education, we need to examine Franklin's career, his social and educational philosophy, and his plan for an English grammar school in Philadelphia.

Franklin's Career

Benjamin Franklin's career reveals him to a self-made and largely self-educated person who won success because of his own ambition and common sense. Franklin was the son of Josiah Franklin, a small businessman who was a manufacturer of soap in Boston. Benjamin Franklin's formal education was limited to a year in the Boston grammar school and some private writing and arithmetic lessons. More important than his limited formal schooling was his practical training as an apprentice to his brother in the printing trade. As a young man, Franklin pursued his own self-education, which led him to read the works of such English authors as Locke, Defoe, and Bunyan. John Locke's theory of knowledge, which stressed human sense experience as the source of ideas made a deep impression on Franklin, who implemented Lockean empiricism in his own work.

Although Franklin's claims to success were many, a brief survey of these reveals his wide-ranging interests. Like many members of America's rising middle class, Franklin devoted himself to organizing and joining societies that contributed to the good of the community. Like the modern businessman who holds memberships in the Rotary Club and Chamber of Commerce, Franklin was an active member in Philadelphia's civic organizations. For Franklin, however, these organizations served to bring together like-minded individuals to discuss and debate matters of intellectual, scientific, and political significance. At a time when higher education was limited to the study of classical languages, these civic and intellectual associations were agencies of informal education that made Philadelphia one of America's leading intellectual and scientific centers.

For example, Franklin helped to organize the Junto, a discussion group that examined and debated current scientific and political ideas. Believing in the importance of self-education, he organized a voluntary subscription society to support a lending library for Philadelphia. In 1743, he helped to organize the American Philosophical Society for the purpose of stimulating inquiries in natural philosophy and science. Because of his efforts, Philadelphia began to attract scientists, scholars, and philosophers. A man who prized both theory and practice, Franklin was comfortable with, and stimulated by, the company of such gifted individuals.

A man of many interests, Franklin was also attracted to politics and gained a reputation that extended from Philadelphia throughout the colonies. From 1753 to 1774, he served as postmaster general of the colonies. In 1774, he proposed the Albany Plan of Union, which held portents of things to come. While ostensibly the plan sought to rally the colonies against the French and Indian threat, it also was intended to stimulate in Americans the sentiments that they were a common people who possessed a distinctive national identity and were not provincials living in a disconnected string of colonies. One of Franklin's significant contributions to the new republic came during the revolutionary struggle when he served as ambassador to France from 1776 to 1785. Popular both at the French court and in French intellectual circles, he succeeded in winning France's recognition of the United States as a sovereign nation and gained a military alliance with that nation that was crucial in turning the military tide against Britain. As an elder statesman, Franklin, as a delegate from Pennsylvania to the Constitutional Convention in 1787, was instrumental in working out the various compromises needed to create the U.S. Constitution.

Franklin's Educational Philosophy

Franklin's educational philosophy encompassed a number of diverse theoretical strands. In many ways, he was the progenitor of the American race of inventors, individuals who created the scientific, industrial, and technological breakthroughs out of their own sense of initiative, curiosity, and self-made genius. While not great theoretical or scientific researchers, these inventors applied common sense to solving intellectual and practical problems. Franklin, in some respects, anticipated self-made inventors and entrepreneurs such as Alexander Graham Bell, Thomas A. Edison, and Henry Ford. Like these famous inventors, Franklin used an experimental trial and error method. In other respects, Franklin as an intellectual was conversant with the Enlightenment's rationalistic and scientific thinking.

Franklin also personified the aspirations and emerging values of the middle classes—the merchants, businessmen, entrepreneurs, and professionals who were dissatisfied with the political and educational institutions of the old order. Searching for new political, social, and educational modes for expressing their values and satisfying their needs, the middle classes sought progress and prosperity. Franklin's educational proposals, like his political ideas, expressed the aspirations of his class. His educational ideas reflected his rationalism, his utilitarianism, and his sense of American nationalism.

As a natural scientist and inventor, Franklin believed, as did the Enlightenment philosophers, that science could solve the problems of human life and society. Like John Locke, he believed that knowledge came from the senses, observation, and experimentation.

While a theorist in the mode of Enlightenment rationalism, Franklin embodied the American propensity for practicality and utilitarianism. While ideas were interesting intrinsically, they also had to do something, to accomplish some goal or end, and to be tested in human experience.[6] When applied to life and society it was hoped that ideas would make a profit. In other words, knowledge was to be applied to human affairs, economy, and society. In *Poor Richard's Almanac*, as well as in his educational proposals, Franklin emphasized the practical and utilitarian as well as the scientific.

Franklin, as a nationalist, wanted to develop a sense of American political and cultural identity. During his lifetime, many colonists saw themselves as Virginians, Pennsylvanians, and New Yorkers rather than Americans. Before the

---

[6] Robert Ulich, "Benjamin Franklin," in *A History of Educational Thought* (New York: American Book Co., 1950), pp. 225-41.

revolution, loyalties were to a particular colony. After the revolution, loyalties often were to a particular state rather than to the nation. To survive as a nation, Franklin realized that Americans needed a common identity and institutions.

Franklin's Educational Proposals

Although Franklin was a self-educated man who learned through his own efforts and continuing study, he also valued formal education or schooling. He disliked, however, traditional schooling, particularly secondary and higher education, for its obsession with Greek and Latin classics and for its disregard of the natural sciences and useful subjects. For Franklin and those who shared his educational opinions, the building of a new nation required persons who were prepared to open new frontiers, not only of settlements, but also of thought.[7]

In 1749, Franklin's *Proposal Relating to the Education of Youth in Pensilvania* proposed establishing an English-language grammar school in Philadelphia.[8] The general aims of Franklin's *Proposals* were: (1) to create a school in which English, rather than Latin, would be the language of instruction; (2) to devise a curriculum that embodied scientific and practical skills and knowledge; (3) to prepare persons who would make useful contributions to society, politics, government, and the occupations and professions.

Franklin, who was aware of the relationship between learning and its environment, wanted the school to be well equipped with laboratories and workshops that contained books, maps, globes, and scientific apparatus for experiments. Unlike many of the homely and uncomfortable schools of the time, the proposed school would be a well-designed, -lighted, and -ventilated building, located in a pleasant natural setting, surrounded by gardens.

Unlike the limited curriculum of the Latin grammar school, Franklin's English school would offer a broad and varied program. Teachers were to emphasize both the practical and the ethical elements of the skills and subjects that they taught. The proposed curriculum included:

The English language, with emphasis on grammar, composition, rhetoric, and public speaking.

Elementary art work, which was defined as utilitarian skills such as carpentry, shipbuilding, engraving, printing, painting, cabinetmaking, carving, and gardening.

Mathematics, which included arithmetic, geometry, astronomy, and accounting.

---

[7]Franklin's educational philosophy and proposals are analyzed in John Hardin Best, ed., *Benjamin Franklin on Education* (New York: Bureau of Publications, Teachers College, Columbia University, 1962).

[8]For Franklin's proposal for an English grammar school, see Leonard Labaree, ed., *The Papers of Benjamin Franklin* (New Haven: Yale University Press, 1961) IV: 102-8. Also, see Best, op cit., pp. 126-58.

History, which was to emphasize both facts and values; it included the study of biography to provide moral lessons, the study of the world's great orators, Greek and Roman history, the history of Great Britain and its colonies, and the history of religions and morality.

Geography, which was designed to enhance an understanding of navigation and commerce and involved working with maps and globes.

Languages, which were to be based on future career needs, for example, future ministers were to study Latin and Greek; physicians would study Latin, Greek, and French; and merchants would study French, German, and Spanish.

Natural science and agriculture, which were innovative additions to the curriculum, incorporated Franklin's belief that science could be applied to life and society.

In addition, the students would be introduced to the study of technology, machines, commerce, invention, and manufacturing. Character formation and values would receive attention in that good manners, etiquette, ethics, and morals would be cultivated. The curriculum was completed by an emphasis on physical education, health, and exercise.

The curriculum outlined in Franklin's proposed English grammar school resembled and anticipated the programs that would be offered in nineteenth-century academies and twentieth-century high schools.

The Plan of Studies

Franklin also established some guidelines on admission requirements and the sequence of studies that the students were to follow in the English grammar school. The students admitted to the school were males, at least eight years of age, and were to demonstrate competence in dividing words into syllables and in demonstrating legible handwriting.

The First Class.   Students enrolled in the first class were to learn the rules of English grammar. The master was to pair students of similar ability. Each student would give ten spelling words to his partner each day. In that way, both boys would actually learn to spell twenty words per day. The students would learn to read by reading short stories. The master would explain the meaning of difficult words to the students, who would copy them in their own books and thus create their own dictionaries.

The Second Class.   Students in the second class would pay particular attention to proper modulations of voice, according to the author's sentiments and the nature of the subject. Students would be expected to give an account of the parts of speech, sentence construction, the important rules of grammar, and the author's intention. The master would first read the story and then the students would imitate him. The reading assignments would vary so that students could become familiar with various styles and types of prose and verse. In an age that stressed rote learning and memorization, Franklin emphasized the importance of understanding the meaning and interpreting what was being read. The master and the students also were to discuss the moral principles contained in the stories being read.

The Third Class.   Students in the third class were to learn to speak properly and gracefully. Bad habits of speech, incorrect grammar, foreign accents, and improper phraseology were to be identified and corrected. The students were to memorize and deliver short speeches from Roman and other history and parliamentary debates. These orations were to be delivered with proper gestures, emphasis, and appropriate style. Scenes in tragedies and comedies were to be acted out since they contributed to public-speaking abilities.

To begin their study of history, Franklin recommended that students first memorize short chronological tables containing the dates of principal epochs and events. Among the historical works to be read were Rollins's ancient and Roman histories, and the histories of the colonies. The master was to identify examples of morality and ethics that could be impressed upon students. Students would be motivated in their historical study by weekly competitions in which prizes would be awarded to those who gave the best account of the names, dates, events, and lessons.

The third class would also be introduced to commerce, manufacturing, and science. The practical objective of the study was to enable future merchants to better understand the principles of trade and commerce. Those who would be craftsmen and manufacturers would be exposed to various tools, techniques, and materials.

The Fourth Class.   In the fourth class, students would concentrate on writing and composition. According to Franklin, writing one's own language was necessary to good public speaking. In their writing, students were to write legibly and use correct punctuation. Showing his practical bent, Franklin advised students to write letters to each other on common occurrences, various subjects, and hypothetical business matters. For example, they could write short reviews of books they had read recently. They were to write letters of congratulation, compliment, request, thanks, recommendation, admonition, consolation, and excuse. The letters were to be natural, clearly written, and without affectation or high-flown phrases. The letters of Sir William Temple were to be used as models. The master was to comment on and correct these letters with an emphasis on clear expression and conciseness.

Ethics and values were to be cultivated by examining and discussing Dr. William Johnson's *Ethica Elementa, or First Principles of Morality*. Students of the fourth class would also study geography and practice using globes and maps.

The Fifth Class.   In the fifth class, students would write essays in prose and verse, using the *Spectator* as a model. To encourage clarity and concise expression, students would practice writing précis and paraphrases. Lessons in speaking and reading would continue. Samuel Johnson's *Noetica, or First Principles of Human Knowledge* would be studied.

The Sixth Class.   The sixth class would continue the lessons initiated in the preceding five classes. Studies in history, rhetoric, logic, morality, and natural philosophy would continue. The students would read and explain the best of the English writers such as Tillotson, Milton, Locke, Addison, Pope, and Swift. They would read articles and essays in the *Spectator* and the *Guardian*. They would be exposed to classical thought through translations of Homer, Virgil, Horace, Cyrus, and Telemachus. There would also be lessons in arthmetic, accounting, natural science, drawing, and mechanics.

The Significance of Franklin's Proposals

While the English grammar school that Franklin proposed was established, it did not flourish for various reasons. Most likely, the headmaster assigned to the school was unwilling to implement the innovations required for the school's success. Such has been the case with other educational innovations. When educators are assigned to implement innovations, they often revert to the security of the familiar and distort the innovation so that it resembles traditional schooling.

Franklin's educational proposals are most significant in that they embody the emergent trends of the revolutionary and early national periods and also anticipate the course of future education. His proposals, with their emphasis on scientific and utilitarian subjects and methods, broke sharply with the classical tradition. Their respect for the vernacular showed that the English language would become the language of educated persons involved in building a new nation. Finally, Franklin's proposals pointed the way to a more comprehensive educational institution that would offer students a varied curriculum suited to the needs of an emerging and developing nation.

THOMAS JEFFERSON

Like Benjamin Franklin, Thomas Jefferson was a product of the eighteenth-century Enlightenment and of the experience that was unique to America. In this section we shall examine Jefferson's life and career, his social and political philosophy, and his ideas and plans for education.

Jefferson's Early Life and Education

Thomas Jefferson was born in 1743 into the wealthy planter class of slave-owners who dominated the society and politics of colonial Virginia. A member of the Virginia gentry he enjoyed the security of inherited wealth and the confidence of an assured social position.[9] He was the son of Peter Jefferson, a recognized surveyor and cartographer, who owned a plantation in Albermarle County, near the Blue Ridge Mountains. Jefferson's mother was a member of the socially prestigious Randolph family. Peter Jefferson, a member of Virginia's House of Burgesses, was a staunch Whig who favored self-government and representative institutions.[10]

Thomas Jefferson began his formal education at a Latin school conducted by a Reverend Douglas; he later attended a school conducted by the Reverend James Maury in Fredericksville Parish.

In his *Autobiography*, Jefferson wrote that he was a "correct classical scholar" who found the Greek and Roman literature a source of delight. Jefferson's higher education was at the College of William and Mary, where he studied natural science and mathematics as well as the classics and philosophy. Particularly impor-

Thomas   Jefferson   (1743-1826), the third president of the United States founded The University of Virginia (New York Public Library collection).

[9] Max Beloff, *Thomas Jefferson and American Democracy* (New York: Collier Books, 1962), p. 23.

[10] Saul K. Padover, *Thomas Jefferson and the Foundations of Freedom* (New Jersey: D. Van Nostrand, 1965), p. 3.

tant was his study with Dr. William Small, who introduced him to George Wythe, with whom he studied law for five years after college. Jefferson's tutelege under Small and Wythe involved literature and political philosophy.[11] After graduating from William and Mary, Jefferson read law in Wythe's office. As he studied law, Jefferson drew up a study list of subjects that a future lawyer should know. He found Latin and French essential and mathematics and natural philosophy useful. Jefferson also worked out a plan for studying that involved reading in the natural sciences, law, politics, history, literature, rhetoric, and oratory. His regimen for preparing for the law was successful and he was admitted to the bar.

As a result of his education, Jefferson had become a man of wide interests. He was well versed in both Greek and Latin authors, and was acquainted with Epicurean and Stoic philosophy. Among his intellectual interests was natural science, which, like Franklin, he believed could be applied to human affairs. Political philosophy was also a subject of interest, and he read the works of Locke and Montesquieu. Unlike Franklin, Jefferson had the benefits of formal learning and an education at one of the leading colonial colleges.

Jefferson was elected to Virginia's House of Burgesses in 1769. He was elected to the Continental Congress in 1775. During those revolutionary years, Jefferson was in the forefront of the movement for American independence. In "A Summary View of the Rights of British America," Jefferson argued that neither king nor Parliament could deny Americans the natural rights to which they were entitled as free-born Englishmen.[12] In 1776, he was assigned to the committee to draft the Declaration of Independence. Jefferson prepared the Declaration, which asserted the American right to revolt against a king who was denying them their natural rights of "life, liberty, and pursuit of happiness."

During the Revolutionary War, Jefferson struggled to advance civil liberties by bringing Virginia's laws into conformity with republican principles. As a member of the Virginia legislature, he introduced legislation that abolished entail and primogeniture. He also introduced the Bill for Religious Freedom and the Bill for the More General Diffusion of Knowledge.

Jefferson's Bill for Religious Freedom was a declaration of intellectual and spiritual independence that provided for the full religious freedom which he believed necessary to liberate human intelligence. Concerned with advancing the civic literacy needed by citizens of the republic, Jefferson introduced the following three educational bills: (1) for the greater diffusion of knowledge to more of the people; (2) to amend the charter of William and Mary to remove theological control and to modernize the curriculum; and (3) to establish a public library in Richmond. (Jefferson's educational ideas and proposals will be examined in greater depth in other sections of this chapter.)

---

[11] Fawn M. Brodie, *Thomas Jefferson: An Intimate History* (New York: W. W. Norton & Co., Inc., 1974), p. 60.

[12] Padover, *Jefferson and the Foundations,* p. 82.

Jefferson as a Political Leader

Before analyzing Jefferson's educational ideas, let us examine his contributions to American political life. An early proponent of civic education, Jefferson's own experiences contributed to his concept of education for life in a republic.

After serving in the Continental Congress from 1783 to 1784, Jefferson was delegated to negotiate commercial treaties for the United States in Europe. While abroad, Jefferson reaffirmed his commitment to the uniqueness of the American experience and to republican principles of government. He was, however, cosmopolitan in outlook and associated with some of the leading political, literary, and philosophical personalities of France. While he was truly a transatlantic personality, Jefferson would later admonish young Americans to forget the ways of Europe and to complete their educations in America.

In 1789, Jefferson returned to the United States to serve as Washington's secretary of state. Because of differences with Alexander Hamilton, the secretary of the treasury, Jefferson left Washington's cabinet and organized his own political party, the Democratic Republicans. Opposing the Federalist party's tendency to a strong central government, Jefferson developed a political philosophy that stressed: (1) a limited role for the federal government, (2) states' rights and, (3) greater popular participation and representation. Jefferson's political philosophy had educational implications that encouraged civic education and greater political literacy among the population. For him, it was necessary that the electorate make intelligent decisions between contending political parties and candidates.

In 1796, Jefferson was elected vice-president, having been defeated by John Adams in the presidential election. When the Federalist-dominated Congress passed the Alien and Sedition Acts, Jefferson viewed them as a massive assault on republican principles. In opposition, Jefferson encouraged the Kentucky and Virginia Resolutions, which defended the compact theory, a limited federal government, and states' rights and sovereignty. These resolutions asserted Jefferson's political belief in decentralized government.

In the presidential election of 1800, Jefferson was the victorious candidate. His presidency reaffirmed popular republican principles against the Federalist party's inclination to centralization and oligarchy. In 1804, he was reelected to a second term as president. After leaving the presidency, Jefferson retired to Monticello. He then led the movement for the establishment of the University of Virginia, pursued his intellectual avocations and scientific inquiries, and wrote. Thomas Jefferson died on July 4, 1826, fifty years after his Declaration of Independence proclaimed the right of Americans to be a free and independent people.

Jefferson's Philosophy of Civic Education

Thomas Jefferson was a man of many talents: political ideologist, natural scientist, educational theorist, and president of his country. What is significant about Jefferson and many of the leaders of the early national period was their ability to see events, movements, and institutions in relationship to each other. For

Jefferson, politics, society, and education were interconnected. A healthy republic, or polis, needed a system of education that prepared citizens to participate in government by their decisions and their ballots.

Jefferson trusted his fellow men and believed that they were capable of using political power intelligently and responsibly. It was this trust that made self-government a possibility. Human intellect was to be nurtured in an institutional environment, by a government that encouraged human freedom.

A disciple of the Enlightenment, Jefferson believed that Nature had endowed human beings with reason, a sense of justice, and with the natural rights of "life, liberty, and the pursuit of happiness." Since human beings were so endowed, Jefferson had no hesitation or reservation about their right to, and their ability to, govern themselves. Self-government did not occur automatically or easily, however. People had to be educated as citizens to make the decisions and to elect representatives who would act for them in the legislatures and in the Congress. While not everyone was prepared to be a government official, all could use their intelligence to elect capable leaders. While not everyone could be a legislator, everyone was qualified to "choose the legislators." While most people were not educated in the law to be judges, they were "to serve as jurors."[13]

Jefferson's political philosophy revealed some of the basic conflicts that would face the American republic from its inception to the present day. While he affirmed "the best government to be that which governs least," he was equally convinced that "the welfare of the whole is the proper purpose of the state."[14] During his presidency, particularly at the time of the Louisiana Purchase, Jefferson experienced the tension that arose from a philosophical commitment to limited government and a need to use federal powers to advance the national interest for the common good.

Jefferson, who held an optimistic view of the common people's ability for self-government, also recognized that the success of government by the people rested on an educational foundation. If the majority of the people remained uneducated, then democracy would degenerate into mob rule. The theme that a republic required educated citizens was evident in Jefferson's political-educational philosophy. It also was a theme that would appear in the latest movement for common schools in the first half of the nineteenth century.

Jefferson's political philosophy and his corollary educational ideas rested on the premise that a balance between majority rights and minority interests could be achieved if the people were "enlightened" by education. The best defense against tyranny is to "illuminate as far as practicable, the minds of the people at large." For Jefferson, education of the people permeated his political and social ideology. Convinced that liberty required a well-educated populace, he asserted that "If a nation expects to be ignorant and free in a state of civilization, it expects what never was and never will be."[15]

[13] Padover, *Jefferson and the Foundations,* p. 152.

[14] Beloff, *Jefferson and Democracy,* p. 202.

[15] Padover, *Jefferson and the Foundations,* p. 75.

While Jefferson believed that all citizens were equal in their natural right to self-government, he did not believe that all individuals were equal in their abilities. There were, he held, differences among individuals, particularly in their intellectual abilities. Jefferson's distinction between equal rights but unequal abilities posed a political problem that he hoped to resolve through civic education. As his "Plan for the More General Diffusion of Knowledge" reveals, the problem could be resolved by: (1) providing a general education for all people in the literary and the common branches of knowledge; (2) providing a more advanced and specialized education for those of greater intellectual ability. He trusted that most citizens would be sufficiently enlightened to elect those who were suited to and prepared for positions of government.

Jefferson considered education the only "sure foundation" for the maintenance of the republic. The selection and education of gifted young men would furnish the invaluable leadership for the "instruction, the trust, and the government of society." This "natural aristocracy" would rest on "talent and ability" rather than, as in Europe, birth, social class, or wealth.[16]

In addition to the balance needed between a generally educated body of citizens and a gifted group of leaders, Jefferson's philosophy of civic education emphasized the cultivation of civic virtues and responsibility among all the citizens of the republic. A republic needed civically virtuous citizens since self-governing individuals needed to have a mutual confidence and respect for the rights of others, especially a trust that a majority would not abuse or persecute members of a minority.

Jefferson prescribed an education that would cultivate in citizens the "principles and practices of virtue."[17] His recognition that a generalized sense of morality must permeate the citizens of the republic identified an issue that has concerned American educators since the founding of the United States. How can civic loyalties and commitments best be cultivated in the young? While some have stressed patriotic indoctrination, Jefferson took a more enlightened view. For him, self-government meant a generalized commitment to democratic institutions and processes rather than blind obedience.

JEFFERSON'S EDUCATIONAL DESIGNS

So far we have examined Jefferson's early life and education, his contributions as a political leader, and his philosophy of civic education. Let us turn now to his proposals that most directly relate to schooling or formal education: (1) his Bill for the More General Diffusion of Knowledge; (2) his plan to reorganize William and Mary College; and (3) his work to establish the University of Virginia.

---

[16] Ibid., p. 184.

[17] Roy J. Honeywell, *The Educational Work of Thomas Jefferson* (Cambridge, Mass.: Harvard University Press, 1937), p. 125.

The Bill for the More General Diffusion of Knowledge

In 1779, Jefferson introduced a "Bill for the More General Diffusion of Knowledge" to the Virginia legislature. Underlying his bill were the assumptions that: (1) republican government requires the general education and civic literacy of citizens; (2) the function of organized education, or schooling, is primarily civic or political rather than religious; (3) the state government should control the schools rather than the church or the federal government. Jefferson's bill, which anticipated the American educational ladder, pointed to a cumulative and consecutive arrangement of schools. Specifically, it provided for the establishment of elementary, or ward, schools and secondary, or grammar, schools, the completion of which could lead to attendance at the College of William and Mary.

According to the bill, Virginia's counties were to be divided into wards, units of local government. In each ward, a school within walking distance of all children in the area was to be built. The curriculum in the ward schools was to consist of reading, writing, arithmetic, and the histories of Greece, Rome, England, and the United States. All white children, both boys and girls, were to attend and receive a publicly supported education for three years without paying additional tuition. Jefferson's proposal departed from traditional school practice in that girls were to be admitted to elementary schools. He did not, however, provide for their attendance at grammar schools or the college. After receiving the minimum three years of publicly supported schooling, children could continue to attend on a tuition basis, payable by their parents or guardians. The bill contained a significant provision based on Jefferson's belief that a republic needed to identify individuals of intellect and talent who would benefit from additional educational opportunities. The overseer or trustee of each ward was to select the most able student in each elementary school who was unable to pay tuition and to provide that student with a scholarship to attend one of the twenty grammar schools that were to be established in the state.

The second level of schools provided by Jefferson's bill were the secondary, or grammar, schools. Twenty grammar schools (actually college preparatory schools) were to be established to provide a curriculum consisting of Latin, Greek, English grammar, geography, and higher mathematics. In addition to paying students, the scholarship students who had been identified at each ward school would receive three additional years of schooling at public expense. The selective process was then applied to the scholarship students; the most promising of them would be selected for six years of publicly supported schooling and the rest would be dismissed. Annually, the twenty most intellectually promising students would be publicly supported and enabled to complete grammar school. At the end of the six years of grammar school, the lower ten of the twenty students would become teachers at the ward schools; the remaining ten, the most intellectually able, would then enter William and Mary to begin their higher education.

Although Jefferson's bill was defeated on the grounds that it would be too costly, it was significant for its educational principles. It sought to establish the principle of state-supported elementary schooling. It provided for scholarships based on intellectual ability to economically needy but intellectually gifted students.

Jefferson sought to broaden the educational base of society and to identify and develop for the public good the "aristocracy of worth and genius," which he described as "the most precious gift of nature."[18] It marked the beginning of a struggle to provide educational opportunities on the basis of merit rather than birth or social and economic status.

Jefferson's Plan to Reorganize William and Mary

In 1779, Jefferson developed a plan to reorganize the College of William and Mary and its curriculum. He proposed to reduce the influence of theology in the curriculum and to introduce more modern subjects. Jefferson proposed a curriculum revision by which the College would offer:

> *Ethics,* which was subdivided into moral philosophy, natural law, law of nations, fine arts, poetry, oratory, and literary criticism.
>
> *Law,* which included municipal law, common law, equity, merchant law, maritime law, and economics.
>
> *History,* which was subdivided into civil and ecclesiastical branches.
>
> *Mathematics,* including the higher branches of the subject, such as algebra, geometry, and statistics.
>
> *Natural science,* which was subdivided into chemistry, mechanical physics, hydrostatics, pneumatics, agriculture, natural history, zoology, botany, and geology.
>
> *Ancient languages,* including Hebrew, Chaldean, Syrian, and Anglo-Saxon.
>
> *Modern languages,* especially French, Italian, and German.

Jefferson cooperated with President Madison of the College of William and Mary and accomplished many of his proposed changes in the curriculum.

Jefferson: Father of the University of Virginia

After leaving the presidency in 1809, Jefferson devoted much of his intellect and energy to the establishment of the University of Virginia. He surveyed the site of the university, planned the buildings, and supervised their construction. He continually sought funds from the legislature to complete the task. He helped to shape the policies on admission standards, curricula, organization, and governance. Regarding the establishment of the university as his most significant lasting work, Jefferson wrote, "I contemplate the University of Virginia as the future bulwark of the human mind in this hemisphere."[19] Because of his efforts, the university opened in March of 1825. Among his goals was the establishment of a modern university free from any restrictive affiliation to a particular religious creed.

[18] Ibid., p. 9.

[19] Honeywell, *Educational Work,* p. 153.

BENJAMIN RUSH

Like Franklin and Jefferson, Benjamin Rush was a leader in the movement to achieve American independence from Great Britain. A member of the revolutionary generation, Rush urged the conscious creation of a distinctive American character and culture. A persistent advocate of American cultural nationalism, he sought to devise an educational plan that would encourage and then reinforce a unique American identity.

Rush's Career

Benjamin Rush was born on January 4, 1746, in Philadelphia. His career as a physician, revolutionary, Founding Father, and intellectual, which spanned some sixty-seven years, won him fame and influence both in America and Europe. Like Franklin and Jefferson, Rush's ideas were shaped by the ideology of the Enlightenment. He was a member of that unique generation of Americans who were interested in and contributed to many areas of knowledge.

Rush attended the College of New Jersey from 1759 to 1760. He then studied and began practicing medicine. In 1766, he went to Scotland to complete his medical education at the University of Edinburgh, a leading medical school. He also studied Scottish "common sense" realist philosophy. After completing his medical education he returned to America, where he resumed his medical practice. His pioneering research and writing on medicine earned him the title of "Father of American Medicine." His medical research stimulated his interest in experimental science. His memberships in the Society for Promoting Political Enquiries and the American Philosophical Society brought him into association with theorists and scientists who helped sharpen his philosophical and educational insights. He developed an educational philosophy that emphasized the diffusion of republican and scientific knowledge, principles, and methods.

Committed to the revolutionary cause, Rush served as a member of the Continental Congress and signed the Declaration of Independence. He believed that the political revolution had to have a cultural and educational phase that would turn former colonials into Americans.[20] For him, the revolution was but the "first act of the great drama."

Although Americans had altered their "forms of government," they had yet "to effect a revolution in . . . principles, opinions, and manners." His desire to bring about such a republican transformation in American citizens stimulated Rush to enter the realm of educational theory.

Rush as an Educational Theorist

Essentially, Rush's educational theory expressed a broad commitment to a form of citizenship education that stressed cultural nationalism. For Rush, Ameri-

---

[20] Hyman Kuritz, "Benjamin Rush: His Theory of Republican Education," *History of Education Quarterly*, 7 (Winter 1967): 437.

can citizens had to be committed to a patriotic love of their country. Since the United States was a new and developing nation, nationalistic impulses had to be nurtured consciously, especially in the young. In fact, Rush wanted to develop a sense of an American national identity, character, and culture. Rush's advocacy of cultural nationalism was significant in that it anticipated: (1) the movement to create national school systems that took place in Europe and America in the nineteenth century; (2) the use of nationalism as an element in creating national unity that occurred throughout the nineteenth and twentieth centuries, particularly in newly independent countries.

Rush's philosophy of cultural nationalism did not advocate a chauvinistic and unyielding patriotism. It was rather a complex synthesis of several strands of thought. Rush's educational theory was notable for its (1) reliance on materialism and Scottish common-sense realist philosophy, (2) advocacy of American cultural nationalism, (3) integration of republican and scientific principles, (4) advocacy of women's education, and (5) antagonism to the classical curriculum.

Both Rush and Jefferson recognized that the United States, as a new nation, required its own style of education. Like Jefferson, Rush believed that a republican society required general popular literacy and enlightenment. In *Thoughts upon the Mode of Education Proper in a Republic* (1786), Rush proposed a plan for a national system of education to foster republicanism, scientific temperament, and American cultural nationalism.[21] Like Jefferson, he sought to develop a philosophy of civic education to disseminate republican knowledge and values. Rush wanted a system of education that would cultivate good physical and moral habits, proper manners, and republican principles. Rush's medical research convinced him that intellectual and moral development were influenced by physiological factors and that educators needed to arrange and organize instruction according to the laws of human physical development. His nationalist orientation also caused him to call for the elimination of the residues of "European monarchical and aristocratic" society that impeded the development of a uniquely American culture.[22]

Rush's educational philosophy was based on a materialist strain of thought derived from the Enlightenment and Scottish common-sense realism. His materialism was influenced by such philosophers of the French Enlightenment as Condorcet, d'Holbach, and La Mettrie, who believed that reality could be explained adequately by the existence and nature of matter. According to these materialists, human knowledge was derived from sense experience. In 1786, Rush, addressing the American Philosophical Society, relied on a materialist argument to argue that the physical condition of the brain influenced memory, imagination, and morality.[23] In 1812, Rush further developed his materialist position in his *Medical Enqueries and Observations upon Diseases of the Mind*. Rush's attempt to connect human

[21] L. H. Butterfield, ed., *Letters of Benjamin Rush* (Princeton, N.J.: Princeton University Press, 1951), I: 388.

[22] Kuritz, "Benjamin Rush," p. 433.

[23] Merle Curti, *The Growth of American Thought* (New York: Harper & Row, Pub., 1951), p. 164.

physiology to behavior was an early effort to suggest a psychology of education and of learning.

Although committed firmly to a cultural nationalistic conception of education based on many aspects of Enlightenment ideology, Rush rejected deism and the principle of separation of church and state. He was convinced that republican and scientific principles should be based on religious beliefs.

In his *Autobiography*, Rush reminisced that his first schoolmaster, a Dr. Finley, impressed upon him that religious and moral values were necessary to a proper and virtuous life.[24] Throughout his life, Rush emphasized the importance of religious values. While believing that ideas originated in sensory experience, he rejected the materialist and deist position that denigrated the role of a Supreme Being in the creation and operations of the universe. For Rush, both Christian revelation and science were compatible sources of authority. Unlike Jefferson and others of the revolutionary generation, Rush took a moderate position on the issue of separation of church and state.

Rush's acceptance of religious truth was compatible with his adherence to Scottish common-sense realism. This philosophy was developed during the eighteenth century in the Scottish universities by Francis Hutchinson, Thomas Reid, and Adam Ferguson. Reid, in his *Inquiry into the Human Mind* (1764), argued that certain "original and natural Judgments" not based on sensation or reflection "serve to direct us in the common affairs of life." While sensation was the source of ideas, human beings also possessed a "common sense," which was the basis of human reflection.[25] This God-given common sense was the power upon which human beings arranged and sorted out their sensory experiences.

Samuel Smith, president of Princeton University and proponent of Scottish common-sense realism, maintained in his "Lectures on Moral and Political Philosophy" (1812) that human beings possessed both external and internal senses. External senses provide knowledge of the outside world, knowledge that passes through the nerves and becomes ideas in the mind. Internal sensations, including those of the mind itself, originate such first principles as the idea of God, the existence of the soul, the certainty of the will, and moral values.[26] Following the theories of Reid and Smith, Rush, believing that God had endowed human beings with faculties to guide moral behavior, was convinced that morality was inextricably linked to religion.

Rush attempted to create an educational synthesis that would integrate religion, science, republicanism, and American nationalism. While he did not believe any particular church or creed should dominate education, he disagreed with Jefferson's view that sectarian religion interfered with scientific and educational

[24] George W. Corner, ed., *The Autobiography of Benjamin Rush: His "Travels Though Life" Together with His Commonplace Book for 1789-1813* (Princeton, N.J.: Princeton University Press, 1948), pp. 28-33.

[25] Russell B. Nye, *The Cultural Life of the New Nation, 1776-1830* (New York: Harper Torchbook, 1963), p. 34.

[26] Ibid., p. 35.

inquiry and research. Unlike Jefferson, he advocated church-related schools that would offer an education that integrated morality with religious beliefs.

In *Thoughts Upon the Mode of Education Proper in a Republic*, Rush wrote that in a republic the only "foundation for a useful education" rests in "religion." Without such a foundation, "there can be no virtue, and without virtue there can be no liberty, and liberty is the object and life of all republican governments."[27]

In this work, Rush explored the use of education to promote American cultural nationalism. He believed that the new republic needed a uniform educational system to cultivate a sense of American identity and citizenship. Like Jefferson, he wanted youth educated within the United States. He denounced the tradition by which upper-class families sent their sons to Europe for their higher and professional education. Americans should establish their own educational system to prepare their youth to be citizens of a new land with its own unique culture. In relation to civic education, American schools were to: (1) encourage a sense of American cultural identity in the young; (2) once such a sense of identity was established, they were to perpetuate it by transmitting the American cultural heritage to the oncoming generations.

As a cultural nationalist, Rush believed that education should inculcate a love for the United States. He was so committed to creating an American nationality that he wrote that the American student should be taught "that he does not belong to himself, but that he is public property." While the American student should love his family, Rush admonished that he must be taught to "forsake, and even forget them, when the welfare of his country requires it."[28] Rush's rhetoric on behalf of cultural nationalism came dangerously close to the chauvinism that was practiced in totalitarian nations in the twentieth century. Fortunately, however, elsewhere in his writings, Rush tempered his nationalistic impulses with his equally compelling beliefs in science and scientific inquiry.

Rush's admonitions for nationalistic loyalty did not imply blind obedience. Patriotism was joined with science and enlightenment. While their duties to the republic were to be impressed upon students, these duties were to be joined to republican principles. Students were to be impressed with the view that only the guarantees of life, liberty, and property could be secure in a republic. The science of government, like the other sciences, was of a progressive nature. A true son of Enlightenment ideology, Rush argued that the American nation could be the source of universal progress. However, American youth had to be prepared to meet the challenges of life in a republican society. For republican institutions to function progressively, they had to be continually modified.

Since the Revolution had created new responsibilities, it was necessary to devise curricula and modes of instruction that suited the education of a new citizenry. Rush's *Observations on the Study of Latin and Greek* (1791), argued that these classical languages were unsuited to a republican education because their

[27] Dagobart D. Runes, ed., *The Selected Writings of Benjamin Rush* (New York: Philosophical Library, 1947), p. 88.

[28] Ibid., pp. 87-90.

aristocratic nature confined them to only "a few people."[29] In a developing nation with new frontiers to conquer, four or five years of valuable time should not be spent in studying dead languages. For Rush, the American people, in their westward march, should concentrate on exploring and developing the continent's resources. Education should be adapted "to carry forward these explorations with enterprise and haste."[30] Recalling his own classical language, Rush regretted studying Latin and Greek. Because American prosperity depended on science, Rush believed that the elimination of Latin and Greek from the school curriculum would produce a scientific revolution. According to Rush, students of Latin and Greek acquired habits prejudicial to scientific study. Classical study took time away from scientific inquiry. Rush's antipathy to classical languages was so great that he claimed that the "nation which shall first shake off the fetters of these ancient languages will advance further in knowledge and happiness in twenty years than any nation in Europe has done in a hundred."[31]

Rush wanted American schools to educate citizens embued with the spirit of American nationalism. This goal, he believed, could be advanced if youth were instructed in the history of ancient republics, in the progress of liberty, and in the deleterious effects of tyrannical governments. True civic education required that future citizens study the laws governing human progress and those conditions that either repressed or liberated humankind. Rush believed that a sense of common national identity could be cultivated by a common education that fostered "regularity and unison of government" and converted Americans into "republican machines."[32]

As a cultural nationalist, Rush also was interested in women's education, a subject neglected by most theorists. In his *Thoughts on Female Education*, Rush proposed a liberal education for women, arguing that the success of America's republican experiment depended on the proper education of the nation's women. Women, he said, possessed the same mental capabilities as men and needed the same general education. Since as mothers they would influence the attitudes of youth, women needed a civic education in order to impart republican values to their children.

Like Jefferson, Rush was interested in education at all levels, from elementary schooling to higher education to professional education. In an essay *To the Citizens of Philadelphia: A Plan for Free Schools* (1787), he argued that it was a public responsibility to provide a primary education to poor children. Private corporations were to be chartered by the state of Pennsylvania to raise funds for such free schools. Rush was also interested in higher education and was instrumental in establishing Dickinson College, under Presbyterian auspices, at Carlisle,

---

[29] Allen O. Hansen, *Liberalism and American Education in the Eighteenth Century* (New York: Macmillan, 1926), pp. 52-53.

[30] Ibid., p. 53.

[31] Hansen, *Liberalism and American Education*, p. 54.

[32] Runes, *Selected Writings*, p. 92.

Pennsylvania, in 1784. Unlike Jefferson, however, Rush believed that colleges should be affiliated with and supported by religious denominations. Such an alliance between higher education and organized religion, he thought, would foster the progress of the republic.

Benjamin Rush was a person of varied talents, as were Franklin and Jefferson. While he shared many of the ideological perspectives of the Enlightenment, he was committed to the integration of republican and religious principles. He saw education as a means of developing a common nationalistic consensus that would create an American character and cultural identity.

NOAH WEBSTER

The career of Noah Webster (1758-1843) is revealing in that the development and alteration of his ideas on education paralleled significant trends in educational thinking in the United States from the revolutionary era to the establishment of common schools in the mid-nineteenth century. Webster, "father of American grammar and the American dictionary," in his early career was a confirmed apostle of a self-conscious American cultural nationalism. While Washington, Franklin, and Jefferson had won political independence from Great Britain, Webster—like Benjamin Rush—sought to achieve cultural independence from England. His early efforts were directed to establishing a uniquely American form of the English language to be used throughout the United States. From 1776 to the early years of the nineteenth century, Webster, like other leaders of the revolutionary generation, worked to create a distinctive American character and national identity.

In the early 1800s, a change occurred in Webster's outlook that caused him to view language and education as instruments of cultural conservation and social control instead of social change and innovation.[33] This change in Webster's thinking reflected the fact that American independence was secure. For him, as well as for other educational theorists, the central task was now to preserve the nation by establishing strong political and educational institutions. According to Webster's educational ideology, schools were to serve as agencies of social control by inculcating values of loyalty, obedience, and duty to established authorities. Thus, Webster came full circle from a revolutionary to a conservative outlook. Let us examine Webster's impact on American language and institutions.

Noah Webster was born on October 16, 1758, in West Hartford, Connecticut, the son of Noah Webster, Sr., and Mercy Stelle Webster, a descendant of William Bradford. His father was a farmer, justice of the peace, and militia captain. As a child, Noah Webster learned the New England virtues of industriousness, seriousness, and frugality, values that he would later incorporate in his educational writings. He attended the local elementary school, where he studied the usual sub-

---

[33] Richard M. Rollins, "Words as Social Control: Noah Webster and the Creation of the *American Dictionary," American Quarterly,* 28 (Fall 1976): 415-30.

jects and read the *New England Primer.*[34] He received private tutoring from the local Congregationalist minister, the Reverend Nathan Perkins, who prepared him for entrance to Yale College, which he attended from 1774 to 1778. Although he had initially planned a legal career, reduced financial circumstances caused him to become a schoolmaster, a career that would move him into educational theory and textbook writing. In 1789, Webster taught school in Glastenbury and in the following year in Hartford. His earnings as a teacher enabled him to read law with Oliver Ellsworth, who later became Chief Justice of the Supreme Court. Webster was admitted to the bar in 1781 but chose to remain a teacher.[35]

Webster's classroom experiences moved him to write his opinion on education. Webster, believing that educational reforms were needed, observed that: (1) Americans believed in the power of education but were unwilling to support schools with adequate funding; (2) as a result of false economy, textbooks were scarce, teachers were poorly trained and underpaid, and school facilities were crude and uncomfortable. Webster's recommendations for needed reforms in education were similar to those made by contemporary educators. He argued that: (1) teachers should receive improved training; (2) class sizes should be no more than twenty-five students per teacher; (3) subjects should be presented in an interesting style; (4) students should be motivated to achieve academically.

After the Revolution, Webster turned to broader social, political, and educational issues. In the 1780s and 1790s, his optimistic belief in the power of a progressive American nationalism convinced him that America would be the "site of a future Utopia."[36]

Webster, like Rush, argued enthusiastically for the United States' complete separation from all things foreign. A proponent of a self-conscious American nationalism, he argued for a system of education that would advance a purely American culture. Again, like Rush, Webster believed that the most effective means of national development depended on a "general diffusion of science" among the American people.[37]

Webster, believing that cultural independence was necessary to maintain political independence, saw a strong connection between language and nationality. Recognizing "a national language" to be the "bond of national union," Webster wanted to develop a distinctive American language and literature.[38] According to Webster, now that the American people had declared their political independence from England, they needed to declare their linguistic independence as well. Realizing that a sense of national identity was conveyed through a distinctive national

[34] Harry R. Warfel, *Noah Webster, Schoolmaster to America* (New York: Macmillan, 1936), p. 9.

[35] Ervin C. Shoemaker, *Noah Webster, Pioneer of Learning* (New York: Columbia University Press, 1936), p. 21.

[36] Rollins, "Words as Social Control," p. 416.

[37] Shoemaker, *Noah Webster,* p. 44.

[38] Henry Steele Commager, "Schoolmaster to America," in *Noah Webster's American Spelling Book* (New York: Teachers College, Columbia University, 1958), p. 6.

language and literature, Webster set out to reshape the English language used in the United States into a uniquely American language. He believed that an American language would (1) eliminate residues of European usage, (2) develop into a uniform speech free of localism and provincialism, and (3) promote cultural nationalism. The creation of an American language would become the linguistic cement of national union. He believed that his proposed American language would have to be taught deliberately and systematically to the young in the nation's schools. In the early national period, Webster argued for the Americanization of the schools. As they learned an American language, children also would learn to think and to act as Americans.

To advance a self-conscious cultural nationalism, Webster wanted American textbooks to be free of pro-British orientation. Determined to write American textbooks for American schools, Webster began working on his three-part series, which contained a speller, a grammar, and a reader, to replace the English texts then in use, Daniel Fenning's *The Universal Spelling Book* (1756) and Thomas Dilworth's *The New Guide to the English Tongue* (1754). Webster's *A Grammatical Institute of the English Language, Comprising an Easy, Concise, and Systematic Method of Education, Designed for Use of English Schools in America in Three Parts* was published in 1783. The titles of later editions were shortened to *The American Speller* and *The Elementary Spelling Book,* commonly referred to as "The Blue-Back Speller" or "Webster's Old Spelling Book."[39]

In preparing these books, Webster had the objectives of developing a standard American pronunciation and an accurate method for instructing children in the language. By standard pronunciation, Webster meant pronunciation patterned after the "most accurate scholars and literary gentlemen" that was free of those "odious distinctions of provincial dialects, which are the objects of reciprocal ridicule in the United States."[40] Webster's textbooks, particularly his spelling book, were well received and were used extensively in the schools. It has been estimated that fifteen million copies of the speller had been sold by 1837. The popularity of Webster's speller stimulated the American enthusiasm for the spelling bee as a social and educational event.

The early editions of Webster's textbooks emphasized nationalistic themes. Later editions, taking a more conservative value orientation, stressed obedience, loyalty, and duty to established authorities. Schooling came, for him, to mean instilling discipline and curbing unruly passions. In addition to their value orientation, Webster's textbooks devoted attention to public speaking, oratory, and elocution, which enjoyed popularity among Americans. The emphasis on public speaking reflected the general respect that Americans had for the ministry and the law, both of which required oratorical skills. With the extension of suffrage, oratory also became important in political campaigns.

[39] Shoemaker, *Noah Webster,* pp. 67-70.

[40] Noah Webster, *A Grammatical Institute of the English Language, Part I* (1783) (Menston, Eng.: Scholar Press, 1968), p. 6.

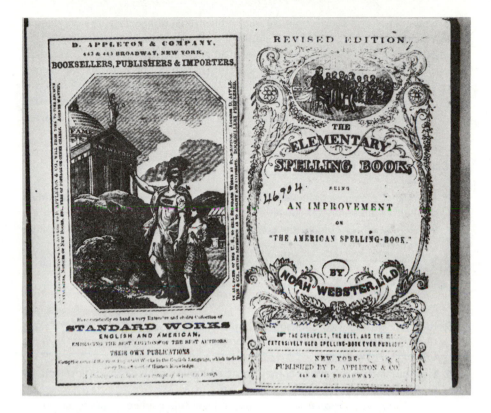

An illustration from Noah Webster's widely and long used *American Spelling Book.* (From Leroy V. Goodman, ed., A Nation of Learners. Washington, D.C.: G.P.O., 1976, p. 7. Library of Congress Collection.)

Noah Webster's great work was his *American Dictionary of the English Language.* Completed in 1825, Webster devoted twenty-five years of constant effort to preparing his monumental achievement that contained 70,000 entries. Webster hoped that his dictionary would correct the errors that come from a "misunderstanding of words."[41] By the time his great *Dictionary* appeared, Webster was no longer a revolutionary. He had become a conservative who saw both language and education as instruments to promote moral order and social and political stability.

CONCLUSION

The theorists of the revolutionary generation, especially Franklin, Jefferson, Rush, and Webster, sought to create a political and educational outlook that was suited to republicanism. Their act of creation involved a turning away from the monar-

[41] Rollins, "Words as Social Control," p. 424.

chical and aristocratic social, political, and educational concepts of the old regime. While rejecting part of the European world view, they embraced the ideology of the Enlightenment. The theories of the revolutionary generation shaped American education in the nineteenth century. Foremost among these formative themes were: (1) a secular orientation to schooling, (2) the need for civic education to prepare future citizens for political responsibilities, (3) the need to include science in the curriculum and, (4) the use of schooling to form an American cultural identity.

DISCUSSION QUESTIONS

1. Identify the major components of the Enlightenment ideology and comment on their implications for education.
2. What implications does the contract theory of government hold for civic education?
3. Examine the educational implications of the Enlightenment doctrine of Progress.
4. Contrast the Enlightenment concept of deism with the doctrines of Puritanism.
5. Identify the major components in Franklin's *Proposals Relating to the Education of Youth in Pensilvania* and compare them to the contemporary high school curriculum.
6. How did Jefferson's philosophy of civic education provide for both selectivity and equality?
7. Define *cultural nationalism* and analyze how this concept shaped the educational ideas of Benjamin Rush and Noah Webster.
8. Contrast the principle of separation of church and state in terms of the Puritan and the revolutionary perspectives.
9. In what ways was Noah Webster a transitional figure in American education?
10. To what extent has a common American culture developed in the United States? Use the cultural nationalist theme of the educational theorists of the revolutionary era as a framework for your discussion.

RESEARCH TOPICS

1. In an interpretive essay, analyze the concept of Progress as used by the theorists of the Enlightenment and relate your analysis to education.
2. Read a biography of Benjamin Franklin and prepare a sketch that examines the forces that shaped his outlook on society and education.
3. Read a biography of Jefferson and prepare a sketch that examines the forces that shaped his outlook on society and education.
4. Analyze the concept of cultural nationalism in the writings of the leaders of the revolutionary generation.

5. Read several books or sources on the American and French revolutions. Compare and contrast cultural nationalism in these two historical events.
6. Examine Noah Webster's spelling books and other educational materials and identify the values that they conveyed.
7. Read several well-selected histories of American literature; determine if the themes portrayed by writers on noneducational subjects paralleled or diverged from those of writers on education.

REFERENCES AND READINGS

Anchor, Robert. *The Enlightenment Tradition*. New York: Harper & Row, Pub., 1967.

Babbidge, Homer D., Jr. *Noah Webster: On Being American, Selected Writings, 1782-1828*. New York: Praeger, 1967.

Becker, Carl. *The Heavenly City of the Eighteenth-Century Philosophers*. New Haven: Yale University Press, 1932.

Beloff, Max. *Thomas Jefferson and American Democracy*. New York: Collier, 1962.

Best, John H. *Benjamin Franklin on Education*. New York: Teachers College, Columbia University, 1962.

Brodie, Fawn M. *Thomas Jefferson: An Intimate History*. New York: W. W. Norton & Company, Inc., 1974.

Butterfield, L. H. *Letters of Benjamin Rush*. Princeton, N.J.: Princeton University Press, 1951.

Conant, James B. *Thomas Jefferson and the Development of American Public Education*. Berkeley: University of California Press, 1962.

Corner, George W., ed. *The Autobiography of Benjamin Rush: His "Travels Through Life" Together with His Commonplace Book for 1789-1813*. Princeton, N.J.: Princeton University Press, 1948.

Crocker, Lester G. *Rousseau's Social Contract: An Interpretive Essay*. Cleveland: Case Western Reserve University Press, 1968.

Frankel, Charles. *The Faith of Reason: The Idea of Progress in the French Enlightenment*. Oxford, Eng.: Oxford University Press, 1948.

Gay, Peter. *The Enlightenment: The Science of Freedom*. New York: W. W. Norton & Co., Inc., 1977.

Hansen, Allen O. *Liberalism and American Education in the Eighteenth Century*. New York: Macmillan, 1926.

Heslop, Robert D. *Thomas Jefferson and Education*. New York: Random House, 1969.

Honeywell, Roy J. *The Educational Work of Thomas Jefferson*. Cambridge, Mass.: Harvard University Press, 1937.

Koch, Adrienne, ed. *Great Lives Observed: Jefferson*. Englewood Cliffs, N.J.: Prentice-Hall, 1971.

Leavitt, Robert Keith. *Noah's Ark, New England Yankees, and the Endless Quest*. Springfield, Ill.: Merriam Company, 1947.

Lee, Gordon C. *Crusade Against Ignorance: Thomas Jefferson on Education*. New York: Teachers College, Columbia University, 1961.

Lehman, Karl. *Thomas Jefferson: American Humanist*. New York: Macmillan, 1974.

Lewis, Jan. *The Pursuit of Happiness: Family and Values in Jefferson's Virginia*. Cambridge, Eng.: Cambridge University Press, 1983.

Locke, John. *Two Treatises of Government*. Ed. Peter Laslett. New York: NAL, 1965.

Malone, Dumas. *Jefferson the Virginian*. Boston: Little, Brown, 1948.

____. *Thomas Jefferson as Political Leader*. Berkeley: University of California Press, 1963.

Manning, D. J. *Liberalism*. New York: St. Martin's, 1976.

Nye, Russell B. *The Cultural Life of the New Nation, 1776-1830*. New York: Harper Torchbooks, 1963.

Padover, Saul K. *Thomas Jefferson and the Foundations of American Freedom*. Princeton, N.J.: D. Van Nostrand, 1965.

Pollard, Sidney. *The Idea of Progress: History and Society.* Baltimore: Penguin, 1971.

Rollins, Richard M. *The Long Journey of Noah Webster.* Philadelphia: University of Pennsylvania Press, 1980.

Runes, Dagobert D., ed. *The Selected Writings of Benjamin Rush.* New York: Philosophical Library, 1947.

Shoemaker, Ervin C. *Noah Webster, Pioneer of Learning.* New York: Columbia University Press, 1936.

Wager, Warren W. *World Views: A Study in Comparative History.* Hinsdale, Ill.: Dryden Press, 1977.

Warfel, Harry R. *Letters of Noah Webster.* New York: Library Publishers, 1953.

___. *Noah Webster: Schoolmaster to America.* New York: Macmillan, 1936.

Watkins, Frederick M. *The Age of Ideology: Political Thought from 1750 to the Present.* Englewood Cliffs, N.J.: Prentice-Hall, 1964.

Webster, Noah. *American Spelling Book.* New York: Bureau of Publications, Teachers College, Columbia University, 1962.

Yolton, J. W. *John Locke and the Way of Ideas.* Oxford, Eng.: Oxford University Press, 1956.

3
EARLY NINETEENTH–CENTURY EDUCATIONAL ALTERNATIVES

The first three or four decades of the nineteenth century saw the introduction of European educational innovations into the United States. Foremost among these new methods was the monitorial method devised by the English Quaker educator, Joseph Lancaster. The period also saw attempts by William Maclure to introduce Pestalozzian educational methodology and by Robert Owen to introduce communitarian education into the New World. While the introduction of monitorialism met with some limited successes, the essential pattern of schooling that developed in the nineteenth century arose from the common school movement, which is discussed in the following chapter, and not from the various educational alternatives that are the present subject. The study of these alternatives illustrates how the nation was searching, albeit in a nonsystematic way, to find an appropriate educational pattern for a new and developing country.

THE SOCIAL, POLITICAL, AND ECONOMIC CONTEXT

The educational alternatives of the early nineteenth century are best seen in their relationship to the social, political, and economic context of the time. States such as New York, Pennsylvania, and Massachusetts were experiencing the early stages of industrialization. While industrialization would become a national phenomenon after the Civil War, sufficient industrial development had occurred in the larger northeastern cities to differentiate them from the rural South and West. With their larger and more concentrated populations, cities such as Philadelphia and New York explored school alternatives other than the one-room district school found in New England.

To the large eastern cities came the country's immigrants—especially Irish, Germans, and others. The children of the immigrants, as well as those of the workers and tradesmen of the older stock, needed schooling. The emerging middle class of industrialists, entrepreneurs, businessmen, and professionals was motivated to support some kind of schooling for the lower socioeconomic classes. Their willingness to support schooling came from mixed motives: (1) a genuine altruism that compelled them to support the education of children as a good and worthy undertaking; (2) a belief that a literate population would be disinclined to embark on revolutionary or radical activities that threatened the status quo; (3) finally, a prevailing opinion that literate, trained, and disciplined persons would be productive workers. (These same social, civic, and economic motives also influenced many of the proponents of common schools.) However, in Middle Atlantic states such as New York and Pennsylvania, which lacked a tradition of state support for schooling, educational efforts were largely philanthropic rather than supported by public taxation.

Philanthropic support for education meant that certain wealthy, well-disposed persons, either as individuals or in association, would contribute financially to support schools. Sometimes this support fully funded a school; at other times, it was partial. In most cases, philanthropic efforts provided only rudimentary and brief schooling for children fortunate enough to find their way into a classroom. While many of the chief supporters of philanthropic education were persons of wealth and social status, there were also grassroots educational efforts. In the larger cities of the northeast, tradesmen had founded workingmen's associations, progenitors of trade unions, to further their economic and social goals. Some of these workingmen's associations supported libraries and schools for their members and their children. The case of William Maclure, a wealthy philanthropist who tried to promote Pestalozzian education, is interesting, since he supported workingmen's institutes, libraries, and schools.

Several generalizations can be made regarding private and philanthropic efforts in education in early nineteenth-century America:

1. Most of the private and philanthropic efforts took place in the Middle Atlantic states, such as New York and Pennsylvania, where the principal cities were experiencing early industrialization and immigration.
2. During the colonial era, these Middle Atlantic states developed a tradition of parochial and private rather than state-supported schooling such as in the New England states of Massachusetts, Connecticut, and New Hampshire.
3. The basic support for educational alternatives came from private sources such as wealthy philanthropists or working men's associations.
4. The education provided by philanthropic efforts was rudimentary, basic, and sporadic.

With these generalizations in mind, let us now examine some of the major educational alternatives to common schooling in the early nineteenth century.

MONITORIAL EDUCATION

The monitorial method, an approach to large-scale education, was used in several nations in the early nineteenth century. Essentially, under monitorial education, a master teacher trains and employs a number of teaching assistants, or aides, called monitors, to impart a basic skill or subject to students. For example, the master or senior teacher might instruct his aides in the letters of the alphabet; the aides, after learning the particular lesson, would then provide that particular instruction to a group of students. The process could then be repeated for other lessons.

Although variations of monitorialism have been used from ancient to modern times, it was the early nineteenth-century version, associated with the English educators Andrew Bell and Joseph Lancaster, that had the greatest impact on American education. Monitorialism seemed to be tailored to the educational needs of a developing country such as the United States. It promised to provide basic literacy on a large scale at low cost.

English Origins

As indicated earlier, the version of monitorial education popular in the first three decades of the nineteenth century was associated with two rival English educators, each of whom claimed to have devised the method independently of the other. The Reverend Andrew Bell, a clergyman of the Church of England, claimed that he had devised the method to bring literacy and the Christian Gospel to the people of Madras, India, where he was a missionary. Bell found that by training assistants, or monitors, he could teach large numbers of people. Upon returning to England, Bell introduced his educational method as a means of educating the growing populations of the British cities.

Of even greater signifiance in the importing of monitorial education to the United States was Joseph Lancaster (1778-1838). While Bell's version of monitorialism was used in Anglican parish schools, Lancaster's was adopted in the schools maintained by Protestants who had dissented from the Church of England. Lancaster himself was a Quaker and taught in schools that functioned under Quaker auspices.

Lancaster wanted to develop an educational system and method that would enable students to learn the basic skills efficiently and economically. He knew that the majority of English children would have only a few years available for their education. For the multitudes of child laborers, schooling had to be "worked into" their schedule as factory or mill hands. In his own school, Lancaster began to train some of the older boys as monitors to assist him in instruction and in administrative tasks.

An essential feature of Lancaster's system was his use of monitors or teaching assistants, who were more advanced students, to provide instruction to less advanced beginners. An attractive feature of monitorialism was its cheapness; only one master teacher was needed to operate a school that might enroll hundreds of students. In addition, Lancaster stressed economy of time. In order for every minute of the school day to be used efficiently, he devised carefully planned schedules. In many respects, monitorialism developed into a quasi-military system of training according to carefully prescribed schedules and lesson plans. This need for scheduling and planning caused Lancaster to write a number of books and manuals describing his method of school organization and instruction.[1]

Lancaster's monitorialism appealed to philanthropists and other public leaders on both sides of the Atlantic. English philanthropists, such as the Duke of Bedford and Lord Somerville, encouraged his efforts as a way to provide inexpensive and mass schooling to the children of the growing urban working classes. In the United States, New York's Governor DeWitt Clinton, a proponent of internal improvements, saw Lancaster's monitorial system to be an educational improvement that was suited to the needs of a developing nation. In the United States, monitorialism proved most attractive in the larger cities in states where local schooling was underdeveloped. Lancastrian monitorialism was truly a transatlantic educational movement that drew adherents both in Europe and America.

In *The British System of Education*, Lancaster, whose motto was "a place for everything and everything in its place," meticulously described the architecture, organization, curriculum, and methodology to be used in monitorial schools. Monitorial schools were to follow a single design. Each room was a square or parallelogram with single desks facing the front; the master's desk was located on an elevated platform, from which he could observe all activities. The edges of the desks were to be rounded so that students leaving class would not injure themselves when they bumped into them. Also, the desks were bolted down so that they could be arranged in orderly rows, which facilitated taking attendance and sweeping classroom floors.

Lancaster's design for schools put the master teacher at the center of the educational stage and allowed him the maximum opportunity to closely supervise the instruction. The curriculum consisted of the basic skills of reading, writing, arithmetic, and Scripture study. There was no instruction in denominational religion, however. Students were to receive such instruction at their own particular church.

Lancaster's rather complex system of classifying students into homogeneous ability groups was based on a simple principle that there were two essential categories of students: those who were learning to read and do arithmetic, and those who were practicing basic skills that they had previously learned. For monitorialism

---

[1] Among Lancaster's widely circulated books were: *Improvements in Education as It Respects the Industrious Classes of the Community* (London: Darton and Harvey, 1805); *The British System of Education: Being a Complete Epitome of the Improvements and Inventions Practiced at the Royal Free Schools* (London: Royal Free Schools, 1810); *Instruction for Forming and Conducting a Society of the Children of the Labouring Classes of the People According to the General Principles of the Lancastrian, or British Plan* (London: Royal Free Schools, 1810).

to function effectively, it was important that students be organized into ability groups. In this way, a monitor could work with a group of students of similar ability and particular lessons could be keyed to that group.

Monitorial education emphasized the learning of the basic skills of reading, writing, and arithmetic. Following careful organization, Lancaster grouped students into a series of classes.[2]

READING CLASSES IN MONITORIAL SCHOOLS

Class	Educational Objective
1	To learn the alphabet
2	To learn words or syllables of two letters
3	To learn words or syllables of three letters
4	To learn words or syllables of four letters
5	To learn words or syllables of five letters
6	To read Scriptural stories and to begin spelling
7	To read the Bible
8	To continue reading the Bible

WRITING CLASSES IN MONITORIAL SCHOOLS

Class	Educational Objective
1	To print the alphabet
2	To write the alphabet and words of two letters
3	To write words of three letters
4	To write words of four letters
5	To write words of five and six letters
6	To write words of two syllables and more
7	To learn a spelling series [designed by Lancaster]
8	To continue spelling exercises

ARITHMETIC CLASSES IN MONITORIAL SCHOOLS

Class	Educational Objective
1	To make and combine units of 10
2	To practice simple addition
3	To learn compound addition
4	To learn simple subtraction
5	To learn compound subtraction
6	To learn simple multiplication
7	To learn compound multiplication
8	To learn simple division
9	To learn compound division

[2]The outlines illustrating Lancastrian instructional organization were created by the author but are based on Lancaster's *The British System of Education* (1810).

10	To learn reduction [a series of lessons particular to Lancaster]
11	To practice the rule of three
12	To practice and review previously learned lessons

Children progressed from class to class as they mastered the particular skill. As a result, a child might be in the fourth class in reading but in the first in arithmetic. Entering students, upon successfully passing an examination, were placed in the appropriate reading or writing class. In arithmetic, however, students had to complete all of the classes in the sequence designed by Lancaster, who believed that he had developed a unique method of mathematical education.

Methodology

Lancaster devised a specific instructional method that was to be followed by the monitors. For example, in learning the alphabet, students were divided into groups of twenty and practiced printing and reading with the aid of a monitor. They used a special table as wide as a desk but longer, with one edge left bare so that they could rest their left arms on it while they worked with their right hands at the far end of the surface. The far end was designed as an oblong sandbox with the bottom painted black. White sand overlaid the box and the children traced the letters of the alphabet with their fingers in the sand, the black surface showing through in the form of the letter traced. Since the children sat close together, those who did not know the particular letter could copy from those who did. The monitor deliberately paired the children so that each child who did not know the lessons was seated next to one who did. The monitor also tutored beginning students by tracing the letter for them; they would then trace the letter in the outline left by the monitor. After the children had made each of the letters, the monitor smoothed the sand with a flat iron and a new letter was presented.

The use of the sand table to teach writing illustrates Lancaster's desire to reduce the cost of schooling. Instead of providing or requiring paper, pens, ink, or copybooks that were expendable after a single use by the student, the system employed sand, which could be used repeatedly. The same cost-effectiveness applied to the use of large wall charts rather than books to teach reading.

For each instructional phase, Lancaster developed a corresponding methodological sequence that was to be followed by the monitors. Since following the prescribed sequence was so important for the smooth functioning of monitorialism, it did not allow for divergent teaching nor departures from the approved lesson plan, no matter how compelling the motivation. Critics condemned its regimented routine.

Motivation and Discipline

Lancaster, who carefully worked out a detailed curriculum and precise methodology, also sought to apply his principles of order and structure to questions of motivation and discipline. As a Quaker, he rejected the harsh and cruel practice of corporal punishment that was regularly practiced in early nineteenth-century schools. However, his use of emulation and isolation could be as cruel in a psychological way.

Rejecting the use of the lash or the rod, Lancaster devised a series of tags or signs, to be hung on the student's neck, that defined and announced his misdeed. Such public punishment was designed to make an example of the miscreant. For example, a chronic truant would be seized at his home by his classmates, who were to bring him to school by force, if necessary. Serious repeaters might be tied to a post or tied in a blanket and forced to spend the night in the school.

Using a rudimentary form of behavior modification. Lancaster used rewards and emulation to reinforce desired behavior. High achievers were awarded badges of merit that publicly proclaimed their scholastic attainment. In addition, students who completed their lessons correctly were given tickets that could be accumulated and redeemed for prizes such as toys, balls, kites, or books.

Lancastrianism in the United States

As indicated earlier, Lancastrian monitorialism appealed to certain philanthropic and political leaders in the United States. Monitorialism—like the later Pestalozzian, Froebelian, Herbartian, Montessorian, and British Primary School movements—was yet another example of the transference of educational ideas from Europe to America. Joseph Lancaster came to the United States to promote his method in 1818, leaving financial and sectarian issues behind in England. His method, however, had preceded his arrival. Lancastrian schools were functioning in New York as early as 1806 and in Philadelphia in 1807.

In New York, Lancastrian monitorial education drew the enthusiastic support of Governor DeWitt Clinton, who eloquently proclaimed the English educator as the "benefactor of the human race," who had the noble mission of redeeming the "poor and distressed of this world from the power and dominion of ignorance."[3]

Clinton, a promoter of internal improvements to develop agriculture, industry, and transportation, believed Lancastrianism would advance America's educational system. He believed monitorial education would serve as an inexpensive, effective, and immediate solution to New York's need for mass education.[4] In the 1820s and 1830s, Lancastrian schooling attracted a large following. While Lancastrian schools occasionally received some public subsidies, they were founded primarily by philanthropists or by subscription societies. Proponents of Lancastrianism developed an extensive literature to advertise and publicize the method.

The Decline of Lancastrianism

Lancaster's monitorial schools flourished in several regions of the United States and then rapidly declined in the late 1830s and 1840s. There were several

[3] As cited in Carl F. Kaestle, *Joseph Lancaster and the Monitorial School Movement* (New York: Teachers College Press, Columbia University, 1973), p. 153.

[4] For example, see *Manual of the Lancastrian System of Teaching Reading, Writing, Arithmetic, and Needlework as Practiced in the Schools of the Free-School Society of New York* (New York: Samuel Wood and Sons, 1820).

reasons for the decline of monitorialism. Organizationally, it was better suited for large cities with masses of students rather than for America's small towns and rural areas, where the prevalent mode of organization was the one-room school. In the self-contained one-room school, a single teacher taught a group of students of varying ages and abilities. Individualized recitation was the dominant method. Homogeneous ability grouping, as advocated by Lancaster, was not practical in such settings. Educational critics condemned monitorialism for being limited to the rudiments of literacy rather than providing a more thorough educational foundation. They also rejected as inept and limited the extensive use of monitors to educate other students.

Although Lancastrianism declined in both England and America, its significance as an educational response to industrialization should not be overlooked. Just as the factory assembly line was designed for mass production, the Lancastrian school was designed for mass education. The logic of the factory system that moved production from small-scale handicrafts to large-scale manufacturing could also be found in monitorial schooling. The assembly line of the factory was based on the division of labor principle, with workers performing limited but specialized functions.[5] Large-scale factory organization brought with it the concept of a supervisor, or foreman. The educational counterpart of the factory foreman was the master teacher who supervised an entire school and the monitors who performed specialized instructional functions. Like the factory worker, the monitors often did not understand, nor even need to know, the purpose of the entire enterprise. The very architecture of Lancaster's schools was factorylike. The organizational plan of the school, with its grouping and differentiation, were factorylike as well. Rather than being an educational deadend, as construed by many educational historians, Lancastrian monitorialism may have been the model for the factorylike urban schools that emerged in the United States in the late nineteenth century.

WILLIAM MACLURE AND SCHOOLS OF INDUSTRY

If Lancastrianism had become the dominant model of school organization in the United States, it would have provided mass literacy education. It is unlikely, however, that the educational alternative suggested by Lancaster would have encouraged social or economic mobility. In contrast to Lancaster's monitorialism, the educational ideas of William Maclure (1763-1840) suggested a model that encompassed: (1) using research in the basic sciences as a framework for economic development; (2) creating schools of industry for the agricultural and industrial working classes so that they could gain both economic and political power; (3) introducing the Pestalozzian method of education to the United States as the most effective approach to popular education. Although Horace Mann's concept of the common school would become the dominant educational model, Maclure's

---

[5] Eric Midwinter, *Nineteenth-Century Education* (New York: Harper & Row, Pub., 1970), pp. 25-30.

social and educational ideas presented an alternative educational model for the United States in the early nineteenth century.

Maclure, who was of Scottish ancestry, amassed a fortune in trade. In 1796, while on a business trip to the United States, he decided to become an American citizen. When he retired from business in 1800, he was free to engage in scientific and geological exploration, educational innovation, and other philanthropic pursuits.[6] Making Philadelphia his headquarters, Maclure traveled widely to conduct geological surveys. He explored the eastern half of the United States, collecting geological specimens and recording his observations on the soils and minerals of the region. Although an amateur scientist, Maclure intended that his research be related to America's potentiality for agricultural and industrial development.[7] In 1809, Maclure published a geological map and observations of the United States. Because of his pioneering work in geology, Maclure gained scientific recognition, served as president of the Academy of Natural Science from 1821 to 1843, and was also president of the American Geological Society.

Maclure's geological research was just part of his larger design for American economic development, in which scientific and industrial education would play a large role. In particular, Maclure predicted that the Mississippi valley would become, because of its rich soil and temperate climate, a region of immense agricultural and industrial productivity. As a result, much of Maclure's scientific and educational philanthropy was directed to the development of the American heartland.

In addition to his American geological expeditions, Maclure traveled extensively in Europe, from Spain in the south to Lapland in the north, observing not only geology but also social, economic, political, and educational institutions and conditions. Keenly interested in educational innovation, he was impressed by the experiments of the Swiss educator, Johann Heinrich Pestalozzi, at Burgdorf and Yverdon. Concluding that Pestalozzi's method should be implemented in the United States, he unsuccessfully sought to persuade Pestalozzi to introduce his method to America. Maclure, however, did succeed in bringing a number of Pestalozzian educators to the United States. Among them was Jospeh Neef, who was to popularize Pestalozzi's method and to establish Pestalozzian schools.[8]

In addition to introducing innovative educational methods such as Pestalozzianism, Maclure also believed that basic scientific research was needed for the agricultural and industrial development of the United States. He also imported and subsidized a group of scientific scholars, such as Thomas Say and Charles-Alexandre Lesueur. Maclure hoped to forge a synthesis of the scientific and educa-

---

[6] J. Percy Moore, "William Maclure—Scientist and Humanitarian," *Proceedings of the American Philosophical Society*, 91, no. 3. (August 29, 1947): 234.

[7] W. H. G. Armytage, "William Maclure, 1763-1840: A British Interpretation," *Indiana Magazine of History*, 47, no. 1 (March 1951): 2.

[8] For a discussion of Maclure's and Neef's efforts to introduce Pestalozzianism, see Gerald L. Gutek, *Joseph Neef: The Americanization of Pestalozzianism* (University: University of Alabama Press, 1978).

tional worlds that would unite basic scientific research and knowledge with the Pestalozzian educational method.[9] Maclure was convinced that such a synthesis would generate the practical education needed to develop America's natural resources and stimulate social and political change.

Maclure's Theory of Social and Educational Change

Maclure believed that knowledge was power and that popular education was the necessary instrument for diffusing this power to the working classes. According to Maclure, all societies were divided into two classes: the minority which was composed of idle, wealthy, nonproducing property owners, and the majority, which was composed mostly of producers who actually created goods and services. The non-producing ruling class lived parasitically at the expense of the producers. The drone-like idle owners, who exploited the labor of others, maintained themselves in power by controlling political, legal, and educational institutions that functioned in their interests. While the producers labored, the profits of their labor were expropriated to sustain the class of nonproducers. Maclure broadly defined the producing classes to include farmers and workers as well as scientists and educators. Maclure's pre-Marxist theory argued that society rested on an economic base. Whoever controlled that base also controlled the social institutions, including schools. While Maclure recognized the existence of class hostility, unlike Marx he believed that economic and social control could shift to the producers by political and educational processes rather than class warfare. Maclure believed that American representative political institutions could be the instruments by which the working classes might gain the social and political control to which their numbers entitled them. It was necessary, however, for the working classes to have an education that illuminated rather than obscured social, political, and economic realities.

In the United States, despite its formal representative institutions, wealthy nonproducers controlled the government. The American electoral processes presented an opportunity for working classes to organize and to win power. The key to political consciousness rested in education. Unfortunately, just as the wealthy producers controlled government so did they control schooling. Maclure charged that the schools and colleges of early nineteenth-century America offered an education that was church controlled and classically oriented and unsuited to the needs of the working classes. Maclure reasoned that schools of industry could be created; these schools would offer a scientific and utilitarian curriculum that would prepare workers to become more effective economic producers and political activists.

Maclure was a caustic critic of America's traditional educational institutions. Traditional elementary schooling, based upon the memorization of the catechism, he rejected as worthless. He also rejected classical education, based on Latin and Greek, as equally worthless and designed for the elite classes who controlled the secondary schools and colleges. While elementary schooling indoctrinated working-

---

[9]For Maclure's views on science and education, see William Maclure, *Opinions on Various Subjects* (New Harmony, Ind.: School Press, 1831).

class children to believe that they lived in the best of all possible worlds, higher education produced idle dilettantes who were not expected to earn their own living.

For Maclure, scientific knowledge that dealt with man's discovery and use of natural resources was most useful. Biology, botany, geology, chemistry, and physics were significant sciences that could educate people to use their resources intelligently. Science was particularly useful to the citizens of the United States, a country blessed with great water, soil, and mineral resources. What was needed, then, was basic scientific research. Maclure wanted the members of his scientific community, such as Lesueur, Say, and Troost, to investigate America's natural resources, catalog them, describe them, and indicate their uses.

Along with his emphasis on scientific knowledge, Maclure believed that new kinds of schools were needed to disseminate scientific knowledge to the workers and their children, who would then learn to apply it to life's practical occupations. If knowledge were power, then it had to be applied. Knowledge could not be idle; it had to be used. To this end, Maclure planned to create schools of industry that would instruct the producers in agricultural and industrial skills. Once the working classes were armed with basic scientific knowledge and with the techniques for applying it, they could then effectively seek political power. Upon winning such power through the electoral process, the government, legal, and educational institutions could be completely transformed.

Throughout his life, Maclure, with rather limited success, supported scientific research and educational innovation. He founded schools of industry, workingmen's institutes, and free libraries. Although his plan for schools of industry resembled the later movement for land-grant colleges, Maclure's immediate impact on American educational development was limited; nevertheless, it was an interesting alternative. In 1824, Maclure would join forces with the English utopian socialist, Robert Owen, in a bold social and educational experiment in communitarianism at New Harmony, Indiana.

COMMUNITARIAN EDUCATION

While Lancastrian monitorial schooling can be viewed as an educational alternative that followed the factory model of early industrialism, Robert Owen's concept of communitarian education presented still another possibility.

Robert Owen (1771-1858) was variously a socialist, a proponent of cooperatives, and a founder of utopian communities as well as an advocate of communitarian education. For him, the ideal society was a cooperative community of common life, property, and education. Owen's experiences from 1799 to 1824 as the manager of a cotton mill in the factory town of New Lanark in Scotland shaped his communitarian ideology. He had taken a typical factory village and had transformed it into a model community. In contrast to the grime, crime, and exploitation that characterized British industrial life in the early nineteenth century, Owen had brought cleanliness, order, and education to the lives of the mill workers. New

Lanark and its schools had attracted scores of visitors and had given Owen both a reputation and an audience. He came to be known as the "benevolent Mr. Owen," a humane and responsible capitalist whose social altruism did not jeopardize profits.

Once his reputation was secure as a successful reformer, Owen became recognized as an expert on the condition of the industrial working classes. In his *Report to the Committee of the Association for the Relief of the Manufacturing and Labouring Poor* (1817) and *Report to the County of Lanark* (1820), Owen proposed solutions to problems of periodic unemployment and inadequate poor relief. He wrote that humankind was experiencing a great cultural transformation in the form of an industrial civilization. Although the factory system had increased productivity, its benefits were unequally distributed because of an archaic and irrational individualism based on private property. Periodic unemployment, Owen reasoned, was not an inevitable result of industrial modernization, as Adam Smith and David Ricardo had argued, but was rather an unnecessary consequence of a competitive and exploitative economy.

In his *Report to the County of Lanark*, Owen urged the communitarian reorganization of society into self-supporting "Villages of Unity and Mutual Co-operation," for all social classes and not just the dependent poor. In these villages, the accommodations, arranged in a parallelogram of buildings, would meet all the residents' requirements. Owen's Village of Unity matured into a comprehensive communitarian ideology that he attempted to implement at New Harmony, Indiana, from 1825 to 1828. The Scottish factory town of New Lanark and the American frontier village in Indiana were to be linked by the transatlantic bonds of Owen's communitarian ideology.

In Owenite theory, the cooperative community was the major agency of social change and reconstruction. As members of an ethical joint family united by social instead of blood relationships, all community members would enjoy the fruits of increased productivity. Community property, goods, and services would be commonly held, administered, and distributed. Once the model community had been created, Owen predicted its success would be emulated by satellite cities that would encircle the earth. Linked by rapid communication and transportation systems, all men, Owen prophesized, would soon dwell in a world community, a global village, of socially related communities of cooperation. Although Owen's communitarianism had many meanings, it was: (1) a system of cooperative human relationships, regarded as the most effective means of promoting human happiness and progress; (2) a system of communal ownership and governance; (3) a comprehensive plan for institutional reform; and (4) a system of both informal milieu education and schooling. Owen's communitarian ideology envisioned the alteration of such basic institutions as marriage, family, property, government, law, and schooling into communal agencies. In his *New View of Society*, Owen proclaimed his basic psychological and sociological principle that human character was the product of the interaction of man's original nature with the environment. Arguing that human character could be improved through environmental manipulation,

Owen believed the controlled community to be the most efficacious milieu to perfect human personality and society. As Owen stated:

> . . . man at birth is wholly formed by the power which creates him, and that his subsequent character is determined by the circumstances which surround him, acting upon his original or created nature—that he does not in any degree form himself, physically or mentally, and therefore cannot be a free or responsible agent: the first practical effects of this knowledge must be, to banish from the mind of man all ideas of merit or demerit in any created object or being—to extirpate from his constitution all the feelings to which such ideas give rise.[10]

In propagandizing for a "New Moral World," Owen assumed the posture of a social prophet sounding the call of the coming millennium. The communitarian society of the future was to be the consequence of historical inevitability. As a prophet, Owen believed that he had correctly interpreted the course of history and of social change. A scientific and secular millennium—a thousand years of peace, progress, and prosperity—was dawning for all mankind. The millennial sense of historical inevitability caused Owen to discount the necessity of political organization and revolutionary tactics and to rely exclusively on education.

Owen was a self-proclaimed social prophet who saw his mission to be preaching the "good news" of communitarianism to a receptive world audience. His task was to convert people from the erroneous dogma of private property to communitarian social and economic theory. When men had been enlightened by the truth of the new social science, people of all classes would unite to effect social change. Thus, Owen did not preach violent revolution but was predicting the coming of a major social transformation from individual property and ownership to the communal ownership of the cooperative commonwealth.

New Harmony:
The Alternative of Communitarian Education

From 1825 to 1828, Robert Owen and his associates attempted a brief but educationally significant communitarian social experiment at New Harmony, Indiana.[11] In *Backwoods Utopias*, Arthur Bestor, a noted historian of American communitarianism, called the coming of Owen, William Maclure, Thomas Say, Joseph Neef, and others to New Harmony "one of the significant intellectual migra-

---

[10] Robert Owen, "The Social System," in *The New Harmony Gazette,* 2, no. 15 (January 10, 1827): 113.

[11] A number of books have appeared on Owen's New Harmony community. Among them are George B. Lockwood, *The New Harmony Movement* (New York: Appleton, 1905); Arthur E. Bestor, Jr., *Backwoods Utopias: The Sectarian and Owenite Phases of Communitarian Socialism in America: 1663-1829* (Philadelphia: University of Pennsylvania Press, 1950); idem, *Education and Reform at New Harmony: Correspondence of William Maclure and Marie Duclos Fretageot, 1820-1833* (Indianapolis: Indiana Historical Society Publications, 1948).

tions of history." It represented the transfer of scientists, naturalists, and educators to the Indiana frontier. In New Harmony's schools, Maclure and Neef sought to establish an outpost of Pestalozzian pedagogy. While the design for a communitarian utopia on the American frontier was Owen's, it was William Maclure who promised to establish a Pestalozzian school system to educate the children of these utopians.

Robert Owen's Experiment

In 1825, Owen purchased the Posey County town of New Harmony, Indiana, from the Rappites, a communal sect of German Pietists.[12] Owen already enjoyed a reputation as a social and educational reformer because of his program at New Lanark where he had established a child-centered community school that emphasized permissiveness, sensory training, and activities instead of language learning. Owen decided to transfer his philanthropic activity to the United States, which he considered more hospitable to social innovation than tradition-bound England. In 1824, Owen journeyed to the United States to purchase Rapp's New Harmony. He visited numerous educational institutions, including those conducted by William Maclure's associates in Philadelphia. Maclure had earlier met Owen at New Lanark in 1824. Although impressed by Owen's educational and social reforms at New Lanark, Maclure felt that Owen's plan at New Harmony was hastily contrived and naïvely optimistic. While Owen planned a utopia, Maclure remained convinced that genuine social reform would come only gradually as generations of children were educated according to Pestalozzi's method.

Nevertheless, Maclure and Owen joined forces. Although both Owen and Maclure agreed to cooperate, spheres of authority were blurred and financial liabilities were vaguely determined. It was generally assumed that Owen would direct the general community while Maclure organized its schools.

Although generally neglected by educational historians, Maclure was an early student of comparative education. From 1804 to 1805, he visited German, Swiss, and French schools and had met both Emmanuel Fellenberg and Johann Heinrich Pestalozzi. Although impressed by Fellenberg's efficient operations at Hofwyl, Maclure found the cooperative spirit of Pestalozzi's school at Yverdon more congenial. Maclure shared Pestalozzi's view that education served social, economic, and political, as well as pedagogical purposes. Finding ignorance to be the chief cause of social evil and poverty, both Maclure and Pestalozzi held that societal reform could be achieved only by gradual educational means. Maclure, who hailed Pestalozzianism as the most effective method for diffusing useful knowledge, believed that the open American environment would be receptive to the system of natural education.

Maclure, who was firmly committed to Pestalozzian education, was convinced that genuine social and economic reform depended on providing children with use-

[12] For treatments of Owen, see G. D. H. Cole, *Robert Owen* (Boston: Little, Brown, 1925); Rowland Hill Harvey, *Robert Owen: Social Idealist* (Berkeley: University of California Press, 1949); Robert Owen, *The Life of Robert Owen, by Himself* (New York: Knopf, 1920).

ful knowledge. He wrote that he "stumbled upon the Pestalozzian system," which he held to be the best system "for the diffusion of useful knowledge." Further, he regarded the United States "as the place" where it was "most likely to succeed."[13]

The Pestalozzian Presence at New Harmony

The third person whose presence was felt at New Harmony was a man who had never been there, the Swiss educator, Johann Heinrich Pestalozzi (1747-1827).[14] Maclure, who financed the educational activity at New Harmony, was dedicated to disseminating Pestalozzianism in the United States. Although his own ideas on education had developed independently of Pestalozzi, Robert Owen, too, found Pestalozzi's educational method to be congenial. What was this method of education that won the allegiance of Maclure and his scientists and teachers at New Harmony?

The Pestalozzian method was devised by the visionary Swiss educator, Johann Heinrich Pestalozzi, who was initially motivated to develop a system of education that would prepare the poor of his native Switzerland to lead healthy, happy, and productive lives. At first, he worked with orphan and poor children at schools he conducted at Neuhof and Stans. He then established educational institutes at Burgdorf and Yverdon which attracted a number of educators eager to study the method.

Theoretically, Pestalozzi's initial inspiration came from reading Rousseau's novel, *Emile*, which told of how a boy was educated according to nature's principles. Pestalozzi, struck with the idea that nature provided the laws of human growth and development, proceeded to "psychologize" instruction according to natural laws. While conducting his schools, Pestalozzi sought to popularize his ideas by writing. Among his books, one in particular seemed appropriate to Owen's New Harmony community. *Leonard and Gertrude*, a novel, told of how a decaying Swiss village was restored to moral and economic vitality through the workings of natural education.[15] In the fictional village of Bonnal, an energetic housewife, Gertrude, educated her children according to the natural principles of education. The life of the village had been in a state of decline as drunkenness and idleness corrupted the town's life. However, Gertrude's energetic efforts brought the town back to moral life and freed it of its corrupting influences. At the center of reform was the newly constructed village school where lessons were learned according to the natural method of education.

Pestalozzi's natural method of education consisted of two phases: the general method and the special method. Because of his work with emotionally scarred and

[13] William Maclure to Marie D. Fretageot, May 22, 1820, in Arthur E. Bestor, Jr., ed., *Education and Reform at New Harmony: Correspondence of William Maclure and Marie Duclos Fretageot, 1820-1833* (Indianapolis: Indiana Historical Society Publications, 1948), p. 301.

[14] Treatments of Pestalozzi's life and method are Kate Sibler, *Pestalozzi: The Man and his Work* (London: Routledge and Kegan Paul, 1965) and Gerald L. Gutek, *Pestalozzi and Education* (New York: Random House, 1968).

[15] Johann H. Pestalozzi, *Leonard and Gertrude*. Trans. by Eva Channing (Boston: D.C. Heath and Co., 1891).

culturally disadvantaged children, Pestalozzi concluded that before any specific learning could take place the school had to become a pervasive atmosphere of love and emotional security. Before children could learn specific skills and tasks, they had to trust the teacher and the teacher in turn needed to love them. Pestalozzi's general manager sought to cultivate children's moral sensibilities. The moral, he believed, developed from loving relationships based on trust and emotional security. As his experience in dealing with children deepened, Pestalozzi came to the conclusion that the establishment of an environment of love and emotional security was a necessary condition for any kind of education. The school, itself, became an extension of the loving home environment. Once the general method had been made to operate in the school, it was possible to use the special method, which he based on what he called the "Anschauung" principle which meant conceptualization, intuition, or impressionism. Essentially, Pestalozzi believed that all knowledge came to human beings by the senses.

Stressing sense impressionism, Pestalozzi devised his object lesson which was the framework of the special method. Instead of beginning instruction with reading, writing, and arithmetic, the special method emphasized that instruction should begin with form, number, and sound. Children were to (1) identify the form of objects by studying their design or their shape; (2) to count the number of objects present; and (3) to name the objects.

After thoroughly studying the objects in their environment, children would gradually be led to writing, arithmetic, and reading. Pestalozzi always emphasized that the process of learning should be slow and gradual—nothing should be hurried or introduced before the child mastered the preceding phase of the lesson.

Like the later progressive educators, Pestalozzi emphasized that learning should begin in children's immediate environment rather than with something remote to their experience. For example, he encouraged frequent field trips or excursions into the countryside surrounding the school. Once children had become thoroughly familiar with their environment, it was possible for them to replicate the major features of that environment in models in which the actual objects' features such as streams and hills were reproduced in miniature form. After this had been done, then children could create maps of their immediate region.

The following methodological strategies were part of Pestalozzi's philosophy of education: (1) All learning comes from the senses; (2) Instruction should begin with the concrete before proceeding to the abstract; (3) Instruction should begin with the particular before going to the general; (4) Instruction should begin with the easy before proceeding to the difficult; and (5) Instruction should proceed from the simple before going to the complex.

During his European travels, Maclure visited Pestalozzi and his school at Burgdorf. He was convinced that Pestalozzian education was ideally suited to his plans for disseminating useful knowledge to the working classes. Maclure eagerly accepted Pestalozzi's special method based on sensation. Sensation was the method used in scientific research. Eminently practical and utilitarian, the object lesson could serve scientific and vocational purposes. Importantly, Pestalozzi's special method avoided the abstract and highly verbal learning associated with classical study that Maclure strongly opposed. So Maclure was strongly determined that the Pestalozzian method would be used in the New Harmony schools. Here Pestalozzian teachers would practice the method of the Swiss educator. New Harmony would become a pedagogical beacon which would illuminate the development of education in the United States.

New Harmony as a Communitarian Experiment

Education at New Harmony can be examined only within the communitarian context of the experiment. Nineteenth-century communitarians like Owen believed that the small, voluntary, experimental community would effect the reform of its residents. Since social regeneration was to be accomplished peacefully, education was to be the chief instrument of reform.

Since he believed that personal and social regeneration could be secured through education, Pestalozzi's sociological and pedagogical theories suited the communitarian impulse. Pestalozzi's book, *Leonard and Gertrude*, told of the social redemption of a village of simple Swiss peasants by natural education. To such convinced Pestalozzians as Maclure and Neef, Owen's experimental community was a suitable environment to establish Pestalozzi's system.

The educational efforts of the New Harmony reformers were based on their particular social, political, and economic beliefs. Owen's reform programs at New Lanark used education to improve the living conditions of his textile workers. Maclure believed that utilitarian education would liberate the energies of the working masses and enable them to secure political power.

Owen, founder of the New Harmony community, saw social reconstruction as a total process. He believed that the community, as an informal educational agency, was a more potent force for social reform than formal schooling. As an educational agency in the broad sense, the successful model community would inspire the establishment of other communities according to the paradigm. For Owen, the school as a formal institution would reflect the reformed values already established within the community. While the school alone could not build a new social order, it could perpetuate it by transmitting communitarianism to succeeding generations.

Maclure, director of New Harmony's schools, relied more on formal education as a means of reform than did Owen. Pessimistic about reforming adults, Maclure believed that genuine social change would occur as children received a scientific and utilitarian education.

New Harmony as an Experiment in Popular Education

The schools of Maclure's New Harmony educational system can be viewed in several ways: as instruments of social reform, as vehicles for diffusing Pestalozzianism, as practical and utilitarian industrial institutions or, as an isolated prototype of the common school. In terms of the latter, Maclure's efforts anticipated Mann's common school crusade for popular education. New Harmony's schools, like the later nineteenth-century common school, were nonsectarian institutions open to all community children.

Although somewhat similar to the common school movement, New Harmony's embryonic experiment in popular education represented a more basic educational shift. The Harmonist revolt against classical learning was also a rebellion against a society dominated by aristocratic Southern planters and Northern capitalists. Owen and Maclure's anticlassicalist and unconventional educational experiment, conducted on the American frontier, was really a nonviolent revolution on behalf of the agricultural and industrial working classes. Maclure and Owen rejected the classical Greek and Latin language curriculum as an obsolete educational residue that had grown irrelevant in a developing society. While some businessmen might share this anticlassical bias, they could not accept the communitarian antipathy to private property and profit. Owen and Maclure saw popular education as a nonviolent instrument for ameliorating the condition of the working classes during the dehumanizing stages of early industrialization. Their educational efforts were directed not only to practical and utilitarian schooling but to fundamental social, economic, and political reconstruction.

In contrast to New Harmony's utopian socialists, the common school leaders Mann and Barnard enlisted the support of businessmen for universal popular education. Holding that wealth was produced by applying social intelligence to the exploitation of natural resources, Mann told businessmen that their investment in common schooling could increase their profits. Commenting on Barnard's strong inclination to ally popular education with private property, Curti said, ". . . he seems to have sanctioned what was virtually the indoctrination of the teachers of youth with capitalistic theory."[16] While Mann and Barnard used common schooling to reduce social and economic class antagonisms, Maclure saw popular education as a means of liberating the working class from upper-class exploitation.

New Harmony as a Community of Equality

Owen's New Harmony communitarians opposed private property as the source of all social evils. They believed that common property and popular education would be the "great equalizers" that would break down barriers to progress produced by unequal social classes and distinctions. On May 1, 1825, the Preliminary Society of New Harmony was formed "to improve the character and conditions of its own members, and to prepare them to become associates in independent communities, having common property." Ten months later, on February 5, 1826, an overly optimistic Owen proclaimed the Community of Equality. The constitution adopted by the community members revealed their basic social and educational convictions as they committed themselves to "equality

[16] Merle Curti, *The Social Ideas of American Educators* (Paterson, N.J.: Littlefield, Adams, 1959), p. 154.

of rights" and "equality of duties" within a "cooperative union" and a "community of property." According to their constitution:

> ... man's character, mental, moral, and physical, is the result of his formation, his location, and ... the circumstance within which he exists.
>
> ... man is powerful in action, efficient in production, and happy in social life, only as he acts cooperatively and unitedly.
>
> All members of the community shall be considered as one family, and no one shall be held in higher or lower estimation on account of occupation. There shall be similar food, clothing, and education, as near as can be furnished, for all according to their ages; and, as soon as practicable, all shall live in similar houses, and in all respects be accommodated alike. Every member shall render his or her best services for the good of the whole, according to the rules and regulations that may be hereafter adopted by the community. It shall always remain a primary object of the community to give the best physical, moral, and inellectual education to all its members.[17]

New Harmony's constitution restated Robert Owen's views on property, community, environment, and education. It was in this communal context that Maclure's Education Society sought to establish the schools that were to educate a new, utopian generation.

Maclure's Boatload of Knowledge

Although agreeing to cooperate with Owen, Maclure was more committed to popularizing Pestalozzianism and to establishing agricultural and industrial schools. Maclure brought his Philadelphia intellectuals to New Harmony as the nucleus of a major scientific and educational center. Maclure's followers were to teach in the schools and do scientific and pedagogical research. In time, their scientific and educational findings were to be disseminated across the United States. Maclure shipped his extensive library, scientific instruments, and natural history collection to New Harmony and organized the individuals who were to advance his program. Maclure brought his Pestalozzian associate, Joseph Neef, to lead the New Harmony schools.

Maclure gathered his band of intellectuals for the journey from Philadelphia to the Indiana frontier. At Pittsburgh, they boarded a keelboat, *The Philanthropist*, and embarked on the Ohio River for the last stage of their journey. Owen referred to the migration of Maclure's Philadelphia intellectuals as the "boatload of knowledge." With Maclure was Thomas Say and Charles Lesueur, naturalists; Marie Duclos Fretageot and Phiquepal d'Arusmont, Pestalozzian teachers; Gerard Troost, a Dutch geologist; Robert Dale Owen, the son of the project's originator; Captain Donald Macdonald, a friend of Owen and a former English army officer; and

---

[17] Lockwood, *New Harmony Movement,* pp. 286-87.

Stedman Whitwell, an architect. Aboard *The Philanthropist* was the nucleus of the Education Society and the general faculty of New Harmony's schools.

The Owen-Maclure Controversies

In the course of the New Harmony experiment, the basic differences that existed between the major figures, Owen and Maclure, surfaced. By the spring of 1827, the Owenite community was on the brink of disintegration, as Owen and Maclure quarreled over financial and educational matters. Their financial disputes weakened the community. Since the community had been organized on the basis of common ownership, it was ironic that so much effort was devoted to property litigation.

The differences between Owen and Maclure extended to educational issues. Owen criticized Maclure's educators, charging them with improperly organizing the schools. To achieve communitarian indoctrination, Owen proposed a new system of social education that consisted of three weekly evening lectures to be attended by the entire community, children as well as adults. Lectures on various trades and occupations would replace the systematic instruction in mineralogy, chemistry, and mechanics. No distinction was to be made between teacher and student; practical experience was the only prerequisite for lecturing. Visual aids, maps, and globes were to be used in teaching geography and other subjects.[18]

Owen's plans for social education undermined Maclure's efforts. Owen was coming under the influence of Lancastrian monitorialism, which asserted that a trained teacher could quickly train students in particular subjects or skills. Hastily prepared monitors would then teach other students. At the time of the New Harmony experiment, monitorialism was becoming popular in the larger American cities of Philadelphia and New York. Pestalozzians like Maclure and Neef opposed a system that relied on unprepared teachers. They could not accept an educational system that relied on haste instead of the slow, thorough, and deliberate learning emphasized by Pestalozzi.

Owen's plan of social education made the lecture into the central instructional phase. Owen was becoming increasingly obsessed with rhetoric as a means of social and educational reform. Maclure, who had always opposed excessive concentration on verbalism, complained that Owen was proposing a "parrot" method by which children would repeat words without understanding them. Such a step would retard, rather than advance, Pestalozzi's progressive method of natural education.

Owen's plan of social education also minimized the importance of expertise in educational method and competence in subject matter. Neef, for example, was thoroughly prepared in Pestalozzian methodology. Say, Lesueur, Troost, and the other naturalists were competent research scientists. In minimizing the importance of pedagogical and scientific training, Owen claimed that practical experience was the only requirement for lecturing. In implementing his plan on social education, Owen found that he was still forced to rely on Maclure's Education Society for

[18] Bestor, *Backwoods Utopias,* pp. 192-93.

much of the instruction. Like many of Owen's proposals, the plan for social education was abandoned after only a few lectures. Nevertheless, the gulf between Owen
and the Education Society had widened.

As a result of the confusing financial litigation between Owen and Maclure,
the community was in the throes of complete disintegration. The relationship
between the school and the community also collapsed. When the Education Society
requested payment for education on the basis of labor for labor, the Agricultural
Society refused to render either goods, services, or money for the tuition of its children. The Mechanics' Society completely repudiated any obligation to the Education Society.

The Educational Significance of New Harmony

Owen failed to create a utopia in Indiana. His experiment was short-lived and
lacked the communal consensus needed to hold it together. Where such communities have succeeded in the United States, they usually have been sustained by
religious commitments rather than by political or sociological ideologies.

New Harmony was the location of one the first early infant schools in the
United States. Owen, who had established an infant school at New Lanark, was a
pioneer proponent of early childhood education. He believed that young children
needed a special environment that exposed them to socializing activities, stories,
and games, as well as some intellectual experiences.

Following Maclure's predilection for schools of industry, New Harmony's
schools provided extensive vocational education. Maclure was vitally interested in
establishing such practical institutions to educate working-class children. Each student in Neef's higher school was to learn some trade or craft.

New Harmony's schools were open to all of the community's residents. Although recognizing education as a vital community component, the Owenites did
not develop a formula for school support. In fact, the members of the Agricultural
and Mechanics' Societies refused to pay for the education of their children. Owen
and Maclure's socialistic experiment furnished little support for the common school
movement that Mann and Barnard advanced later in the nineteenth century. The
New Harmony schools also offered equal education to both boys and girls. They
were in advance of most of the schools in the United States in the matter of equal
educational opportunity for both sexes.

Although many aspects of New Harmony's educational system were far in
advance of most American schools, the community suffered from isolation. While
much was known and reported about Owen's social theories, little was known
about the schools. The charges that the community was socialistic and antireligious
prejudiced many against the experiment and blunted the possible impact of
Pestalozzianism. It was not until the second half of the nineteenth century that a
more formal version of Pestalozzian object teaching gained popularity. It was the
more conservative Edward Sheldon of the Oswego Normal School, rather than
Maclure, who was the recognized popularizer of Pestalozzian education in the
United States.

The greatest achievement of New Harmony was intellectual, in a broad rather than pedagogical sense. Maclure brought a number of scientists to New Harmony who contributed to the natural sciences. After the failure of Owen's community, Maclure established a School of Industry at New Harmony, whose excellent printing press published research in the natural sciences.

The work of Owen and Maclure should not be dismissed by educators. In New Harmony's schools can be found the transference of European educational philosophies of Pestalozzi and Fellenberg to the United States. Neef's, Owen's, and Maclure's emphasis on experience, activities, and interest anticipated the Progressive Education Movement of the early twentieth century. The views of Owen and Maclure also suggested the theories of social reconstructionist educators who sought to use schools as instruments for building a new society.

FRANCES WRIGHT

Frances Wright (1795-1852), an early nineteenth-century feminist and antislavery reformer, had visited Owen's New Harmony community. Convinced of the wisdom of Owen's communitarian doctrines, she established a community for freed slaves at Nashoba in Tennessee. Wright conceived of Nashoba as a biracial community in which black and white children would attend integrated schools. The children of former slaveowners were to be instilled with respect for manual labor and taught useful trades. Black children would learn the responsibilities needed for citizenship.[19] Like New Harmony, Nashoba was a brief episode, lasting only from 1827 to 1828. However, it embraced a vision of things to come.

In addition to her attacks on slavery and demands that women be accorded equal rights, Frances Wright, like William Maclure, argued for a system of popular education. From 1828 to 1831, Wright and Robert Dale Owen, the eldest son of Robert Owen, were coeditors of *The Free Enquirer*, a New York newspaper that advocated women's rights, working-class solidarity, and a system of popular and useful education.

In her articles, Wright argued that all American children needed equal, universal education under state auspices. With Robert Dale Owen, she organized an Association for the Protection of Industry and the Promotion of Popular Instruction. The association's primary purpose was to work toward public education.

For Wright and Owen, public education was to be "free from sectarian and clerical influences and from aristocratical distinction." It was to cultivate "in the rising generation those habits of industry, those principles of sound morality, those feelings of brotherly love, together with those solid intellectual acquirements,

---

[19] Cecilia Morris Eckhardt, *Fanny Wright: Rebel in America* (Cambridge, Mass.: Harvard University Press, 1984), p. 127.

which are necessary to secure for all the fair exercise of those equal political rights set forth in the institutions of the land."[20]

Frances Wright, who was antagonistic to church-related schools, became embroiled in controversy with religious groups. While she and Owen were able to muster some support for their educational proposals, they succeeded more in raising the consciousness of the working classes on behalf of public schooling than in actually creating a system of schools. Unlike the more politically adroit Horace Mann and Henry Barnard, who made strategic compromises with church leaders and business interests for common schooling, Wright and Owen held fast to their principles. As forceful advocates of working-class education, women's rights, and the abolition of slavery, they were propagandists for popular education.

CONCLUSION

In the era before the common school movement, several alternative patterns of schooling were introduced to the United States. The popular monitorial system, designed by Joseph Lancaster, growing out of the assembly-line model of the factory, promised efficiency at low cost. Robert Owen and his communitarian ideology saw education as an agency of social reconstruction. William Maclure and Frances Wright were advocates of useful knowledge for the working class. The major impetus for public education would come, however, with the common school movement.

DISCUSSION QUESTIONS

1. Examine the concept of philanthropy in education. To what extent was philanthropy derived from the Puritan notion of stewardship? Did early nineteenth-century philanthropy differ from stewardship?
2. Examine the socioeconomic context of monitorialism. In what ways was monitorialism a transatlantic educational movement?
3. How was Lancaster's educational system a prototype of later urban school administration and supervision?
4. Compare and contrast the functions of the Lancaster's monitor with those of the contemporary teaching aide.
5. In what ways did William Maclure envision education to be an instrument of economic development and social change?
6. Examine Owen's communitarianism as a transatlantic philosophy that had impact in both Great Britain and the United States.

[20] *The Free Enquirer* (September 23, 1829), p. 377.

7. Examine the New Harmony experiment as a case study in communitarian education.
8. What impact did the early nineteenth-century alternatives to common schooling have on American educational history?

RESEARCH TOPICS

1. Several of the educational methods of the early nineteenth century, particularly monitorialism, Owenism, and Pestalozzianism, originated in Europe and were popular in both Europe and North America. Consult several sources on European educational history and compare the uses of these methods in Europe and the United States.
2. Read accounts of monitorialism written by Lancaster or other proponents of the system. Comment on the degree to which these accounts suggested a routinized pattern of schooling.
3. Examine William Maclure's opinions and extrapolate from them his concepts of education as an instrument of economic growth and social change.
4. Identify the scientific or educational contributions made by one of the following persons who were subsidized by William Maclure: Joseph Neef, Marie Duclos Fretageot, Thomas Say, Charles Lesueur, Gerard Troost.
5. Read Owen's autobiography or a carefully selected biography. From your reading, identify Owen's views on education.
6. Describe the communal educational efforts at New Harmony or at similar communities.
7. Investigate the efforts of Frances Wright on behalf of women's rights and popular education.

REFERENCES AND READINGS

Barlow, Thomas A. *Pestalozzi and American Education.* Boulder: Este Es Press—University of Colorado Libraries, 1977.
Bestor, Arthur E., Jr. *Backwoods Utopias: The Sectarian and Owenite Phases of Communitarian Socialism in America: 1663-1829.* Philadelphia: University of Pennsylvania Press, 1950.
___. *Education and Reform at New Harmony: Correspondence of William Maclure and Marie Duclos Fretageot, 1820-1833.* Indianapolis: Indiana Historical Society Publications, 1948.
Butt, John, ed. *Robert Owen: Aspects of His Life and Work.* New York: Humanities Press, 1971.
Cole, G. D. H. *Robert Owen.* Boston: Little, Brown, 1925.
Eckhardt, Celia M. *Fanny Wright: Rebel in America.* Cambridge, Mass.: Harvard University Press, 1984.
Gutek, Gerald L. *Joseph Neef: The Americanization of Pestalozzianism.* University: University of Alabama Press, 1978.
___. *Pestalozzi and Education.* New York: Random House, 1968.
Harrison, J. F. C. *Quest for the New Moral World: Robert Owen and the Owenites in Britain and America.* New York: Scribner's, 1969.

Harvey, Rowland H. *Robert Owen: Social Idealist.* Berkeley: University of California Press, 1949.

Johnson, Oakley C. *Robert Owen in the United States.* New York: Humanities Press, 1970.

Kaestle, Carl F. *Joseph Lancaster and the Monitorial School Movement.* New York: Teachers College Press, Columbia University, 1973.

Lockwood, George B. *The New Harmony Movement.* New York: Appleton, 1905.

Maclure, William. *Opinions on Various Subjects.* New Harmony, Ind.: School Press, 1831.

Midwinter, Eric. *Nineteenth-Century Education.* New York: Harper & Row, Pub., 1970.

Owen, Robert. *The Life of Robert Owen, by Himself.* New York: Knopf, 1920.

Pitzer, Donald E., ed. *Robert Owen's American Legacy.* Indianapolis: Indiana Historical Society, 1972.

Pollard, Sidney, and Salt, John., eds. *Robert Owen: Prophet of the Poor.* Lewisburg, Pa.: Bucknell University Press, 1971.

Silber, Kate. *Pestalozzi: The Man and His Work.* London: Routledge and Kegan Paul, 1965.

Stiller, Richard. *Commune on the Frontier: The Story of Frances Wright.* New York: Crowell, 1972.

Wilson, William E. *The Angel and the Serpent: The Story of New Harmony.* Bloomington: Indiana University Press, 1964.

4
THE COMMON SCHOOL MOVEMENT

The common school movement, which took place in the first half of the nineteenth century, from about 1820 to 1860, was a complex and significant occurrence not only in American education but also in American society, politics, and culture. In this chapter, we shall examine the movement's historical context and phases of development. We shall also discuss how America's common school movement differed from contemporary European educational movements and then go on to examine the movement's leaders, the ways in which common schools were established, and the overall significance of the movement.

Essentially, the American common school movement sought to establish tax-supported, locally controlled elementary schools that would be open and available to children living in the various school districts created in the process. Following the earlier tradition of educational decentralization established in New England, the common school movement resulted in state systems of schools rather than in a national school system, as was the case in many European nations. As a result of the common school movement, thousands of small local school districts were established throughout the United States. These schools, elementary in nature, offered such primary branches of instruction as reading, writing, arithmetic, spelling, history, and geography. Their milieu and their instructional materials were permeated by a value core that followed a generalized version of Protestant Christianity.

The term "common school," still used in many states to designate a public school, in the nineteenth century referred to a school that was open to all children, both boys and girls, whose parents or guardians lived in the particular school district. "Common" did not connote an inferior school for inferior students. It meant a school that was used by all the people, open to all children, and supported by all citizens. It also referred to a school that offered common branches of instruction. The term "public" also describes common schools, which formed the first rung in the evolving American education ladder, a ladder that would eventually link elementary, secondary, and higher educational institutions into a statewide network of publicly supported schools.

The legal framework of the common school movement was found in the Constitution of the United States and in the various state constitutions. Although the United States Constitution did not directly address education or schooling, the Tenth Amendment's reserved powers clause delegated power over education and schooling to each of the states. In their constitutions, the states generally expressed their commitment to education and to schooling. In the years immediately after the Union was established, the various states did little to implement their general educational commitment. When the common school movement began in earnest in the early 1830s, it originated in those states that already had a tradition and some experience with publicly supported or state-related schooling; it then slowly proceeded to states that lacked such a tradition.

In the early national period, from 1800 to 1820, the patterns of school establishment varied from state to state and from region to region. Although the political and educational philosophy that supported common schooling was national in scope, the realities of implementation were state and local. Constitutionally, the states were the designated legal agencies for education. The states tended to delegate much of the responsibility for establishing and maintaining common schools to the local districts. Although more will be said about the actual establishing process later in the chapter, the general regional pattern for establishing common schools was as follows: (1) The New England states, especially Massachusetts, Connecticut, and New Hampshire, moved more rapidly than other states to establish common schools. (2) The Middle Atlantic states, with their strong tradition of support for private and parochial school alternatives, moved more slowly and experimented with alternatives to publicly supported common schooling. (3) The Southern states, because of a tradition that regarded schooling as a private matter and because of their pattern of race relations, did not establish common school systems until the Reconstruction period after the Civil War. (4) The Northern states, lying in the Ohio and Mississippi River valleys, tended to follow the New England pattern.

THE HISTORICAL CONTEXT

The historical context of the common school movement revealed a varied and often inconsistent mosaic of political, social, economic, and educational crosscurrents. Although several historians have attempted to analyze this important development in American life, the common school movement still needs a comprehensive and

An illustration of the *New Third School Readers*, a nineteenth century text.   *(From Leroy V. Goodman, ed., A Nation of Learners. Washington, D.C.: G.P.O., 1976, p. 182. National Institute of Educational Collection.)*

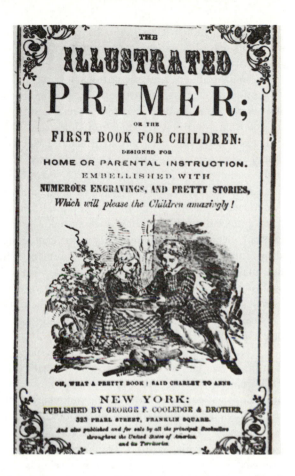

The Illustrated Primer, a first book for children, used in the late nineteenth century. *(From Leroy V. Goodman, etc., A Nation of Learners. Washington, D.C.: G.P.O., 1976, p. 99. Library of Congress Collection.)*

adequate treatment. Let us look briefly at some of the major trends, forces, and personalities that were part of the common school movement in the United States. In many respects, the common school movement was as significant to the course of national development as such important events as the Civil War and Reconstruction, industrialism and modernization, and populism and progressivism.[1]

Revolutionary and Enlightenment Impulses

Previous chapters have examined the impulses derived from the eighteenth-century Enlightenment and from the revolutionary and early national periods that helped shape American educational thought. Here we shall discuss: (1) the Enlightenment and revolutionary impulses that stimulated common schooling; (2) the

[1] The standard histories of American education examine the common school movement. The definitive work is Lawrence A. Cremin, *The American Common School: An Historical Conception* (New York: Teachers College Press, Columbia University, 1951). A readable and historically accurate account is Frederick M. Binder, *The Age of the Common School, 1830-1865* (New York: John Wiley, 1974).

trend toward industrialization, urbanization, and modernization that accompanied common schooling; and (3) the common school's relationship to American social and political reform.

Enlightenment and revolutionary impulses suggested that a popular form of education that encouraged American nationalism and the application of science to life would advance the progressive development of the American people. Franklin, an advocate of utilitarian education; Jefferson, who wanted education to promote citizenship; and theorists such as Rush and Webster all wanted to create an educational system to serve America's unique needs. Underlying these revolutionary and early national impulses was a desire to separate church and state and school and church. This trend from the period of independence advanced the secularization of American education. While these ideological trends had an impact on the common school movement, it was somewhat muted. The most significant impact of Enlightenment ideology was the motivation for civic education, or education for citizenship. The American common school movement sought to cultivate citizenship and nationalistic loyalty to the United States. However, as indicated, the common school movement, while national in its ideological scope, was a local and state rather than a national movement in implementation. Underlying the movement, however, was the ideological belief that common schools could advance generalized citizenship and nationalism.

Many of the theorists of the early republican period, rebelling against the dominance of classical languages over formal education, argued for scientific and utilitarian instruction. The common school movement, especially in its emphasis on basic skills and subjects, fulfilled in a rudimentary but evolutionary way the demand that schooling be utilitarian and functional and contribute to national development.

Finally, the impulses stimulated by the Enlightenment and the revolution encouraged a secularization of American education that led eventually to a separation of the churches from the common schools. During the common school movement, however, these secular tendencies were more theoretical than implemented in practice. The zenith of the common school movement also coincided with a series of major religious revivals of Protestant Christianity in the United States, especially among evangelical denominations. These revivals muted the trend to secularization. The leaders of many Protestant denominations agreed to abandon parochial schools in exchange for common schooling that expressed a commitment to Christianity. While the emergent common schools were separated from direct denominational control, they encouraged a generalized commitment to the ethics and values of a common evangelical Christianity.

The Early Industrialization of the United States

The first half of the nineteenth century, the era of the common school movement, saw the first stage of America's Industrial Revolution. These seeds of industrialism would grow and slowly transform the United States from an agrarian-rural society into an urban, industrial, and increasingly modern society. Industrialization would increase American productivity and would contribute to the urbanization of the United States by creating large cities with burgeoning populations.

Concurrent with the industrialization and urbanization processes transforming America's social order, the United States also experienced massive immigration. In the early years of the nineteenth century, the majority of immigrants still came from Northern Europe—from Great Britain and the Scandinavian countries. After the 1830s and 1840s, large numbers of immigrants arrived from Ireland and Germany. Irish immigration was spurred by the devastating potato famine on that island, and German immigration was stimulated by the failure of liberal and republican forces in the revolutions of 1848. Later in the nineteenth century, immigration patterns shifted again and millions began to arrive from Southern and Eastern Europe, especially Italy and Russia. There was also an influx of Poles, Slovaks, Czechs, Serbs, Croats, Slovenes, and others who had been submerged in the Austro-Hungarian Empire.

Although industrialization increased the gross national product and brought about economic growth, it also generated complex social and economic problems. At root, these social problems were aggravated by the dislocation and resettlement of people in a haphazard, unplanned way. Social dislocation gave rise to the following problems and trends: (1) The increasing urban population included large numbers of children, collected in central locations, who required schooling. (2) The factories, mills, and enterprises of an industrializing and modernizing society needed educated managers and trained workers. (3) The populations of the Northern states became increasingly heterogeneous in terms of ethnicity and language as large numbers of non-English-speaking immigrants settled them. (4) In certain areas of the country, particularly in the large northeastern cities, Protestant domination was challenged by a growing Roman Catholic population.

These changing economic, social, and religious patterns occurred concurrently with the common school movement. Although it is difficult to interpret the impact of such immense social changes on the common school movement, certain generalizations can be made. Common schooling was an effort to modernize and make more efficient the various patterns of American elementary education. It was an effort to create new educational structures of an institutional nature to meet the needs of a modernizing society. As a response to the reforming impulses of the Jacksonian period, the establishing of common schools created greater educational opportunities for lower socioeconomic classes. Common schools were, in this instance, conduits of upward social and economic mobility.

While common schools were agencies of upward social and economic mobility, they were also instruments of social control over the lower socioeconomic classes by dominant English-speaking, upper-class Protestants. Social control, in this context, meant imposing by institutionalized education the language, beliefs, and values of the dominant group on outsiders, especially on the non-English-speaking immigrants. Common schools were expected to create such conformity in American life by imposing the language and ideological outlook of the dominant group. For example, by using English as the medium of instruction, the common schools were expected to create an English-speaking citizenry; by cultivating a general value orientation based on Protestant Christianity, the common schools were expected to create a general American ethic. As such, the common schools were to be agencies of Americanization, which meant the imposition of prescribed values on an increasingly heterogenous multicultural population.[2]

While the forces of industrialization, urbanization, and immigration were beginning to transform the United States from an agrarian into a modern society, the process was slow and uneven. Agricultural and rural interests were strong throughout the nineteenth century, especially in the state legislatures and the Congress. As the northeastern states were experiencing the beginnings of industrial modernization, the westward movement was continuing as successive waves of settlers occupied the Western territories. The social concepts that were transported to the West were essentially those of rural New England. Farmers, often living in isolated homesteads, established thousands of one-room rural schools, taught by a single teacher. These homely and simple schools were the outposts of American civilization on the regions of the frontier and would remain such, in some localities, until the early twentieth century. If common schooling meant Americanization in the large cities of the northeast, it had a different meaning on the frontier. It meant an effort to keep alive literacy, citizenship, and civilization in the wilderness.

Many of the basic organizational patterns governing common schools in nineteenth-century America were established in the nation's rural areas and small towns. The small, independent school district governed by locally elected trustees or board members had rural origins. Even in the large cities, the patterns of school governance remained essentially those of small-town and rural America.

In rural and small-town America, the local elementary or common school, often a one-room building painted white or red and located as near as possible to the geographical center of the school district, was valued as a community neighborhood educational institution. In many instances, the school, as the only public building in the vicinity, gave the community its corporate and community identity. Indeed, Fuller has called the local rural school districts "laboratories of democracy" in which Americans learned "how to make laws" and "to govern themselves." In the early nineteenth century, local rural school boards established district attendance boundaries, conducted school elections, levied taxes, and appointed and licensed teachers.[3]

The Common Schools and American Reform

While the common schools were instruments of Americanization, of advancing industrialization and urbanization, and of social control of the lower socioeconomic classes by the dominant group, they were also products of the great

[2]David Nasaw, *Schooled to Order: A Social History of Public Schooling in the United States* (New York: Oxford University Press, 1979), pp. 37-43.

[3]Wayne E. Fuller, *The Old Country School: The Story of Rural Education in the Middle West* (Chicago: University of Chicago Press, 1982), pp. 45-46.

reform movements of the first half of the nineteenth century. The 1830s and the 1840s, the zenith of the common school movement, was also the time when various reforms associated with the Jacksonian period swept much of the United States.[4] Like many currents of this transforming but unsettling age, the great reform movements were varied. At times, they were part of a common spirit of reform and reinforced each other. At other times, they ran in different directions. Some of the reform movements failed and others succeeded. As a reform movement, schooling, like the abolition of black slavery, was one of the great movements for social change in the United States.

Historians have heralded the first half of the nineteenth century, the Age of Jackson, as the era of the common man. At the national level, Andrew Jackson's politics stressed the principle of rotation in public office. Leadership was no longer limited to a financial oligarchy as envisioned by the Federalist Alexander Hamilton; nor was the national leadership in the hands of an aristocracy of intellect as recommended by Thomas Jefferson. Rather, national leadership, as well as state and local offices, went increasingly to those who won elections. The entry of the common man into leadership positions was accompanied by an extension of suffrage. Many states, especially those on the frontier, reduced or eliminated property requirements for voting. Elections were increasingly decided by popular vote. Jacksonian popular democracy had an educational corollary that provided for the education of the common people in common schools. A broader conception of citizenship meant that more people had to be prepared for citizenship by an educational system that was common to all. The common school was the educational reform that accompanied the political reforms associated with popular democracy.

In addition to popular democracy, there was a demand that governments— federal, state, and local—encourage internal improvements—that is, digging canals, developing roadways, and building a transportation system to link the various sections of the United States to improve commerce and advance national development. While the government's role in effecting internal improvements was hotly debated, such improvements were part of the modernization process. Common schooling was the educational improvement that accompanied the material kinds of internal improvements. As these internal improvements were debated, so was common schooling.

The movement for common schooling originated in the northeastern region of the United States, particularly in the New England states of Massachusetts, Connecticut, and New Hampshire, where Calvinism's gloomy injunctions were being transformed, especially in intellectual circles, into more humanistic religious sentiments seeking to uplift individuals by educating them. The Unitarian perspective of such common school leaders as Horace Mann, and the Transcendentalism of Ralph Waldo Emerson generated a reforming impulse that abandoned the church pulpit for the floor of the town meeting and the legislative chamber of the state.

---

[4]Henry Steele Commager, *The Era of Reform, 1830-1860* (Princeton, N.J.: D. Van Nostrand, 1960).

The inherited Calvinist tradition that saw educated persons as stewards for humanity was an impulse not only in the common school movement but in the movements for penal reform, temperance, and abolitionism as well. There was a sure and unmistaken view that if people were educated to know what was right, then they would do what was right. In this way, the common school movement sought not only to educate but also to uplift and to reform.

THE COMMON SCHOOL COMPARED
TO OTHER EDUCATIONAL SYSTEMS

In the past, American educational historians have emphasized the distinctiveness and uniqueness of the common school. Emphasizing its egalitarian and democratic origins, they stressed the common school as the foundation of America's educational ladder. While these historians were correct in their assessment, they often neglected the degree to which the American common school movement both coincided and differed with attempts to establish national elementary or primary school systems in Europe, especially in England, France, and Prussia.

In the first half of the nineteenth century, Prussia, the United States, England, and France undertook efforts to establish systems of primary or elementary schools. While it is an exaggeration to claim that these nations were establishing national systems of education, they were seeking to create some sort of primary school system. The movement toward universal elementary education was not located in one nation but was an ongoing development in those nations that were experiencing industrial modernization. Each nation developed its own style and institutional structure in terms of its own traditions and cultural, political, and economic context.

Political and educational leaders who wanted to achieve nationwide elementary schooling in their own countries often looked to other countries for successful models. Visitors with an educational mission often traveled to Prussia to examine that nation's school system. Germany did not exist as a national entity until 1871; what came to be the German Empire, united under Prussian leadership in 1871, was then a collection of independent and sovereign nations of which Prussia was the largest and most powerful. When it recovered from the Napoleonic wars, Prussia sought to achieve hegemony over the other German states by embarking on a concerted program of efficient national administration. As a result, the Prussian army, civil service, postal service, and schools were operated in an efficient and coordinated manner. In their efforts to create a strong and unified nation, the Prussian leaders assigned an important role to the nation's schools. Since they were state supported, the central government dispatched inspectors to visit the schools to make sure that they were meeting standards. The result was administrative efficiency and educational uniformity. The Prussians, too, were borrowers of educational ideas; they sent emissaries to visit schools in other countries where educational innovation was occurring. For example, the Prussian government sent teachers to study with the famous Swiss educator, Johann Heinrich Pestalozzi. Fichte, in his *Addresses to the German Nation*, advocated the introduction of Pestalozzian educational methods as instruments not only of educational reform but of national regeneration as well.

Attracted by Prussia's educational achievement, educators from other nations, especially the United States, France, and England, journeyed to Prussia to examine its school administration and organization. These visitations by foreign educators to Prussia were an early beginning of comparative education and the use of comparative study to encourage educational borrowing from other countries.

Of particular importance to the American common school proponents was the French interest in Prussian schools. Francois Guizot, minister of education in the government of King Louis Phillippe, was embarking on a program to establish government-supported primary schools.[5] Guizot dispatched Victor Cousin to study Prussian schools and to report back to him. Guizot, using information gathered by Cousin, succeeded in securing legislation that established a system of national primary schools in France in 1833. Although the French primary schools differed from the American common schools in many respects, they served a similar purpose in providing instruction in the basic subjects of reading, writing, and arithmetic and in instilling nationalism in the children of the two countries. They differed, however, in that while the centralized French primary schools were controlled by the national government, the American common schools were locally supported and controlled.

American common school leaders, such as Horace Mann and Henry Barnard, made it their business to visit Europe and to inspect schools on that continent. In the nineteenth century, there was a transatlantic flow of ideas from Europe to America. The United States, still much in the position of being a developing nation, was seeking to borrow selectively from Europe. Of particular interest to the American educators were European innovations in school administration and in instruction methodology. Henry Barnard, in particular, in his *American Journal of Education*, introduced the innovative ideas of such European educators as Pestalozzi, Fellenberg, Froebel, and others to American educators.

In much the same way that Guizot had sent Victor Cousin to Prussia, the Ohio legislature dispatched Calvin Stowe to visit Prussian schools and prepare a report that could be used to organize schools in Ohio. Stowe's report provided a comparative stimulus to common schooling in Ohio and in the United States.

While Prussia, France, and the United States moved forward in creating elementary schools, England was also beginning to make some movement, albeit hesitantly, in that direction. In England, however, the movement was much slower due to the English tradition that viewed schooling as primarily a private responsibility. By the 1830s, however, the changing English political and economic situation

[5] John E. Talbott, *The Politics of Educational Reform in France, 1918-1940* (Princeton, N.J.: Princeton University Press, 1969), pp. 3-5, 21; and Douglas Johnson, *Guizot: Aspects of French History, 1787-1874* (Toronto: University of Toronto Press, 1963), pp. 2-9.

was becoming more favorable to supporting education. Stimulated by the reforming impulses of utilitarian philosophy and liberal ideology, Parliament enacted a series of reforms. Modifications of the Poor Law in 1834 increased the number of pauper schools; the Factory Act of 1833 required that working children reserve two hours for schooling each day. Also in 1833, Parliament decided to aid elementary education by granting £10,000 to the Foreign Bible Society for schools maintained by these associations.[6]

The examples of other nations provided an impetus to America's common school movement. The connective link in this transatlantic movement to establish elementary school systems was the recognition by some political leaders that literacy and competency in basic skills was necessary in cementing national cohesiveness, stimulating industrial modernization and productivity, and in bringing about patriotic loyalty to the nation-state. The American common school leaders were quick to point out that while Europe's school systems contained elements that could be imported and imitated in the United States, they sought to emulate neither Prussian militarism and uniformity nor French bureaucratic centralization. Mann, Barnard, and other proponents of common schooling argued that the creating of American common schools should take place within the political and educational traditions and framework that were unique to the United States. In summary, the following comparisons and contrasts can be made between the European and American efforts to create elementary school systems:

1. Prussian and French efforts to create national elementary school systems were led by leaders in the national or central governments; in the United States, leadership for common schools arose largely at the state or local levels.

2. The control of the Prussian and French systems was located at the national level in the central government; in the United States, control—based upon the Constitution—was located in the various states, which in turn delegated large areas of responsibility to local school districts.

3. Although the national elementary school systems of Prussia and France contributed to national unity, patriotism, and productivity, they were not designed to serve as vehicles of upward socioeconomic mobility for large sections of the population. In these European countries, elementary schools were a distinct track separate from college preparatory institutions. The upper socioeconomic classes attended distinctive preparatory, secondary, and higher institutions. In the United States, the common elementary schools became the foundation of the American educational ladder. Later in the nineteenth century, this ladder included publicly supported secondary schools that linked elementary schools to higher institutions and facilitated upward social and economic mobility.

4. Finally, there was a strong element of social control operating in nations that established elementary school systems. Dominant political, social, and economic classes used these schools to encourage conformity to the ideas and values that perpetuated the status quo and preserved their dominance.

[6]Eric Midwinter, *Nineteenth-Century Education* (New York: Harper & Row, Pub., 1970), pp. 31-38.

LEADERSHIP

As indicated earlier, the leadership of the common school movement in the United States came from a wide range of individuals and organizations at the state and local rather than the national level. Here, we shall identify and describe the role played by these individuals and organizations.

Organizations

American society has exhibited a propensity for forming organizations that advance certain causes or special interests. Establishing common schools was high on the agendas of several of these organizations. Educational organizations and societies, which included teachers and supporters of popular schooling, worked to propagate the program for common schooling. The American Lyceum Society was organized by Josiah Holbrook in 1826 and was committed to the common school ideal; it arranged lecture series throughout the country featuring prominent speakers such as Ralph Waldo Emerson. In the midwestern states, the Western Literary Society supported common schools. Other groups advocating a variety of reforms such as penal reform, aid for the insane, temperance, peace, and abolition, added common schooling to their agendas. Particularly in the Northeastern states, the memberships of these reformist organizations were interlocking; members of one reform group often held memberships in other reform organizations. Individuals attracted to reformist societies tended to support similar causes and to support reform-minded candidates for public office.

Some of the organizations and individuals who supported common schooling used journalism as well as public speaking to popularize their cause. Publications such as William Russell's *American Journal of Education* featured articles on European educational methods and on efforts in the various states to enact common school legislation. Pro-common school journalists, writing in the popular press or in periodicals devoted to educational subjects, helped to create a climate of opinion favorable to publicly supported universal education.

Political Leaders

The leaders of the common school movement were often politicians who supported the establishment of common schools as part of their political platforms. The list of individuals who combined political and educational leadership is a long one. For example, Horace Mann and James Carter in Massachusetts, Henry Barnard in Connecticut, Calvin Stowe in Ohio, Thaddeus Stevens in Pennsylvania, Ninian Edwards in Illinois, Robert Dale Owen in Indiana, and leaders in other states combined educational and political careers. Many of these individuals, as members of state legislatures, took on the cause of promoting common schools. They were instrumental in their states in introducing and in enacting legislation to establish common schools. Several of them, such as Horace Mann, alternated between political and educational offices. These common school leaders recognized the necessary relationships between politics and education and between legislation and schooling.

HORACE MANN

One of the leading proponents of common schooling was Horace Mann. Although many labored for common schools, Mann (1796-1859) is regarded as the foremost statesman of the movement that eventually led to the American public school system. This Massachusetts lawyer, politician, and educator popularized and laid the foundations of common school education through his position as secretary of the Massachusetts Board of Education.[7]

Horace Mann was born on May 4, 1796, in the small Massachusetts town of Franklin, where his father, Thomas Mann, was a farmer.[8] At the end of the eighteenth century, life in Massachusetts was still dominated by the religious intensity of orthodox Calvinism. In Franklin, the Calvinist creed was preached by the Reverend Nathaniel Emmons, an imposing and severe figure. During adolescence, Mann came to question the austere doctrine of Predestination that stressed human depravity. Although he later rejected Calvinism, his early training influenced his intellectual and personal temperament.[9]

Mann's youth in a small Massachusetts town convinced him of the value of hard work, diligence, and seriousness. In many ways, his attitude embodied the Protestant work ethic, which stresses work and productivity. He came to hold the view that children should be educated to respect ethical values and that the school has a duty to forge and educate good, hard-working men and women.

Mann's own education in the town school was brief and erratic. After learning to read in school, he became a steady consumer of the few volumes in the town library. Primarily, he was a self-educated man. His own self-tutelage was sufficient to gain him admission to Brown University in Providence, Rhode Island, in 1816. Mann's exposure to higher education broadened his intellectual perspective. Attracted to the concepts of liberal humanitarianism, he joined a reform-oriented literary society, the United Brothers, which discussed the crucial social and political ideas of the day.

While a student at Brown University, Mann was also exposed to the Transcendentalist philosophy. American Transcendentalism, along with its religious affiliate, Unitarianism, was an idealist, humanitarian, and reformist philosophy that emphasized the inherent goodness of human nature and the possibility of human perfectability. Transcendentalists such as William Ellery Channing, Ralph Waldo Emerson, Henry David Thoreau, and Nathaniel Hawthorne believed in the possibility of personal regeneration and social reform. To advance human perfectability, the Transcendentalists encouraged popular and public education. Reflecting the

---

[7] The definitive biography of Mann is Jonathan Messerli, *Horace Mann: A Biography* (New York: Knopf, 1972). A brief and readable work is Robert B. Downs, *Horace Mann: Champion of Public Schools* (New York: Twayne, 1974).

[8] E. I. F. Williams, *Horace Mann: Educational Statesman* (New York: Macmillan, 1937), p. 1.

[9] Lawrence Cremin, ed., *The Republic and the School: Horace Mann on the Education of Free Men* (New York: Bureau of Publications, Teachers College, Columbia University, 1957), p. 4.

Transcendentalist enthusiasm for education, Mann in his valedictory address at the Brown commencement in 1819 stressed the progressive character of the human race and maintained that education, philanthropy, and republicanism could remedy many of the defects of human civilization.[10]

The Puritan ethic of his boyhood and the Transcendentalist impulse of his young manhood exerted a powerful influence on Horace Mann's evolving philosophy of education. Although rejecting Calvinism's dour belief in human depravity, he found Puritanism's stress on the diligent life irresistible. From Transcendentalism, he accepted the view that humankind was basically good and that life held a higher if sometimes obscure meaning. When Puritanism and Transcendentalism were joined, the mixture produced the ideology that a meaningful life was characterized by constant efforts at personal and societal reform.

After graduating from Brown, Mann prepared for a legal career and was admitted to the Massachusetts bar in 1823. At age 31, Mann launched his political career, promising that he would "do something for the benefit of mankind."[11] Elected to the Massachusetts legislature in 1827, he supported reform causes such as railroad expansion, the funding of public institutions for the mentally ill, and the prohibition of alcoholic beverages.

Mann was elected to the Massachusetts Senate in 1853, where he supported legislation for common schools. In 1834, he supported legislation to establish a permanent school fund to be derived from the sale of public land and state taxes. When the legislature established a permanent board of education in 1837, Governor Everett appointed Mann to the board, of which he became secretary.

From 1837 until 1848, Mann was secretary of the Massachusetts Board of Education. Under his leadership, Massachusetts became a model state for school establishment, organization, and administration. In fact, Mann was often referred to as the "father of the common school movement" in the United States. Recognizing that education closely related to political life, Mann saw publicly supported common schools as having an important role in the civic education of the young in preparing them to take their places as responsible citizens of the republic. Considering school administration to be a form of political leadership, he developed a consensus style of educational leadership and administration. For him, consensus meant that diverse and frequently conflicting special interest groups had to be reconciled to support the common school. He was able to convince businessmen, workers, farmers, and members of different religious denominations that public education would benefit all by advancing a common knowledge and a prosperity that was in the public interest.

To publicize the need for common schools and to work for the improvement of public education, Mann founded and edited the *Common School Journal* from 1839 to 1852. He wrote twelve annual reports, which remain classic statements of the public school philosophy. He organized teachers' conventions and institutes,

---

[10] Williams, *Horace Mann*, pp. 16-18.

[11] Cremin, *Republic and the School*, p. 5.

where he inspired teachers with his educational and social theories. He argued for and helped organize the first public normal school in the United States; this was built in Lexington, Massachusetts, in 1839 and served as a model for other teacher preparation schools. Mann believed that the survival of common schools depended on well-educated and competently prepared teachers. He wanted teachers to be professionals who mastered not only subject matter but also the art of teaching. Normal schools, he believed, could impart techniques for arranging learning material and adapting it to the student's needs and readiness. Horace Mann was determined to elevate teaching from the lowly status of schoolkeeping to that of a profession of educational leaders.

In 1848, Mann resigned his post as secretary to seek election to the seat in Congress vacated by the death of the former president, John Quincy Adams. As a member of Congress, he espoused the abolitionist cause and worked to end slavery in the United States. In 1852, he was defeated for reelection. The next year, in 1853, Mann accepted the presidency of Antioch College in Yellow Springs, Ohio. A new institution, Antioch was committed to such innovations as coeducation, nonsectarianism, and equal opportunities for blacks. Here, he continued to work for educational advancement until his death in August 1859.

Mann's Conception of the Common School

Because of his background, inclination and character, Mann's career was devoted to public service and education. He believed the common school to be a training ground for citizenship in the American republic. He was thoroughly committed to the republican conception that the best polity was one where people governed themselves through elected officials and representative institutions. Since such a society would succeed, he believed, only if its citizens were literate, educated, and responsible, it had a definite need for a free universal public school system.[12] Public educational institutions should strive to educate responsible leaders and citizens who would not fall victim to the excesses of mob rule and demagoguery. To instill republican principles, he argued that common schooling should teach the rudiments of government, the Constitution, and good citizenship while avoiding political partisanship. Not only did the common school have a political role in the American republic, Mann also believed that it would become the basic cultural agency of American civilization; it would develop into the instrument by which Americans would become acquainted with the basic sources of their heritage.

Mann's concept of the common school was based upon his philosophy that American education should prepare children to be responsible citizens in a republican society. Mann did not want state-supported education in the United States to become a dual-track school system like that of Europe. In the European dual system, primary schools were used to educate lower-class children in reading, writing, arithmetic, and religion; grammar, or higher secondary, schools were used

---

[12] Merle Curti, *The Social Ideas of American Educators* (New York: Littlefield, Adams, 1959), pp. 101-38.

to prepare upper-class children for college and for positions of political, social, and economic leadership. The common school in the United States, he believed, was to be a school for all children of all citizens.

Mann saw the common school as an integrative agency for bringing children together in a unifying social institution. His model of the common school was integrationist in that it would be attended by children of varying class backgrounds and religions. Mann's common school was also a public institution, supported by public funds, administered by publicly elected officials, and responsible to the community.

For the common school to weld together a common community, Mann also believed it should cultivate shared basic knowledge in those who attended it. He believed the common school curriculum should encompass the elementary subjects and skills needed to successfully perform the duties of social, economic, and political life. The curriculum should therefore include the skills needed for everyday life, for ethical behavior, and for responsible citizenship.[13] Education for everyday life included reading, writing, spelling, arithmetic, history, and geography—the tools needed by practical businessmen, skilled working men, and independent citizens.

The values that Mann wanted the common schools to inculcate were derived from the moral codes of his own upbringing, his exposure to Transcendentalism, and his persistent belief in republican government. Essentially, he believed that common schools should prepare individuals who would and could earn a living, pay taxes, and support their families. The moral values that Mann stressed were those of hard work, effort, honesty, diligence, thrift, literacy, respect for property, and respect for reason. Neither radical nor revolutionary, he defended the right of private property and individual initiative. His ethics were those of individualism, personal initiative, and private property. Mann's individualism was neither selfish nor ruthless, however. Men of property and wealth had a special responsibility to support schools, to improve living and working conditions, and to work for social reform.

While Mann wanted common schools to instill a sense of ethical behavior in those who attended them, he opposed the inculcation of any single denominational religious doctrine. He knew that the specific tenets of one denomination would offend members of other sects. His problem, then, was that of cultivating ethics in a religiously neutral school. Some of his critics said then—and say now—that this cannot be done. Nevertheless, Mann tried to steer a course that would avoid sectarianism. His compromise was to teach those values common to all Christian denominations. His common Christianity compromise satisfied many, but not all, of the Protestant denominations. However, Roman Catholics, who came in large numbers to Massachusetts in the mid- and late nineteenth century, rejected common Christianity as a common Protestantism. Of the various compromises Mann engineered to win acceptance of the common school ideal, that of a common Christianity proved least durable. Roman Catholics preferred to create their own

[13] Cremin, *American Common School,* pp. 62-63.

separate school systems. Others who felt that common schooling should be religiously neutral argued, and later achieved, a public school system that was separate from religious denominationalism.

HENRY BARNARD

Henry Barnard (1811-1900), who served as secretary of the Connecticut State Board of Education from 1838 to 1842, had a career that paralleled Horace Mann's. In addition to leading common school forces in Connecticut, Barnard served as state commissioner of public schools in Rhode Island (1845-1849), chancellor of the University of Wisconsin (1858-1860), and United States commissioner of education (1867-1870). Throughout the nineteenth century, Barnard was America's prominent educational statesman. As an educational journalist and editor, he popularized public education through the *Connecticut Common School Journal* and the *American Journal of Education* and kept Americans informed on educational developments. He also introduced teachers to the ideas of European educational reformers such as Pestalozzi, Froebel, Herbart, and Fellenberg.

Like Mann's, Barnard's life coincided with the industrialization of America. His emphasis on a utilitarian curriculum was directly related to the continuing industrialization of American life. Industrialization required the preparation of an entrepreneurial class who could manage business affairs intelligently and profitably. It also required trained and disciplined workers who were capable of learning the skills needed for industrial productivity. These needs were essentially economic in character, and Barnard believed that a functional curriculum would satisfy them. Barnard also believed that the common school should educate for responsible citizenship. Urging civic education, he stressed love of country and its traditions, heritage, and heroes.

As a result of his inspections of district schools, Barnard was concerned with improving the quality of common schooling. While knowledge of reading, writing, and arithmetic were necessary foundations, Barnard believed common schools should also emphasize good health, accurate observation, clear reflection, and wholesome values that stressed the practical application of knowledge to life. Barnard urged teachers to avoid unnecessary abstractions. Barnard's first annual report as secretary to the Connecticut Board of Common School Commissioners in 1838 advised Connecticut teachers on subjects ranging from writing to religion.[14] The primary branches of learning should not be neglected, he wrote, since reading, writing, and arithmetic were necessary foundations of later schooling and a successful life. For Barnard, the most important subject was English, which included spelling, reading, speaking, grammar, and composition. Instead of being confined to long lists of words learned by repetition, spelling should be integrated with reading and writing. The practical uses of arithmetic should be stressed.

[14] John S. Brubacher, *Henry Barnard on Education* (New York: McGraw-Hill, 1931). Brubacher provides a skillful introduction and editing of Barnard's annual reports.

Barnard warned against the confusion that could result from rapid teacher turnover. The loss of continuity, and therefore of time, resulting from changing teachers retarded the progress of the school, he pointed out. Condemning the practice of boarding teachers in rural districts, Barnard suggested that teachers be allowed a regular home of their own so that they could devote part of their time to regular study.

As an educational administrator, Barnard realized that the quality of instruction provided by the common schools depended on the professionalization of teaching. Like Mann, Barnard urged deliberate and adequate teacher preparation, the establishment of normal schools, and increased financial rewards for teachers.

SOCIAL AND ECONOMIC FORCES

While particular organizations and individual leaders were in the forefront of the common school movement, less defined and more diffused social and economic

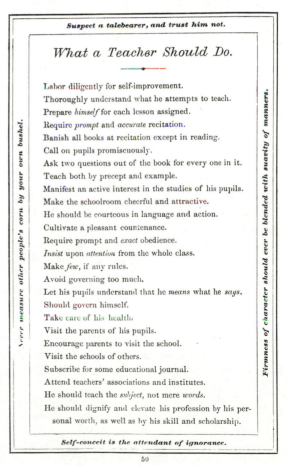

Admonitions on being a proper teacher. *(From D.W. Fish, ed., The American Educational Series, A Full Course of Practical and Progressive Text-Books; and ALMANAC. New York: Juison, Phinney, Blakeman & Co., 1867, p. 50.)*

Suspect a talebearer, and trust him not.

What a Teacher Should Do.

Labor diligently for self-improvement.
Thoroughly understand what he attempts to teach.
Prepare *himself* for each lesson assigned.
Require *prompt* and *accurate* recitation.
Banish all books at recitation except in reading.
Call on pupils promiscuously.
Ask two questions out of the book for every one in it.
Teach both by precept and example.
Manifest an active interest in the studies of his pupils.
Make the schoolroom cheerful and attractive.
He should be courteous in language and action.
Cultivate a pleasant countenance.
Require prompt and *exact* obedience.
Insist upon *attention* from the whole class.
Make *few*, if any rules.
Avoid governing too much.
Let his pupils understand that he *means* what he *says*.
Should govern himself.
Take care of his health.
Visit the parents of his pupils.
Encourage parents to visit the school.
Visit the schools of others.
Subscribe for some educational journal.
Attend teachers' associations and institutes.
He should teach the *subject*, not mere *words*.
He should dignify and elevate his profession by his personal worth, as well as by his skill and scholarship.

(Left margin: Never measure other people's corn by your own bushel.)

(Right margin: Firmness of character should ever be blended with suavity of manners.)

Self-conceit is the attendant of ignorance.

50

forces also contributed to the public school cause. The rising middle classes, especially the business and professional classes of the northeast, saw common schools as a means of promoting a literate, stable, and trained population that could serve the advancing industrialization and commercialization of the United States. They envisioned common schools as a means of indoctrinating the work ethic and in promoting the social and political stability they believed was needed for national economic productivity. Since the business sector was influential in shaping educational policy and in financing, it was important that it support the movement.

While the common school movement enjoyed support in professional and business sectors, it was also endorsed by many working-class leaders. Although trade and craft unions were still in their embryonic and primitive states in the early nineteenth century, a loose network of small trade unions, or working men's associations, existed. Some workingmen's associations had established reading rooms, libraries,and even schools for their members. Workingmen's associations saw common schooling as a means of creating popular educational institutions that could improve the social and economic condition of their members.

For members of workingmen's associations, universal education was a means of bringing about social change rather than social control. Prolabor newspapers such as New York's *Free Enquirer*, edited by Frances Wright and Robert Dale Owen, agitated for popular education. Many union leaders believed that knowledge was power and that proper education would help the working classes gain political power.[15]

William Maclure (1763-1840), scientist, geologist, and philanthropist (see Chapter 3), was a leading proponent of workers' education. His *Opinions on Various Subjects* argued that schools of industry should be established for the American working classes.[16] These schools were to educate workers' children to recognize their genuine political and economic interests. An opponent of classical education, Maclure's curriculum emphasized basic sciences and their practical application to agriculture and industry. He encouraged Pestalozzian teachers such as Joseph Neef to immigrate to the United States to introduce this new method, which he regarded as the most effective form of education.[17] Maclure was a pioneer proponent of the philosophy that education could induce social and economic change.

In addition to the positive reasons that caused businessmen, factory owners, professionals, workingmen, and laborers to join in an ill-defined coalition to support common schools, many were also motivated by fear. Early nineteenth-century America, as indicated earlier, was experiencing profound social and economic changes. The waves of new immigrants from Southern and Eastern Europe appeared to threaten established American values. Along with immigration, the fragility of

[15] Arthur M. Schlesinger, Jr., *The Age of Jackson* (New York: NAL, 1958), p. 66.

[16] William Maclure, *Opinions on Various Subjects* (New Harmony, Ind.: School Press, 1831), I: 65-70.

[17] Gerald L. Gutek, *Joseph Neef: The Americanization of Pestalozzianism* (University: University of Alabama Press, 1978), pp. 18-29.

law and order in the burgeoning cities and on the Western frontier and the basic structural alternations in social patterns contributed to a pervasive anxiety. This anxiety was felt not only by members of the socioeconomic establishment but by others who regarded themselves as members of older American stock. Those who feared that the emerging new social order might weaken their socioeconomic position saw the proposed common schools as an agency of social stability. They hoped that common schools would Americanize immigrants and train disciplined, productive laborers. From this rather inchoate fear came a range of conflicting expectations for the proposed common schools:

1. Members of the older Protestant, English-speaking stock wanted common schools to Americanize new immigrants by imposing established ideas and values and the English language on them.
2. Commercial and business interests wanted common schools to prepare literate and trained workers who would acquire and practice the old Puritan values of hard work, punctuality, industriousness, and productivity.
3. Workingmen, craftsmen, laborers, and farmers hoped that the common schools would make popular education available to them and to their children and thus enhance their upward mobility.

These new expectations, although often conflicting, were joined with the ideology of the early national period that saw common schools advancing a common patriotism, loyalty, and devotion to the American republic.

OPPONENTS OF COMMON SCHOOLING

A general mood and readiness for common schools existed and was supported by a wide range of leaders and organizations. But common schools also had their antagonists. History tends to record the names of proponents for change, if they succeed, rather than their opponents. Let us turn to the opponents of common schools and examine their motives.

While many educational leaders supported common schools, there were also educators who opposed both the concept and the movement. Frequently, these opponents were associated with the private and independent schools; however, some private school educators supported the movement and worked to convert their institutions into common schools. Seeing the common schools as a threat to their institutions' existence, some private school educators feared that schools supported by public taxes would soon monopolize education in the United States. For them, common schools would bring a popularization and commonness to education that would lower admission requirements, lower academic standards, and weaken the curriculum. Believing that alternative private schools were preferable to a public school system, they saw independent schools competing for students and in their own style providing a distinctive education, free from standardization and commonness.

If some politicians supported common schools, others opposed them. If there was a loosely formed political coalition for common schools, there was also a loose and ill-defined group of opponents. Tax-conscious individuals who saw common schools as an unnecessary luxury did not believe that education was a financial responsibility of the public. They argued that those who had children to be educated should pay for that education. It was not a burden to be shared by the community. Believers in limited government feared that publicly supported schools would be a step in creating a powerful government apparatus that would eventually indoctrinate the young. For them, common schooling was a dangerous intrusion into the private life of citizens. In addition to these opponents, those who wanted to preserve their unique ethnicity, language, or religious beliefs felt that common schools would threaten their existence by creating a common language, morality, and religion. For example, non-English groups saw common schools as a step toward eradicating their ethnic and linguistic heritage and traditions. Roman Catholics feared that common schools could be the instruments of converting their children to Protestantism.

If some businessmen supported the common school concept, there were others who wanted inexpensive schools supported either by private philanthropy or by tuition paid by their users. Looking for less expensive educational alternatives, they hoped that the Lancasterian monitorial system might provide massive but cheap instruction.

In the political struggle that took place across the United States in the first half of the nineteenth century, the victory in the long run was won by common schooling proponents. Their opponents might win an occasional battle but their efforts were simply delaying tactics, not a final victory.

ESTABLISHING AND GOVERNING COMMON SCHOOLS

Although the movement to enact legislation for compulsory publicly supported and controlled education varied from state to state and from region to region, some general patterns were discernible. As early as 1827, Massachusetts enacted legislation that made the support of schools by taxation compulsory. Other New England and Midwestern states followed the Massachusetts model. The enactment of legislation for tax-supported public schools advanced more slowly in the Middle Atlantic states. Most of the Southern states did not enact such laws until the Reconstruction period after the Civil War.

While there were variations, the process of establishing publicly supported common schools occurred in four major phases. First, the state legislature enacted permissive legislation that recognized local districts as legal units which could elect boards of education and levy school taxes, if the majority of voters resident within the district so agreed in referenda. The important point was that the state, by means of permissive legislation, recognized and established the school district as a unit with legal and taxing powers.

Second, the state, while still not requiring the organization of local districts, encouraged their formation by providing grants of monies from the general school fund to districts voting to levy taxes for public schools. State funds came from permanent school funds derived from the sale of public land, state taxes or lotteries, and allotments from federal revenues.

Third, the state legislatures established compulsory, but still not completely free, public education. While the state required the formation of school districts, the tax support generated was often inadequate to provide elementary education for all the children living in a school district. As a result, districts often resorted to the *rate bill*, a tuition fee levied upon parents according to the number of children attending the district school. The tuition payments supplied by the rate bill supplemented funds derived from public sources.

Fourth, state legislatures established compulsory and completely tax-supported public education as increased sources of revenue became available for school support. The growth of industry in the eastern states provided an increased tax base in revenue derived from industrial properties. As more people moved into the western states, the establishment of a stable community life facilitated the collection of taxes for those schools. Occasionally, the surplus income of the federal government derived from the tariff would be distributed among the states and used for the common school fund. As more money became available for school financing, the rate bill was gradually discontinued, and elementary school attendance was facilitated.

The model of the common school was developed in rural America and painstakingly perfected on the frontier as well as in the more populous eastern states. In many respects, the basic pattern of local control and local governance originated in the democratic milieu of frontier rural America.

School Boards in Rural Areas

Following the New England pattern, school districts in midwestern and western states had elected boards of education, consisting of three members elected for three-year terms. Each of these boards had a president or chairman who moderated or chaired the meetings, a secretary or clerk to record the minutes and maintain the records, and a treasurer to collect and disburse the district's funds. It was important that records be accurately maintained since the district's share of state funds was allocated according to the number of children who attended school.

The Country School Curriculum

In most of the nation's rural schools, the curriculum was not an elaborate program but consisted of the common branches of learning, with an emphasis on reading, writing, spelling, and arithmetic. The McGuffey readers, which enjoyed wide usage, stressed common values derived from a generalized version of Protestantism. In addition, some districts offered instruction in American history, geography, health, and music.

Throughout most of the nineteenth century, rural schools were plagued by the "textbook problem." Lacking standardized textbooks, the children brought their own readers, arithmetics, geographies, and spellers with them from home. These books were often inherited from one generation to the next. Because of the many kinds of books being used, teachers in rural schools relied on the individual recitation. As the school day ended, they made individual homework assignments. During the next day, the students would recite these lessons individually to the teacher. Although this made for a primitive kind of individualized instruction, it resulted in little group work or simultaneous instruction. Depending upon the size of the class, each student might have only a few minutes of the teacher's time. The problem of organizing instruction in the rural schools was complicated further in that all students in the district, particularly in small districts, would attend a single school. This meant that a wide range of ages was represented, sometimes ranging from six to fourteen or older.

As the century neared its end, the pattern of graded schools that had been adopted in the larger city districts began to have an impact on the smaller rural schools. In the larger urban districts, students were grouped according to age into what became the conventional eight grades. To capture the textbook market, publishing companies designed series of books to be used at the various grade levels. Teachers in rural schools, following the urban pattern, began to organize instruction around textbook series, usually the reading series, the most popular of which were the McGuffey readers. Emulating the McGuffey and other readers, publishing companies developed readers for other common school subjects. By the 1880s, the grade system was used to separate elementary school pupils into the three broad classifications of primary, intermediate, and upper grades that also came to be the pattern for teacher preparation, examination, and certification.

Efforts to Centralize Rural Schools

As the Midwestern and Western territories were settled, thousands of local districts, many of which had but one school, were organized. State officials and professional educators, especially professors of education in normal schools, argued that these small school districts were causing inefficient and costly duplication. Despite incentives to consolidate, local school districts often resented and resisted consolidation, preferring to remain as autonomous as possible. Throughout much of the nineteenth century, the consolidation of smaller school districts into larger ones proceeded very slowly. It was not until the early twentieth century that consolidation advanced. Several factors influenced consolidation in the twentieth century: (1) a decrease in the number of farm families, which made it difficult to maintain one-room neighborhood schools; (2) improved transportation and roads, which facilitated the busing of students to larger consolidated schools; and (3) financial inducement, often in the form of larger grants-in-aid from some of the state governments.

The County Superintendent of Schools

Since school district consolidation was often resisted by local districts throughout much of the nineteenth century, the office of the county superintendent of schools, which developed at mid-century in many states, helped bring about some degree of educational standardization and uniformity. An elected official, the county superintendent was responsible for: (1) collecting statistics on the number of school-age children in the various districts of the county and reporting these figures to the state superintendent of schools; (2) apportioning the county and state funds among the school districts according to their average daily attendance; (3) adjudicating disputes among school districts over boundaries; (4) conducting licensing examinations for teachers; (5) visiting schools within the county and making recommendations for their improvement; (6) organizing and conducting county-wide teacher institutes for teacher in-service training.[18]

THE DEVELOPMENT OF CATHOLIC SCHOOLS

Roman Catholic schools, conducted by religious orders and communities such as Dominicans, Franciscans, and Jesuits, existed in the colonial period. In the early republic, the Catholic population, located primarily in Maryland and Kentucky, was predominantly of English extraction. However, the Roman Catholic Church for much of its history in the United States was an immigrant church, and its parish schools served the needs of an immigrant population.

Catholic efforts to establish parochial schools as an educational alternative to the public schools gained momentum on the eve of the common school movement of the late 1830s and 1840s. While common school leaders such as Mann, Barnard, and others found a "common Christianity" to be a compromise solution to the claims of contending denominations for a place in the public schools, Catholic bishops, priests, and laity soon found that common Christianity in reality meant common Protestantism.

While Catholics were resisting common Christianity, the large numbers of immigrants in the 1830s and 1840s, especially the Irish who located in the Eastern cities, encountered nativist anti-Catholicism. Between 1830 and 1850, more than a million Irish had immigrated to the United States. Disagreements between Catholics and Protestants reached such an explosive point in Philadelphia in 1844 that forty people were killed during summer riots.

In their various councils during the 1830s and 1840s, Catholic bishops established the rationale for what would become the Catholic school system. At the Third Provincial Council in Baltimore in 1837, the bishops urged the support of

---

[18]Fuller, *Old Country School*, pp. 133-34.

Catholic schools in order to "make them as perfect as possible, in their fitness for the communication and improvement of science, as well as for the cultivation of pure, solid, and enlightened piety."[19] In 1852, the Plenary Council, meeting at Baltimore, urged that parish schools be established in connection with the parish churches in the various dioceses. Thus, the Catholic school system, based on the local parish or parochial schools, had its origins in the United States.

CONCLUSION

The common school movement established the concept of state-supported and publicly controlled popular education in the United States. Building upon traditions established in New England, the common school movement—although originating in the states of the northeast—was reshaped by the westward-moving frontier. The district school was carried westward and in rural America became a focus for the practice of participatory democracy. Although the motives of the proponents of common schooling varied, the end result was that elementary education was made available to large numbers of children. In terms of the growth of educational institutions, the basic rung—the elementary level—of what would become the public school system was established.

The eventual success of common schooling secured the proposition that the school had an important role to play in nation building and in shaping the national consciousness. The vision of Jefferson, Rush, and other early leaders of schools unique to the needs of a republican society was realized. The religiously neutral orientation of public schools that grew out of the compromise of a "common Christianity" eventually yielded to a secular system of schools. While the role of religious denominations diminished, the concept that schooling should exercise a larger political and societal role increased.

The common school concept was based on an emerging consensus that included residues of the Puritan ethic, republicanism, evangelical Protestantism, and capitalistic entrepreneurship. While an odd mixture at first glance, these elements had a consistency about them. They valued economic productivity, representative political institutions, and moral themes of honesty, hard work, diligence, and application.

In its basic outlines, the establishment of common schools implemented the commitment expressed as an ideal in many state constitutions that each state was the responsible agency for education. Along with the state role, common school establishment also was based on the principle of taxation and local control.

DISCUSSION QUESTIONS

1. Define the common school concept. Is the concept relevant to contemporary American society?

[19] Glen Gabert, *In Hoc Signo? A Brief History of Catholic Parochial Education in America* (Port Washington, N.Y.: Kennikat Press, 1973), pp. 24-29.

2. Examine the ideological, social, political, and economic context of the common school movement.

3. How did common schooling reflect both secular trends and religious values?

4. Were the common schools agencies of social mobility or social control?

5. Consider the common school movement in the context of general reform in nineteenth-century America.

6. Compare and contrast the common school movement in the United States with the development of primary or elementary schools in other Western countries.

7. Analyze the political and legal framework for public schooling in the United States.

8. Analyze Horace Mann's concept of common schooling. Is his concept relevant to contemporary public schools in the United States?

9. Analyze the arguments for and against common schools that were debated during the first half of the nineteenth century.

10. Identify the general phases in the establishment of common schools.

RESEARCH TOPICS

1. Research the establishment of common schools in your state, and write a paper that outlines the major phases.

2. Determine if any one-room schools remain in your locality. If so, visit them and prepare a description of the building.

3. Using local history resources, examine the origins of a local public or parochial school system.

4. Read several well-chosen histories of Western education or books on comparative education. Write an essay comparing the origin and development of the American common schools with the school system of another country.

5. Research the history of common school legislation in your state and develop an outline of the major laws and events relating to that subject.

6. Identify a common school leader in your state. Prepare a short biographical sketch of this individual.

7. Read a biography of Horace Mann. Prepare a paper that analyzes his style of leadership and his efforts on behalf of common schools.

8. Examine the McGuffey readers; prepare a content analysis that examines the essential values that they conveyed.

REFERENCES AND READINGS

Binder, Frederick M. *The Age of the Common School, 1830-1865.* New York: John Wiley, 1974.

Brubacher, John S. *Henry Barnard on Education.* New York: McGraw-Hill, 1931.

Commager, Henry S. *The Era of Reform, 1830-1860.* Princeton, N.J.: D. Van Nostrand, 1960.

Cremin, Lawrence A. *The American Common School: An Historical Conception.* New York: Teachers College Press, Columbia University, 1951.

___. *American Education: The National Experience, 1783-1876.* New York: Harper & Row, Pub., 1980.

___. *The Republic and the School: Horace Mann on the Education of Free Men.* New York: Bureau of Publications, Teachers College, Columbia University, 1957.

Culver, Raymond B. *Horace Mann and Religion in the Massachusetts Public Schools.* New Haven: Yale University Press, 1929.

Curti, Merle. *The Social Ideas of American Educators.* Paterson, N.J.: Littlefield, Adams, 1961.

Downs, Robert B. *Horace Mann: Champion of Public Schools.* New York: Twayne, 1974.

Fuller, Wayne E. *The Old Country School: The Story of Rural Education in the Middle West.* Chicago: University of Chicago Press, 1982.

Gabert, Glen. *In Hoc Signo? A Brief History of Catholic Parochial Education in America.* Port Washington, N.Y.: Kennikat Press, 1973.

Gutek, Gerald L. *Joseph Neef: The Americanization of Pestalozzianism.* University: University of Alabama Press, 1978.

Lannie, Vincent. *Henry Barnard: American Educator.* New York: Teachers College Press, Columbia University, 1974.

Mann, Horace. *Lectures and Annual Reports on Education.* Cambridge, Mass: Cornhill Press, 1867.

___. *Lectures on Education.* Boston: Idel and Dutton, 1855.

Mann, Mary Peabody. *The Life and Work of Horace Mann.* Washington, D.C.: National Education Association, 1937.

___. *The Life of Horace Mann, by His Wife.* Boston: Lee and Shepard, 1867.

Messerli, Jonathan. *Horace Mann: A Biography.* New York: Knopf, 1972.

Midwinter, Eric. *Nineteenth-Century Education.* New York: Harper & Row, Pub., 1970.

Nasaw, David. *Schooled to Order: A Social History of Public Schooling in the United States.* New York: Oxford University Press, 1979.

Schlesinger, Arthur M., Jr. *The Age of Jackson.* New York: 1958.

Williams, E. I. F. *Horace Mann: Educational Statesman.* New York: Macmillan, 1937.

5

THE DEVELOPMENT OF AMERICAN SECONDARY EDUCATION

Over the course of time, secondary schools in Western culture have been viewed in various ways. Traditionally, they have been seen as educational institutions that prepared youth for entry into colleges and universities. In the American educational experience, especially in the late seventeenth, eighteenth, and early nineteenth centuries, secondary schools were construed to be college preparatory institutions. By the mid- and late nineteenth century, the dominance of the college preparatory function of secondary schooling was challenged by other conceptions, especially by those who wanted secondary schools to perform more functional, developmental, or personal services for an adolescent population with a variety of educational needs. We shall examine the changing nature of American secondary education by treating the following major themes:

1. the inherited European conception of secondary education;
2. the Latin grammar school;
3. the academy;
4. the emergence of the American high school; and
5. the efforts to define American secondary education.

In describing the development of American secondary education, we shall present an overview of institutional evolution from the Latin grammar school of the eigh-

teenth century, through the academy of the nineteenth century, to the comprehensive high school of the late nineteenth and early twentieth centuries. While we
have treated these institutional developments in a single chapter in order to provide
a coherent discussion of the sequence of events, we have not followed a strictly
chronological order.

INHERITED EUROPEAN CONCEPTS

The colonists who came to North America from Europe imported a conception of
secondary education in much the same way that they brought with them ideas
about elementary and higher education. To understand the historical development
of American secondary education, we must realize that these inherited and originally European concepts have persisted and have had a continuing impact on
modern American education. These traditional concepts were challenged by educational forces that wanted to reconstruct secondary schools into more flexible and
multifunctional institutions. However, this tendency has often been deflected by
the persistence of traditional conceptions of education.

The ideas of secondary education that the Europeans brought with them had
a long history. During the Greco-Roman and medieval periods, there were schools
that were "secondary" in that those who attended them had already had a primary education. The concepts of secondary schooling that had an impact on
American education came most directly from the Renaissance and Reformation
periods, however.[1]

The Renaissance humanist schools were designed to prepare the sons of the
upper classes for leadership positions in the church and state. Castiglione, who
wrote a treatise on the education of the courtier, prescribed the training appropriate to prepare a young man to serve his lord.[2] Although their ethical orientations
differed, both Erasmus and Machiavelli commented on the education of princes.
The Renaissance classical humanist schools were selective and enrolled only the
sons of the elite who were being prepared for positions of leadership. Their curriculum was oriented to the study of the classical languages and literature—Latin and
Greek—which were the marks of an educated person. The general educational
orientation of the classical humanist schools was transported to North America in
the institutional form of the Latin grammar school.

During the late stages of the Renaissance, the Protestant Reformation
occurred. Such leaders of the Protestant Reformation—Zwingli, Calvin, Luther, and

---

[1] Most of the standard histories of Western education describe education during the
Renaissance and Reformation. For example, see R. Freeman Butts, *The Education of the West:
A Formative Chapter in the History of Civilization* (New York: McGraw-Hill, 1973), pp. 183-
292; Gerald L. Gutek, *A History of the Western Educational Experience* (New York: Random
House, 1972), pp. 99-138; Christopher J. Lucas, *Our Western Educational Heritage* (New York:
Macmillan, 1972), pp. 271-323.

[2] Baldesarre Castiglione, *The Book of the Courtier,* tr. Charles S. Singleton (New York:
Doubleday, 1959).

Melanchthon—agreed that classical humanist schools offered the best preparation for future ministers of the church and leaders of the state. To the classical language curriculum, they added the creeds of the particular Protestant denomination that established and supported the school. In France, the classical humanist school that emerged was the *lycée*, in Germany, the *gymnasium*, and in Italy, the *liceo*. The Latin grammar school, the humanist school that developed in England, was used as a preparatory school by both Anglicans and Puritan dissenters. The Latin grammar school was transported to North America by the Puritans of New England and the Anglicans of Virginia.

THE LATIN GRAMMAR SCHOOL

The Latin grammar school, based on antecedents from the Renaissance and Reformation, was established by the American colonists to prepare youth for entry into colonial colleges. In many ways it was more properly a preparatory than a secondary school, since students were admitted at age eight or nine after they had learned to read and write in English. Although some students in New England entered the Latin grammar school from the elementary district or town schools, this was not the usual pattern. For most students, the Latin grammar was their first exposure to formal schooling. The Latin grammar school did, however, perform the role conventionally delegated to secondary institutions by preparing students for college admission.

The curriculum of the Latin grammar school stressed the study of the Latin and Greek languages and their literatures. Much of the instruction was geared to the memorization of Latin grammar, taught by means of Ezechial Cheever's *Accidence* and the study of various nomenclatures. By studying the *Accidence*, the students learned the principles and rules of Latin grammar. The nomenclature provided lists of words, the vocabulary, with which to construct sentences. After mastering the necessary rules of Latin grammar and after acquiring a vocabulary, the students were led by their masters through the works of Julius Caesar, Sallust, Cicero, Horace, Juvenal, and Vergil. The students spent the great majority of their six years of study in learning the Latin classics. They devoted much less time to studying Greek. The Latin grammar school curriculum was determined by college admission requirements. This reflected the long-standing pattern in which the curriculum of the higher institution dominated that of the lower institution.

At the beginning of America's early national period, what approximated secondary schooling—the Latin grammar school and its curriculum—exhibited the following characteristics:

1. a purpose and orientation that was college preparatory
2. a curriculum based on the Latin and Greek languages and literature and
3. the dominance of an instructional method that stressed memorizing literary materials.

Finally, as a college preparatory institution, the Latin grammar school was oriented to preparing students for college admission so that they could eventually enter law or the religious ministry, the two professions that enjoyed high status at the time. As an educational institution, the Latin grammar school functioned largely in the historical and cultural context of the European Renaissance and Reformation. While serving as an outpost of Western culture, it did not reflect the economic and political realities of the settlement and development of North America. For example, its curriculum was not oriented to skills and subjects that would further the development of the continent's natural resources. Science and the scientific temperament and method were absent, and the impetus of the Enlightenment was generally ignored. Since the ideals and values of republicanism were missing from the institution's classical curriculum, the Latin grammar school did not contribute to the building of the nation.

THE ACADEMY

In the first half of the nineteenth century, the academy emerged, eclipsed, and replaced the Latin grammar school as the dominant institution of secondary education in the United States. Recall from Chapter 2 that Benjamin Franklin had argued for an English-language grammar school in Philadelphia in 1749. Franklin's proposed school was to have a practical, utilitarian, and scientific curriculum. Further, instruction was to be in English, the principal subject, rather than Latin and Greek. When the academy developed, many of the features suggested by Franklin could be found in the institution.

As an educational institution, the academy reflected the major social and economic trends taking place in the United States. The academy attained dominance in the Age of Jackson, that period during the 1830s and 1840s when popular democracy was triumphant in the United States. With its emphasis on popular elections, rotation in office, and the beginnings of political patronage, it was the time when the common man entered government.[3] Like the trend toward a more open and participative political process, the academy seemed to make secondary education more available and accessible to larger numbers of people.

According to Theodore Sizer, the academy was the social and educational institution that exemplified the optimism of the American people during the enthusiastic interlude between the Revolution and the Civil War, a period of great faith in the possibilities of improving the human condition through social reform.[4] The expansive liberalism of Jacksonianism generated a climate in which the new academies could provide increasing educational opportunities by open enrollment and nonstructured curricula. It was the age of the common man, of frontier individualism, of class mobility, and of popular sovereignty.

[3] Arthur M. Schlesinger, Jr., *The Age of Jackson* (New York: NAL, 1949).

[4] Theodore R. Sizer, *The Age of the Academies* (New York: Bureau of Publications, Teachers College, Columbia University, 1964), p. 1.

The nineteenth century also saw great economic development, growth, and productivity in the United States. The Jacksonian period was the era of the entrepreneur and the small businessman. During this era, laissez-faire economic individualism and private enterprise reigned supreme. As profit-making institutions, academies competed for students by offering the subjects that the public demanded. Practical courses related to business, such as bookkeeping and accounting, entered the curriculum. To stay in operation, the academies—like other businesses—had to turn a profit. There was a proliferation of academies, with some academically inadequate institutions competing for a larger number of students.

The movement to establish academies was also stimulated by the religious revivalism of the nineteenth century. Protestantism, in general, experienced an evangelical awakening. In particular, the more evangelical denominations, such as the Methodists and Baptists, actively established churches and academies. Most of the Protestant denominations were content with the common school and with the "common Christianity" that shaped the values of that institution. While many denominations were no longer directly involved in elementary schooling, they turned to secondary schooling and vigorously established academies. Roman Catholics followed the trend of establishing academies, which were usually conducted under the auspices of religious communities of priests, brothers, or sisters. The Jesuits founded academies for young men; the Sisters of Charity, the Ursulines, and others founded academies, or "finishing schools," for young women. In general, the academies conducted by the religious denominations were private schools governed by their own self-sustaining boards of trustees; they offered a secondary education permeated by religious beliefs and values.

As indicated, the development and growth of academies in nineteenth-century America arose from mixed motives. These various political, economic, social, and religious motivations produced a range of institutions that varied in purpose, educational philosophy, curriculum, and academic quality.

ACADEMY ORGANIZATION AND CONTROL

The academies varied in terms of their organization, control, and support. The major categories were: (1) institutions that were private, entrepreneurial, "for profit" schools of a nonreligious nature; (2) institutions that were operated under the control of, and with the support of, religious denominations; and (3) academies that had limited public financial support and were controlled, usually partially, by local, county, and state government units.

Academies generally were governed by boards of trustees or directors who were responsible for establishing general policies and for attracting revenues. In some cases, the governing board was self-perpetuating in that its members appointed their successors. If the institution was church-related, the sponsoring denomination might name the board. Academies that were semipublic usually had a number of public officials on their boards.

Various titles such as headmaster, principal, or president designated the head of the academy. The headmaster was responsible for enforcing the policies established by the board of directors, for the day-to-day operations, for the organization of the curriculum and scheduling of courses, for the employment of teachers, and for maintaining the quality of instruction. Headmasters were often ministers in the various denominations and were expected to be paternalistic father figures for both faculty and students. This was especially true in boarding schools.

Academy Curricula

One of the distinguishing and also troublesome characteristics of the academy was its relatively unstructured curriculum. To stay in business and attract students, academies were quick to respond to the needs of the educational marketplace by offering courses for which there was a student demand. Unfortunately, they offered a wide range of subjects that often overextended the academic competency and instructional energies of their faculty. As a result, the academic quality of the academies was uneven and often poor.

The programs offered by the academies were organized into the following categories:

1. the *college preparatory curriculum*, which concentrated on the classical languages required for college admission;
2. the *English-language curriculum*, designed for students who would end their formal education at the secondary level; and
3. the *normal curriculum*, for students preparing to teach in common or private elementary schools.

In addition to these three major curricula, there were also military academies whose curricula included military history, the study of military tactics, and discipline. Some of the officers serving on both sides of the Civil War were graduates of military academies.

While the courses offered by many of the academies clustered into these three basic groups, there were also a number of curricular hybrids that featured a wide range of subject matter. The list of courses offered by academies was long and varied. Among the courses offered were:

Latin and Greek: the classical languages and literatures.
English: grammar, composition, literature, declamation.
Natural sciences: botany, zoology, natural history, chemistry, physics, and geology.
History: ancient, medieval, English, and American.
Modern languages: French, Spanish, German, Portuguese, and Italian.
Commercial subjects: bookkeeping and accounting.
Mathematics: basic computation, algebra, geometry, and related studies.
Music and Art.

In addition to curricular offerings of a general nature, there were also more specialized courses. The academies and seminaries for young ladies featured the domestic sciences, embroidery, needlework, art, music, singing, and dancing. The normal curricula, designed for prospective teachers, included the history and philosophy of education, the principles of teaching, and often some experience in teaching in a demonstration school.

Not only were the curricula of the academies varied, but there were no uniform means of assessing the length, content, and quality of the courses offered. Some courses were offered for only a few weeks; others lasted a half year or a year. No uniform standards existed that could be applied to the academic programs of the various academies. There were no accrediting agencies that could attest to the quality of the programs offered. As the nineteenth century approached its midpoint, the conditions of secondary education were free but chaotic.

THE EMERGENCE OF THE HIGH SCHOOL

In the second half of the nineteenth century, particularly after the Civil War, the high school emerged, first to rival the academy and then to eclipse it as the dominant institution of American secondary education. The appearance of the high school was significant in the history of American education because it linked the public elementary or common school and the state-supported college and university. It completed the American educational ladder and made it possible for American youth to be educated in a fully articulated and sequential system of public schools. While some private academies continued to operate, the majority of them were replaced by the high school.

The social, economic, and political developments that occurred in the second half of the nineteenth century provided the context for the high school's rise. After the Civil War, the industrialization of the United States proceeded rapidly, especially in the North and the East. The era of industrialization saw the rise of the factory system with its mass production processes. Industrialization stimulated the growth of large cities such as New York, Chicago, Philadelphia, and others. The expanding industrial productivity of the United States created a larger tax base that could support a more extensive school system. In addition, a more sophisticated industrial system required a more extensively educated and highly trained worker.

Industrial society created new demands for an expanded system of secondary schools that would offer a more functional curriculum. However, the leaders of secondary education were slow to react to these new social and economic demands. They had inherited from the academy a rather confused educational situation. In the 1870s and 1880s, the academies were replaced by the emerging public high schools. The trend to establish public high schools was stimulated by America's transition from an agrarian-rural to an industrial-urban society. By the turn of the century, the United States was experiencing a major economic transformation; the economic base was shifting from the individual entrepreneur to the large corpora-

The Illinois Institute for the Education of the Deaf and Dumb illustrating school architecture of the late nineteenth century. *(From Edward A. Fay, ed., Histories of American Schools for the Deaf, 1817-1893. Washington, D.C.: The Volta Bureau, 1893.)*

tion. The educational counterpart of entrepreneurship, the academy, was forced to yield to the public high school, an institution that was better equipped to satisfy the educational consumerism of a modernizing and increasingly corporate society.

The Growth of the High School

Although free high schools had existed in the United States since the founding of the English Classical School of Boston in 1821, it was not until the latter half of the nineteenth century that the public high school came to dominate American secondary education. During the 1880s, the number of high schools surpassed the number of academies. In 1890, the United States commissioner of education reported that 2,526 public high schools were enrolling 202,063 students, in comparison to the 94,391 students enrolled in 1,632 private academies.[5]

The emergence of the high school was related to the socioeconomic modernization of the United States. Life in an industrializing and urbanizing society required a more extensive education that would prepare individuals for specialized professions and skilled occupations of an increasingly corporate social order. One effect of industrialization was that young people required a longer period of

---

[5] Edward Krug, *The Shaping of the American High School* (New York: Harper & Row, Pub., 1964), I: 5.

116

preparation before joining the work force. In the past, farm life—with its chores—had brought them directly into the world of work. As a result, high schools began to function as institutional intermediaries between the activities of adult society and the child's world. Some educators began to envision the new high school as a multipurpose institution that would introduce adolescents—by a series of planned intermediate stages—to the activities and demands of the larger society.

America's industrialization required a more sophisticated and comprehensive knowledge of the natural, physical, and social sciences. The basic literacy provided to children by the common elementary school, while necessary, was not a sufficient preparation for their intelligent participation in an industrial society.[6] Over time, the high school curriculum would expand as a consequence of the knowledge and skills required in a transformed nation.

Although the economic requirements of industrial society were significant factors in the emergence of the public high schools, there was also present a more humanistic interpretation of the psychological and social needs of adolescents. A more affluent economic base could support an education that developed persons as well as trained workers. In particular, the research and teaching of G. Stanley Hall, a pioneer psychologist in the field of adolescence, focused attention on the educational needs of adolescents.

The emergence of high school education was a continuation of the common school movement. The common school movement in the early nineteenth century had established the state's responsibility for tax-supported elementary education; as the movement to extend the state's role in secondary education gained momentum, some of the earlier controversies regarding publicly supported schooling resurfaced.

Although several court cases are relevant to establishing the legality of public taxation for high schools, the decision of Justice Thomas C. Cooley in Michigan's Kalamazoo case clearly established a judicial precedent. The case occurred when some taxpayers brought suit to prevent the Kalamazoo Board of Education from levying a tax to support a high school. These claimants argued that the high school curriculum, which was primarily college preparatory, did not merit support by public taxation. Why, they asked, should taxpayers pay for the education of the small minority of students that were being prepared for college admission? In upholding the right of the Kalamazoo school board to levy taxes for the support of a high school, Judge Cooley argued that the state was obliged not only to provide elementary education but also to maintain equality of educational opportunity. Since the state was already maintaining public elementary schools and colleges, he ruled, it was inconsistent for it not to provide the transitional stage that enabled students to proceed from elementary to higher education. Justice Cooley thereby affirmed the prerogative of the board of education to tax for the support of the high school.

Cooley's, and similar decisions in other states encouraged state legislatures to

---

[6] George S. Counts, *Secondary Education and Industrialism* (Cambridge, Mass.: Harvard University Press, 1929), p. 26.

enact legislation that permitted local boards of education to establish and support high schools. Following their approach to common schooling, state legislatures first encouraged and then required the establishment of high schools. As a result, it was possible for students to attend a complete sequence of educational institutions, from kindergarten through elementary and high schools to colleges and universities, within the framework of publicly supported and controlled schools.

Standardizing the Curriculum: The Committee of Ten

The institutional and curricular patterns of the American high school were defined in the period from 1880 to 1920. In the early years, a series of controversies occurred over the nature and purpose of the new secondary institution. These controversies focused on the curriculum. Was it to remain college preparatory, as had been traditionally true of secondary schooling? Or was the high school to be a multipurpose institution, meeting a variety of educational needs of a diverse adolescent population? Should its curriculum stress traditional college preparatory subjects, or should it offer a range of industrial, commercial, vocational, and social programs?

The high school inherited the curricular problems of the academy, its institutional predecessor, which had offered a multiplicity of ill-defined curricula and courses. Often within the same high school could be found such curricula as the ancient classical, the business-commercial, the shorter commercial, the English terminal, the English-science, and the scientific. In order to standardize the high school curriculum, the National Education Association in 1892 established the Committee of Ten, which was composed of five individuals associated with colleges and universities, a public school principal, two private school headmasters, United States Commissioner of Education William Torrey Harris, and committee chairperson Charles W. Eliot, president of Harvard University.[7] Since the majority of the committee represented higher education, it was no surprise that it favored reinforcing the high school as a college preparatory institution.

Charles Eliot, who chaired the Committee of Ten, was one of the nation's leading spokesmen for higher education. His interests also extended to elementary and secondary education. In particular, he was concerned with improving the efficiency of the schools, making better use of the time students spent in school, and increasing students' freedom of choice by introducing the elective system, which permitted them to choose their courses. As head of the committee, he vigorously guided its research and investigation into the scope and function of secondary education. Under Eliot's guidance, the committee's recommendations clustered around two of Eliot's basic concepts: (1) the early introduction of basic subject matter in the elementary grades; (2) uniformity in the subjects studied and in the instruction given to college preparatory and terminal students.[8]

[7]*Report of the Committee on Secondary School Studies* (Washington, D.C.: GPO, 1893).

[8]Krug, *Shaping of the American High School,* I: 17.

The Committee of Ten recommended eight years of elementary and four years of secondary education. For the high school, four separate curricula were recommended: classical, Latin-scientific, modern language, and English. While each curriculum included foreign languages, mathematics, English, science, and history, the major differences were that the English and modern language curricula permitted the substitution of modern languages for Latin and Greek and that the Latin-scientific emphasized mathematics and science.

In its report, the committee identified the subjects appropriate to high school study as being English and foreign languages such as Latin, Greek, German, French, and Spanish; mathematics such as algebra, geometry, and trigonometry; natural sciences such as descriptive astronomy, meteorology, botany, zoology, physiology, geology, and physical geography; and physical sciences such as physics and chemistry. The committee recommended the intensive study of selected topics and periods from American and Western history. It also emphasized that high school students study intensively a relatively small number of subjects for longer periods of time instead of a large range of courses for shorter periods of time. Every subject was to be taught in the same way and to the same extent to all students, regardless of their career goals.

The report of the Committee of Ten illustrates the tendency of the higher institution, the college, to dominate the lower, the high school. Although the committee stated that the high school was not exclusively a college preparatory institution, its recommendations stressed courses designed for college entry. Using the psychology of mental discipline as a theoretical rationale, the committee claimed that the subjects recommended could be used profitably by college preparatory students as well as by those who would end their formal education with high school graduation. These scientific, language, and historical subjects, it was claimed, would train their powers of observation, memory, expression, and reasoning.

Standardization by Accreditation

The relationship of the high school curriculum to college admission was a major problem of institutional articulation in the 1890s. Specification of admission requirements was the mechanism by which the higher institution controlled the lower one. In 1895, the North Central Association was established, with a combined membership of colleges and secondary schools, to forge closer ties in the North Central states.[9] In 1899, the National Education Association established the Committee on College Entrance Requirements. To resolve the controversy over electivism, which permitted students to choose their subjects, the committee proposed a set of constant subjects, a curricular core, to be required of all students without reference to their future educational or career destination. Once the core requirements were completed, students were free to elect the remainder of their program.[10] The committee used the term "unit" to designate a course acceptable

[9]Calvin O. Davis, *A History of the North Central Association of Colleges and Secondary Schools* (Ann Arbor, Mich.: North Central Association, 1945).

[10]Krug, *Shaping of the American High School,* I: 141-42.

for graduation. A subject studied for four or five periods a week during an academic year in secondary school was defined as a unit of study. The constants recommended in the core group were four units of foreign languages, two of mathematics, two of English, one of history, and one of science.

The Committee on Unit Courses of the North Central Association specified in 1902 that, to be accredited, high schools had to require fifteen units of course work for graduation. Each unit was defined as a course covering a school year of not less than thirty-five weeks, taught in four or five periods of at least forty-five minutes per week. Furthermore, all high school curricula and requirements for college entrance were to include as constants three units of English and two units of mathematics.[11]

Following the model of the North Central Association, other regions established accreditation agencies such as the New England Association, the Middle States Association, the Northwest Association, the Western Association, and the Southern Association. Historically, accreditation associations have used two approaches regarding college entrance requirements: admitting any student who passes the College Entrance Examination Board examinations or admitting graduates of accredited high schools.

Reorganizing Secondary Education

In 1918, the National Education Association established the Commission on the Reorganization of Secondary Education to reexamine the scope and function of the high school. The commission's report recognized the need for greater articulation and cooperation between educational institutions. Chaired by Clarence Kingsley, the commission issued the "Cardinal Principles of Secondary Education," which identified the following objectives of secondary education: vocational preparation, citizenship, worthy use of leisure, and ethical character.[12] The major task of the high school was to translate these principles into curricular programs.

In contrast to the almost exclusive emphasis of the earlier Committee of Ten on academic subjects, the commission's perspectives were broader in societal terms. For example, the commission argued that the high school was an agency of social integration as well as a college preparatory institution. The American high school was to be a comprehensive institution. If the adjective "common" was subject to continuing interpretation when used to explain the public elementary school, the term "comprehensive" would also be defined in varying ways. In the early twentieth century, when the commission prepared its report, the "comprehensive high school" meant a secondary school that: (1) was comprehensive in a social sense in that it integrated adolescents of different racial, religious, economic, ethnic, and social classes in the same institution: (2) was comprehensive in an academic sense by educating students who were pursuing different curricula—college preparatory, vocational, clerical, or terminal—within a single institution.

[11] Davis, *History of the North Central Association,* p. 49.

[12] National Education Association, *A Report of the Commission on the Reorganization of Secondary Education* (Washington, D.C.: GPO, 1918), pp. 10-16.

A girl's gymnasium class typical of the late nineteenth century. *(From Edward A. Fay, ed., Histories of American Schools for the Deaf, 1817-1893. Washington, D.C.: The Volta Bureau, 1893.)*

The important social and educational significance of the comprehensive high school was that it represented an institutional effort to continue the democratic equalizing tendency of the "ladder concept" in secondary education. The American comprehensive high school was equalitarian only in a formal institutional sense; there were many factors that made it an elitist and highly selective institution: (1) The vast majority of the children of immigrants did not complete high school but rather "dropped out" to earn income for their families as soon as it was legally possible to do so. (2) A high school education was still designed as college preparation; as a result, the majority of those attending were white young men who were members of the upper-middle or upper classes. (3) The great majority of black Americans did not attend high school. (4) Even for those who attended high school, particularly in the large cities, there was considerable tracking according to curriculum identification and specification. Despite the rhetoric and intentions of the Commission on the Reorganization of Secondary Education, the high school was less than a comprehensive institution.

Despite the high school's lack of comprehensiveness, a comparison of the reports of the Committee of Ten and the Commission on the Reorganization of Secondary Education reveals that some major changes had occurred in educational attitudes between 1893 and 1918. In this short span of twenty-five years, significant transformations in American life and education were beginning to change the nature of the secondary school curriculum. While the Committee of Ten had been dominated by college academicians, the Committee on the Reorganization of Secondary Education was controlled by professors of education and educational administrators. While the academic professors had viewed the high school curriculum as college preparatory, the members of the 1918 commission, in contrast, saw the high school curriculum in broader social, economic, personal, and civic terms. The commission members regarded the high school as an institution in which adolescents would define their goals and pursue their interests. While the Committee of Ten regarded the high school as subordinate to college interests, the commission members viewed secondary education as serving a widely varied adolescent population.

During its development as an educational institution, the nature of the high school was subject to ongoing controversy. Between 1880 and 1920, strong arguments were made to maintain the high school as a strictly college preparatory institution. However, equally determined, but more diffuse arguments remonstrated that the high school should be a multifunctional "people's college."

From 1880 to 1920, the high school was primarily college preparatory, emphasizing Latin, modern foreign languages, mathematics, science, English, and history. However, some educators such as G. Stanley Hall objected strongly to the college preparatory view, arguing that the high school should be more concerned with the education of adolescents. For educators like Hall, the high school was the institutional extension of the elementary school. Because of Hall's and others' efforts, some educators began to view the high school as a school for adolescents rather than a strictly college preparatory institution. Others, like David Snedden, launched the "social efficiency " movement. A reaction against the high school's college orientation, social efficiency used a utilitarian criterion to define the curriculum. According to social efficiency educators, the inclusion of any subject in the high school curriculum was justified only as it prepared students to be citizens, wage earners, parents, and consumers.

THE DEVELOPMENT
OF THE COMPREHENSIVE HIGH SCHOOL

In 1880, the high school population numbered 110,277; by 1920 it had risen to 2,382,542.[13] Despite its increasing attendance, educators such as George S. Counts believed that the high school was still a selective institution and that a close relationship existed between the parents' occupational status and high school attendance. Many more children of native-born parents attended than did those of immigrant parents. In *The Selective Character of American Secondary Education*, Counts, who concluded that the high school was serving primarily the upper socio-

---

[13] William M. French, *American Secondary Education* (New York: Odyssey Press, 1957), p. 100.

economic classes, argued for an extension of educational opportunity, and urged that the high school deliberately open its doors to all students.[14]

William French, in *American Secondary Education*, reinforced Counts's analysis. French found that between 1880 and 1920 the selectivity of the high school was reinforced by three factors: (1) Many immigrants from Eastern and Southern Europe lacked an educational tradition that was conducive to secondary schooling. (2) Hidden costs in the form of books, supplies, transportation, lunches, and clothing kept many adolescents from high school. And (3), many rural districts, lacking an extensive financial base, had difficulty in establishing high schools.[15]

By the mid-1920s, the essential contours of the American comprehensive high school were apparent. It was an institution that offered a range of curricula to an adolescent population of differing interests, aptitudes, and inclinations. Although college preparation remained a continuing high school function, secondary school educators were devising more programs for youth whose formal education would end with the high school diploma. As the high school assumed its institutional form in the 1920s, four basic patterns of curricular organization could be identified: (1) the college preparatory program, which included courses in the English language and literature, foreign languages, mathematics, natural and physical sciences, and history and social sciences; (2) the commercial or business program which offered work in bookkeeping, shorthand, and typing; (3) industrial, vocational, home economics, and agricultural programs; (4) a modified academic program for terminal students.

Despite some organizational variations, the typical high school pattern followed a four-year attendance sequence, encompassing grades nine, ten, eleven, and twelve, and was attended by the fourteen-to-eighteen age group. There were exceptions, however, in that in some reorganized six-year institutions students attended a combined junior-senior high school after completing a six-year elementary school. The two-year junior high school, comprising the seventh and eighth grades, also began to appear in some urban districts.

THE JUNIOR HIGH SCHOOL

The junior high school, as an elaboration of American secondary education, was an institutional response to important social, political, and economic trends that were having an impact on American society during the period from 1900 to 1920. These first two decades of the twentieth century were marked by: (1) massive immigration from Southern and Eastern Europe to the large cities of the United States; (2) the continuing industrialization of the United States; (3) the recognition, as a

[14] George S. Counts, *The Selective Character of American Secondary Education* (Chicago: University of Chicago Press, 1922), p. 152.

[15] French, *American Secondary Education*, pp. 101-2.

result of the Spanish-American and First World wars, that the United States was a world power; (4) the impact of behavioral science, particularly psychology, on education and society; and (5) the impact of progressive education and philosophy on American schools. These trends, which eventually transformed American society, also stimulated a reorganization of American secondary education.

Among the critics of eight-four school systems (eight years of elementary and four years of secondary schooling) were the proponents of industrial education who believed that this pattern of organization was not preparing enough skilled craftsmen and technicians for an increasingly industrialized and technological society. Believing that American schools needed to modernize their organizational, curricular, and instructional patterns, proponents of industrial education contended that the eight-year elementary, or graded school, was based on America's preindustrial past. They also believed that the high school was still dominated by its traditional college preparatory curriculum. Impressed by the impact of industrial education in Germany, proponents of industrial education believed that schooling should be an agency of efficient industrial productivity.

In 1906, advocates of industrial education organized the National Society for the Promotion of Industrial Education (NSPIE) to promote their cause. The NSPIE wanted to reorganize the school system by creating institutions that would offer curricula differing from those of the traditional elementary and college preparatory secondary schools.

While the NSPIE was agitating for educational reorganization, some professional educators were also questioning the traditional eight-four system. Identified with the social efficiency movement, Frank Spaulding and Franklin Bobbitt urged the application of scientific management to education; they believed that curriculum construction should be based on measurable outcomes that had social or economic consequences. Like the industrialists who wanted education to respond to economic needs, social efficiency educators wanted schooling to be justified economically and socially. Not surprisingly, the aims of the social efficiency educators and the industrialists were often similar. The proponents of industrial education were active at the state and national levels. Using the argument that industrial training would prepare American youth for a wide range of useful occupations, this group and their allies in Congress secured enactment of the Smith-Hughes Act in 1917 to promote vocational education.

In addition to the NSPIE and the social efficiency educators, educators of a more traditional academic ideology saw the junior high school as a means of beginning academic work earlier than had been done in the elementary school. Educators of this group saw the junior high school as a way of implementing the Committee of Ten's recommendation to begin secondary education two years earlier and thereby reduce elementary school from eight to six years.[16]

While industrial education was a major goal of the NSPIE, certain professional educators sought to create new structures to facilitate students' transition not only

[16] Nelson Bossing and Roscoe Cramer, *The Junior High School* (Boston: Houghton Mifflin, (1965), p. 14.

from elementary to secondary education but also from childhood to adolescence. Concerned that the upper years of elementary schooling, particularly seventh and eighth grade, were too repetitious of earlier grades, they wanted to replace the old reading, arithmetic, spelling, and vocabulary reviews with different educational experiences. While they agreed that different educational experiences were needed, they did not always concur that an earlier introduction of academic subjects or increased vocational training was desirable. These educators derived their concept of educational reorganization from research into the nature of adolescence; from such research, they saw a need for educational institutions that followed the patterns of human growth and development. These educators were inspired by the work of G. Stanley Hall (1846-1924), whose pioneering studies, *Adolescence* (1904) and *Educational Problems* (1911), described the implications of adolescent development on education. While these theorists viewed the high school as an institution for adolescents, they also believed that a unique educational institution was needed for preadolescence, a period of human growth distinct from childhood.

Early Junior High Schools

The trend of reorganization that occurred in school districts throughout the United States brought with it several kinds of intermediate, or junior high, schools. In 1910, the Cleveland, Ohio, system established an "intermediate industrial school" for fourteen-to-sixteen-year-old students, with a curriculum that included vocational courses for boys and home arts for girls. In that same year, a prototype of today's junior high school was created by Superintendent Frank Bunker in Berkeley, California, where grades seven through nine were reorganized as an "introductory high school." Bunker based his concept for the introductory high school on: (1) the characteristics of adolescence; (2) the need for a more gradual transition between elementary school and work; (3) the need to alleviate over-crowded central schools; and (4) a need to construct a curriculum based on the future occupations of students.[17] The curriculum of the Berkeley introductory high school included vocational courses such as typewriting, bookkeeping, stenography, commercial law, elementary banking, manual training, domestic science, business arithmetic, and business English.[18]

Although junior high schools like those of Cleveland and Berkeley were established throughout the country, there was little agreement among educators as to curricular scope and the grades to be included in a reorganized school plan. While some districts identified the seventh and eighth grades as appropriate for junior high school instructions, other school districts used a variety of organizational patterns such as the 6-6, 7-5, 7-4, 6-2-4, and 6-3-3 plans. While there was organizational diversity, the general trend was for a six-year elementary school, a three-year

---

[17] Frank P. Bunker, *Reorganization of the Public School System* (Washington, D.C.: GPO, 1916), pp. 108-9.

[18] W. Richard Stephens, "The Junior High School: A Product of Reform Values, 1890-1920," a paper presented at the Midwest History of Education Society, Chicago, Illinois, October 27-28, 1967, p. 16.

senior high school, and an intermediate school—the junior high school, composed of the seventh, eighth, and ninth grades.[19]

By 1920, several educators had written authoritative books about the junior high school.[20] Leonard Koos, in particular, described the major functions of the junior high school as:

1. retaining students in school by reducing the attrition rate and easing the transition from elementary to high school;
2. economizing instructional time by introducing certain secondary level subjects earlier and by eliminating unnecessary repetitious reviews of subjects studied in elementary school;
3. recognizing and providing for individual differences in ability, interests, environment, age, and development;
4. providing more extensive personal, career, and occupational guidance;
5. beginning vocational instruction by providing a range of vocational activities, training, and experiences;
6. recognizing the nature and impact of adolescence on education;
7. beginning subject matter departmentalization earlier and thereby increasing teaching specialization; and
8. increasing students' educational and socialization opportunities by providing a variety of physical, social, recreational, athletic, and educational activities.[21]

The trend of school reorganization, marked by an increase in the number of junior high schools, continued over the next fifty years. In 1930, there were 16,460 regular high schools, 1,842 junior high schools, and 3,287 junior-senior high schools. In 1952, there were 10,168 four-year high schools, 3,227 junior high schools, 1,760 senior high schools, and 8,591 junior-senior high schools. In 1959, there were 6,044 high schools on the 8-4 system, 1,407 high schools on the 6-2-4 system, 1,651 senior high schools on the 6-3-3 system, 5,027 junior high schools on the 6-2-4 and 6-3-3 systems, and 10,155 junior-senior high schools on the 6-6 system.[22] At mid-century, the junior high school was a well established and widely acknowledged part of America's educational ladder. Although some districts still followed the 8-4 pattern, most school systems had been reorganized to incorporate the junior high school.

[19] Francis T. Spaulding, O. Z. Frederick, and Leonard V. Koos, *The Reorganization of Secondary Education,* National Survey of Secondary Education, Monograph 5, United States Office of Education Bulletin 17, 1932 (Washington, D.C.: GPO, 1935), pp. 27-29, 38-44.

[20] Noteworthy examples are Leonard V. Koos, *The Junior High School* (New York: Harcourt, Brace, 1920); and Thomas H. Briggs, *The Junior High School* (Boston: Houghton Mifflin, 1920).

[21] Koos, *Junior High School,* pp. 13-85.

[22] Robert E. Potter, *The Stream of American Education* (New York: American Book Co., 1967), p. 376.

CONCLUSION

The institutional development of American secondary education spanned several centuries. The Latin grammar school, a preparatory institution, was transported to North America in the seventeenth and eighteenth centuries from Europe. In the early nineteenth century, the academy, a multipurpose private institution, replaced the Latin grammar school as the dominant secondary school. After the Civil War, the public high school slowly replaced the academy. These episodes were institutional reponses to broader social changes. For example, the industrialization of the United States contributed to the emergence of the high school. Progressivism in education also influenced the reform of American secondary education and the development of the junior high school.

DISCUSSION QUESTIONS

1. Identify and examine the European antecedents of preparatory education that were transported to North America in the colonial era.
2. Examine the role and functions of the Latin grammar school.
3. How did Jacksonian democracy stimulate social and educational change?
4. How did the academy reflect laissez-faire economic theory and the spirit of entrepreneurship?
5. Describe the organization, governance, and curriculum of the nineteenth-century academies.
6. Identify and analyze the socioeconomic and educational factors that contributed to the emergence of the public high school.
7. Examine the areas of continuity between the common school and the high school movements.
8. What was the educational significance of the Kalamazoo case?
9. Examine the impact of the Committee of Ten on the high school curriculum.
10. Compare and contrast the recommendations of the Committee of Ten and the Commission on the Reorganization of Secondary Education.
11. Compare and contrast the reports of the Committee of Ten and the Commission on the Reorganization of Secondary Education with more recent national reports on secondary education.
12. Identify and analyze the factors that led to the establishment of the junior high school.

RESEARCH TOPICS

1. Examine several histories of Western education; from your reading, prepare a general survey of the concepts inherited from Europe that helped to shape preparatory education in North America.

2. Beginning with contemporary relationships between the high school and the college, trace the historical impact of the higher educational institution on the lower educational institution.

3. Examine state or local histories to determine if academies existed in your locality. If an academy exists or existed in your area, prepare a short historical sketch of the institution. Determine if it fits the general patterns described in the chapter.

4. If they are available in your college or university or local history archives, examine the catalogues and circulars of local academies. Determine if the curriculum described corresponds to the treatment in the chapter.

5. Research the origins of the first public high school in your locality.

6. Using published documents, examine the contemporary college preparatory curriculum. Compare and contrast it with the curriculum prescribed by the Committee of Ten.

7. Research the origins of the first junior high schools in your locality.

REFERENCES AND READINGS

Bossing, Nelson, and Cramer, Roscoe. *The Junior High School.* Boston: Houghton Mifflin, 1965.

Briggs, Thomas H. *The Junior High School.* Boston: Houghton Mifflin, 1920.

Commission on the Reorganization of Secondary Education. *Cardinal Principles of Secondary Education.* Bulletin No. 35. Washington, D.C.: U.S. Bureau of Education, 1918.

Conant, James B. *The American High School Today.* New York: McGraw-Hill, 1959.

____. *Slums and Suburbs.* New York: McGraw-Hill, 1961.

Counts, George S. *Secondary Education and Industrialism.* Cambridge, Mass.: Harvard University Press, 1929.

____. *The Selective Character of American Secondary Education.* Chicago: University of Chicago Press, 1922.

Davis, Calvin O. *A History of the North Central Association of Colleges and Secondary Schools.* Ann Arbor, Mich.: North Central Association, 1945.

French, William M. *American Secondary Education.* New York: Odyssey Press, 1957.

Gross, Ronald, and Osterman, Paul. *High School.* New York: Simon & Schuster, 1971.

James, Thomas, and Tyack, David. "Learning from Past Efforts to Reform the High School," *Phi Delta Kappan,* 64 (February 1983): 400-6.

Koos, Leonard. *The Junior High School.* New York: Harcourt, Brace, 1920.

Krug, Edward A., ed. *Charles W. Eliot and Popular Education.* New York: Teachers College Press, Columbia University, 1961.

____. *The Shaping of the American High School.* Vol. I. New York: Harper & Row, Pub., 1964.

____. *The Shaping of the American High School, 1920-1941,* Vol. II. Madison: University of Wisconsin Press, 1972.

National Education Association. *Report of the Committee of Ten on Secondary School Studies.* New York: American Book Co., 1894.

Passow, Harry A. *Secondary Education Reform: Retrospect and Prospect.* New York: Teachers College Press, Columbia University, 1976.

Popper, Samuel H. *The American Middle School: An Organizational Analysis.* Waltham, Mass.: Blaisdell, 1967.

Prescott, William M., et al. *The Emergent Middle School.* New York: Holt, Rinehart & Winston, 1968.

Sizer, Theodore. *The Age of the Academies.* New York: Bureau of Publications, Teachers College, Columbia University, 1964.

6

THE DEVELOPMENT
OF AMERICAN
HIGHER EDUCATION

We turn now to a review of the origins and development of American higher education from the colonial period until the early twentieth century. We shall present
an historical overview of the growth of colleges and universities in the United States
and examine the following major developments: (1) the transplanting of European
concepts of higher education in North America; (2) the origins of state colleges and
universities, as well as denominational institutions, during the early national period;
(3) the impact of the Morrill acts on the establishment of land-grant colleges and
universities; (4) the formative stages of the modern research-oriented university;
and (5) the rise and development of junior and community colleges.

As in Chapter 5 on secondary education, we shall examine the foundations
and development of higher education as a set of significant American educational
institutions. Although we shall observe a general chronological framework, our
treatment of the subject is topical. More recent developments in higher education
are discussed in later chapters.

TRANSPLANTED EUROPEAN CONCEPTS

American higher education originated in the seventheenth- and early eighteenth-
century colonial period. In Great Britain's North American colonies, the founding
of colleges emulated the institutional models of Oxford and Cambridge, the leading

English universities. In England, students admitted to these prestigious insitutions first completed preparatory studies in "public schools" such as Eton, Rugby, and other boarding schools, which resembled Latin grammar schools. The students at Oxford, Cambridge, and other English colleges and universities were males, the sons of upper-class and aristocratic families. Drawn from England's aristocratic elite, these students pursued a liberal arts curriculum and followed this with professional studies in law, medicine, or theology. In addition to preparing scholars, lawyers, physicians, and ministers, English universities also performed a cultural and political mission. Their educational styles and curricula were designed to provide the British Empire with well-rounded, liberally educated, articulate, and versatile English gentlemen who were capable of serving sovereign, country, church, and empire.

Medieval Antecedents of Colonial Colleges

Colonial colleges, like their English prototypes, borrowed much of their administrative, organizational, and curricular structures from medieval universities. The medieval university was the institutional product of the complex forces characterizing the revival of learning in the twelfth and thirteenth centuries. The revival of learning that stimulated the rise of the medieval university is traceable to several significant historical events. Between 1100 and 1200, there was an influx of knowledge into Western Europe from Arabic sources. The Arab world, for centuries, was a repository for much of the Greek scholarship that had fallen into obscurity or was thought lost to Western civilization. From the Arab scholars, the works of Aristotle, Euclid, Ptolemy, and the Greek physicians entered the libraries of medieval scholastics. Along with the rediscovery of ancient learning, the new arithmetic and texts of Roman law stirred the ferment of the medieval intellectual world. In particular, this newly discovered knowledge created a professional base of study for law and medicine.[1] These new areas of specialized study brought scholars together in the medieval university.

There are several reasons for the rise of the medieval university: (1) a significant revival of learning occurred in the twelfth and thirteenth centuries; (2) the introduction of Arabic scholarship and the rediscovery of ancient Greek texts stimulated new intellectual questions; and (3) a commercial revival renewed city life and encouraged a more cosmopolitan world view.

Originally, the medieval university was not a collection of buildings or a campus but a guild, or a corporation, of professors and students; it was a coming together of teachers (the masters) and students at a central location. In many respects, the medieval university resembled a guild that prepared students, or apprentices, to be masters, or professors. Upon completing the necessary requirements, aspiring students could join the body of scholars. In addition to preparing professors, the medieval university also provided training in the three great professions of law, medicine, and theology.

[1] Charles H. Haskins, *The Rise of Universities* (New York: Cornell University Press, 1957), pp. 8-9.

To be admitted to a university, applicants had to speak and read Latin, the language of instruction. Originally, the curriculum was based on the *trivium* and the *quadrivium* of the seven liberal arts. Completion of the arts course prepared students for professional study in law, medicine, or theology. The *trivium* consisted of grammar, rhetoric, and logic; the *quadrivium* consisted of arithmetic, geometry, astronomy, and music. This slender curriculum was enlarged during the twelfth-century renaissance with the addition of Ptolemy's astronomy, Euclid's geometry, and Aristotle's metaphysics. As the medieval university developed, so did its curriculum. The faculty regulated the subjects and the length of courses.

The arts course was prerequisite for professional study in theology, law, and medicine. According to the medieval view of education, the curriculum was arranged in a pyramid of studies. The student progressed upward from the arts course, at the base, through philosophy and finally at the summit reached theology, the queen of scholastic studies.

The scholastic method centered around books, lectures by the professors on the texts, and disputations by students under the supervision of the masters. The professor lectured, interpreted, and commented on the text. The student followed the text and recorded the professor's interpretations and comments. The plan of the lecture followed syllogistic logic.

The rector emerged as one of the most important officials of the university. Elected by the arts faculty, the rector presided at meetings of the entire university at which all the faculties were represented. The faculties of the university were those of law, theology, medicine, and arts. The term "faculty" first meant a subject of study; it later denoted a corporate body of masters who taught a given subject. Each faculty had the privilege of conferring degrees. Then as now, the degree was the sought-after prize. The license to teach, the *licentia docendi*, was the initial academic degree. Later, the bachelor's degree became a stage toward the master's or doctor's degree. Although there is confusion regarding the distinction between the master's and the doctor's degree, it is generally believed that the titles of master, doctor, and professor were synonymous. *Magister* was the prevailing title used in the faculties of the theology, medicine, and arts.[2]

Students formed groups and rented houses as collective residences. The practice grew that a master, chosen by the student housing group, would be invited to live in the house as its principal resident. Rich students preferred to live in their own houses with their own servants and perhaps a hired tutor. Gradually, these housing groups developed into colleges. The college was at first an endowed boarding house. The founder of the endowment would select a master to direct the house. The object of the endowment was to secure board and lodgings for needy students who could not pay for it themselves. Eventually the colleges were absorbed directly into the university.

The medieval university was also distinguished for its cosmopolitan spirit. The very fact that students could travel from place to place and from country to

---

[2] Hastings Rashdall, *The Universities of Europe in the Middle Ages* (Oxford, Eng.: Oxford University Press, 1895), I: 22.

country indicates that the learning of the period transcended national or linguistic boundaries. Evidence of this is indicated by the use of Latin as the scholar's universal language. The medieval university was the institutional progenitor of Oxford and Cambridge, the universities that were the models for higher education in the British colonies in North America.

The Influence of the Renaissance and Reformation

The medieval university grew to institutional maturity under the aegis of Roman Catholic scholasticism. The renaissance and the Protestant Reformation of the fifteenth and sixteenth centuries that altered intellectual and educational perspectives, especially in England, also produced changes in higher education. Relying less on Aristotle and his logic as the basis of intellectual authority, Renaissance humanists sought to return to what they regarded as purer and more authentic classical texts. Even more significant for the English universities and for the colleges in North America was the Protestant Reformation, which saw higher education as an instrument for creating a theology and a ministry that was faithful to the reformed religion.

The Renaissance classical scholars emphasized the importance of humanistic studies and stressed Greek and Ciceronian Latin as the languages of educated people. With the Protestant Reformation, religion became a dominant force as various denominations sought to use higher education to inculcate doctrinal conformity and to train an educated ministry. The colonial conception of higher education, as transmitted to the New World from England, was derived from the scholasticism of the medieval university, the classical humanism of the Renaissance, and the denominational zeal of the Protestant Reformation.

Establishing Colleges in the Colonies

The Puritan colonists in Massachusetts brought with them strong preconceptions about higher education. Soon after arriving in Massachusetts, they institutionalized these preconceptions by establishing Harvard College in 1636. A description of Harvard, written to promote the institution, clearly stated its Puritan founders' educational rationale:

> After God had carried us safe to *New England*, and we had builded our houses, provided necessaries for our liveli-hood, rear'd convenient places for Gods worship, and settled the Civil Government: One of the next things we longed for, and looked after was to advance *Learning* and perpetuate it to *Posterity*; dreading to leave an illiterate Ministery to the Churches, when our present Ministers shall lie in the Dust. And As we were thinking and consulting how to effect this great Work; it pleased God to stir up the heart of one Mr. *Harvard* . . . towards the erecting of a College. . . .[3]

[3]*New England's First Fruits* (London: Henry Overton, 1643), p. 12.

The education of future Puritan clergymen was the primary motive of Harvard's founding fathers; over 70 percent of the graduates of Harvard in the 1640s became ministers.[4]

Harvard's establishment united three colonial preconceptions about higher education: (1) the idea that the liberal arts were necessary for a liberal education as well as for professional preparation; (2) the idea that classical studies were necessary for "a gentleman's education;" and (3) a confirmation of the belief in religious control of higher education for doctrinal conformity and to prepare ministers.[5]

Based upon these preconceptions, the Harvard curriculum was developed. In the first year, the student studied such classical authors as Tully (Cicero), Isocrates, Homer, and Vergil; the Greek Testament; the catechism; rhetoric; Hebrew grammar; logic; and disputation. The second year brought additional recitations in logic, Greek, and Hebrew grammar, and saw natural philosophy introduced. The third year included more Greek recitation and the introduction of physics, metaphysics, ethics, and geography. Disputations on physical, metaphysical, and ethical questions were continued. The fourth year brought the study of arithmetic, geometry, and astronomy; a review of grammar, logic, and natural philosophy; and continued philosophical disputation.

By the early eighteenth century, Harvard was beginning to be influenced by the liberal intellectual outlook associated with the Enlightenment, as theology at the college came to bear the imprint of deism. As a protest against Harvard's liberalizing theology, the more conservative Congregationalists established their own institution at New Haven in 1701, when Cotton Mather persuaded Elihu Yale to give the initial endowment. Those who sought admission to Yale had to demonstrate competency in reading Cicero and Vergil and the Greek Testament. They also had to be able to write Latin prose and understand basic arithmetic. The liberal arts curriculum was followed at Yale, as it was at other colonial colleges. However, in the decades after its founding, Yale sought to maintain a doctrinal conformity to conservative Congregationalism.

In the colonial South, the plantation-owning class sent their sons to England for higher studies in the liberal arts and the professions. In Virginia, demand for an institution of higher learning led to the granting of a royal charter establishing the College of William and Mary in 1693. Thomas Jefferson's interest in higher education later contributed to the reorganization of William and Mary's curriculum in 1779 to include natural philosophy, mathematics, law, anatomy, medicine, moral philosophy, fine arts, and modern languages.

In the Middle Atlantic colonies, Princeton was chartered in 1746 in New Jersey as a Presbyterian educational institution. King's College, later Columbia, was

---

[4] Samuel Eliot Morison, *Three Centuries of Harvard* (Cambridge Mass.: Harvard University Press, 1936), pp. 189-91.

[5] R. Freeman Butts, *The College Charts Its Course* (New York: McGraw-Hill, 1939), p. 47.

chartered in 1754 to serve New York's Anglicans; it soon acquired a reputation for its tolerant admission policies and liberal curriculum.

The establishment of a college in Philadelphia in 1755, which became the University of Pennsylvania, was encouraged by Benjamin Franklin, who advocated a utilitarian curriculum and educational diversity. Franklin argued that useful and scientific studies should be integrated into the educational programs. With the Reverend William Smith, formerly of the University of Aberdeen, as president, the curriculum included traditional as well as scientific subjects useful for trade and commerce.[6] Smith, a proponent of the Scottish ideas on higher education, brought about some innovation in American higher education in the period preceding the Revolutionary War.

Although there were variations among the colleges during the colonial period, they exhibited some general features in terms of entry requirements, curricula, and methodology. They required applicants to be versed in Latin and Greek. These entry requirements sustained the Latin grammar school as the dominant college preparatory institution. The eighteenth-century colonial college curriculum included the following:

First year:	Latin, Greek, logic, Hebrew, and rhetoric
Second year:	Greek, Hebrew, logic, and natural philosophy
Third year:	Natural philosophy, metaphysics, and moral philosophy
Fourth year:	Mathematics, and review in Latin, Greek, logic, and natural philosophy[7]

The enrollment in the colonial colleges came primarily from the economically favored and socially prominent classes. College presidents and trustees were constantly searching for endowments, bequests, and other forms of financial support.

The Scottish University Influence

While the greatest impact on American colonial colleges came from the English universities of Oxford and Cambridge, the concept of higher education that developed in Scotland also influenced American higher education. The years immediately prior to the American Revolution saw a significant immigration of Scots and Scotch-Irish to North America. True to their Calvinist persuasion, the Presbyterian ministers who accompanied these immigrants were committed to establishing academies and colleges in the New World. In Scotland, universities such as Saint Andrews, Glasgow, Aberdeen, and Edinburgh were centers of utilitarian social service, scientific research, and educational reform. In particular, Aberdeen and Edinburgh, unlike Oxford and Cambridge, were deeply influenced by Enlightenment philosophers and scientists. Educators such as William Smith, Francis Alison,

---

[6] Thomas H. Montgomery, *A History of the University of Pennsylvania from Its Foundation to A.D. 1770* (Philadelphia: George W. Jacobs, 1900), pp. 236-39.

[7] Frederick Rudolph, *The American College and University: A History* (New York: Knopf, 1962), pp. 25-26.

and John Witherspoon brought many Enlightenment ideas to America. Witherspoon developed a synthesis of Newtonian empirical science and Christian religious concepts at Princeton.[8]

To these Scottish universities also came a number of young Americans seeking college degrees and professional training. Benjamin Rush, a founder of American medical education, was one of these Americans who studied in Scotland. After studying medicine in Edinburgh, he returned to Pennsylvania to introduce the new learning at the College of Philadelphia.

Princeton, in New Jersey, was especially influenced by the educational philosophy of the Scottish universities. While its curriculum still stressed classical languages and literature, it also featured more modern courses in science, geography, astronomy, moral philosophy, and mathematics. Its emphasis on sense realism, observation, and experimentation contrasted with the reliance on deductive reasoning that was common to higher education during the colonial period. Among the most significant Scottish contributions to American higher education were: (1) an emphasis on the college as an academic and scientific community; (2) a view that higher education should stress science as well as theology; and (3) an orientation that knowledge could be applied to economic development.[9]

THE EARLY NATIONAL PERIOD

The American Revolution created a nationalistic enthusiasm for a uniquely American form of higher education. The establishment of a national university under federal auspices was proposed at the Constitutional Convention. Although supported by Washington, Jefferson, and Madison, the proposal failed. Throughout his career, Washington advocated establishing a national university. Jefferson, too, was a proponent of such an institution.

Though a national university was not established, the early national period experienced an enthusiasm for founding colleges. In addition to the existing private colleges, new state colleges were chartered. As the Northwest Territory and the Louisiana Purchase were organized into territories and then admitted as states, the various state governments established their own state universities; their efforts were encouraged by the federal policy of granting land for educational purposes from the national domain.

The land-grant precedent had been established by the Ordinances of 1785 and 1787, enacted by the Continental Congress prior to the Constitution's ratification. The Ordinance of 1785 reserved the sixteenth section of each township of the Northwest Territory for education, and the Ordinance of 1787 expressed a federal commitment to encourage "schools and the means of education." The use of

[8]John S. Brubacher and Willis Rudy, *Higher Education in Transition* (New York: Harper & Row, Pub., 1968), p. 15.

[9]Douglas Sloan, *The Scottish Enlightenment and the American College Ideal* (New York: Teachers College Press, Columbia University, 1971), p. 225.

revenues from the abundant frontier land to aid education was a convenient federal policy, since it did not increase taxation. The establishment of state universities was directly encouraged by the federal land-grant policy, which granted two townships of land for institutions of higher learning to each state as it entered the union. Ohio was the first to benefit from this policy; the Ohio Enabling Act, which provided land grants to higher education, set a precedent for other states that later entered the union.

The early national period saw the establishment of the first state universities: the University of Georgia (1785), the University of North Carolina (1789), the University of Tennessee (1794), and South Carolina College (University of South Carolina, 1801). These states were followed by others, who ventured enthusiastically to establish colleges. In the new state colleges, two major trends were discernable: a lessening of denominational religious influence, and the beginning of a gradual movement toward a more diverse curriculum. For example, by 1795, the University of North Carolina had moved beyond the classical curriculum to offer courses in the English language and literature, mathematics, and American government. At the time of their establishment, many of the early state colleges were located in small towns. The location of a college was often based on political decisions rather than on careful planning. Some of the colleges, lacking a network of preparatory feeder schools, had to maintain their own secondary departments and schools to prepare students to meet the college entry requirements, which were usually based on competency in Latin. Library holdings were generally small. After their brief period of enthusiasm for establishing colleges, state legislators gave them inadequate attention and financial support.

Thomas Jefferson and the University of Virginia

The University of Virginia, established in 1825, was one of the first major American institutions of higher learning to deviate from the older patterns of organization, control, and curriculum. Largely the conception of Thomas Jefferson, who regarded it as one of his most significant accomplishments, the University of Virginia was to be free of religious control and was to promote scientific inquiry and progress.

Jefferson's concept of the purpose and nature of the University of Virginia served as a model for the modern state university. As indicated in Chapter 2, Jefferson was committed to the idea that education was vital to the success of American republican political institutions. He believed, however, that American schools and colleges needed to incorporate science and scientific inquiry and methods into their curricula. Such educational reform would enhance both personal liberty and national development as well.

After completing his terms as president of the United States, Jefferson steadfastly devoted his energy to founding the University of Virginia. The establishment of the university in 1825 marked a significant change from the older classical patterns. Jefferson's philosophy of the state university was asserted in the "Report of the Rockfish Gap Commission," which stated that each generation inherits knowledge from the preceding generation, adds its own discoveries, and then transmits an increasing body of knowledge to its posterity.[10] Influenced by the Enlightenment doctrine of Progress, Jefferson firmly believed that education was the instrument that would give humankind control of its future.

Jefferson wanted the University of Virginia to be an institution that would permit its students to enroll in courses that were relevant to their future professional careers instead of rigidly following a prescribed regimen of studies. Quite liberal in his orientation, Jefferson advocated that the University of Virgina should steadfastly follow the principle of academic freedom.[11]

The University of Virginia embodied several characteristics that would emerge later in other state institutions of higher learning. Among these features were: (1) state, rather than church or private, control and support; (2) an increasingly scientific rather than classical and theological curriculum; (3) the introduction of some degree of student election or choice of subject; (4) the origin of a secular instead of a religious perspective. These characteristics could also be found in varying degrees in other state colleges and universities. It should be remembered, however, that the early state colleges and universities that were established prior to the Morrill Act of 1862 responded to change only very gradually and maintained many of the inherited colonial conceptions of higher education.

Denominational Colleges

The first half of the nineteenth century was marked not only by the founding of state colleges and universities but also by an intensification of religious demoninationalism. The evangelical spirit of the great religious revivals that swept the frontier areas was also responsible for the establishment of numerous denominational academies and colleges. As the frontier moved west, ministers of the various churches migrated along with their congregations. At times, ministers and priests led the westward advance as missionaries and then remained to serve the small towns that grew up in the Midwest and West. The impact of denominationalism can be seen in the number of colleges that were established in the first half of the nineteenth century. When American independence was proclaimed, only nine colleges were functioning; by the outbreak of the Civil War in 1861, more than 200 colleges were operating, and most of them were under denominational control.[12] The religious revivals and the growth of evangelical Protestantism before the Civil War had influenced American higher education in a number of ways: (1) American Protestants, like their European counterparts, generally valued an educated ministry, and even denominations that questioned "too much book-learning" began

---

[10] Roy J. Honeywell, *The Educational Work of Thomas Jefferson* (Cambridge, Mass.: Harvard University Press, 1931), p. 248.

[11] Robert D. Heslep, *Thomas Jefferson and Education* (New York: Random House, 1969), p. 108.

[12] Donald G. Tewksbury, *The Founding of American Colleges and Universities before the Civil War* (New York: Bureau of Publications, Teachers College, Columbia University, 1932), p. 15.

to establish colleges. (2) The proliferation of religious denominations stimulated a competition that extended to establishing colleges. (3) Denominational colleges were viewed as a way to educate the faithful and to build religious commitment in the young. These denominational colleges did not restrict themselves to religious education but also offered courses in the liberal arts and practical subjects. Like the state colleges, the denominational institutions often had to establish academies to prepare their own students at the secondary level. Presbyterians, Congregationalists, Roman Catholics, Methodists, Lutherans, Christian Disciples, Baptists, Episcopalians, Quakers, and Mormons were among the sects that founded a number of small liberal arts colleges.[13]

The Dartmouth College Case

As indicated earlier, the first half of the nineteenth century witnessed significant changes in higher education. New state colleges and universities were being established, and the number of denominational colleges was increasing. While these changes were taking place, the older colonial-era colleges continued to function. In the early nineteenth century, there was some confusion over matters of control, governance, and support. In New Hampshire, these issues produced a controversy that was settled in the Dartmouth College case in 1819. The controversy over the control of Dartmouth College stemmed from political contention between the Federalists, who controlled Dartmouth's board of trustees, and the Jeffersonian Democratic-Republicans, who controlled the New Hampshire state legislature. In 1816, the Democratic-Republican majority in the legislature sought to take control of Dartmouth by changing its charter, annulling the original provisions, and establishing a new institution called the University of New Hampshire. The Federalist-controlled board of trustees contended that the action of the state legislature was unconstitutional in that it violated the college's original charter. Daniel Webster, who argued the case before the Supreme Court, won a decision favorable to the trustees that affirmed the original charter. According to Chief Justice John Marshall, the charter granted to Dartmouth by King George III was a contract; and under the Constitution, the binding force of contracts could not be impaired. Marshall's decision upheld the Constitution's contract clause, applied it to the Dartmouth case, restored control of the college to its board of trustees, and returned it to its status as a private educational institution.

The Dartmouth College decision of 1819 had far-reaching significance for both educational and national development. It protected the continued existence of independent, privately controlled colleges by ending state efforts to establish control over such institutions by legislative action. It sanctioned a dual system of private and state colleges and universities in the United States. Marshall's decision meant that private institutions, though contributing to the public good, could

---

[13] For a discussion of the evolution of denominational higher education, see Allan O. Pfinster, "A Century of the Church-Related College," in William Brickman and Stanley Lehrer, eds., *A Century of Higher Education: Classical Citadel to Collegiate Colossus* (New York: Society for the Advancement of Education, 1962).

remain under private control. It protected the right of private colleges to exist outside state control once the charter had been issued. It also had the side effect of slowing down the growth of public higher education, since state institutions could no longer be shaped from already existing private colleges. Most significantly, private colleges were free to shape their own destinies.

The Yale Report of 1828

Although several significant developments had occurred in the establishment, control, and governance of higher education, the college curriculum was generally resistant to innovation. Then, as now, institutions of higher learning were more resistant to change than elementary or secondary schools. Despite the efforts of leaders like Thomas Jefferson at the University of Virginia, the curricula of the most prestigious colleges and universities remained cast along traditional forms. An important document that supported traditional higher education was the Yale Report of 1828. The Yale Report, prepared by President James L. Kingsley, was written as a rebuttal to those critics who were challenging the traditional collegiate curriculum. The authors of the report relied heavily on "faculty" psychology, which maintained that the mind was composed of faculties such as reason, memory, and imagination. According to this psychology, education should be a form of mental discipline that would train these mental faculties for their proper uses. The wide use of drill as an instructional method derived its academic strength from this theory.[14]

The Yale Report of 1828 gave faculty psychology its last great rationale as a basis for the classical curriculum. According to Kingsley, higher education should: (1) be a substitute for parental control; (2) provide mental discipline; (3) vigorously exercise and train students' mental faculties; (4) form a proper character. In defense of the traditional curriculum, the report's authors contended:

> In the course of instruction in this college, it has been an object to maintain such a proportion between the different branches of literature and science, as to form in the student a proper *balance* of character. From the pure mathematics, he learns the art of demonstrative reasoning. In attending to the physical sciences, he become familiar with facts, with the process of induction, and the varieties of probable evidence. In ancient literature, he finds some of the most finished models of taste. By English reading, he learns the powers of the language in which he is to speak and write. By logic and mental philosophy, he is taught the art of thinking; by rhetoric and oratory, the art of speaking. By frequent exercise on written composition, he acquires copiousness and accuracy of expression. By extemporaneous discussion, he becomes prompt, fluent, and animated. It is a point of high importance that eloquence and solid learning should go together; that he who has accumulated the richest treasures of thought, should possess the highest powers of oratory.[15]

[14] Richard Hofstadter and C. Dewitt Hardy, *The Development and Scope of Higher Education in the United States* (New York: Columbia University Press, 1952), p. 14.

[15] "Original Papers in Relation to a Course of Liberal Education," *American Journal of Science and Arts,* 15 (January 1829): 300-01.

Not only did the Yale Report uphold the traditional college curriculum, it also reasserted the importance of the classics, especially Latin and Greek, in forming the truly educated person. Knowledge of the classics, as an important part of early discipline, was regarded as necessary for entry to higher learning.

In upholding the traditional curriculum, the Yale Report considered higher education to be a general training of mental faculties and a general cultural education instead of a specialized preparation for particular professions. In answering criticisms that the curriculum was unrelated to economic, social, and scientific developments and needs, the report's authors stated that the goal of a genuine higher education was "not to teach that which is peculiar to any one of the professions but to lay the foundation which is common to all." A classical education would develop a mind enriched by general knowledge and would impart to a gentleman "an elevation and dignity of character" that would enhance his role in the community.[16]

While the Yale Report was an eloquent argument for a traditional classical higher education, it did not satisfy the restlessness of businessmen, industrialists, and farmers for a curriculum that was relevant to commerce, industry, and agriculture.

THE MORRILL ACTS AND LAND-GRANT COLLEGES

In the mid-nineteenth century, several forces converged to bring about a major innovation in American higher education: the land-grant college and university. As noted, industrial and agricultural spokesmen were calling for a new direction in higher education that would make colleges and universities more attuned to American national development. In addition, politicians from the Western states on the frontier were urging greater federal involvement in higher education. (The land-grant concept had been used earlier to finance both common schools and state colleges.) The federal government also had become involved in several projects in higher education.[17] For example, military academies at West Point and Annapolis had been established under federal auspices to train army and naval officers for the nation's defense. In 1857, the Columbia Institute for the Deaf, later named Gallaudet College, was established with federal assistance. After the Civil War, Howard University was established to provide higher education for the newly freed blacks. These various federal ventures into higher education were not part of a general movement aimed at solving specific educational problems.

The movement to establish land-grant colleges and universities during the 1850s demonstrated a recognition that economic development was related to and

---

[16] Ibid., pp. 308-9.

[17] For additional reading on the federal government's role in higher education, see Hollis P. Allen, *The Federal Government and Education* (New York: McGraw-Hill, 1950); Richard G. Axt, *The Federal Government and Financing Higher Education* (New York: Columbia University Press, 1952); Homer D. Babbidge and Robert M. Rosenzweig, *The Federal Interest in Higher Education* (New York: Columbia University Press, 1962).

An illustration of Southern Illinois Normal University, in Carbondale, Illinois in 1879). *(From The Year-Book of Education for 1879. New York: E. Steiger, 1879.)*

somewhat dependent on educational innovation. In addition to economic development, Allan Nevins, in *The State Universities and Democracy*, has pointed out that the social and political motive for equality of opportunity also stimulated the land-grant college movement.[18] For many of the farmers and laborers in the 1850s and 1860s, equality of opportunity required an education that would improve their economic condition. Finding the existing liberal arts colleges unresponsive and irrelevant to their needs, members of the agricultural and industrial organizations urged the establishment of a new institution, the industrial college. For example, Jonathan Baldwin Turner, in the early 1850s, proposed the establishment of a state industrial university in Illinois that was to be financed by federal land grant. In 1853, the Illinois legislature petitioned Congress to endow a system of industrial

[18] Allan Nevins, *The State Universities and Democracy* (Urbana: University of Illinois Press, 1962), p. 17.

colleges. Justin S. Morrill, a Vermont congressman, introduced the first of two land-grant acts to finance agricultural and mechanical education, without excluding scientific and classical studies. The first act, a protest against the domination of higher education by the classics, sought to encourage agricultural and industrial education at the collegiate level. When Congress passed the first Morrill Act, President Buchanan vetoed it. When the bill returned to the president's office in 1862, Abraham Lincoln signed it. The first act granted 30,000 acres of public land to each state for each senator and representative it had in Congress according to the apportionment of the census of 1860.[19] The income from this land was to support at least one college whose primary mission was agricultural and mechanical instruction. In states lacking adequate acreage of public land, the grant was paid in federal script—i.e., certificates based upon the public domain. The funds were to be used to establish a land-grant college.

The second Morrill Act, passed in 1890, provided a direct cash grant of $15,000, to be increased annually to a maximum of $25,000 to support land-grant colleges and universities. It also provided for the support of land-grant colleges for black students in states that prohibited their enrollment in existing land-grant institutions. The federal government specified that colleges receiving support were to provde instruction in agricultural and mechanical subjects and in military training.

As a result of the Morrill acts, land-grant institutions have been established throughout the United States. In some states, land-grant agricultural and mechanical colleges are part of the state university. Examples of such universities are Maine, founded in 1865, Illinois and West Virginia in 1867, California in 1868, Nebraska in 1869, Ohio State in 1870, Arkansas in 1871, and the Alaska Agricultural College and School of Mines in 1922. Seventeen Southern states established separate land-grant colleges for black students under the provisions of the Second Morrill Act of 1890.

THE FORMATION OF THE UNIVERSITY

The history of American higher education reveals a continuous interaction between transplanted European concepts and the American environment. The modern American university resulted from the imposition of the German graduate school upon the four-year undergraduate college. German universities such as Berlin, Halle, Göttingen, Bonn, and Munich, with their emphasis on *Lehrfreiheit und Lernfreiheit*, freedom to teach and freedom to learn, exercised a great influence on American higher education at the end of the nineteenth century. Many American professors, who completed their education with study in a German university, introduced German research concepts into American higher education. For example, university presidents such as Daniel Coit Gilman of Johns Hopkins and Charles W. Eliot of

---

[19] Benjamin F. Andrews, *The Land Grant of 1862 and the Land-Grant College* (Washington, D.C.: GPO, 1918), pp. 7-8.

Harvard worked to transform their institutions into centers of graduate study and research. At the Johns Hopkins University, founded in Baltimore in 1876, instruction was modeled along the lines of the German university as distinguished scholars conducted research seminars for graduate students. The methods of Johns Hopkins were followed by the graduate schools of Harvard, Yale, Columbia, Princeton, and Chicago.[20] Thus, the German emphasis on scholarship and research came to dominate the American university, as distinguished professors devoted themselves to the pursuit of truth and the advancement of knowledge.

By the end of the nineteenth century, the American university reached its basic definition as it came to encompass the undergraduate college of liberal arts and sciences, the graduate college, and the professional colleges of law, medicine, education, agriculture, engineering, nursing, social work, theology, dentistry, commerce, and other specialized areas.

Charles Eliot

The career of Charles Eliot, Harvard's president from 1869 to 1909, reveals his efforts to modernize higher education as he transformed Harvard University from a classically oriented institution into one that prepared its graduates for the professional needs of a complex and technological society.[21] A Harvard graduate, Eliot had studied the classics, mathematics, and chemistry. While touring Europe in 1863, Eliot visited French and German universities and polytechnical institutes. Returning to the United States, Eliot recommended that some selected aspects of European institutions be incorporated into American universities. While he believed that some European innovations would be useful, he steadfastly argued that the American university should meet the unique needs of the United States, a nation that was changing from a rural-agrarian to a rapidly modernizing technological society.

During the forty years that he was Harvard's president, Eliot's leadership helped to modernize not only his own university but American higher education as well. Historically, American college and university presidents had been recruited from the ranks of distinguished clergymen who conducted their presidencies in a ministerial or paternalistic fashion. In contrast, Eliot believed that the modernization of universities required a concept of the presidency that was both executive and managerial. In fact, Eliot saw his role to be that of managing a highly complex educational corporation that incorporated undergraduate, graduate, and professional education.[22] As Harvard's president, he worked for greater efficiency, higher standards, and greater student freedom of choice. As a firm proponent of articulation between educational institutions, he worked to end the ivory tower isolation

[20] Abraham Flexner, *Universities: American, English, German* (New York: Oxford University Press, 1930), pp. 73-74.

[21] Hugh Hawkins, *Between Harvard and America: The Educational Leadership of Charles W. Eliot* (New York: Oxford University Press, 1972), pp. 30-32.

[22] Ibid., p. 52.

of higher education from elementary and secondary schools. As chairman of the National Education Association's Committee of Ten, he worked to develop closer working relationships between high schools and colleges (see Chapter 5).

In seeking to enlarge student freedom of choice in course selection, Eliot worked to reduce curricular prescription and to encourage the elective principle at Harvard in the 1870s. As a result, students were free to elect a certain number of courses rather than following a totally prescribed curriculum. The elective principle, Eliot believed, would encourage undergraduate specialization by stimulating the development of new fields of specialized study, as professors concentrated on their areas of expertise rather than on mandatory general courses.

Critics of Electivism

Eliot's campaigns to encourage the elective principle and specialization at Harvard raised the ire of traditionally minded educators, who believed that the purpose of higher education, especially at the collegiate or undergraduate level, was to prepare intellectually able generalists who had studied the arts and sciences. Eliot's opponents were humanists, who believed that language and literature were important subjects in preparing the liberally educated generalist. In the twentieth century, Irving Babbitt, in particular, criticized Eliot's electivism at Harvard. Babbitt reiterated the philosophy that classical study would educate a genuinely broad cultural taste and intellectual discipline.[23] For Babbitt, the essential purpose of higher education was to transmit enduring cultural values from generation to generation through a general liberal education.

Robert Hutchins, in *Higher Learning in America* (1936), attacked not only specialization but what he regarded as confusion in American higher education.[24] Hutchins, who was president of the University of Chicago during the 1930s, accused the modern university of neglecting a genuinely intellectual education to appease the special interests of donors, students, big business, football-oriented alumni, and politicians. Contending that modern universities had degenerated into "service stations," Hutchins claimed that the sole purpose of higher education was the pursuit of intellectual truth. Overspecialization had caused scholars to focus their work on narrow objectives; such specialization had limited the intellectual vision that a university needed to be a community of scholars. Also, Hutchins condemned a rising anti-intellectualism that had developed from emphasizing strictly utilitarian over theoretical and speculative intellectual studies.

Critics of Hutchins's philosophy of higher education saw it as a retreat to an ivory tower mentality that isolated the university from the realities of social and technological change. Rather than pursuing purely intellectual pursuits, they believed, higher education should provide the specialized knowledge and methods needed in a technological and scientific age.

---

[23] Irving Babbitt, *Democracy and Leadership* (Boston: Houghton Mifflin, 1952), p. 302.

[24] Robert M. Hutchins, *Higher Learning in America* (New Haven: Yale University Press, 1936).

The broad educational issues raised by Eliot at Harvard and Hutchins at the University of Chicago have reverberated throughout American higher education's history. Essentially, the debate has produced the following continuing questions:

1. Should the mission of higher education be to prepare liberally educated generalists or highly trained specialists?
2. Should the curriculum prescribe a general core of studies for all students or should it feature specialized programs and elective subjects based on student professional goals and interests?

By the beginning of the twentieth century, some American universities had developed into recognized centers for scholarship and research. The German research model and the thrust to professional studies combined to create a new focus in graduate education that added to the complexity of higher education in the United States.

JUNIOR AND COMMUNITY COLLEGES

While the American college and university were being transformed by forces of intellectual, social, and technological change in the late nineteenth and early twentieth centuries, a new institution—the junior college—was emerging to take its position on the American educational ladder. The impetus for a new, two-year collegiate institution came from two sources: university administrators who wanted to remove the first two years of undergraduate education to institutions other than their own; and high school administrators who wanted to provide their graduates with advanced instruction. These two administrative initiatives were joined with the broad thrust of socioeconomic forces that called for the establishing of colleges that would be convenient to students and provide them with opportunities for advanced education beyond secondary schooling.

Initially, the impetus to establish junior colleges originated in the late nineteenth century with university presidents such as Henry A. Tappan of Michigan, William W. Folwell of Minnesota, William Rainey Harper of Chicago, and David Starr Jordan of Stanford, who argued that the first two undergraduate years of college were more appropriate to secondary than to higher education. Arguing that the first two years of undergraduate education should be offered elsewhere than in the existing four-year college, these university presidents were not especially interested in creating a new institution. However, they wanted to free their universities from performing what they considered to be secondary education functions so that their faculties could devote more time to graduate level education and research. In 1892, President Harper of the University of Chicago took the initiative and separated the first two and last two years of undergraduate instruction into the Academic and University Colleges. In 1869, these designations were changed to the "junior" and the "senior" colleges.[25]

[25]James W. Thornton, *The Community Junior College* (New York: John Wiley, 1966).

In 1901, Joliet Junior College, a public institution, was established in Joliet, Illinois. Under the direction of Superintendent J. Stanley Brown, high school graduates were encouraged to take postgraduate work without additional tuition.[26] Although Brown's primary objective was to provide courses whose credits could be transferred to four-year institutions, Joliet Junior College also began to offer terminal courses and programs of a vocational nature. By the early twentieth century, junior colleges were beginning to offer diverse programs to meet the needs of a changing society.

By the mid-1920s, the concept of the junior college was well established. Leonard V. Koos, a professor of education at leading universities such as Minnesota and Chicago, produced the first major systematic rationales and surveys of the new institution. As of 1922, Koos had identified 200 public and private junior colleges enrolling more than 16,000 students.[27]

As Koos surveyed the status of junior colleges some two decades after the founding of the pioneer institution in Joliet, he identified the following major purposes of the new colleges: (1) to provide college level courses that would be transferable to four-year institutions; (2) to provide opportunities for "rounding out" students' general education; (3) to provide occupational preparation; (4) to popularize higher education by reducing its cost and bringing it nearer to the students' homes.[28]

As is true of new and developing educational institutions, the junior college experienced a period of definition and redefinition in its earlier period. As indicated, the two-year college was initially the idea of university presidents who wanted to divert the responsibility for educating first- and second-year undergraduates to other institutions. According to this concept, the junior college would offer general liberal arts courses. In 1925, the American Association of Junior Colleges reaffirmed that junior colleges would offer two years of collegiate instruction of a quality equivalent to the first two years of a four-year college. The association, however, broadened its curricular conception to include the personal, social, civic, and vocational needs of students.[29] As the functions of the junior college became more diverse, it gradually developed into a multipurpose educational institution for the entire community and was no longer an upward extension of the high school or a downward extension of the four-year college.

During the late 1920s, junior colleges began to develop more extensive vocational and technical education programs. One of the most extensive terminal, or semiprofessional, programs was developed at Los Angeles Junior College, which offered fourteen separate terminal programs in 1929, its inaugural year.[30] Junior colleges throughout the country also increased their offerings of terminal programs.

[26] Elbert K. Fretwell, Jr., *Founding Public Junior Colleges* (New York: Teachers College Press, Columbia University, 1954), pp. 11-12.

[27] Leonard V. Koos, *The Junior-College Movement* (Boston:Ginn and Co., 1925). p. 13; and *The Junior College* (Minneapolis: University of Minnesota, 1924).

[28] Koos, *Junior-College Movement*, pp. 17-22.

[29] Thornton, *Community Junior College*, p. 51.

[30] Ibid., p. 52.

Several factors stimulated the emphasis on collegiate vocational and technical education. In 1917, Congress enacted the Smith-Hughes Act to provide federal aid to vocational education. Although it primarily assisted high school programs, the act also encouraged vocational education programs in junior colleges in states where they were an extension of secondary education. During the 1920s, a number of educators subscribed to the theory of social efficiency, which held that each subject of study could be justified only in terms of its economic and social utility. Since vocational and technical subjects had an obvious economic utility, they were prime candidates for an expanding junior college curriculum.

By the 1920s, the concept of the junior college had become well established in the United States. Subsequent decades, particularly the 1950s and 1960s, would witness an enormous expansion of junior colleges. During those decades, junior colleges would be transformed into community colleges.

CONCLUSION

Higher education in the United States, like elementary and secondary education, began with the transporting of European concepts of the college and university to North America during the colonial era. The westward-moving frontier and the concepts of a distinctive American nation reshaped these inherited institutional patterns. The land-grant colleges and universities created by the Morrill acts were responsive to the agricultural and industrial needs of a developing society. In the late nineteenth century, the research model of the German university was introduced to American higher education. The result was a more sophisticated research orientation. A later development was the emergence of the junior college, a product of industrial America.

With the essential institutional framework that had developed at the beginning of the twentieth century, Americn higher education would continue to grow. Later chapters will examine the continuing development of American higher education.

DISCUSSION QUESTIONS

1. Examine the European antecedents of the American college.
2. Analyze the catalogues of the college of arts and sciences in your college or university at five-year intervals over a given period of time. Determine areas of curricular continuity and change.
3. Examine the concept of higher education within the Puritan world view.
4. Examine the role of the land-grant concept in supporting institutions of higher learning.
5. How was the University of Virginia a model for the modern state university?
6. What was the significance of the Dartmouth College case?
7. Examine the philosophy of education that was implied in the Yale Report.

8. What social, economic, and political changes contributed to the enactment of the Morrill acts?
9. Examine the efforts of Charles Eliot to modernize higher education.
10. Examine the socioeconomic trends that contributed to the rise of the junior college.

RESEARCH TOPICS

1. Examine several good histories of European colleges and universitites. In a short paper, identify and analyze the influences of European higher education on American colleges and universities.
2. Examine the origins and development of the liberal arts curriculum.
3. Prepare a review of the standard treatments of the rise of universities provided by Charles Haskins or Hastings Rashdall.
4. Select a colonial college and research its history. Prepare a short institutional history that identifies the major developments in the pre-Civil War period.
5. Research and write a short institutional history of a state college or university in your state.
6. Research and write a short institutional history of a private college or university in your state.
7. Identify the colleges and universities in your state that are governed and supported by religious denominations.
8. Read a biography or autobiography of a nineteenth- or early twentieth-century college or university president. From your reading, comment on the style of leadership and administration portrayed.
9. Prepare a short historical sketch of the origins of a community college in your locality.

REFERENCES AND READINGS

Allen, Hollis P. *The Federal Government and Education.* New York: McGraw-Hill, 1950.
Andrews, Benjamin F. *The Land Grant of 1862 and the Land-Grant College.* Bulletin No. 13. Washington, D.C.: GPO, 1918.
Axt, Richard G. *The Federal Government and Financing Higher Education.* New York: Columbia University Press, 1952.
Babbidge, Homer D., and Rosenzweig, Robert M. *The Federal Interest in Higher Education.* New York: Columbia University Press, 1962.
Babbitt, Irving. *Democracy and Leadership.* Boston: Houghton Mifflin, 1952.
Brickman, William F., and Lehrer, Stanley, eds. *A Century of Higher Education: Classical Citadel to Collegiate Colossus.* New York: Society for the Advancement of Education, 1962.
Brown, Hugh S., and Mayhew, Lewis B. *American Higher Education.* New York: Center for Applied Research in Education, 1965.
Brubacher, John S., and Rudy, Willis. *Higher Education in Transition: An American History: 1636-1956.* New York: Harper & Row, Pub., 1958.

Brunner, Henry S., *Land-Grant Colleges and Universities, 1862-1962.* Washington, D.C.: GPO, 1962.

Butts, R. Freeman. *The College Charts Its Course: Historical Conceptions and Current Proposals.* New York: McGraw-Hill, 1939.

Eddy, Edward, Jr. *College for Our Land and Time: The Land-Grant Idea in American Education.* New York: Harper & Row, Pub., 1956.

Flexner, Abraham. *Universities: American, English, German.* New York: Oxford University Press, 1930.

Fretwell, Elbert K., Jr. *Founding Public Junior Colleges.* New York: Bureau of Publications, Teachers College, Columbia University, 1954.

Haskins, Charles H. *The Rise of Universities.* New York: Cornell University Press, 1957.

Hawkins, Hugh. *Between Harvard and America: The Educational Leadership of Charles W. Eliot.* New York: Oxford University Press, 1972.

Hofstadter, Richard, and Hardy, C. Dewitt. *The Development and Scope of Higher Education in the United States.* New York: Columbia University Press, 1952.

Koos, Leonard V. *The Junior College Movement.* Boston: Ginn and Co., 1925.

McConnell, T. R. *A General Pattern for American Public Higher Education.* New York: McGraw-Hill, 1962.

Medsker, Leland L. *The Junior College: Progress and Prospect.* New York: McGraw-Hill, 1960.

Morison, Samuel E. *The Founding of Harvard College.* Cambridge, Mass.: Harvard University Press, 1935.

____. *Three Centuries of Harvard.* Cambridge, Mass.: Harvard University Press, 1936.

Nevins, Allan. *The State Universities and Democracy.* Urbana: University of Illinois Press, 1962.

Perkins, James A. *The University in Transition.* Princeton, N.J.: Princeton University Press, 1966.

Rashdall, Hastings. *The Universities of Europe in the Middle Ages.* Oxford, Eng.: Oxford University Press, 1895.

Ross, Earle D. *Democracy's College: The Land-Grant Movement in the Formative Stage.* Ames: Iowa State College Press, 1942.

Rudolph, Frederick. *The American College and University: A History.* New York: Knopf, 1962.

Sloan, Douglas. *The Scottish Enlightenment and the American College Ideal.* New York: Teachers College Press, Columbia University, 1971.

Tewksbury, Donald G. *The Founding of American Colleges and Universities before the Civil War.* New York: Bureau of Publications, Teachers College Press, Columbia University, 1932.

Thornton, James W. *The Community Junior College.* New York: John Wiley, 1966.

Thwing, Charles F. *A History of Higher Education in America.* New York: Appleton, 1906.

Tiedt, Sidney W. *The Role of the Federal Government in Education.* New York: Oxford University Press, 1966.

7

THE CIVIL WAR, RECONSTRUCTION, AND THE EDUCATION OF BLACK AMERICANS

In this chapter, we shall examine the conditions, problems, and issues related to the education of black Americans. We begin with a brief description of the condition of black slaves in the antebellum South. We then analyze the proslavery defense of Southern ideologues and the abolitionist attack on the South's "peculiar institution." The discussion goes on to survey the Reconstruction era (1865-1877), when black children were admitted to the newly established public schools in the South.

The philosophy of education developed by Booker T. Washington at Tuskegee Institute is next analyzed. We conclude with the blacks' rising disenchantment with Washington's gradualistic position on civil rights and the challenge raised by W. E. B. DuBois.

AMERICAN BLACKS BEFORE THE CIVIL WAR

From 1800 to the beginning of the Civil War in 1861, black slavery was an accepted and fiercely defended social and economic condition in the South. Let us briefly examine the origins and development of African slavery in the United States.

African slavery in North America began in 1619, when twenty blacks were brought to Jamestown to work on the Virginia plantations. By the time of Southern secession in 1860, black slaves numbered about four million. The major reason for the growth of American slavery was economic.[1] The Southern states—ranging from the Tidewater counties of Maryland and Virginia, to North and South Carolina, to the flatlands of Mississippi and Alabama—formed a vast agricultural region, much of it semitropical, suited to the cultivation of staple crops such as tobacco, rice, and cotton. Grown as products for export to Europe and the Northern states, these staple crops, especially cotton, brought about a system of agricultural economics in which large aggregates of land were given over to the cultivation of a single crop. The large plantation, in contrast to the small New England family farms, emerged as the agricultural unit, and a labor-intensive system of cultivation arose that required a large work force. The growing need for plantation labor was satisfied by a flourishing slave trade in which Africans were seized by force or sold into slavery to work on the plantations of America's South.

Slavery

For the majority of blacks who were slaves on Southern plantations, life was a process of being conditioned to accept white superiority and black inferiority. Fearful of slave revolts such as the one that occurred against the French on the island of Haiti in 1791 and the one led by Nat Turner in 1831, white plantation owners instituted a conditioning process that was intended to make blacks docile, obedient, and compliant.[2]

The results of this process were mixed both for the black slave and the white master. Some blacks fell into line, worked hard, and demonstrated loyalty to the plantation family. Others resisted and attempted to flee to free states and territories or to join in abortive slave uprisings. For the majority, the strategy was outward submission but inward rejection of a degrading human and social system. For the majority, discontent took the form of passive resistance marked by deliberate work slowdowns or inefficiency.

An important cultural and educational influence on blacks was religious experience. Afro-American Christianity was: (1) an expression of evangelical Protestantism, (2) an incorporation of elements of African religious traditions, and (3) an expression of the Biblical search for freedom. These aspects of Afro-American Christianity took denominational form in the various Baptist churches and in the African Methodist Episcopal Church.[3]

The worship services of blacks were both a form of religious experience and of informal education. Sermons and songs, expressed in Biblical allusions, carried the freedom message. Often, the message was expressed indirectly and referred

---

[1] Eugene D. Genovese, *The Political Economy of Slavery: Studies in the Economy and Society of the Slave South* (New York: Pantheon, 1965); and Robert W. Fogel and Stanley L. Engerman, *Time on the Cross: The Economics of American Negro Slavery* (Boston: Little, Brown, 1974), examine the economics of slavery.

[2] Vincent Harding, *There Is a River: The Black Struggle for Freedom in America* (New York: Harcourt Brace Jovanovich, 1981), examines black resistance to slavery.

[3] Albert J. Raboteau, *Slave Religion* (New York: Oxford University Press, 1978), examines black religious experience during slavery.

to the deliverance of the Israelites from Egyptian bondage. Of significance for informal education, black religious activities: (1) developed preachers and church elders as a leadership group, (2) provided a set of sustaining spiritual and ethical values, (3) created a strong oral tradition that stressed the spoken word as a powerful educational agency. In addition to religion, black family life and kinship relationships helped to sustain black culture during the slavery era.[4]

Although not recognized legally, most slaves lived in stable, monogamous marriage relationships, with children growing up in two-parent households. Family relationships and marriages could be broken, however, by the sale of a family member. Within the nuclear family, children learned from their parents the strategies of surviving plantation life. Kinship relationships were highly valued, with relatives forming a support system. Kinship ties meant that members of the extended family could depend on each other for support. Thus, the occupations of the plantation economy, religious experience, and family and kinship relations constituted an informal educational process for blacks trapped in the web of slavery.

The education of the black slaves in the South was primarily by informal means, because the slaveholding states had enacted laws forbidding their formal schooling. The tasks performed by slaves in the plantation economy ranged from those of fieldhands to skilled craftsmen. Slaves performed many of the tasks that were normally done by lower-middle-class workmen in the free states. Some slaves became skilled carpenters, blacksmiths, weavers, and seamstresses; others were proficient bookkeepers, typesetters, and machinists.

A small minority of slaves learned to read and write through informal and often "accidental" ways. Some blacks learned to read as they sorted their master's newspapers or set type in print shops. Some black children were pupils in "play schools" conducted by their owner's children, who, playing the role of "teacher," taught their students to read. Many, forbidden to read, did so clandestinely. Frederick Douglass recalled bribing white boys with bread to give him lessons in *Webster's Spelling Book.*[5] For a few slaves, learning was a part of plantation life. For others, it was a forbidden undertaking that was punished severely if discovered.

As antislavery opinions, stimulated by abolitionist organizations, grew in the Northern states, the slaveholding Southern states enacted laws to prevent blacks from receiving even the rudiments of formal schooling. The following are examples of laws enacted by slaveholding states to prohibit the education of blacks: In 1817, Missouri barred blacks from schools; in 1819, Virginia forbade the teaching of reading and writing to blacks; in 1831, Georgia made it unlawful for any black or white person to teach a black to read or write; in 1832, Mississippi made it illegal for five or more blacks to meet for educational purposes; in 1832, Florida prohibited all meetings of blacks, except for religious purposes.[6]

[4] See Herbert C. Gutman, *The Black Family in Slavery and Freedom, 1750-1925* (New York: Random House, 1976), for a treatment of family relationships during slavery.

[5] Henry A. Bullock, *A History of Negro Education in the South, from 1619 to the Present* (Cambridge, Mass.: Harvard University Press, 1967), p. 11.

[6] Carter G. Woodson, *The Education of the Negro prior to 1861* (Washington, D.C.: Associated Publishers, 1919), pp. 159-67.

The Ideological Battle over Slavery

From the 1840s until the Civil War, the issue of slavery divided Americans in what was referred to as the "sectional crisis." Antislavery sentiments in the Northern free states were met by a rising positive defense of slavery in the South that no longer apologized for the necessity of slavery but proclaimed the institution to have salutory social, economic, and political effects. Let us look at some of the events and personalities in the sectional conflict over slavery and analyze their educational implications.

In 1831, William Lloyd Garrison, a publicist and journalist, began publication of *The Liberator*, an abolitionist magazine, in Boston.[7] Garrison and his associates condemned slavery as a national disgrace and called for its abolition. White abolitionists such as Garrison encouraged and supported black resistance. In particular, the gifted black orator Frederick Douglass, a former slave, was a featured speaker at antislavery meetings. In its early years, the abolitionist movement faced hostility on its Northern home ground and repugnance in the South. Gradually, abolitionists became a significant force, especially when antislavery groups joined forces with Northern politicians such as Charles Sumner, who were bent on blocking the extension of slavery into the western territories.

A series of political events kept the slavery issue before the nation from the late 1840s until the firing on Fort Sumter in 1861. With the end of the Mexican War (1846-1848), the new territories that came to the United States posed a challenge to the political compromise of keeping the free and slave states equally balanced. A "proviso" introduced by Pennsylvania congressman David Wilmot in 1846 would have banned slavery in any territories acquired from Mexico; Southern senators and congressmen responded by claiming that slavery could be extended to any territory of the United States. The crisis was resolved temporarily by the strategies of Senators Henry Clay of Kentucky and Stephen Douglas of Illinois, who secured passage of the Compromise of 1850. This agreement admitted California as a free state, provided for popular sovereignty in the territories of New Mexico and Utah by which the residents would determine the slavery issue, and enacted a more stringent fugitive slave law. The new fugitive slave law, which required federal officers to aid slaveholders in recapturing escaped slaves, aroused the ire of abolitionists.

The plight of fugitive slaves was the plot of Harriet Beecher Stowe's novel *Uncle Tom's Cabin*, which enjoyed tremendous popularity throughout the North. Stowe's novel portrayed the slavery issue in emotional and simple terms of right and wrong and good and evil. Stowe told of the cruel sale of Uncle Tom and his separation from his wife and children. The character of Simon Legree personified the slaveowner as a cruel and inhuman beast. *Uncle Tom's Cabin* is a noteworthy example of the power of informal education in shaping public opinion. The book

---

[7]Significant treatments of Garrison are John L. Thomas, *The Liberator: William Lloyd Garrison* (Boston: Little, Brown, 1963); Aileen S. Kraditor, *Means and Ends in American Abolitionism: Garrison and His Critics on Strategy and Tactics* (New York: Pantheon, 1967).

captured the emotions of its readers and was also enacted as a play throughout the North.

If Garrison's journalism and Stowe's novel succeeded in arousing Northern passions against slavery, they also succeeded in marshalling Southerners to develop a proslavery rationale. James D. B. DeBow launched *DeBow's Review* in 1846, and it became a vehicle for proslavery sentiments and arguments.[8]

Articles written by Edmund Ruffin, A. J. Roane, and other Southern apologists attacked abolitionism and presented the ideological defense of slavery. Roane wrote that an insidious anti-Southern campaign of indoctrination was being waged against Southern institutions by Northern preachers, politicians, and common school leaders. *Uncle Tom's Cabin* was condemned for distorting the reality and positive features of slavery. Stowe and other abolitionists were viciously condemned as dupes of ambitious politicians, unrealistic utopians, or fanatics seeking to destroy the white population of the South by inciting slave insurrections.

Edmund Ruffin (1794-1865), an agricultural publicist and one of slavery's most vociferous defenders, used the columns of *DeBow's Review* to propose the secession of the Southern states from the Union. Ruffin, who had also developed an ideological rationale for slavery, asserted that the Southern socioeconomic system had created a superior civilization, similar to that of ancient Athens; it had produced a leadership elite that included statesmen such as George Washington, Patrick Henry, Thomas Jefferson, and John C. Calhoun.[9] Ruffin was to fire the first shot on Fort Sumter and then to die by his own bullet, a suicide, when Lee surrendered at Appomattox.

The commentary in *DeBow's Review* also defended slavery on Biblical, economic, and social terms, claiming that it benefited both blacks and whites. The outlines of the proslavery ideology were as follows:

1. Slavery was sanctioned positively in the Old Testament; abolitionists, seeking to found a new "transcendental religion" in place of Christianity, were attacking slavery to inculcate their own version of morality.
2. Slavery was a system of labor exchange that secured "life-maintenance" for the slave and "life-labor" for the master. Ensuring "homes, food, and clothing for all," it was a superior social and economic system to the Northern factory system, which allowed people to starve during periods of economic recession.

Through the 1850s, the posture of Northern antislavery and Southern proslavery ideologues hardened. Pamphlets, tracts, speeches, and newspapers presented the issue increasingly in terms of moral rights and wrongs. The ideological skirmishing that preceded the actual battles of the coming Civil War can be seen as a vast effort at persuasion by means of informal education.

[8] Ottis C. Skipper, *J. D. B. DeBow: Magazinist of the Old South* (Athens: University of Georgia Press, 1958).

[9] Edmund Ruffin, "Consequences of Abolition Agitators," *DeBow's Review,* 23 (1857): 267-68, 549-84.

The actual war began after Abraham Lincoln's election in 1860 and inauguration as president in 1861. On April 12, 1861, a Confederate artillery battery opened fire on Union forces at Fort Sumter in Charleston harbor. For four long and bloody years, the armies of the Confederacy battled against the Union army; the fratricidal struggle ended with General Lee's surrender to General Grant on April 9, 1865. Five days later, Abraham Lincoln was assassinated by John Wilkes Booth at Ford's Theater in Washington on April 14, 1865. The stage was now set for the restoration of the South to its place in the Union.

RECONSTRUCTION

The period from 1865 to 1877 has been called Reconstruction, a time when the defeated Confederate states were to be reintegrated into the political, economic, social, and educational life of the nation. Here, we shall identify the most significant features of political reconstruction and concentrate on the educational aspects of the process. The Reconstruction period has been subject to much partisan interpretation. From about 1890 to the 1940s, historians often referred to Reconstruction as America's tragic era—a time of lawlessness and corruption. According to this interpretation, the defeated South was the helpless victim of ambitious Northern radical Republican politicians who ventured southward to make their fortunes with all of their possessions in a carpetbag. The "carpetbaggers" found ready allies in "turn-coat" Southerns, called "scalawags." These political adventurers used the newly enfranchised former slaves, the freedmen, for their own purposes. This version of Reconstruction was portrayed in motion pictures such as *The Birth of a Nation* in 1915 and *Gone with the Wind* in 1939. It also found its way into the pages of many elementary and secondary textbooks.

After the 1940s, the carpetbag-scalawag version of Reconstruction was challenged by able historians such as C. Vann Woodward, John Hope Franklin, and others. According to these historians, the Reconstruction era in the South was one of notable achievements. For example, in many states the Reconstruction legislatures—containing many black legislators—enacted laws for uniform taxation, improved transportation systems, and established common schools.

Political Reconstruction

Lincoln's successor, Andrew Johnson, a native of Tennessee, attempted to steer a moderate course toward the former Confederate states. According to Johnson's plan, each state that had seceded was to: (1) declare its act of secession illegal, (2) repudiate the Confederate debt, and (3) ratify the Thirteenth Amendment abolishing slavery. Once the state convention had taken these three acts, then the former Confederate state would be restored to its full political rights.

The Southern legislatures that were elected under the Johnson phase of Reconstruction were dominated by small white farmers who, while antiplanter, were often also antiblack. For the most part, freedmen were not given the vote. In addition, several states enacted Black Codes, which restricted the freedom of movement and employment of blacks. A series of so-called apprenticeship laws forced blacks to work, often without a choice of employment.

The Republican majority in Congress, led by Senator Charles Sumner of Massachusetts and congressman Thaddeus Stevens of Pennsylvania, challenged President Johnson's version of Reconstruction. This group, known as "Radical" Republicans, pursued a policy that would bring the black population to full citizenship, including suffrage, and exclude many former Confederates from participation in the political process. Over Johnson's opposition and veto, the Radical Republicans established the Freedmen's Bureau to assist the former slaves in securing education, legal aid, and employment, and enacted the Civil Rights Act of 1866 to guarantee to freedmen "full and equal" benefit of the law. Most significant among the Radical Republican initiatives were two amendments to the Constitution: The Fourteenth, ratified in 1866, and the Fifteenth, ratified in 1869. Of great significance for civil rights both during Reconstruction and in later years, especially during the civil rights movement of the 1950s, the Fourteenth Amendment: (1) made the federal government responsible for guaranteeing equal rights and due process under the law to all Americans, (2) granted national citizenship to all persons born or naturalized in the United States, and (3) expressly forbade the states to deprive any person of "life, liberty, or property, without due process of law." The Fifteenth Amendment prohibited denying the right to vote because of race, color, or past condition of servitude.

In addition to these legislative initiatives, Congress also passed the Reconstruction Act over Johnson's veto in 1867; this act placed the former Confederate states under military rule and garrisoned federal army units in the South. It is against this framework of political reconstruction that we now consider educational Reconstruction.

Educational Reconstruction

Educational Reconstruction had three major emphases: (1) assistance from the federal government to newly freed blacks through agencies such as the Freedmen's Bureau; (2) assistance to the freedmen from Northern philanthropic and missionary societies; (3) legislation relating to schools enacted by the state legislatures in power during Reconstruction.

In March 1865, Congress created the Bureau of Refugees, Freedmen, and Abandoned Lands, as an emergency organization to assist former slaves in adjusting to freedom. The bureau continued to function until 1872, when its congressional support ended. Under the leadership of General O. O. Howard, the Freedmen's Bureau established schools throughout the South. In 1865, some 71,000 students were attending bureau schools; four years later in 1869, some 114,000 were in attendance.

The Freedmen's Bureau schools were a copy of the New England common school in terms of their curriculum and moral outlook. They were usually staffed by Northern school teachers, who brought with them their educational ideas, methods, and goals. It was in these schools that a small cadre of black teachers was trained.

During its existence, the Freedmen's Bureau would support schools to the extent of $5,000,000. Slowly, a rather makeshift network of freedmen's schools was created under the bureau's auspices. The schools followed a New England curriculum of reading, writing, grammar, geography, arithmetic, and music, especially singing. As in their Northern counterpart, the freedmen's schools relied on the standard textbooks such as Webster's spelling book and the McGuffey readers. The school day usually began with Bible reading.

In addition to importing the New England common school curriculum, the Northern teachers also added a new dimension called "industrial training." Somewhat inflated in scope, the term "industrial" referred to a variety of practical utilitarian activities designed to develop the freedmen's economic productivity. In the judgment of Northern white educators, industrial education would prepare the blacks for the occupations they were most suited to perform in the South. Since blacks had traditionally been engaged in manual labor, the curriculum was designed to train farmers, mechanics, seamstresses, and laundresses. Thus, a system of "Negro education" emerged that kept the freedmen at the manual labor level.

Industrial education was a basic undertaking at the Hampton Institute, where Booker T. Washington developed his educational ideas under the tutelage of his mentor, General Samuel C. Armstrong. Industrial education, in addition to normal, or teacher, preparation, became an important element in the black secondary and higher schools and institutes that developed in the South.

The teachers in the bureau schools brought to the freedmen their conception of the Puritan ethic as well as the common school curriculum. Schooling was to inculcate the values of thrift, industriousness, perseverance, punctuality, and diligence. If these values had made the North prosperous, they would be just as efficacious for the black population of the South, reasoned the Northern educators.

The curriculum that emerged in the Freedmen's Bureau schools also had political overtones. Conducted under the auspices of the federal government and supported by the Radical Republicans in Congress, the bureau's schools developed a version of civic education for black children that often included units on the Republican party, the importance of voting, and the veneration of Lincoln.

Almost all Southern whites resisted Reconstruction and resented the Freedmen's Bureau schools, the Northern teachers, and the curriculum offered to black children. This prejudice against educating blacks derived from the earlier Slave Codes, which forbade teaching slaves to read or write. This historic view, when combined with Southern white anxieties based on the defeat in the Civil War and the pervasive social and economic transformation wrought by Reconstruction, created an antipathy to the bureau's schools and teachers. The Northern schoolteacher was a particular target of white distrust. New England school-teachers were alien intruders whose "mischievous" lessons would "disturb the good feeling between the races."[10]

In addition to the Freedmen's Bureau schools and frequently in alliance with them, Northern philanthropic societies also joined in educating the freedmen in the South. Foremost among the philanthropic societies was the American Missionary Association; though it was nonsectarian, it enjoyed the financial and moral support of Protestant denominations such as the Congregationalists and Methodists.[11] It was under the auspices of the American Missionary Society that the impetus for black secondary and higher education originated. In particular, the Hampton Institute in Virginia and Fisk University in Tennessee would serve as models for black institutions of higher learning.

Philanthropic organizaions sent funds to the South to create a complete educational system for blacks. George Peabody, a banker and philanthropist, established a fund that gave over $2,000,000 to promote black education in the South. Peabody's fund, supplemented with later grants from the Slater and Rocke-feller funds, were especially useful in supporting black institutes and colleges.[12]

The Emergence of the Southern School System

While the Freedmen's Bureau and the philanthropic societies created the initial stimulus for black schools in the South, it was the legislation passed by state legislatures in the Reconstruction era that created a common, or public, school system in the South. The establishing of tax-supported public schools was one of the lasting achievements of state government in the South.

The common school movement, which had begun in New England and had shaped public schooling in the Northern states, had only a slight impact on the South. Although a few states such as North Carolina had provisions for public schooling, little or nothing had been done to create a system of publicly supported schools in the South. During the early Reconstruction period under the Johnson administration, some states began to establish public school systems—but for white students only.

During the next stage of Reconstruction, from 1868 to 1877, when the South was under military occupation, a genuine common school system was established. A series of constitutional conventions held in the Southern states examined the need for public schools and how to establish them. Eventually, each state legislature passed some type of enabling law to establish a public school system. The educational efforts of the Freedmen's Bureau and the philanthropic societies had created a foundation for the new public schools. On the eve of the establishment of public schools in the South, 2,677 bureau schools were functioning, with 3,300 teachers and slightly more than 150,000 students in regular attendance.[13]

---

[10] Henry L. Swint, *The Northern Teacher in the South, 1862-1870* (New York: Octagon Books, 1967), pp. 81-85.

[11] Ibid., pp. 11-20.

[12] Henry A. Bullock, *A History of Negro Education in the South, from 1619 to the Present* (Cambridge, Mass.: Harvard University Press, 1967), p. 121.

[13] Henry A. Bullock, *History of Negro Education*, p. 53.

As the various state legislatures drafted public school legislation, the issue shifted from that of establishing public schools for both black and white children to the organization and racial composition of such schools. The debate focused on whether public schools should be racially mixed or segregated. Although some blacks favored mixed schools, the general trend of the legislation was to segregated schools.

Many black legislators initially wanted integrated schools established and opposed the creation of a racially segregated system. These legislators correctly foresaw that black schools were unlikely to receive equal financial aid from the state. Whites, on the other hand, objected to the "social consequences" of mixed schools.

South Carolina, Florida, Mississippi, and Louisiana established schools without reference to separate or mixed schools. However, Reconstruction's end terminated any attempt at mixed schools in the South. North Carolina and Alabama legislated for total segregation in 1876, South Carolina and Louisiana in 1877, Mississippi in 1878, and Virginia in 1882, while Texas legalized segregation as early as 1873.[14]

The End of Reconstruction

Reconstruction officially ended in 1877, when the newly elected president, Rutherford B. Hayes, withdrew federal military forces from the South. Hayes's decision to end military occupation was based on the disputed presidential election of 1876 when Hayes, the Republican candidate, and Samuel Tilden, the Democratic, were locked in a very close contest. The electoral votes from several key Southern states were disputed. In return for Southern white support, Hayes received the disputed electoral vote and won the presidency. In return, Southern whites secured the promise that Reconstruction would end.

From the post-Reconstruction era until the end of World War I, from about 1877 to 1919, progress for black Americans was slow and uneven. Popular attitudes, stimulated by pseudoscientific Social Darwinism, saw blacks as innately inferior. Those whites who remained sympathetic to blacks were generally paternalistic and preached nonpolitical doctrines of self-help and self-initiative. The prevailing attitude was that progress for blacks would have to be gradual and result from the slow but steady processes of education.

During the late 1870s and 1880s, the federal government moved away from its policy of promoting the civil and educational rights of blacks. Recall that immediately after the Civil War (1) Congress established the Freedmen's Bureau in 1865 to assist former slaves both materially and educationally; (2) the Civil Rights Bill of 1866 transferred the protection of person and property from the state to the federal government; and (3) the Fourteenth Amendment, guaranteeing the privileges and immunities of national citizenship, prohibited states from depriving

---

[14] Recommended sources for the "mixed" versus segregated school issue are Ellis M. Coulter, *The South During Reconstruction, 1865-1877* (New Orleans: Louisiana State University Press, 1947); and Edgar W. Knight, *The Influence of Reconstruction on Education in the South* (New York: Arno Press, 1969).

persons of life, liberty, and property without due process of law. After Reconstruction, however, the Radical Republicans, who had engineered the enactment of the problack civil rights legislation, were replaced by a conservative coalition of Northern probusiness Republicans and states' rights Southern Democrats. This conservative coalition was either disinterested in or opposed to civil rights legislation.

From the late 1870s through the early 1900s, a system of racial segregation was established in the South that was to remain until the civil rights movement of the 1950s. During this period, blacks were effectively disenfranchised throughout the South.

Race relationships in the South were influenced by the politics of the 1880s and 1890s, particularly by the use of the People's party, or Populists, as a third force, competing for votes with the Republicans and Democrats. Primarily a farmer's party, the Populists initially sought to create an alliance between black and white farmers and laborers against what they regarded as the entrenched power of the moneyed class of large landowners and industrialists. By the 1890s, Populist leaders saw that their attempts to create a racially integrated political party were having the reverse effect of driving white voters away. Populist leaders such as Thomas Watson of Georgia then became ardent segregationsits, who led the movement to completely disenfranchise black voters. When the Populist movement declined after the election of 1896, many leaders of the party moved into the Democratic party and often took the leadership away from the more paternalistic "Bourbon" Democrats. What resulted was an activist and radical segregationism that disenfranchised blacks through literacy and property requirements, and created and enforced by law strictly segregated social and educational facilities. Disinterested in Southern racial relations or supporting segregation themselves, many Northern politicians in both the Republican and Democratic parties refused to intervene at the federal level in Southern social relations.

In the Southern states, various strategems such as the white primary, the poll tax, literary tests, and the Grandfather clause (which required a current voter to verify that his grandfather had voted prior to 1865), eliminated large numbers of black voters. In addition to legal restrictions, blacks who attempted to vote were often intimidated by secret societies such as the Ku Klux Klan.

In addition to the segregationist political order that was being erected in the South, a series of decisions by the Supreme Court eroded the legal protection that the Thirteenth, Fourteenth, and Fifteenth amendments had given to blacks. In the *Slaughter House* case of 1873, the Court ruled that the Fourteenth Amendment had not been designed to federalize the privileges and immunities of state citizenship. The Court's decision in *Hall* v. *De Cuir* in 1878 upheld state segregation laws in interstate commerce. Most important, in *Plessy* v. *Ferguson* (1896), which ruled that separate accommodations on railway trains did not violate the Thirteenth Amendment, the Supreme Court gave legal sanction at the highest level to the "separate-but-equal" doctrine that was to govern racial relations for the next fifty-eight years until reversed by the *Brown* decision in 1954.

The separate-but-equal doctrine held that racially segregated institutions, facilities, and services, including educational ones, did not violate civil rights or due process provisions. The legal fiction was that racially separate or segregated institutions, including schools, were to receive equal support and provide equal services. The social, educational, and economic reality, however, was that the institutions and services provided for whites received greater support than those for blacks.

In terms of its effects on public schooling in the South, the separate-but-equal doctrine contributed to the solidification of a dual system of schools that segregated blacks and whites. From 1880 to 1900, white enrollments doubled, as children from lower socioeconomic families enrolled in increasing numbers. Simultaneously, conservative Democrats lowered taxes and reduced revenues for public education. The small white farmers, who had supported Populism and were now supporting the agrarian wing of the Democratic party, diverted funds from black schools to improve the schools attended by their own children.

Educational Ideology in the Post-Reconstruction Era

In the post-Reconstruction period, educational efforts for black Americans were the product of an amalgamation of religious zeal, doctrines of self-help, paternalism, and industrial training. Immediately after the Civil War, Northern abolitionist and missionary societies, often with the assistance of the federally sponsored Freedmen's Bureau, sent teachers, ingrained with the values of New England's Protestant ethic, to educate newly freed blacks. These Northern teachers, often bitterly resented and resisted by Southern whites, taught the basic skills of reading, writing, arithmetic, and the values of industriousness, cleanliness, thrift, and punctuality to black children. Their opponents claimed that they also carried with them the political ideology of Radical Republicanism.

The educational efforts of the Northern teachers in the South were supported financially by philanthropist businessmen such as George Peabody and John Slater, who defined black education as a practical training for industry rather than a preparation for citizenship or higher education. Because of prevailing social attitudes and the nature of its fiscal support, black education in the South took on the elements of industrial training and paternalism.

While schooling for blacks was initially an invention of Northern white missionary societies and industrial philanthropists, Southern white business leaders, who advocated a new, industrialized South, also supported industrial education and manual training for blacks as a means of providing a trained and docile work force. According to Southern white business spokesmen like Henry Grady and Henry Watterson, the formula for black education was: (1) provide black children with a rudimentary education in basic literacy and skills; (2) cultivate values that contributed to order and industry; (3) create a protected but subservient status for blacks in the South; and (4) detach blacks from political activist movements and labor organizations. The outlines of industrial education were emerging by the late 1870s and would form the basis of the educational philosophy articulated by Booker T. Washington, who would become the leading spokesman for blacks in the United States.

BOOKER T. WASHINGTON AND TUSKEGEE IDEA

Booker Taliaferro Washington (1856-1915) was born a slave on a plantation in Franklin County, Virginia. *Up from Slavery*, Washington's autobiography, recounts his reminiscences of a childhood spent in bondage and then the experience of freedom.[15] In 1872, Washington was admitted as a student to the Hampton Institute, a school for blacks, which followed a philosophy of industrial education developed by its head, General Samuel C. Armstrong. At Hampton, students could earn their tuition, room, and board by working. Washington, working as a janitor, graduated from Hampton in 1875 as a brick mason. He then taught school for three years. Armstrong, who regarded Washington as a protégé, invited him to return to Hampton as his secretary and as an instructor. At Hampton, Washington became a disciple of Armstrong's philosophy of industrial education, which stressed the "uplifting" of blacks by practical and utilitarian training and the Puritan values of hard work, perseverance, and diligence to one's task.

Samuel C. Armstrong and Industrial Education

Samuel Chapman Armstrong, a former officer in the Union army, founded Hampton Institute in 1868 to provide agricultural and industrial education for blacks. Armstrong's program was based on the following assumptions:

1. The inculcation of moral values was a more important component of black education than intellectual pursuits.
2. By adhering to the Yankee "virtues of industriousness and thrift," blacks could win a measure of economic independence that would enable them to become tradesmen, save money, buy land, and create stable families.
3. Full participation as citizens was not an immediate but a remote goal that would have to be achieved very slowly and gradually.[16]

The Hampton model of industrial and agricultural training attracted the financial backing of white philanthropists such as John F. Slater, who created a fund to support schools that instructed black youth in the manual trades. The rationale of industrial education, which Washington would develop more fully at Tuskegee, won the grudging acquiescence of Southern white politicians and industrialists of the "New South," who saw it as a means of creating an industrial and agricultural work force without threatening the post-Reconstruction power structure. It also gained the financial support of Northern philanthropists, who saw it as a means of extending the Protestant work ethic to the black population. Emerging black leaders such as Washington were prepared to collaborate with their white sponsors in order to begin the creation of a black education system.

---

[15] Booker T. Washington, *Up from Slavery* (New York: Bantam, 1967); originally published in 1901.

[16] August Meir, *Negro Thought in America, 1880-1915: Racial Ideologies in the Age of Booker T. Washington* (Ann Arbor: University of Michigan Press, 1963), pp. 87-90.

Founding the Tuskegee Institute

In 1881, Alabama's governor, Rufus Cobb, signed the legislation authorizing the establishment of a black normal school at Tuskegee, with an annual appropriation of $2,000. The trustees of the new normal school accepted General Armstrong's recommendation of Booker T. Washington as principal. Washington opened Tuskegee Institute on July 4, 1881, with an initial enrollment of thirty-seven students.[17]

Under Washington's administration, the institute grew from a single building in 1881 to a sizeable academic institution of 123 buildings, located on 2,300 acres. Ten years after its founding, Tuskegee had a faculty of 88 instructors and some 1,200 students.[18] Even more important than its physical plant was the influence that Tuskegee gained in black education. Tuskegee graduates, steeped in Washington's educational philosophy, were employed as administrators and teachers at similar institutions throughout the country.

The Tuskegee Philosophy of Education

Washington's success in creating a respected industrial school in the deep South during an era of intense racial tension was based on his administrative and political acumen, which tied the philosophy of industrial education to a policy of accommodation with the white power structure. Washington's success at Tuskegee gave him a national platform from which he became the spokesman for his race.

Educationally, Washington was a convinced proponent of industrial education. He argued that it was ideally suited to the needs of Tuskegee's students and to black students in the South:

> First, we have found the industrial teaching useful in giving the student a chance to work out a portion of his expenses while in school. Second, the school furnishes labour that has an economic value and at the same time gives the student a chance to acquire knowledge and skill while performing the labour. Most of all, we find the industrial system valuable in teaching economy, thrift, and the dignity of labour and in giving moral backbone to students.[19]

Industrial education for blacks, however, should not be considered in isolation from the national thrust for manual and trade education that was occurring in other sections of the country. The general tenets of industrial education, to which Washington as well as other advocates of industrial education subscribed, were:

1. Industrial training was a method of inculcating simple but systematic manual skills that could be applied to industry.

[17] Louis Harlan, *Booker T. Washington: The Making of a Black Leader, 1856-1901* (New York: Oxford University Press, 1972), p. 122.

[18] Booker T. Washington, *The Future of the American Negro* (Boston: Small, Maynard, 1900), pp. 108-110.

[19] Ibid., pp. 111-12.

2. Industrial training was a practical and useful alternative to "bookish" schooling that was separated from the activities of real life.
3. Industrial training was a means of cultivating the values of efficiency, punctuality, thrift, and a sense of the importance of time in the children of people who were relative newcomers to an industrializing society. In other words, such training was particularly appropriate in preparing the children of blacks and immigrants from Southern and Eastern Europe for the work force of a modernizing nation.

In developing his educational program at Tuskegee, Washington followed the general principles of industrial education but reformulated them to fit what he perceived to be the racial and economic climate of the South in the post-Reconstruction era of the 1880s and 1890s. There were several elements involved in his reformulation: (1) his own self-perception as an educational leader, (2) the existing racial climate, and (3) the economic situation.

Booker T. Washington perceived himself to be more than an educational administrator. He believed that he had a semireligious role as the "agent of civilization" who would bring "a better life" to his people.[20] Washington, in perceiving himself as an educational missionary, imbued his work at Tuskegee with a sense of moral mission. At Tuskegee, character building was stressed as an educational objective. Roscoe Bruce, a colleague at Tuskegee, wrote that the institution's program was deliberately designed to transform "the crude, stumbling, sightless plantation-boy" into a man who possessed "an alertness, a resourcefulness, and above all a spirit of service. . . ."[21] Washington himself stressed the values of "cleanliness, decorum, promptness, and truthfulness" in his frequent addresses to Tuskegee's students. Again, these values were not unique to either Washington or the institute. They the same honored values found in the McGuffey readers. However, Washington won approval by accommodating this value orientation to a receptive white audience that was at first regional and then national.

A shrewd and pragmatic administrator, Washington realized that he had to function in the racial and economic climate in which Tuskegee was situated. During the 1880s and 1890s, the forces of white supremacy had regained power in the legislative chambers and court houses throughout the South. In no way did Washington seek direct confrontation with those in political control of the South. While a white supremacist populism dominated the South, the ascendent mode in the North—influenced by a Darwinist social philosophy that reflected the "white man's burden"—was inclined either to outright racism or benign neglect of black political and educational aspirations. Avoiding politics, Washington concentrated on economics. He continually stressed the theme that the Tuskegee philosophy was based upon the "actual life and needs" of those living in the South, "in the shadow of the institution."[22] Washington argued that black and white Southerners lived in a

[20] Idem, ed., *Tuskegee and Its People: Their Ideals and Achievements* (New York: Appleton, 1905), p. 31.

[21] Roscoe C. Bruce, "The Academic Aims," in ibid., p. 67.

[22] Booker T. Washington, *Working with the Hands* (New York: Doubleday, 1904), p. 15.

Booker T. Washington, President of Tuskegee Institute and spokesman for black Americans in the late nineteenth century. *(From Leroy V. Goodman, ed., A Nation of Learners. Washington, D.C.: G.P.O., 1976, p. 140. Library of Congress Collection.)*

symbiotic economic relationship, with each race dependent upon the other. He also alleviated white fears by stating that economic symbiosis did not carry over into social relationships, an area in which the races were to remain separate "like the fingers on the hand." In a practical sense, Washington was seeking to develop economic alternatives for blacks that would provide an escape from the sharecropping system, which left black farmers perpetually indebted.

The Tuskegee Curriculum

Based upon the general principles of industrial education, the Tuskegee curriculum, which Washington designed, embraced three components: agricultural and industrial skills, crafts, and trades; academic subject matter; and values. The first component, agricultural and industrial training, rested on the following rationale: (1) The training should be related to the economic needs of the South and to the occupational possibilities that existed for blacks in the region. (2) The particular trade was to support the student's education at Tuskegee by earning expenses for tuition, room, and board; and it was also to be useful in making internal improvements on the Tuskegee campus. (3) Training in a trade was to lead to the intellectual or academic skills and subjects needed in the particular trade.

(4) Both occupational training and academic learning were to be related to character building and value education.

The occupations for which Tuskegee students were prepared included such trades as: farming, blacksmithing, plastering, carpentry, cooking, mechanical drawing, dressmaking, electrical and steam engineering, housekeeping, canning, nurses' training, painting, shoemaking, printing, and wheelwrighting. Students were assigned to work in one of the various Tuskegee industries; in return, they received a credit that could be applied to their educational expenses.

The second component, academic subject matter, was derived from, and regarded as supporting, occupational training. Responding to criticisms that occupational training limited black employment opportunities to menial trades, Washington argued that Tuskegee's industrial training program was realistically related to intellectual studies. For example, he stated that "Competency in agriculture calls for considerable knowledge of chemistry, and no mechanical pursuit can be followed satisfactorily without some acquaintance with mathematics and the 'three R's.' "[23]

Washington rejected the traditional approach that academic subjects, such as mathematics and science, should be taught separately from their application to the activities of life. Washington's educational methodology resembled Pestalozzian object teaching and the early progressivism of Colonel Francis Parker. In describing the Tuskegee method of education, Washington said:

> I have seen a teacher work for an hour with children, trying to impress upon them the meaning of the words lake, island, peninsula, when a brook not a quarter mile away would have afforded the little ones an opportunity to pull off their shoes and stockings and wade through the water, and find not one artificial island or lake, on an artificial globe but dozens of real islands, peninsulas and bays. Besides the delight of wading through the water, and of being out in the pure bracing air, they would learn more about this, more about these natural divisions of the earth in five minutes than they could learn in an hour in books.[24]

Teachers at Tuskegee were expected to apply academic subject matter to the students' occupational training. While resembling a rudimentary form of progressive education, the essential thrust of the Tuskegee program was specific job training rather than the generalized understanding and appreciation that later progressive educators sought to attain. Nevertheless, similarities exist between Washington's concept of industrial education and the progressive project method.

As indicated earlier, value or character, education permeated the entire Tuskegee program and was inculcated by the example of Washington and his staff, by exhortation, and by the rules, regulations, and routines of the institute. There were frequent inspections of student dormitories for cleanliness and order. Behavior was controlled in a semimilitary fashion by a system of merits and demerits.

[23] Booker T. Washington, ed., *Tuskegee and Its People*, p. 12.
[24] Idem, *Working with the Hands*, p. 159.

Washington in Retrospect

From the late 1880's until his death in 1915, Booker T. Washington was the most influential black leader in the United States. His philosophy of industrial education shaped the goals and the structure of black educational institutions throughout the South. Perhaps his greatest success was that he was able to institutionalize an idea and give it a life after his own death. He succeeded in preparing a cadre of educational disciples and teachers who imitated the Tuskegee educational ideal and recreated it at other black normal schools and institutes.

In strictly pedagogical terms, Washington's philosophy blended progressive and conservative educational themes. "Learning by doing," concomitant learning, and the application of knowledge to life were educational concepts that were similar to those that surfaced during the progressive educational movement in the early twentieth century. Washington's orientation to character formation, however, reflected the stern values of Puritanism rather than the liberating force of student-centered education.

Booker T. Washington's social and racial philosophy was accommodationist and gradualist. He accommodated himself to the segregationist social and educational system that had emerged in the South after Reconstruction. Essentially, Washington was walking a political tightrope in that he sought to reassure whites that black education would not jeopardize their dominant social and political position; he simultaneously sought to provide blacks with a special kind of vocational education that would slowly develop an economic base.

Washington, an articulate spokesman, espoused the educational philosophy of which he was a product. At first at Tuskegee, then in the South, and finally throughout the nation, Washington advanced the doctrines of self-help, personal initiative, and industrial training. His educational and social philosophy did not challenge the prevalent racist and segregationist ideology.

Washington, whose base of operations was deep in the South, claimed that the only feasible solution to racial problems was in an alliance between blacks and the Southern white propertied class and industrialists. While blacks were not to participate in political or labor agitation, Washington hoped that their passive acceptance of subordinate status would eventually gain them separate-but-equal facilities and services, including those that were educational.

Washington's best-known statement of his social and racial philosophy was made at the Atlanta Exposition in 1895, when he urged blacks to stay in the South, learn industrial skills, and avoid political agitation. Slowly and gradually, Southern blacks would move up the economic ladder by becoming skilled craftsmen and laborers. In social matters, blacks and whites could be as separate as the fingers on the hand, but together could be a force for the industrial modernization of the South.

Washington's critics, especially W. E. B. DuBois, challenged the Tuskegee philosophy on broader socioeconomic and political bases. His critics charged that the specific occupational training followed at Tuskegee was a form of caste training that would confine blacks to the lower rungs of American life. By failing to prepare blacks for entry into higher education, Washington's industrial education was blocking their entry into professional and political life. The most serious historical indictment levied against Washington was that he did little to challenge racism, segregation, and the denial of civil rights and educational opportunities to blacks.

W. E. B. DUBOIS

By the early 1900s, Washington's Tuskegee system was under fire from critics who wanted an active leader committed to struggling for civil rights, political equality, and greater economic opportunities for blacks. One of the most articulate challengers to Washington was William Edward Burghardt DuBois (1868-1963), a black sociologist, educator, and civil rights leader.

Early Life and Education

W. E. B. DuBois, the son of Alfred and Mary Burghardt DuBois, was born in Great Barrington, Massachusetts, in 1863. He was of African and French and Dutch ancestry. He attended the elementary and high schools of Barrington, participated in extracurricular activities, and was valedictorian of his high school class in 1884.[25] DuBois's academic record earned him a scholarship at Fisk University in Nashville, Tennessee, which also introduced him to Southern racial attitudes and to the condition of blacks in the South. DuBois began to focus his scholarly attention on the position and status of blacks in American life.

While a student at Fisk, DuBois edited the college newspaper, *The Fisk Herald*, which nurtured his writing skills. In the summer, he taught school in East Tennessee's rural areas and developed his interest in education. In 1903, his *The Souls of Black Folk* was published, which analyzed his impressions of the conditions and impressions of black Americans.

DuBois who demonstrated outstanding academic potential at Fisk, was admitted to Harvard University in 1888, where his instructors included professors who were reshaping the foundations of American intellectual life. For example, DuBois studied under William James and George Santayana in philosophy, Albert Bushnell Hart in history, and William Taussig in sociology. After receiving his bachelor of arts degree, DuBois was admitted to Harvard's graduate school in 1890, where he began research on his dissertation, "The Suppression of the African Slave Trade to America."[26]

Typical of young scholars who sought to enter the professoriate in American universities at the turn of the century, DuBois studied in Germany. At the University of Berlin, he worked under the historians Gustav Schmoller and Adolf Wagner,

[25] W. E. B. DuBois, *The Autobiography of W. E. B. DuBois: A Soliloquy on Viewing My Life from the Last Decade of Its First Century* (New York: International Publishers, 1968), pp. 84-88.

[26] Virginia Hamilton, *W. E. B. DuBois: A Biography* (New York: Crowell, 1972), pp. 35-41.

who were applying historical methods to economic and political issues. DuBois found his study and travel in Europe intellectually stimulating. He also encountered Socialist and Marxist political philosophies and strategies for social change. When he returned to the United States, he completed his dissertation and was awarded the doctorate of philosophy from Harvard University in 1896.[27]

The Forming of a Black Intellectual

Since W. E. B. DuBois and Booker T. Washington became antagonists with differing philosophies and strategies for social and educational change, it is useful to contrast their development as leaders of American blacks. Washington, the older man, born a slave, developed his social and educational perspective in the context of the South, DuBois, born in the North, grew to adulthood in a different context. In contrast to Washington's rather restricted educational opportunities, DuBois enjoyed a more extensive education at leading universities. While Washington was isolationist in his world view, DuBois's study in Germany fostered a cosmopolitanism that influenced his political and educational thinking.

The differences in outlook between Washington and DuBois led to a basic disagreement on the social, political, and educational strategies that black Americans should follow. Washington, responsible for administering Tuskegee, found it necessary to accommodate the demands of the white power structure in the South. Washington, in both education and in politics, began with the immediate, local Southern situation and slowly and gradually moved to larger national issues. DuBois, an academic theoretician and intellectual, taking a larger and more universal world view, developed generalized principles. For example, DuBois held that:

1. Whatever their region of residence, blacks throughout the United States were entitled to the same political, legal, and educational opportunities and rights enjoyed by other Americans.
2. Blacks in the United States did not live in cultural isolation from black people in other parts of the world. Sharing a common racial ancestry and cultural heritage, American blacks and Africans should embrace a pan-African world view.
3. Unlike Washington, who advised blacks to avoid political activism and membership in labor unions, DuBois, who had Marxist inclinations, believed that they shared a common agenda with the American working class to end economic exploitation.
4. Again, unlike Washington, who sought to raise the economic position of blacks by a slow but egalitarian climb up the economic ladder, DuBois believed it necessary to educate an elite leadership group—the "talented tenth"—to be the vanguard of black Americans.

[27]Emma G. Sterne, *His Was the Voice: The Life of W. E. B. DuBois* (New York: Crowell-Collier Press, 1971) pp. 51-52.

Academic and Activist

DuBois combined an academic career in higher education with organizational activism to win political, economic, social, and educational opportunity for blacks. From 1894 to 1896, he was a professor of Latin and Greek at Wilberforce University of Pennsylvania, where he conducted research for his important study, *The Phailadelphia Negro: A Social Study*, published in 1899. From 1897 to 1910, he was a professor of history and economics at Atlanta University. In 1910, he left Atlanta to become director of publicity and research for the National Association for the Advancement of Colored People, the NAACP. He also was editor of *The Crisis*, the NAACP's major publication, a position that he held until 1934, when he returned to Atlanta University.

Just as he had earlier rejected Washington's gradualist position on race relations, DuBois grew impatient of the slow-moving legalism of the NAACP. Attracted to pan-Africanism, he supported colonial independence movements in Africa. In the United States, he joined left-wing political movements such as the Henry Wallace Progressive party of 1948. In 1950 he was the Progressive candidate for United States senator in New York. In 1961 he joined the Communist party of the United States. Leaving the United States during the McCarthy period, he became a citizen of Kwame Nkrumah's Ghana, where he died on August 27, 1963.

THE MOVEMENT FOR EQUALITY

While the movement of blacks for equality of opportunity can be reviewed in the careers of leaders such as Booker T. Washington and W. E. B. DuBois, much of the work was done by organizations such as the Niagara Movement, the NAACP, and the Urban League. In these organizations, black and white Americans joined together to battle against segregationist laws, racism, prejudice, and discrimination.

In 1905, a small group of black and white proponents of full civil rights, who were dissatisfied with Washington's accommodationist policies, met at Niagara Falls, to plan a new and more activist strategy. With DuBois as general-secretary, the group became known as the Niagara Movement. Urging an agenda of political and legal equality, educational opportunity, and full rights of citizenship, the group met periodically, and in 1910 organized as the National Association for the Advancement of Colored People.

Among the leaders of the NAACP were Henry Moskowitz, William English Walling, and Mary White Ovington, a sociologist, as was DuBois, who had a prominent role in the new organization. Ovington, in particular, took the view that the NAACP should pursue an educational policy that would expose the irrationality of racism. Also, she argued that a basic element in bettering the conditions of blacks was to improve the environment in which they lived. A significant aspect of environmental improvement was to reform social and educational institutions, particularly schools. From the date of its organization onward, the NAACP was a biracial organization that pursued a national agenda that included: (1) a campaign to expose racism and the debilitating societal consequences that racial prejudice and discrimination produced; (2) frequent resorts to the legal system to protect the civil rights of blacks; and (3) improving educational opportunities for blacks.

CONCLUSION

From the end of the Civil War in 1865 to entry of the United States in World War I in 1917, the conditions of blacks in American society was shaped largely by white attitudes and the black response to these attitudes. Since the great majority of blacks lived in the South until substantial migration northward began around 1915, the pervasive attitude was that of Southern whites. The entry of Northern politicians and educators during Reconstruction worked to temper these attitudes and to encourage a larger role for blacks in the South. Reconstruction's end saw a return to white supremacy politics and education in the South, to which Booker T. Washington pragmatically accommodated himself. Accommodationist policies were challenged by W. E. B. DuBois and others, who began to campaign actively for full civil rights. Later chapters, dealing with more recent educational history, will examine this crusade for civil rights.

DISCUSSION QUESTIONS

1. Analyze the various forms of Afro-American culture that developed in ante-bellum America.
2. Identify and analyze the elements of the proslavery ideology that developed in the South as a response to abolitionism.
3. Examine the impact of Reconstruction on education in the South.
4. How were educational concepts and practices common to New England introduced into the South?
5. Analyze the concept of industrial education in relationship to black education.
6. Analyze the sociopolitical context that led to the separate-but-equal doctrine. What were the educational consequences of this doctrine?
7. What were the key elements in Booker T. Washington's educational philosophy?
8. What were the key elements in W. E. B. DuBois's educational philosophy?
9. Examine the origins, organization, and strategy of the NAACP.

RESEARCH TOPICS

1. Read the definitive histories of black education by Woodson and Bullock. Compare and contrast their interpretations in a review essay.

2. Prepare biographical sketches of Frederick Douglass, Booker T. Washington, and W. E. B. DuBois.

3. Read and prepare a review of Harriet Beecher Stowe's *Uncle Tom's Cabin* as a vehicle of informal education.

4. Examine several high school American history textbooks that were published in different time periods. Identify and analyze the interpretation of Reconstruction found in these books.

5. Identify a college that originated as an institution for the education of blacks. Prepare a short historical sketch of that institution.

6. Read Booker T. Washington's *Up from Slavery*, and analyze his educational ideas.

7. Read W. E. B. DuBois's *Autobiography*, and examine his educational ideas.

8. Write a character sketch comparing and contrasting Washington and DuBois.

REFERENCES AND READING

Ballard, Allen B. *The Education of Black Folk.* New York: Harper & Row, Pub., 1973.

Bond, Horace M. *The Education of the Negro in the American Social Order.* New York: Octagon Books, 1966.

Broderick, Francis L. *W. E. B. DuBois: Negro Leader in a Time of Crisis.* Stanford, Calif.: Stanford University Press, 1959.

Bullock, Henry A. *A History of Negro Education in the South, from 1619 to the Present.* Cambridge, Mass.: Harvard University Press, 1967.

Coulter, Ellis Merton. *The South During Reconstruction, 1865-1877.* New Orleans: Louisana State University Press, 1947.

Craven, Avery. *Reconstruction: The Ending of the Civil War.* New York: Holt, Rinehart & Winston, 1969.

DuBois, W.E.B. *Black Folk: Then and Now.* New York: Holt, Rinehart & Winston, 1939; reprinted, Octagon Books, 1970.

____. *Black Reconstruction in America: 1860-1880.* New York: Harcourt, Brace, 1935; reprinted, Cleveland: World Publishing Co., 1964.

____. *The Correspondence of W. E. B. DuBois.* 2 Vols. Herbert Aptheker, ed., Amherst, Mass.: University of Massachusetts Press, 1973.

____. *Darkwater: Voices from Within the Veil.* New York: Harcourt, Brace, 1920; reprinted, Schocken Books, 1969.

____. *Dusk of Dawn: An Essay Toward an Autobiography of a Race Concept.* New York: Harcourt, Brace, 1940; reprinted, Schocken Books, 1968.

____. *The Emerging Thought of W. E. B. DuBois: Essays and Editorials from "The Crisis."* Henry Lee Moon, ed. New York: Simon & Schuster, 1972.

____. *The Philadelphia Negro: A Social Study.* Philadelphia: University of Pennsylvania, 1899; reprinted, Schocken Books, 1967.

____. *The Selected Writings of W. E. B. DuBois.* Walter Wilson, ed. New York: English Library, 1970.

____. *The Seventh Son: The Thought and Writings of W. E. B. DuBois.* Julius Lester, ed. New York: Random House, 1971.

____. *The Souls of Black Folk: Essays and Sketches.* Chicago: McClurg, 1903.

____. *W. E. B. DuBois: A Profile.* Rayford Logan, ed. New York: Hill and Wang, 1971.

____. *W. E. B. DuBois Speaks: Speeches and Addresses, 1890-1919 & 1920-1963.* Philip S. Fone, ed. New York: Pathfinder Press.

Ellison, Mary. *The Black Experience: American Blacks since 1865.* New York: Harper & Row, Pub., 1974.

Franklin, John Hope. *From Slavery to Freedom: A History of Negro Americans.* 3rd ed. New York: Knopf, 1967.

Frazier, Thomas R., ed. *Afro-American History: Primary Sources.* New York: Harcourt, Brace, 1970.

Harlan, Louis. *Booker T. Washington: The Making of a Black Leader, 1856-1901.* New York: Oxford University Press, 1972.

___. *Booker T. Washington: The Wizard of Tuskegee, 1901-1915:* New York: Oxford University Press, 1983.

Knight, Edgar Wallace. *The Influence of Reconstruction on Education in South.* New York: Arno Press, 1969.

Matthews, Victoria E. *Black-Belt Diamonds: Gems from the Speeches, Addresses, and Talks to Students of Booker T. Washington.* New York: Fortune and Scott, 1891.

Meier, August, and Rudwick, Elliott M. *From Plantation to Ghetto: An Interpretive History of American Negroes.* New York: Hill and Wang, 1966.

___. *Negro Thought in America, 1880-1915: Racial Ideologies in the Age of Booker T. Washington.* Ann Arbor: University of Michigan Press, 1963.

Swint, Henry L. *The Northern Teacher in the South, 1862-1870.* New York: Octagon Books, 1967.

Thornbrough, Emma Lou, ed. *Black Reconstructionists.* Englewood Cliffs, N.J.: Prentice-Hall, 1972.

Trefouse, Hans L. *Reconstruction: America's First Effort at Racial Democracy.* New York: Van Nostrand, 1971.

Trelease, Allen W. *Reconstruction: The Great Experiment.* New York: Harper & Row, Pub., 1971.

Silberman, Charles E. *Crisis in Black and White.* New York: Vintage, 1964.

Washington, Booker T. *The Auto-Biographical Writings. The Booker T. Washington Papers.* Louis Harlan, ed. Urbana: Univeristy of Illinois Press, 1972.

___. *The Future of the American Negro.* Boston: Small, Maynard, 1900.

___. ed. *Tuskegee and Its People: Their Ideals and Achievements.* New York: Appleton, 1905.

___. *Up from Slavery.* New York: Bantam, 1967. (Originally published in 1901).

___. *Working with the Hands.* New York: Doubleday, 1904.

___, Wood, N.B., and William, Fannie Barrier. *A New Negro for a New Century.* New York: Arno Press and The New York Times, 1969. (Originally published in 1900.)

Webster, Staten W. *The Education of Black Americans.* New York: John Day, 1974.

Woodson, Carter G. *The Education of the Negro prior to 1861.* Washington, D.C.: Associated Publishers, 1919; reprinted, Arno Press and The New York Times, 1968.

Woodward, C. Vann. *The Strange Career of Jim Crow.* 2nd ed. New York: Oxford University Press, 1966.

8

EDUCATION
IN AN EMERGENT
INDUSTRIAL SOCIETY

In this chapter we shall examine the educational and social changes that took place during the 1870s and continued up to the rise of progressivism in the early twentieth century. We focus on the impact of industrialism, urbanization, and immigration on American society and education. We also discuss the spirit of inventiveness and entrepreneurship that characterized America at the turn of the century. As an educational corollary to the rise of industrial and corporate society, school administration, especially in the large cities, imitated models of business efficiency.

The years from 1870 to the beginning of World War I in 1914 saw the United States transformed from a predominantly agricultural to an industrial society. America's industrialization generated momentous alterations in the national character and economy and in the nation's social and educational institutions. While the origins of industrialization can be traced to the mills and factories of the late 1830s and 1840s, the turn of the century, with its wave of applied inventions transformed American life and education.

The emergence of the United States as a modern industrial world power was based on a combination of contributing conditions. The nation was richly endowed with the natural resources necessary for industrial development. It had coal, iron ore, timber, petroleum, and water power, and was building an extensive railroad system that brought raw materials to factories and manufactured products to consumers. Along with plentiful natural resources, there was an abundant supply of cheap labor. Internal migration brought workers who left farms to make their fortune in the cities. Immigration, especially from Southern and Eastern Europe, brought almost 23 million immigrants to the United States between 1870 and 1914. Not only did immigration bring workers, it also brought customers for an expanding market of cheap, mass-produced items.

Closely related to industrialization was the phenomenon of America's urbanization. Cities such as New York, Chicago, and Philadelphia, which were already large at the time of the Civil War, grew into metropolitan population centers. For example, New York City, with a population of 1,174,000 in 1860, numbered in excess of 4,766,000 in 1910. As of 1910, Chicago, the nation's second largest city, had a population of over 2,185,000; and Philadelphia, the third largest city, numbered more than 1,500,000 residents. Large cities at the turn of the century faced myriad problems of providing health, police, transportation, sanitation, and educational services to their burgeoning populations. It was in this period that large centralized urban school systems developed.

At the same time that the United States was industrializing, the rural population began to decline both in numbers and in political influence. Importantly, however, agricultural productivity did not decline but actually increased, primarily through the mechanization of farming by inventions like the combine and the harvester. Agricultural productivity was vital in feeding the nation's industrial cities and was an important export item for foreign markets.

Industrialization was encouraged by federal, state, and local government policies designed to stimulate rather than to control the process. The presidency, for most of the period, was safely in the hands of Republicans such as Rutherford B. Hayes, James A. Garfield, Benjamin Harrison, and William McKinley, who consistently favored big business. Grover Cleveland, the only Democrat in the period to be elected president (in 1884 and again in 1892), was not unfriendly to business interests. Legislation favoring business expansion generally passed a friendly Congress, dominated by probusiness Republican majorities. The courts, too, in their decisions did not interfere with the dominance of business interests.

Government philosophy and policies, largely a mixture of the free enterprise and private property, ideology, combined classical laissez-faire economic theory with the competitive ethic of a popularized Social Darwinism. Generous contributions by business interests to political campaigns generally succeeded in electing officeholders friendly to business. Government policies such as subsidies to railroads, tariffs that reduced foreign competition, guarantees of free enterprise, and an aversion to regulating industry contributed to the business expansion of the new era.

INVENTORS, ENTREPRENEURS, AND CAPITALISTS

Each age produces its own major personalities who are its shaping and formative individuals. For some, these individuals are heroic models and for others villains. The era of industrialization was personified by individuals such as Andrew Carnegie

Prior to the enactment of compulsory attendance and child labor laws, children were often factory laborers.   *(From Leroy V. Goodman, ed., A Nation of Learners. Washington, D.C.: G.P.O., 1976, p. 126. Library of Congress Collection.)*

and John D. Rockefeller. Their role in shaping American society loomed larger than that of many political and educational leaders of turn of the century America. American historians long have debated if Carnegie, Rockefeller, and those like them were "captains of industry" whose corporate genius and creativity modernized the United States, or if they were "robber barons" whose desire for profit despoiled natural resources and exploited human beings. Without entering into this debate, let us say that they were modernizing industrialists whose activities brought the mixed consequences of national economic growth and human exploitation. They were, however, models that many sought to emulate. As such, they were persons of great informal educational importance. The leaders of industrial America were linked to inventors such as Alexander Graham Bell and Thomas A. Edison, whose inventions generated profound industrial and technological change. Such inventors, working in their own makeshift laboratories and demonstrating the American propensity for practicality, were modern-day Ben Franklins. When linked with corporate industrialism, practical invention transformed American life, society, and education. Individuals such as Bell and Edison were heroes to the young people of the time. Like the captains of industry, they were important informal educational models of the new era.

Andrew Carnegie

An important characteristic of the industrial giant was that of being a "self-made" man. A boy, born in humble circumstances and with little formal education, could rise by his own initiative to economic power and prestige. Andrew Carnegie (1835-1919), a Scottish immigrant who came to the United States at age twelve in 1848, personified the myth of the self-made rugged individualist.[1] According to the myth, to advance upward, a young man had to not only work hard but take advantage of any opportunity for success that came his way.

Carnegie, starting as a bobbin boy for $1.20 a week in a Pittsburgh cotton mill, relentlessly climbed the corporate ladder. By age eighteeen, he was the personal telegrapher of an important railroad executive and at twenty-four was promoted to divisional superintendent of the Pennsylvania Railroad. Following the regimen prescribed for self-made men, Carnegie saved his money and invested shrewdly in the steel industry, which he came to dominate. By 1900, Carnegie-owned steel mills, employing 20,000 workers, were earning annual profits of 40 million dollars. In 1901, Carnegie sold his interests to devote himself to philanthropy. While his writings defended the rights of labor, Carnegie's actual practices kept wages low and opposed the organization of labor unions. For example, a strike at Carnegie's Homestead mill was crushed by Pinkerton agents, strikebreakers, and state militia.

The Gospel of Wealth

Upon retiring from steel manufacturing, Carnegie devoted himself to what he called "scientific philanthropy," the giving of large sums of money for purposes that were often educational. In an essay on "wealth," Carnegie put forth his philosophy of scientific philanthropy.[2] According to Carnegie: (1) Following the principle of individualism, wealthy persons should use their accumulated property to elevate the human race instead of distributing it directly to the people themselves in small amounts. (2) The wealthy person, being a steward or trustee for the human race, should use "his superior wisdom, experience, and ability to administer" this wealth as a trust fund for philanthropic purposes. (3) The philanthropist should support projects, especially educational ones, that would enable those who wanted to help themselves to become more industrious.[3] Given priority in Carnegie's philanthropic funding was the founding and support of universities and libraries.

Carnegie's major initial philanthropic effort was to assist in establishing libraries. His general policy was to fund the building of a library if the community

---

[1] Joseph F. Wall's *Andrew Carnegie* (New York: Oxford University Press, 1970) is the definitive biography.

[2] Andrew Carnegie, *The Gospel of Wealth and Other Timely Essays*, Edward C. Kirkland, ed. (Cambridge, Mass.: Harvard University Press, 1962).

[3] Ibid., pp. 20-31.

agreed to tax itself to purchase books and maintain the collection and the facility.[4] This requirement for a community commitment was based on Carnegie's belief that philanthropy should assist those who wanted to help themselves. Throughout the United States, Carnegie free public libraries were established, which Carnegie predicted would "make men not violent revolutionists, but cautious evolutionists; not destroyers, but careful improvers."[5] By the time of his death in 1919, 1,946 Carnegie-supported libraries had been established at a cost of nearly $45 million.[6]

In addition to his interest in uplifting humankind by establishing libraries, Carnegie supported scientific research, pensions for college professors, and colleges and universities. Believing that higher education was too important to be left to professors, Carnegie was pleased that many private American universities were governed by boards of trustees composed largely of successful and affluent businessmen. Antagonistic to classical education, Carnegie argued for polytechnical and scientific training for America's future leaders.

Inventions and Technology

The industrial transformation of the United States was a product of inventions, especially those that applied science to industry. The telegraph and telephone revolutionized communications; the typewriter, cash register, calculator, and adding machine transformed business operations; automatic looms and electric sewing machines transformed textile and clothing production. The range of inventions developed in the 1870s, 1880s, and 1890s, made turn of the century America a vastly different society than it had been in the mid-nineteenth century.

If Andrew Carnegie represented the captain of industry, Thomas Alva Edison (1847-1931) personified American genius, practicality, and inventiveness. With little formal education, Edison, an avid reader, was largely self-educated. To carry on his research, Edison built a laboratory at Menlo Park, New Jersey, where he worked on specific inventions with a team of applied scientists like himself. In 1877, he invented the phonograph. In 1879, using an exhaustive trial-and-error method, he invented the incandescent lamp. Each invention led to other inventions. His experiments led to a complex system by which electricity could be made available to light homes, businesses, and entire cities. By 1900, thousands of electric power stations were supplying the electricity that illuminated the nation.

The Edison success story was an inspiration to many American youngsters. A practitioner who not only studied but used science, Edison epitomized the American ideal of application and utility. Edison became a boyhood hero for Henry Ford, who revolutionized the automobile industry by introducing the moving assembly line for mass production in the 1920s. So impressed was Ford with Edison's work that he built a reconstruction of the Menlo Park laboratory at Green-

---

[4] Ralph Munn, "Hindsight on the Gifts of Carnegie," *Library Journal,* 76 (December 1951).

[5] Wall, *Andrew Carnegie,* p. 821.

[6] Ibid., pp. 828-29.

field Village, near Detroit, where the fiftieth anniversary of the invention of the incandescent lamp was celebrated on October 21, 1929.[7] When Edison died in 1931, Ford eulogized him as a great inventor who succeeded because of "persistence, tireless experiment and downright hard work."[8]

IMMIGRATION

Between 1870 and 1910, immigration patterns shifted dramatically. Until 1890, 85 percent of the European immigrants to the United Stated had come from Northern and Western Europe, primarily from Germany, Great Britain, and the Scandinavian countries. After 1840, a large number of immigrants from Great Britain had been Irish Catholics. For example, of the 2,812,000 European immigrants who entered the United States between 1870 and 1880, only 145,000 had come from Southern and Eastern Europe. After 1890, there was a massive increase in immigration from Southern and Eastern Europe, especially from Italy, Austria-Hungary, and Russia. The polyglot Hapsburg Empire of Austria-Hungary included many submerged nationalities and ethnic groups such as Bohemians, Slovaks, Slovenes, and Croatians who came to the United States in search of an improved standard of living. Poles, Jews, Ukrainians, and others left Russia to escape the repressive policy that the Tsar's regime had imposed on non-Russian ethnic groups. In the decade 1900-1910, 6,224,000 of the total 8,795,000 immigrants had come from Southern and Eastern Europe.

Like the Irish immigrants of the 1840s, the Southern and Eastern European immigrants did not fit the Anglo-Saxon mold of the dominant older stock of Americans. Since they were non-English-speaking and included many illiterates, they posed a significant cultural and educational problem to the institutions of their adopted country. In addition to language and educational problems, the new immigrants experienced the cultural shock of not only being strangers in a strange land but of being rudely transported into an industrial and urban society that differed markedly from their rural peasant villages.

Many of the new immigrants sought to alleviate their cultural shock by seeking the friendship of their own people. They tended to locate, especially in the large cities, in ethnic enclaves, or ghettoes, where they lived with those who spoke the same language and attended the same church, which was often Catholic or Orthodox rather than Protestant. The Roman Catholics, in particular, building on the earlier experience of the Irish, created a system of ethnic parishes and ethnic parish schools. Here children were taught by religious communities of nuns or brothers, often from their native land, and received a bilingual and bicultural education. Seeking to preserve their own ethnic culture, the "new immigrants" established their own newspapers, social groups, and fraternal organizations.

[7] Geoffrey C. Upward, *A Home for Our Heritage: The Building and Growth of Greenfield Village and the Henry Ford Museum, 1929-1979* (Dearborn, Mich.: Henry Ford Museum Press, 1979), p. 22.

[8] Ibid., p. 88.

While the new immigrants sought ethnic security by living in enclaves, forces at work in the dominant white Anglo-Saxon Protestant culture did not encourage an ethnically integrated, multicultural society. The older stock of Americans reacted in several ways. Although some expressed a readiness for pluralism, the spokesmen of the dominant groups, especially in education, urged the assimilation of the immigrants and their children by a policy of Americanism in the public schools. In this way, social integration would be gradual and would not involve ethnically mixed residential areas.

As indicated, the years from 1870 to 1914 were a time of massive migration as new immigrants, from Southern and Eastern Europe and Chinese and Japanese from Asia arrived in the United States. While the new immigrants supplied cheap labor for the national's expanding industries and a large consumer market for mass-produced items, they also generated tensions in American society, politics, and education. For many public school educators, especially those in the large Northern and Eastern cities, education, along with its traditional goals, was directed to the Americanization of the children of the new immigrants. Although a few voices in education would argue for a cultural pluralism that respected ethnic and language diversity, the majority of public schools worked to create a homogenized cultural uniformity.

The theory of Americanization found a strong advocacy in Ellwood P. Cubberley, a nationally recognized school administrator and educational historian. Cubberley clearly believed that the public schools had a mission to assimilate the new immigrants into a nation that would remain not only English-speaking but English-thinking as well. In characterizing the earlier Northern and Western European immigrants, Cubberley found that their racial stock was "not very different from our own" and that they possessed a large degree of "courage, initiative, intelligence, adaptability and self-reliance." In contrast, the Southern and Eastern Europeans, were in Cubberley's opinion, "illiterate, docile, lacking in self-reliance and initiative, and not possessing the Anglo-Teutonic conceptions of law, order, and government."[9]

Cubberley's ideology of Americanization through public schooling rested on preconceptions that saw the American experience as complete and patterned according to an idealized "Anglo-Teutonic" culture. The new immigrants, he believed, were incapable of adding anything of appreciable value to that culture. Indeed, it was necessary to preserve the national culture from dilution. He warned educators that their task was "to assimilate and amalgamate these people" into "our American race." Public schooling would implant in immigrant children "the Anglo-Saxon conception of righteousness, law and order, and popular government."[10]

As the number of immigrants grew, the dominant groups—white middle-class Americans of older stock—relied increasingly on public schools to assimilate immi-

[9] Ellwood P. Cubberley, *Changing Conceptions of Education* (Boston: Houghton Mifflin, 1909), pp. 10-16.
[10] Ibid.

grant children into their version of Americanism. Compulsory school attendance laws, mandated by each state, was one way to ensure that immigrant children attended school. Truancy laws and officers to enforce them were a legal check on those immigrant families who preferred to augment their incomes by sending their children to work. For the immigrant child, the teacher was the agent of American-ization. By using a curriculum and regimen designed to Americanize immigrant children, public schools, especially those in large cities, often stood in sharp con-trast to the immigrant child's home and family life. The foremost means of Ameri-canization was through the English language and literature, which, then as now, dominated much of the curriculum and school day. Although there were a few examples of bilingual education in the 1890s and 1900s, instruction in the majority of public schools was in English. History, civics, and government courses were designed to build a commitment to the American form of government and its politi-cal and legal processes. While any nation's school system tries to reinforce ideas about the superiority of its political system, American history and civics textbooks and curricula offered a selective version of experience that: (1) emphasized Anglo-Saxon and Protestant antecedents while neglecting or ignoring the contribution of other groups to the American heritage; (2) reinforced the Protestant ethic by draw-ing on political, cultural, and literary models generalized from New England's history; (3) stressed the ideal leader as being wealthy, well educated, and free from materialism and special interests.[11] With their concern for deportment, diet, hygiene, and cleanliness the schools were also a social mechanism for changing the behavior of immigrant children, many of whom, like their parents, had been rudely transported from farms and villages to the ghettoes and crowded tenements of America's large cities.[12]

Catholic Schools and Ethnicity

Although there were differences of opinion among the Roman Catholic hierarchy on the degree to which Catholic parochial schools should Americanize new immigrants, a generally pragmatic view prevailed. In many dioceses, church policy permitted, and often encouraged, ethnic parishes and parish schools.[13] The enthusiasm for the ethnic parish and school depended to a large extent upon the traditions that a particular group had toward schooling. For example, Poles and Slovaks were enthusiastic about a parish school that would preserve not only the faith but language, customs, and traditions as well. Parish schools, following ethnic lines, were often staffed by members of religious communities, usually teaching

[11] Frances FitzGerald, *America Revised: History Schoolbooks in the Twentieth Century* (New York: Random House, 1979), p. 67.

[12] For a thorough treatment of the education of immigrant children in a large urban school system, see Selma C. Berrol, *Immigrants at School, New York City, 1898-1914* (New York: Arno Press, 1978).

[13] An excellent case study is James W. Sanders, *The Education of an Urban Minority: Catholics in Chicago, 1833-1965* (New York: Oxford University Press, 1977). Also, see Glen Gabert, Jr., *In Hoc Signo? A Brief History of Catholic Parochial Education in America* (Port Washington, N.Y.: Kennikat Press, 1973).

sisters, who had come to the United States from the immigrants' country of origin. Ethnic parish schools were also encouraged by the Catholic policy of locating the school near the parish church. When the neighborhood was settled on an ethnic basis, as it generally was in the large city, the parochial school reflected the ethnic composition of the neighborhood. As a result, a parochial school often became an Irish, German, Polish, Bohemian, Lithuanian, or Slovak school as well as a Catholic school. Because of the responsiveness of individual bishops to ethnic groups, Roman Catholic schools were often as diverse as the parishes that built and supported them.

Sanders, in his study of Catholic schooling in Chicago, found that the Catholic hierarchy encouraged the establishment of ethnic parishes and ethnic schools that were often bilingual and bicultural.[14] Thus, Catholic immigrants preferred Catholic over public schools that were hostile to ethnic languages and customs. Catholic schools in Chicago, reflecting their different ethnic origins, developed independently of each other as successive waves of immigrants established their own parish schools. First came the French, then the Irish and Germans; these were followed by Poles, Bohemians, Lithuanians, Slovaks, Slovenes, and Croats. While the policy of ethnic permissiveness encouraged the creation of parochial schools, it was a financially costly one and resulted in duplication. Nevertheless, such permissiveness toward ethinic diversity kept the tensions within the polyglot Catholic community from threatening its religious unity.

In the late nineteenth and early twentieth centuries, most of Chicago's Catholic ethnic communities were located in the city's poorer sections. Due to the poverty of many parishioners, Catholic schools had to follow a stringent economy. The various orders of teaching sisters worked at a subsistence level.

DARWINISM AND SOCIAL DARWINISM

Captains of industry, such as Carnegie and Rockefeller, who were engineering America's industrialization according to the model of private corporatism, found a timely and ready-made rationale in the ideology of Social Darwinism. An expensive and often exploitative capitalism found a convenient social science justification in Social Darwinism, which was derived from Darwin's theory of evolution based upon natural selection.

After long research, Charles Darwin, an English natural scientist, published *On the Origin of Species* in 1859.[15] According to Darwin: (1) more individuals of each species were born than could survive; (2) this high birth rate resulted in a continual struggle for existence among these individuals; (3) those individuals who vary in a profitable way enhance their chances for survival; (4) through natural

---

[14] Sanders, *Education of Urban Minority,* pp. 40-55.

[15] Charles Darwin, *On the Origin of Species by Means of Natural Selection; or the Preservation of Favoured Races in the Struggle for Life* (New York: American Publishers Corporation, n.d.).

selection, individuals with the selected variation perpetuate themselves by transmitting it to their offspring. The broad implications of Darwin's thesis suggested an evolutionary and slowly changing universe rather than a static one. The theory of evolution stimulated sharp theological controversies among churchmen, who saw it as a denial of the doctrine of Divine Creation as expressed in the Book of Genesis.

Darwin's theory of evolution in the animal world was borrowed by social theorists and economists who were seeking to create a new social science. Indeed, evolutionary theory became the foundation of the climate of opinion of the "generation of materialism" of the late nineteenth century.[16]

The foremost spokesmen of the Social Darwinist ideology was Herbert Spencer (1820-1903), an English engineer and writer who devoted his life to creating an all-inclusive sociology of knowledge, which he called "a system of synthetic philosophy."[17] Spencer's system, resting on evolutionary theory, applied the "survival-of-the-fittest" concept to economics, politics, society, and education. While enjoying some notice in his native England, Spencer's greatest popularity was in the United States, where his theory of Social Darwinism was acclaimed by Carnegie and other leading industrialists, as well as by academics who were seeking to create a social science free of the constraints of metaphysics and classicism.

Spencer's themes of "the struggle for existence" and "the survival of the fittest" were well fitted to provide an ideology for American industrialists such as Carnegie and Rockefeller. Competition among individuals was nature's way of guaranteeing that victory would go to the fittest—the most clever, most industrious, most entrepreneurial of individuals. According to nature's law, such competition would lead to the gradual but inevitable improvement of humankind and society. The exploitation of natural resources and other human beings was an inevitable part of the process.

Spencer's Social Darwinism also revitalized the classical economic theories of Adam Smith, Thomas Malthus, and David Ricardo. Government was to stay out of the process and act only to ensure that competition was possible. Accordingly, social reform efforts to regulate child labor, improve working conditions, or improve housing were ill-designed attempts "to remedy the irremediable" in that they "interfered with the wisdom of nature."[18]

Social Darwinism conveyed a practical value system that fitted well with the Protestant ethic's doctrines of hard work and stewardship and with the American bent toward an inventive and utilitarian entrepreneurship. Like a modern form of Puritanism, Social Darwinism was suspicious of waste, leisure, and illness. Its call for competition, hard work, punctuality, orderliness, diligence, and the economical use of time was well suited to shops and factories as well as to schools. Schooling,

[16] Carlton J. H. Hayes, *A Generation of Materialism: 1871-1900* (New York: Harper & Brothers, 1941), pp. 9-13, 111-118.

[17] S. J. Curtis and M. E. A. Boultwood, *A Short History of Educational Ideas* (London: University Tutorial Press, 1965), pp. 417-24.

[18] Richard Hofstadter, *Social Darwinism in American Thought* (Boston: Beacon Press, 1955), pp. 6-7.

so conceived, was a means of training up a disciplined work force. Work, inventiveness, and competition developed character. Unemployment was the punishment deserved by the inefficient, shiftless, and wasteful.

The Horatio Alger Myth

The era of the captains of industry and Social Darwinism saw the popularity of the Horatio Alger myth, an important theme in the period's popular culture. The rags-to-riches theme about the poor boy who makes good because of his own initiative, creativity, and industriousness was the format for a series of popular novels written by Horatio Alger (1832-1899).[19] It is estimated that between 100,000,000 and 250,000,000 copies of Alger's books were sold; the success story that they portrayed made them important vehicles of informal education in late nineteenth-century America.

Alger's novels presented the basic theme that a young man of good character can overcome poverty and rise to affluence and power if he is inventive, creative, and moral—which in Algerian terms meant avoiding liquor, tobacco, and pool rooms. Alger's success story depicted a rite of passage from adolescence to maturity as well as from probationary poverty to wealth.

An example of the Alger formula can be found in *Silas Snobden's Office Boy*, a novel about Frank Manton, a poor but industrious office boy who lives with his mother in a crowded tenement in New York. Eager for promotion, Frank possesses all the necessary virtues for success: courage, modesty, ambition, and unfailing honesty. In the course of the story, the hero foils a robbery, returns a valuable wallet to its owner, and rescues a kidnapped child. At the beginning of the novel, Frank earns $4 a week as an office boy; at its end, he receives a reward in the form of a $10,000 certified check, which he invests at 6 percent interest. The novel concludes that Frank, who "is diligent in business, . . . is likely to become a rich man."[20]

Spencer on Education

While Herbert Spencer's Social Darwinism was the regnant ideology in turn-of-the-century America, his ideas on education contributed to a changing conception of curriculum.[21] In the naturalistic tradition of educational reform, Spencer,

---

[19] See the following biographies: Herbert R. Mayes, *Alger: A Biography Without a Hero* (New York: Macy-Masius, 1928); Frank Gruber, *Horatio Alger, Jr.: A Biography and Bibliography of the Best-Selling Author of All Time* (West Los Angeles: Grover Jones Press, 1961); Ralph D. Gardner, *Horatio Alger; or, the American Hero Era* (Mendota, Ill.: Wayside Press, 1964).

[20] Horatio Alger, Jr., *Silas Snobden's Office Boy,* foreward by Ralph D. Gardner (New York: Doubleday, 1973), p. 240. This novel appeared in serialized form in *The Argosy* between 1889 and 1900.

[21] See Herbert Spencer, *Education: Intellectual, Moral, and Physical* (New York: Appleton, 1910); also, Andreas M. Kazamias, *Herbert Spencer on Education* (New York: Teachers College Press, Columbia University, 1966).

like Pestalozzi and Owen before him, criticized the traditional emphasis on Greek and Latin literature. To establish a rational curriculum organization, Spencer asked, "What knowledge is of most worth?" Spencer answered his own query by classifying the significant activities that sustained and were common to human life. He identified the following categories of activities as the basis for a useful curriculum:

1. those that related to self-preservation;
2. those that related indirectly to self-preservation and secured the economic necessities of life;
3. those that related to family life and the upbringing of children;
4. those that related to social and political relationships; and
5. those that were aesthetic and recreational and were for leisure-time pursuits.

Spencer believed that a knowledge of science was necessary for individuals to efficiently perform life's major activities. For example, a knowledge of the principles of health, derived from physiology, was needed for behavior that contributed to self-preservation. Chemistry and physics were basic sciences and economics and engineering were applied sciences that contributed to manufacturing, production, and commerce. Spencer's emphasis on science and its application to commerce was aimed at dislodging the classics from their primary place in the curriculum and replacing them with more modern and utilitarian subjects.

A science class in a nineteenth century school.   *(From Leroy V. Goodman, ed., A Nation of Learners. Washington, D.C.: G.P.O., 1976, p. 5. Library of Congress Collection.)*

SCHOOL ADMINISTRATION

At the turn of the century, school administrators, especially superintendents of urban districts, sought to develop new modes of governance, organization, and control. While school governance in rural districts remained largely in the hands of elected boards who administered one-room schools taught by a single teacher, superintendents in large urban areas had to deal with increasingly complex issues of organizing schools to serve thousands of students, many of whom were the children of new immigrants.

Superintendents in large urban districts, following the captain-of-industry model, sought to become educational executives who stressed managerial and operational efficiency.[22] Following the business corporation model, the organization of big-city schools grew more centralized and complex. For example, central office staff not only increased in size but became more concerned with such managerial functions as supervision, building maintenance, organization of records, and budgeting. Over time, such executive and managerial functions came to require specialized training and certification. Corporate models of school administration

This photograph of Miss Blanche Lamont, with her school at Holca, Montana, October 1893, illustrates the persistence of the one-room school in late nineteenth century America. *(From Leroy V. Goodman, ed., A Nation of Learners. Washington, D.C.: G.P.O., 1976, p. 14. Library of Congress Collection.)*

[22] David B. Tyack, "Pilgrim's Progress: Toward a Social History of the School Superintendency, 1860-1960." *History of Education Quarterly*, 16, no. 3 (Fall 1976): 274-75.

The photograph illustrates an early effort to systematize school procedures. *(From Leroy V. Goodman, ed., A Nation of Learners. Washington, D.C.: G.P.O., 1976, p. 50. Library of Congress Collection.)*

came to dominate the field, although they were resisted by boards in rural school districts.[23]

William T. Harris

At the close of the nineteenth century, the role of the public school leader began to undergo a transformation. The first half of the century had produced individuals such as Horace Mann, Henry Barnard, and others, who, as common school proponents, had entered education as a phase in their political or legal careers. The new leadership, represented by administrators such as William T. Harris (1835-1909), were educational executives who energetically sought to centralize schools into efficiently managed graded systems.[24]

Harris, an urban school superintendent, believed that the large city had a great civilizing potentiality that schools could help to realize. He was convinced that the agencies of city life—libraries, museums, and art galleries—conveniently made available to city children the world's great discoveries in science, art, literature, and history. As a vast classroom, the city would "dissolve clanship and cultivate in its place evidence of opinion and action."[25] Urban schools, in Harris's view, were to aid in the civilizing process.

As a school executive, Harris sought to consolidate the work of the earlier

[23] The resistance of local boards of education in rural school districts is examined in Wayne E. Fuller, *The Old Country School: The Story of Rural Education in the Middle West* (Chicago: University of Chicago Press, 1982), pp. 101-12.

[24] Robert H. Wiebe, *The Search for Order, 1877-1920* (New York: Hill and Wang, 1967), p. 118.

[25] William A. Bullough, "It Is Better to Be a Country Boy: The Lure of the Country in Urban Education in the Gilded Age," *The Historian*, 35 (February 1973): 184.

common school leaders and create public school systems that met the needs of an industrial and urban society.

From 1868 until 1880, Harris was the superintendent of schools in St. Louis, a growing commercial and industrial metropolis.[26] At the crossroads of the nation, St. Louis, located between North and South, was racially and ethnically diverse; it had a large black community as well as a significant immigrant population, especially German-Americans. In this diverse urban setting, Harris established the emerging patterns for school administration for industrial society. Here, where the small one-room rural school was obviously inadequate, Harris tackled problems of organizing, classifying, and structuring a modern school system and won a reputation as an efficient and effective administrator.

Because of his career in St. Louis, Harris gained a national reputation, serving as U.S. commissioner of education from 1889 to 1906. Recognized as the authoritative spokesman on American public education, he was a member of important educational associations and served on national commissions, particularly those of the National Education Association.

Although a practical administrator, Harris was firmly convinced that sound policies should rest on a philosophical base. Harris found that philosophy in the idealism of the German philosopher George Wilhelm Hegel and the American Transcendentalist Ralph Waldo Emerson. Harris's version of idealism integrated older spiritual values with the new industrialism. Using Hegel's dialectic, Harris reasoned that the older spiritual and the newer materialist values were components of an evolving integrative synthesis that united the positive aspects of both. The traditional values, inherited from the Puritans, that stressed hard work, diligence, punctuality, and perseverance were ideally suited to contribute to productivity and efficiency needed in an industrializing society. Under Harris, the schools played an active role in preparing the trained workers and managers required by an industrial economy.[27]

Idealism also provided Harris with a way of viewing the role and functions of institutions, including schools, in the social context of industrialism. He believed that a society had reached a high level of civilization when its life was expressed through social institutions such as the family, state, church, and the school. These social institutions were, he believed, evolving to higher, more complete, and more encompassing forms. In his world view, the school was a crucial institution that prepared individuals to function effectively in a complex and specialized industrial society.

As a society's special institution for promoting civilized life in its younger members, the school was to cultivate such values as self-discipline, civic commitment, obedience to duly established law and order, and a respect for private property. The school's organization and structure were to facilitate the efficient transmission of the curriculum. As a graded, structured, and cumulative sequence

[26] Selwyn K. Troen, *The Public and the Schools: Shaping the St. Louis System, 1838-1920* (Columbia: University of Missouri Press, 1975), pp. 1-4.

[27] Ibid., pp. 161-62.

of studies, the curriculum lifted the child upward from primitive impulses to civilized life.

Harris, impressed with Froebel's kindergarten philosophy, believed that school life should begin with the kindergarten, which was to introduce children to orderly behavior and group participation. After acquiring initial skills in kindergarten, children would be ready for the elementary school curriculum, which Harris called the "five windows of the soul." Consisting of mathematics, geography, literature and art, history, and grammar, the elementary curriculum would give students the tools, information, and insights to participate in, and contribute to, civilization. After completing elementary school, students studied the classics, mathematics, and languages of the secondary curriculum.

As a school executive, Harris believed that efficient instructional methods were needed to transmit subject matter effectively. He admonished teachers to emphasize silence, industriousness, regularity, and discipline in their classrooms and to impress upon students the need to incorporate these behaviors into their daily routines.[28] Public school graduates were to be individuals who respected rather than challenged legitimate authority. Harris's style of school management and classroom discipline encouraged conformity to existing social institutions and standards.

Since Harris and other late nineteenth-century urban school superintendents faced problems of overcrowded classrooms, poorly prepared teachers, and widely divergent student backgrounds, they were convinced that effective instruction would occur only in carefully organized and efficiently administered schools. As superintendent in St. Louis, Harris devoted his energies to careful planning that involved establishing educational priorities and developing efficient management and supervisory procedures. Harris's devotion to planned administration led him to emphasize the classification and grouping of students. What resulted was the graded school, where each year's work was organized and scheduled into an age-specific grade. To make compulsory attendance effective, school administrators had to compile and maintain statistics and attendance reports. Further, the school administrator had to be concerned with the maintenance of the school's physical facilities, lighting, heating, architecture, and ventilation. The end result of Harris's administrative and managerial style was an efficient but centralized uniformity.

Although he viewed the school as the transmitter and preserver of existing social institutions and values rather than as an agency for social change, Harris believed that educational executives had to deal with social issues. While believing that schools should assimilate immigrants into the broad mainstream of American society, Harris wanted Americanization to be gradual, evolutionary, and non-coerced. Using such an evolutionary approach, he encouraged bilingual and bicultural education for St. Louis's large German community, which was designed to integrate German-speaking children into the larger English-speaking society.

In the broad sense, Harris was a consolidator rather than an innovator, who envisioned public schools as institutions that transmitted existing values rather than

[28] William T. Harris, *Compulsory Education in Relation to Crime and Social Morals* (Washington, D.C.: privately printed, 1885), pp. 4-9.

THE FOURTH GIFT.

Froebel's Second Building Box.

The aim of the Fourth Gift is similar to that of the Third; but it gives rise to the observation of similarity and dissimilarity, and allows a very varied and interesting application in the production of forms of *knowledge* (or mathematical forms), of *beauty* (or symmetry), and of *life*.

No. **31**. **A large cube** ($2 \times 2 \times 2$ inches) divided into 8 equal oblong blocks (each $\frac{1}{2} \times 1 \times 2$ inches). In a wooden box, $0.20.

Diagrams and **Directions** for the use of the Fourth Gift are contained in *The Kindergarten Guide*, Number Two. In paper, $0.70.

and, separately, in the special reprint therefrom:

The Fourth Gift. In paper, $0.30.

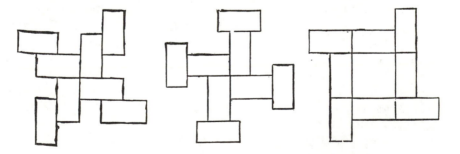

E. STEIGER, 25 Park Place, NEW YORK

Material for use in kindergartens based on Froebel's Fourth Gift. The kindergarten became part of the St. Louis public school system during Harris's superintendency. *(From The Year Book of Education for 1879. New York: E. Steiger, 1879, p. 447.)*

attempting to change them. His greatest achievement was that of channeling the earlier enthusiasms of the common school advocates into patterns of efficient school administration and organization. The work of Harris and the other early urban school superintendents gave American public schooling an organizational design and administrative structure that would shape it in the early twentieth century.

Ella Flagg Young

Ella Flagg Young (1845-1918) served as superintendent of the Chicago public school system from 1909 to 1914. She was one of the first women educators to head a large urban school system. Having come up through the ranks of the turn of the century Chicago system, she sought to administer the large system democratically as well as efficiently.[29] Among her goals for Chicago's schools were: (1) creating a stable salary schedule for teachers; (2) removing the system from political machinations; (3) developing vocational education; and (4) encouraging continuing professional education for teachers.

During Young's administration, the Chicago public school's curriculum incorporated certain progressive tendencies, such as a more extensive manual arts curriculum and more direct learning experiences, especially field trips and excursions. The secondary school curriculum, too, was reshaped to include more vocational education courses in clerical and business occupations, industrial arts, and design. These efforts to improve vocational education reflected the industrial needs

Programme of Exercises for an Ungraded School.

TIME.* From	To	D GRADE.	C GRADE.	B GRADE.	A GRADE.	Time.
8 50	9 00	Opening.........	Exercises........	Roll Call	Rem'ks--Singing.	10
9 00	9 15	*Reading.*....	Reading........	Reading........	Reading..... ...	15
9 15	9 30	Writing.........	*Reading.*	Reading...... .	Reading.........	15
9 30	9 50	Writing.........	Writing..........	*Reading.*.........	Arithmetic	20
9 50	10 10	Out-door	Out-door........	Arithmetic	*Reading.*.........	20
10 10	10 25	....	Recess.	....	....	15
10 25	10 30			Singing all grades.		5
10 30	10 45	*Spelling.*.........	Numbers.	Arithmetic	Arithmetic	15
10 45	11 00	Writing "	*Numbers.*........	Composition.....	Arithmetic	15
11 00	11 20	Writing "	Numbers.........	*Arithmetic.*........	Hist. or Civ. Gov.	20
11 20	11 40	Out.............	Out..............	Arithmetic.......	*Arithmetic*	20
11 40	12 35			Noon.		55
12 35	12 40	....		Singing all grades.....		5
12 40	1 00	*Penmanship.*......	*Penmanship.*......	*Penmanship*	*Spelling.*........	20
1 00	1 15	*Numbers.*..... ...	Place....... ...	Geography......	Geography	15
1 15	1 30	*Writing..*	*Place*	Geography...	Geography	15
1 30	1 50	Tables........	Place...........	*Geography.*..	Grammar.......	20
1 50	2 10	Out.............	Out	*Grammar*	*Geography*	20
2 10	2 25			Recess.		15
2 25	2 40	*Color, size, &c*...	Spelling..... ...	Grammar........	Grammar.......	15
2 40	2 55	Drawing.......	Spelling	Spelling	*Grammar.*......	15
2 55	3 15	Drawing...	*Spelling.*.........	Spelling	Hist. & Civ. Gov.	15
3 15	3 30	Dismiss.........	Dismiss.........	*Grammar.*.......	Spelling	15
3 35	3 50	.. ..	....	*Spelling.*........	*Spelling*	20
3 50	4 00	.. ..	....	*Miscellaneous....*	*Miscellaneous....*	10
4 00	4 05	....	Singing.	Dismission.......		5

*The Recitations are given in *Italic* letters ; the study exercises are shown in Roman.

The schedule illustrates efforts to organize instruction in an ungraded school. *(From E.U.D. DeGraff, The School Room Guide. Syracuse, N.Y.; Davis, Bardeen, & Co., 1878, p. 403.)*

[29] Joan K. Smith, *Ella Flagg Young: Portrait of a Leader* (Ames: Educational Studies Press and Iowa State University Research Foundation, 1979), p. 154.

Classroom furniture of the late nineteenth century.   *(From The Year Book of Education for 1879. New York: E. Steiger, 1879, p. 401.)*

of the city as well as the progressive intention of making school a more direct experience that related to the urban environment.

While Young succeeded in expanding the curriculum, she faced a series of political battles with certain board of education members and with the political establishment. Her efforts to improve teachers' salaries were limited. She also had problems in trying to disentangle the purchase of textbooks and other materials from political control. In addition, her association with friends in the Chicago Teachers' Federation made her suspect to some members of the Chicago Board of Education.

In some respects, Ella Flagg Young's administrative style resembled that of Harris. Both sought to foster a science of school administration that emphasized professional efficiency. By making the superintendent into an educational expert, they hoped to reduce the influence of amateurs and politicians in shaping administrative policy. Such efforts involved the centralization of administration. Harris was skilled in achieving such centralization. Young, in contrast, sought to create an administrative style that incorporated a more democratic approach by working closely with teachers and teacher organizations. It was this tendency to "democratic efficiency" that produced a noteworthy but turbulent tenure in office for Ella Flagg Young.

HERBARTIANISM

At the turn of the century, teacher education in America's normal schools and instruction in many elementary and secondary schools were dominated by Herbartianism, a pedagogical method based on the work of Johann Friedrich

Henry Barnard (1811-1900), a public school leader of the nineteenth century. *(New York Public Library Picture Collection.)*

Herbart (1776-1841). Herbart, a German philosopher, was a professor at the University of Göttingen from 1805 to 1808, and at the University of Königsberg from 1808 to 1833. A prolific author of works on philosophy, psychology, and pedagogy, Herbart's most significant books on education were *General Pyschology* (1806), *A Textbook for Psychology* (1816), *Letters on the Application of Psychology to Education* (1831), and *Outlines of Pedagogical Lectures* (1835).[30]

Herbart believed that the primary function of education was the development of ethical persons. The humanities, especially history and literature, were suited to developing such a sense of ethical awareness. With the encouragement of Herbart's disciples, some of whom were Americans such as Charles DeGarmo and Charles and Frank McMurry, history and literature secured a larger role in the school curriculum.[31]

Along with curricular development, Herbart combined his interests in philosophy and psychology to arrive at several concepts of pedagogical importance. For Herbart, the role of a person's interests was important in motivating learning and in planning and presenting instruction. With experience, a human being developed a knowledge of, and an interest in, many objects and their relationships with each other. Teachers were to harness the "many-sided interests" of learners. The knowledge acquired by experience—a network of stored ideas—became, in Herbart's terminology, the learner's "apperceptive mass." Good teaching, in Herbartian terms, meant that teachers would stimulate the appropriate connections in the mass of ideas and stimulate learners to add to them.

The most popular and most widely adopted Herbartian contribution to American education was the formal steps, or phases, of instruction. As developed by the American Herbartians, a lesson should follow five steps:

1. *preparation*, during which the teacher motivated students by appealing to their interests and creating a state of readiness in them;
2. *presentation*, during which the teacher stated and explained a new idea or set of related ideas to the students;
3. *association*, during which the teacher deliberately related the new knowledge to the students' previous learning;
4. *generalization*, which involved the formulation of the general principle, rule, or definition that was to be derived from the lesson; and
5. *application*, which was a test in which students practiced and mastered the general principle of the lesson.

In the 1880s, Herbart's popularity experienced a revival in Germany when Wilhelm Rein became director of the pedagogical institute and practice school at Jena.

---

[30] Harold B. Dunkel, *Herbart and Education* (New York: Random House, 1969), pp. 1-24.

[31] For accounts of the popularity of Herbart and his method, see Harold B. Dunkel, "Herbart's Pedagogical Seminar," *History of Education Quarterly*, 7, no. 1 (Spring 1967): 93-101; and Val D. Rust and David Starr, "Personalized Teacher Education: The Example of Herbart," *Educational Studies*, 8, no. 3 (Fall 1977): 221-29.

Rein's institute became a center of the Herbartian renaissance and attracted educators from other countries, including the United States. The German revival of Herbartian studies coincided with the development of departments of education, or pedagogy, in American universities and with efforts to raise the quality of teacher education in the country's many normal schools.

Charles DeGarmo, Charles McMurry, and Frank McMurry became the leading American authorities on Herbartianism as a result of their foreign study at Jena. These American Herbartians, determined to make their mark on American teacher education within the context of higher education, set out to create a literature that was both professional, in that it could be used by teachers in their classrooms, and scholarly, in that it earned its authors academic respectability in their colleges and universities. Further, the publications of the American Herbartians came at a time when the Pestalozzian influence was waning and progressivism was but in its embryonic state.

In 1889, DeGarmo published his book on Herbartian principles, *The Essentials of Method*. Charles McMurry published his *General Method* in 1892 and collaborated with his brother Frank in writing *The Method of the Recitation*. These and DeGarmo's *Herbart and the Herbartians* (1895) were the major sources of Herbartianism in the United States.[32]

Until it was eclipsed by John Dewey's Experimentalism and progressive education, Herbartianism dominated the American educational scene, especially from 1880 to 1910. Herbart's pedagogy occupied center stages in teacher education, especially in the normal schools. The directness of the five steps lent itself to lesson planning. Herbartianism was teacher centered and well designed for teachers who wanted to control their classrooms. In the early twentieth century, Herbartianism would be attacked for its formalism and neglect of children's interests and needs; but at the end of the nineteenth century it gave many teachers and school administrators exactly what they wanted.

G. STANLEY HALL

While Herbartianism came quickly to the American educational stage and dominated it for a short time, the work of the American psychologist and educator G. Stanley Hall (1844-1924) was of a longer-lasting significance. Hall made numerous contributions to American education because of his pioneering work in psychology, his leadership of the child study movement, and his explorations into the theory of adolescence.

---

[32] The major publications of the American Herbartians were: Charles DeGarmo, *Herbart and the Herbartians* (New York: Scribners, 1896); Johann F. Herbart, *Outlines of Educational Doctrine,* translated by Alexis Lange and annotated by Charles DeGarmo (New York: Macmillan, 1904); Charles DeGarmo, *Essentials of Method* (Boston: Heath, 1889); Charles McMurry, *The Elements of Method* (Bloomington, Ill.: Public School Publishing Co., 1892); Charles and Frank McMurry, *The Method of the Recitation* (Bloomington, Ill.: Public School Publishing Co., 1897). The definitive analysis is Harold B. Dunkel, *Herbart and the Herbartians* (Chicago: University of Chicago Press, 1970).

Hall, who graduated from Williams College in 1867, began his career as an educator by teaching English and philosophy at Antioch College in Ohio. Attracted to the new field of psychology, he studied with Wilhelm Wundt in Leipzig and earned his doctorate at Harvard. From 1882 to 1888, he taught psychology at Johns Hopkins University, a graduate level institution based on the German research model. In 1889, he became president of Clark University, which was his institutional home until his retirement in 1920. Among Hall's achievements were his leadership in founding *The American Journal of Psychology* and the American Psychological Association. His major publications were *Adolescence* and *Aspects of Child Life and Education.*[33]

Like many intellectuals of the late nineteenth century, Hall was influenced by Charles Darwin's theory of evolution. He believed that evolutionary theory would broaden the scope of psychology and lead to a "genetic" analysis of the stages of human growth and development. His desire to explain the stages of human growth led him to investigate childhood, adolescence, and old age and to expound on the characteristics unique to each stage. For the educators of the late nineteenth and early twentieth centuries, Hall's commentaries on childhood and adolescence—based on psychology rather than the more speculative philosophies of Pestalozzi, Froebel, and Herbart—held the promise of a more scientifically based pedagogy. Hall's attention to adolescence, in particular, dealt with an area hitherto neglected but of great importance for the high school.

Although his belief that human beings recapitulated in their stages of development the history of the human race has long been discredited, Hall made a major contribution by relating the child's educational readiness to psychological and physiological stages of development. According to him, each stage of a child's development, while distinct and unique, was necessarily related to the totality of human development. For each stage, there were appropriate learning and activities. Hall suggested a theme that was developed by the later progressives: that the curriculum should come from the child and be based on her or his interests and needs.

CONCLUSION

The late nineteenth and early twentieth centuries marked America's transition to an industrial society. Industrialization, along with urbanization and immigration, reshaped the older agrarian society. Education formally and informally reflected the new era. Using business efficiency as a model, administrators sought to centralize schooling in large urban areas. The importation of Herbart's method from

---

[33] G. Stanley Hall, *Adolescence* (New York: Appleton, 1905) and *Aspects of Child Life and Education* (Boston: Ginn, 1907); Hall's autobiography is entitled *The Life and Confessions of a Psychologist* (New York: Appleton, 1923); see also Charles E. Strickland and Charles Burgess, eds., *Health, Growth and Heredity; G. Stanley Hall on Natural Education* (New York: Teachers College Press, Columbia University, 1965).

Germany provided a useful pedagogy in America's schools. G. Stanley Hall's studies of childhood and adolescence initiated what would become the reforming education of the later progressive movement.

DISCUSSION QUESTIONS

1. Identify and analyze the educational implications of the transformation of the United States from an agricultural to an industrial society.
2. Analyze Carnegie's concept of scientific philanthropy.
3. How did Thomas A. Edison personify the American success story?
4. Examine the Americanization policy advocated by Ellwood P. Cubberley.
5. Analyze the ethnic and religious origins of Catholic parochial schools in the late nineteenth and early twentieth centuries.
6. Analyze the social and educational implications of Social Darwinism. Compare and contrast Social Darwinism and progressivism.
7. Describe efforts of urban superintendents to modernize school administration.
8. Analyze the administrative style of William T. Harris.
9. Assess G. Stanley Hall's contribution to educational psychology.

RESEARCH TOPICS

1. Read a biography of Carnegie, Rockefeller, or one of the leading American industrialists at the turn of the century. Examine the educational background, career development, and philosophy of the individual in a short essay.
2. Read Carnegie's *The Gospel of Wealth* and write a paper that examines its implications for education.
3. Research the immigration of the late nineteenth century by reading reminiscences, accounts, or diaries of immigrants. Write a paper that describes the immigrant experience.
4. Read a novel or short story by Horatio Alger. Analyze in a short paper the values conveyed as a type of informal education.
5. Read Herbert Spencer on education. Write a paper that analyzes his rationale for curriculum organization.
6. Research the history of a large urban school system in the late nineteenth century. Write a paper that identifies the major events or stages of development in its history.
7. Read a book by one of the American Herbartians. Write a review that analyzes the major Herbartian principles.
8. Read G. Stanley Hall's autobiography, *The Life and Confessions of a Psychologist*. Write a paper analyzing his perceptions of his educational contributions.

REFERENCES AND READINGS

Alger, Horatio. *Silas Snobden's Office Boy*. New York: Doubleday, 1973.
Berrol, Selma C. *Immigrants at School, New York City, 1898-1914*. New York: Arno Press, 1978.
Carnegie, Andrew. *Autobiography*. Boston: Houghton Mifflin, 1920.
____. *The Gospel of Wealth and Other Timely Essays*. Ed. Edward C. Kirkland. Cambridge, Mass.: Harvard University Press, 1962.
____. *Triumphant Democracy*. New York: Scribners, 1886.
Cubberley, Ellwood P. *Changing Conceptions of Education*. Boston: Houghton Mifflin, 1909.
Curtis, S. J., and Boultwood, M. E. A. *A Short History of Educational Ideas*. London: University Tutorial Press, 1965.
DeGarmo, Charles. *Herbart and the Herbartians*. New York: Scribners, 1896.
Dunkel, Harold B. *Herbart and Education*. New York: Random House, 1869.
____. *Herbart and the Herbartians*. Chicago: University of Chicago Pres, 1970.
FitzGerald, Frances. *America Revised: History Schoolbooks in the Twentieth Century*. New York: Random House, 1979.
Fuller, Wayne E. *The Old Country School: The Story of Rural Education in the Middle West*. Chicago: University of Chicago Press, 1982.
Gabert, Glen, Jr. *In Hoc Signo? A Brief History of Catholic Parochial Education in America*. Port Washington, N.Y.: Kennikat Press, 1973.
Gardner, Ralph D. *Horatio Alger; or, the American Hero Era*. Mendota, Ill.: Wayside Press, 1964.
Gruber, Frank. *Horatio Alger, Jr.: A Biography and Bibliography of the Best-Selling Author of All Time*. West Los Angles: Grover Jones Press, 1961.
Hall, G. Stanley. *Adolescence*. New York: Appleton, 1905.
____. *Aspects of Child Life and Education*. Boston: Ginn, 1907.
Hayes, Carlton J. H. *A Generation of Materialism, 1871-1900*. New York: Harper & Brothers, 1941.
Herbart, Johann F. *Outlines of Educational Doctrine*. New York: Macmillan, 1904.
Hofstadter, Richard. *Social Darwinism in American Thought*. Boston: Beacon Press, 1955.
Josephson, Matthew. *The Robber Barons*. New York: Harcourt, Brace, 1934.
Kazamias, Andreas M. *Herbert Spencer on Education*. New York: Teachers College Press, Columbia University, 1966.
Philpott, Thomas Lee. *The Slum and the Ghetto: Neighborhood Deterioration and Middle-Class Reform, Chicago*. New York: Oxford University Press, 1978.
Sanders, James W. *The Education of an Urban Minority: Catholics in Chicago, 1833-1965*. New York: Oxford University Press, 1977.
Smith, Joan K. *Ella Flagg Young: Portrait of a Leader*. Ames: Educational Studies Press and Iowa State University Research Foundation, 1974.
Spencer, Herbert. *Education: Intellectual, Moral, and Physical*. New York: Appleton, 1910.
Strickland, Charles E., and Burgess, Charles, eds. *Health, Growth and Heredity: G. Stanley Hall on Natural Education*. New York: Teachers College Press, Columbia University, 1965.
Troen, Selwyn K. *The Public and the Schools: Shaping the St. Louis System, 1838-1920*. Columbia: University of Missouri Press, 1975.
Wall, Joseph F. *Andrew Carnegie*. New York: Oxford University Press, 1970.
Wiebe, Robert H. *The Search for Order, 1877-1920*. New York: Hill and Wang, 1967.

9
PROGRESSIVISM AND AMERICAN EDUCATION

In this chapter we shall examine the origins, development, and impact of progressivism on American social, political, economic, and educational institutions and processes. As an impulse and phenomenon, progressivism, a complex movement in American history, has been much debated by historians. While agreeing that significant changes in American life and attitudes occurred during the progressive era, historians disagree on the precise chronology of the movement and its broad meaning in American history. An analysis of progressivism's impact on American education is even more complicated. At times, both the general progressive movement and educational progressivism were interrelated and featured individuals who were involved in various social, political, economic, and educational reforms. At other times, progressive education, although a parallel movement, was distinct from the larger national movement.

Chronologically, the progressive era in American life is usually located within the first two decades of the twentieth century. Some historians argue that the progressive era began in the 1890s and ended when the United States entered World War I in 1917. Other historians, contending that the progressive impulse was subdued in the 1920s, construe the New Deal of the 1930s as a renascent progressivism. Progressivism in education, while paralleling the larger national movement chronologically, extended into the early 1950s and still exercises an impact today. Here, we shall examine both the broad context of the progressive era and its educa-

tional implications; we shall also analyze progressive education as a specific movement in educational history.

THE PROGRESSIVE ERA

The period from 1890 to 1920, when the United States experienced the progressive era, was one of profound debate about the quality and direction of American
life. Occurring during a time of intense technological and social change and political, social, and educational ferment, progressivism—as a response to the pressures of
modernization, industrialization, and urbanization—sought to resolve a serious
accumulation of economic, ethnic, and urban-rural tensions. An umbrella movement, progressivism generated numerous reforms that aimed to renew and
regenerate public philosophy and policy.[1]

   Although the motives and achievements of progressives varied, their basic
themes were:

1. Government should regulate economic power in the public interest.
2. Expert knowledge and the scientific method should be applied to solving
   social, political, economic, and educational problems.
3. The national environment should be conserved and its quality enhanced.
4. Political institutions and processes should be reformed to make government
   more efficient.
5. The spirit of community should be revitalized in the burgeoning urban areas.
6. Educational institutions and processes should facilitate democratic participation and scientific efficiency.

Having sketched the origins and basic themes of progressivism, let us now examine
the major processes of the late nineteenth and early twentieth centuries that
exercised a transforming influence on American life, institutions, and education.

Urbanization

   Since the mid-nineteenth century, the population of America's large cities
had become swollen by the arrival of thousands of immigrants from abroad and by
a continuing migration from the hinterland's farms and small towns. In the thirty
years between 1880 and 1910, the nation's urban population tripled, from 15
million to 45 million. By 1920, the urban population had outdistanced the rural
population. The concentration of large urban populations in New York, Chicago,
Boston, Philadelphia, and other metropolitan areas, created unprecedented

---

[1] There are many useful treatments available that examine the progressive era; among them
are: J. Leonard Bates, *The United States, 1898-1928: Progressivism and a Society in Transition*
(New York: McGraw-Hill, 1976); Lewis L. Gould, ed., *The Progressive Era* (Syracuse, N.Y.:
Syracuse University Press, 1974); Arthur Mann, *The Progressive Era* (Hinsdale, Ill.: Dryden
Press, 1975).

demands upon municipal governments for improved services such as public transportation, police and fire protection, sanitation, lighting, and schools.

Problems of a social, political, and educational nature complicated the urbanization process. Urbanization was largely unplanned, and the increasing city population, especially many immigrants, lived in slum tenements. Government in many
large cities was dominated by political machines that depended on ethnic groups for
votes; these machines returned services and jobs through a crude patronage system
that many middle-class citizens regarded as corrupt. Aided by journalistic critics,
social workers, and other reformers, progressives sought to devise political strategies
and policies to reform, plan, and regulate urban government and institutions.

Urban schools suffered many of the same ills that plagued municipal governments. Since the urban population expansion had been unplanned, schools—
especially in the lower socioeconomic attendance areas settled by immigrants—
had become overcrowded and inadequately staffed. Much of the public school
ideology had been shaped in rural or small-town independent school districts.[2]

Many of the patterns and priorities of school governance originating in rural
traditions needed to be reformulated for large urban school districts. Indeed, in
many large cities, political machines influenced the hiring of school administrators
and teachers, who were often selected on partisan party bases rather than on
academic credentials. In addition, to a large extent, the American public school
ideology was based on the English language and Protestant ethic of the older,
established native stock. As a result, immigrant children were often instructed in a
language that they could not understand by teachers who were suspicious of their
"foreign backgrounds."

In addition to the problems that massive urbanization created for schools,
there was also a larger educational issue that stemmed from the modernization
process. For both immigrant and migrant, relocation to the city generated psychic
traumas and social alienation.[3] Many of the immigrants, particularly those from
Southern and Eastern Europe, were transplanted peasants who suffered the cultural
shock of rapidly changing from a traditional to a mobile society whose life-style
and values were still emerging. For the migrants from America's farms and small
towns, the transition to city streets was often almost as traumatic, with the exception of the sense of security that came from speaking English.

Small-town and rural America, like the European village, had provided a sense
of community and belonging, albeit a restricted one, that was lacking in the large
city. Some progressive theorists such as John Dewey and Jane Addams defined the
challenge of modernization to be the recreation of a sense of community in the
urban setting. For educators, such as the administrative theorist and historian
Ellwood P. Cubberley, community meant Americanization and the enculturation

---

[2] Wayne E. Fuller, *The Old Country School: The Story of Rural Education in the Middle
West.* (Chicago: University of Chicago Press, 1982), pp. 79-100.

[3] For a very clear discussion of the complex issue of modernization, see C. E. Black, *The
Dynamics of Modernization: A Study in Comparative History* (New York: Harper & Row, Pub.,
1966), pp. 9-34.

of middle-class values and expectations and the rejection of the multicultural pluralism that was a reality in the American metropolis.

For the nation's educators, especially those who styled themselves progressives, the problems of an urbanizing and modernizing America were: (1) to readapt patterns of school governance and organization into modes and styles that would meet the needs of urban life and society; (2) to create a sense of community in the face of ethnic, racial, and socioeconomic class antagonisms; (3) to undertake curricular reforms that would change instructional patterns to more direct kinds of learning. As they grappled with these problems, progressive educators posed diverse strategies that had significant but often contradictory consequences for America's educational future.

Progressive school administrators, seeking to end the confused and inefficient governance and organizational patterns inherited from rural schooling, devised strategems to make school administration more standardized, efficient, and manageable. As was true of progressives in municipal government, conservation, and other areas, they wanted experts in scientific school management to replace the inefficient amateurs of the past. While they standardized and consolidated schooling, they also succeeded in creating new bureaucracies.[4]

Progressive theorists grappled with varying success with the problem of restoring an American sense of community. Political progressives such as Theodore Roosevelt, Herbert Croly, Woodrow Wilson, and others sought to redefine traditional concepts of American polity and government in evolutionary rather than revolutionary ways. John Dewey and William Heard Kilpatrick, educational progressives, believed that progressive schools as embryonic societies could become the basis for a rekindled American community. Jane Addams, famed social worker and settlement house founder, tried to create agencies to ease the traumas of immigrant assimilation.

The progressive educators who were involved in curricular reform, change, and innovation, ranged from child-centered school advocates such as Carolyn Pratt and Margaret Naumberg, to social reconstructionists like George S. Counts. Curricular innovation was often the most noticeable activity of educational progressives. Later in the chapter we shall examine these various dimensions of progressivism in education.

Economic Regulation and Control

While much progressive activity can be explained in social, cultural, political, or educational terms, it also had an underlying economic dimension. America's modernization was to a large extent the product of the expansion and alteration of American economic life from individual entrepreneurship to the large corporation.

Since the Civil War, American industries and businesses had been growing larger and larger. Business consolidations, mergers, and takeovers had created giant

[4] For treatments of the bureaucratization process, see Michael B. Katz, *School Reform: Past and Present* (Boston: Little, Brown, 1971), and his *Class, Bureaucracy, and Schools: The Illusion of Educational Change in America* (New York: Praeger, 1971).

corporations—many of which were still controlled by single powerful individuals. While corporate bigness contributed to America's modernization, it also concentrated tremendous economic power into a few hands. Much of the energy of progressive reformers went into devising mechanisms to control the trusts and monopolies.

In commenting upon the rapid industrialization of the United States, Lewis Gould has identified the following social injustices that existed at the turn of the century:

1. While only 5 percent of the population owned half of the nation's property, one-third of the population subsisted below the poverty level.
2. A million and a half children under age sixteen were working in mines, factories, and other industries.
3. For many working men, women, and children, an average working week was in excess of sixty hours.[5]

Such economic disparities and wide use of child labor had direct implications for American schooling. Compulsory school attendance laws could be effectively enforced only if there were corollary restrictions on child labor. The general progressive inclination that schooling was desirable and that children should attend school required alliances between progressive politicians and educators in order to secure both compulsory school attendance laws and restrictions on child labor.

More subtle than the school attendance-child labor issue, was that of the growing "corporateness" of American life. Antitrust legislation such as the Sherman and Clayton acts modified the concentration of wealth rather than blocking it. The corporate style of success was emerging as the way to power, prestige, and prosperity. School administrators began to look to corporate models for modes of school governance and organization.

The Conservation of Natural Resources

Among the many themes of the progressive era was that of conserving natural resources and improving the quality of the environment. The conservation movement had economic, educational, social, and psychic implications. The process of industrialization had resulted in the wasting and exploitation of the natural environment and its mineral, water, and forest resources. Deforestation, strip mining, and environmental pollution were the unplanned and often ignored consequences of industrialization. Some progressives such as Gifford Pinchot worked to devise a national policy of conservation that would simultaneously conserve natural resources and allow their use in economic productivity.[6]

Other progressives such as the naturalist John Muir believed that mountains, streams, and forests should be preserved in their pristine state so that future genera-

---

[5] Lewis L. Gould, "Introduction," to *The Progressive Era,* p. 3.

[6] For an insightful and cogent treatment, see James Penick, Jr., "The Progressives and the Environment," in Lewis L. Gould, ed., *The Progressive Era,* pp. 115-31.

tions could be refreshed and renewed by nature. Still other progressives like the Cornell University professor Liberty Hyde Bailey saw conservation as a way of improving the quality of urban life and of restoring the integrity of rural life. With these mixed motives, the conservation movement had an impact on American education that took the following forms:

1. Informally, progressives sought to raise American popular consciousness about the need to conserve natural resources and to create an affirmative public response for conservation policies and an attitude that respected natural resources.
2. Schools began to include curricular units that emphasized conservation, environmental protection, reforestation, and other elements supportive of conservation.
3. Nature study and field trips to parks and woodlands became a popular activity not only in progressive but in many other schools as well.

We shall return to the theme of conservation in this chapter when we discuss the work of Liberty Hyde Bailey.

Progressive Politics and Policies

Progressives could be found in the two major political parties, the Republican and the Democratic. Theodore Roosevelt, a Republican and president from 1901 to 1909, personified moderate progressivism in national politics. During the Roosevelt administration, the Bureau of Corporations was established, the Northern Securities case was pursued, and government regulation of business proceeded. In 1906, the Pure Food and Drug Act was passed. Roosevelt's record in conservation was impressive because of the Reclamation Act of 1902. Woodrow Wilson, a Democrat, was president from 1913 to 1921. An academic, Wilson, a political scientist, had served as president of Princeton University before his entry into partisan politics. One of the new breed of academicians, Wilson's "New Freedom" sought to recast the ideals of Jeffersonian democracy to meet the changing conditions of a modern and industrialized society.

When the major parties appeared impervious to reforms, progressives organized third-party movements. In 1912, Theodore Roosevelt campaigned again for president on the "Bull Moose" Progressive ticket; in 1924, Robert M. LaFollette ran for president on the Progressive ticket. Both of these attempts to create a progressive "third force" failed. Progressives were also active in local and state politics as well as in national politics. Municipal reform, especially in the large cities, was a favorite cause of urban progressives.

Whether in national, state, or local politics, progressives sought reforms to reduce bossism, patronage, and corruption and to open the processes to a more participatory citizen action. They wanted to regulate the processes of industrialism, urbanization, and immigration and make them proceed along constitutional and democratic paths. Not a revolutionary movement, many progressives saw their work as designed to restore honesty and efficiency in government. To open the political processes, they supported the direct election of United States senators, the referendum, the initiative, and the recall. In economics, they endorsed legislation to regulate big business by curbing trusts and monopolies. In education, progressives supported state and national legislation to regulate and minimize child labor. To be effective, compulsory school attendance laws required correlated laws restricting child labor. Once children were eliminated from the work force, there was a greater chance that they would attend school. By 1900, twenty-eight states had enacted laws to regulate and restrict child labor and to improve health and safety conditions for child laborers.

Progressivism's Intellectual Origins

Progressivism's origins coincided with the erosion of the Social Darwinist ideology that had dominated business practices and sociological and educational thought in post-Civil War America. At the same time that Social Darwinism lost its vitality, late nineteenth-century America was experiencing manifestations of discontent with the status quo. For example, in *Progress and Poverty* (1879), Henry George condemned the growing concentration of wealth into fewer hands while poverty victimized larger numbers of Americans. Organizing the Social Gospel movement, reform-minded Protestants asserted that Christians, in the name of social justice, should ameliorate the conditions of the poor. Just as progressive theorists rejected Social Darwinism, reformist Protestant ministers rejected those aspects of the Puritan ethic that saw poverty as a punishment for sin and indolence.

Academic Reformers

In higher education, the Social Darwinism of Spencer and his American disciple, William Graham Sumner, was challenged by a new generation of academics who taught that expert knowledge could be applied scientifically to secure social, economic, and educational reforms. In the 1890s, laissez-faire economic theory was challenged by university scholars who had done their graduate work either in German research universities or in American institutions such as Johns Hopkins and the University of Chicago, which had been patterned after them. In philosophy, John Dewey, trained originally in Hegelian idealism, developed his own version of pragmatism, called instrumentalism, which asserted that the consequences of practice was the true test of ideas. Dewey, who did not restrict his inquiries to academic philosophy, also wrote widely on educational themes. In *Democracy and Education* and in *School and Society*, he argued that education was not only derived from and perpetuated the cultural heritage but was a social process that carried possibilities for larger societal reforms. Dewey's instrumentalism was a stimulus to educators such as William Heard Kilpatrick, George Counts, Harold Rugg, and others who became leaders in progressive education. Like Dewey, William James, psychologist and philosopher, epitomized the progressive academic orientation to relevance and relativism. Rejecting absolute categories of truth and value, James projected an open universe of tentative hypotheses and changing values. For James, the test of ideas was their workability—their consequences—for satisfying human needs and resolving human problems. Truth and values, in James's world view, derived from the push-and-pull of historical forces and were subject to reshaping and reformulation by social processes.

Historians such as Frederick Jackson Turner, Charles A. Beard, and Carl L. Becker threw off not only the Social Darwinist perspective but also the historicism of the German scholar Von Ranke, who called for a completely objective accounting of the past. Progressive historians, believing that each generation created its own interpretation of the past according to present concerns and problems, wrote that history was relevant and relative to social, political, economic, and educational problems. For them, history was an instrument to generate solutions to present problems.[7]

The academic social reformers associated with progressivism made the expert knowledge generated by their research available to solve social problems. Reform-minded politicians enlisted the expert opinion of these scholars in drafting legislation to redress social, political, economic, and educational ills. These academic experts provided the masses of data that served as evidence to accomplish the objectives identified in progressivism's agenda.

THE PROGRESSIVE MOVEMENT IN AMERICAN EDUCATION

The progressive movement in American education remains a controversial episode from both an historical and a pedagogical perspective.[8] As a movement, it has been enthusiastically acclaimed by its advocates and severely criticized by its detractors. As is true of many other educational movements, it has been subjected to gross stereotyping and has been the object of both partisan defense and attack. The commentary that follows traces the course of progressive education through four major chronological phases: (1) the genesis period of progressive education, from 1900 to 1919, when it was part of a general climate of opinion that sought to reform American political, economic, and educational institutions and processes; (2) the period from 1919 to 1930, when progressive education was dominated by child-centered educators associated with private schools who pioneered educational innovation and experimentation; (3) the tumultuous era of the Great Depression and World War II, from 1930 to 1945, during which an internal ideological conflict arose between child-centered educators and social reconstructionists; and (4) the 1950s, which saw major critics charging that progressive education, by then identi-

---

[7] Richard Hofstadter, *The Progressive Historians* (New York: Knopf, 1968).

[8] Although much has been written on progressive education, the definitive work is Lawrence A. Cremin, *The Transformation of the School: Progressivism in American Education, 1876-1957* (New York: Knopf, 1962). The chronology used in organizing this section is adapted from Cremin. For the Progressive Education Association, the definitive work is Patricia Albjerg Graham, *Progressive Education: From Arcady to Academe—A History of the Progressive Education Association, 1919-1955.* (New York: Teachers College Press, Columbia University, 1967).

fied with life-adjustment education, had contributed to the decline of educational standards in the United States. As we shall see, progressive education was really an umbrella movement that united a number of individuals who were opposed to traditionalism, but were unable to develop a comprehensive and coherent educational philosophy. Nevertheless, progressive education produced profound changes in American educational institutions and processes.

During its first phase, from 1900 to 1919, the progressive education movement was part of the general mood of national reform that was expressed in journalism, politics, economics, and religion. Leading figures such as Jane Addams, John Dewey, and Robert LaFollette embraced philosophies and programs that called for educational reform as a part of the general reform of national life. However, let us first examine the patterns of traditional education that the progressives were challenging.

Traditional education can best be seen in the educational philosophy of William Torrey Harris (1835-1909). At the turn of the century, Harris was the elder statesman of American education. Having gained fame as the superintendent of schools in St. Louis, Harris served as the United States commissioner of education from 1889 to 1906. Although he might be identified as a forerunner of the administrative expert, Harris represented traditional educational values and defended the socioeconomic status quo. As the superintendent of St. Louis schools, he had created a model of businesslike efficiency in the administration of a large urban school system.[9] He had standardized administrative procedures, emphasized efficiency, and introduced uniformity. In adapting corporate structure to school organization, Harris was acclaimed for his classification and grouping of students, uniform textbook adoptions, close supervision of instruction, and collection and maintenance of educational statistics. In curricular matters, Harris stressed order, discipline, and work rather than play, and effort rather than interest. For Harris and those who imitated him, the major function of organized education was conservative in that it was to preserve the cultural heritage by transmitting it to the young. Although some administrative progressives might admire Harris's efficiency, curricular progressives rejected his lock-step uniformity and "stand-pat" administrative style.

On the eve of the progressive movement in education, the outlines of American schooling stood in clear relief. In their movement toward organizational maturity, urban public schools had grown excessively formal, routine, and bureaucratic. They generally preserved the status quo and resisted change. Throughout the United States, especially in the rural areas, teachers in thousands of small one-room schoolhouses were still emphasizing memorization, drill, rote learning, recitation, and moral values drawn from the McGuffey readers.

Although the high school had replaced the academy as the dominant institution of American secondary education, most high school students came from the upper social classes. The majority of immigrant children left school as soon as they

---

[9] Selwyn K. Troen, *The Public and the Schools: Shaping the St. Louis System, 1838-1920* (Columbia: University of Missouri Press, 1975).

could, which was usually upon completion of the eighth grade or earlier if permitted by state law. In the Southern and border states, a dual school system
existed, based upon racial segregation sanctioned by law.

It was against this structure of traditional schooling that educational progressivism arose. Like progressivism in politics, the initial progressive forays against
traditionalism were made by journalists writing for newspapers and popular magazines, not for professional education journals.

JOURNALISTIC CRITICS OF TRADITIONAL SCHOOLING

A phenomenon of the progressive era was the journalists who, by their investigative
reporting, served as catalysts of informal education. They investigated and wrote
about slum conditions, unsafe working conditions, child labor, corrupt politicans,
and inadequate schools. The proliferation of inexpensive magazines provided
investigative "muckraking" journalists with a national forum for their articles.
These journalists raised the public consciousness about the evil of corrupt conditions and stimulated a public mood that cried out for reform.

Like Upton Sinclair and Ida Tarbell who wrote muckraking exposés about
corruption in industry and government, education had its equivalent in the investigative reporting of Joseph Mayer Rice (1857-1934), a New York pediatrician who
had studied psychology and pedagogy at the German universities of Leipzig and
Jena. As a progressive commentator, Rice displayed the general tendencies of other
progressive educators. For example, he believed that schools, like other institutions,
needed to be reformed if they were to play a vital role in regenerating American
life. He also believed that scientific principles and methods could be used to create
a science of education that would make schooling an efficient process of learning.[10]

In 1892, Rice was commissioned by Walter Hines Page (1855-1918), a leading
journalist, editor, and later diplomat, to write a series of investigative reports for
Page's *Forum* magazine. Before dealing with Rice's series, let us look briefly at
Page's special interest in progressive reform, including educational reform, which
will explain the climate of reformist opinion that existed in the first decade of the
progressive era. Prior to taking control of the *Forum* in 1891, Page, who had
studied at the new research university of Johns Hopkins, worked on staff of *The
New York World*. He later would be editor of *The Atlantic Monthly* and *The
World's Work*. In his political persuasion, Page, like Woodrow Wilson, believed that
Jeffersonian democracy should serve as the ideological base for reforming modern
American life.[11] Taking a broad view of American reform that encompassed educa-

---

[10] For Rice's views on education, see Joseph M. Rice, *The Public School System of the
United States* (New York: Century, 1893); *The Rational Spelling Book* (New York: American
Book Co., 1898); *Scientific Management in Education* (New York: Publisher's Printing Co.,
1913); *The People's Government* (Philadelphia: Winston, 1915).

[11] For Page's views on progressive reform, see Walter Hines Page, *The Rebuilding of Old
Commonwealths* (New York: Doubleday, 1902); *A Publisher's Confessions* (New York:
Doubleday, 1905); *The Southerner* (New York: Doubleday, 1909).

tion, Page believed that: (1) scientific principles could be applied to agriculture, industry, and education; (2) popular education was a necessary base for an effective political and social democracy; and (3) progressive journalism could both stimulate and inform reform policy and legislation. It was the complementary frame of reference that united the progressive editor, Page, and the progressive journalist, Rice, to undertake an investigative report on the state of American schools.

In January 1892, Rice conducted his investigation by visiting the schools of thirty-six cities and interviewing their administrators, teachers, and parents. From October to June 1982, Rice's *Forum* articles on education appeared and presented the public with the following conclusions:

1. School systems, especially in the large cities, were often controlled by politicians who made key administrative appointments as part of an informal system of political patronage.
2. Instruction, generally dull, routine, and mindless, was characterized by drill, memorization, and rote.
3. Some rare examples of effective schooling were identified as models for educational reform; for example, the enriched curriculum of the Minneapolis schools contained elements conducive to multicultural education; the Indianapolis schools had been separated from political control; Francis Parker's Cook County Normal School had progressively integrated nature study and social activities into the curriculum.[12]

Rice's articles, with the help of Page, reached a wide popular audience and stimulated an attitude conducive to educational reform. It should be noted that the impetus for educational reform first came from outside of the school establishment and then gradually had an impact on the schools. Beyond their immediate impact, Rice's *Forum* articles revealed a number of progressive attitudes in their early stages. For example, (1) educational reform was viewed as part of, and necessary to, the general reform of American life and institutions; (2) the reforming impulse was moderate in tone and texture in that it sought to regenerate existing institutions—in this case schools—rather than bring about radical alterations; (3) a relationship was seen between corrupt politicians and ineffective schools; (4) there was a preconception that the principles of scientific management could be applied to schools as a remedy for political interference by inexpert politicians; (5) successful models of reformed school systems were recommended as springboards for imitative educational reformation; (6) an enriched and liberating curriculum—in terms of social needs and children's interests—was recommended as an alternative to the prevailing instructional routines.

In addition to journalists such as Rice, the spirit of generalized progressive reform was also advanced by influential people such as Jane Addams. Although primarily known for her social settlement work, Addams's interests also embraced political, social, and educational reform.

[12] Lawrence A. Cremin, *The Transformation of the School: Progressivism in American Education, 1876-1957* (New York: Knopf, 1962), pp. 3-7.

JANE ADDAMS
AND THE SETTLEMENT HOUSE MOVEMENT

In the early stage of the progressive era, reform-minded educators, politicians, community leaders, and social workers cooperated in a loose coalition. Although there were different foci of their efforts, they embraced the general mood of reform that characterized progressivism until the U.S. entry into World War I. One of the foremost leaders of reform in this era was Jane Addams (1860-1935), a pioneer social worker who founded Hull House, a settlement house on Chicago's West Side.

Born in the small northern Illinois town of Cedarville, Laura Jane Addams was the daughter of John Addams, a community leader and Republican member of the state legislature.[13] In 1877, she began her studies at Rockford Seminary for Girls, a conservative institution that stressed Protestant ethical values and religious discipline. As a student, she followed the traditional curriculum, enrolling in Latin, Greek, natural science, ancient history, English composition and literature, mental and moral philosophy, French, and mathematics.[14] In 1881, she received her bachelor's degree from Rockford Seminary.

A turning point in Jane Addams's life occurred in 1887 while she was touring in Europe. Visits to London's East End exposed her to sights of urban poverty and despair; she also attended meetings of the striking London matchgirls. Moved to aid the poor, she became involved in Toynbee Hall, a settlement house organized by a group of Oxford intellectuals who were inspired by the philosophies of Ruskin and Tolstoy. Returning to the United States, she founded Chicago's Hull House in 1889, with the collaboration of her long-standing friend, Ellen Gates Starr.

Addams envisioned Hull House as a social and educational center for the impoverished immigrant population living on Chicago's West Side, which included large numbers of Germans, Italians, Irish, Bohemians, and Eastern European Jews. Addams established classes and programs designed to ease the transition of these immigrants, many of whom had come from rural Europe, to live in one of America's rapidly growing cities. Not only did she seek to ease the cultural shock of a strange land and language, but she also sought to encourage their social and economic integration into the new society.

America's growing cities, especially those of the North, were experiencing severe labor unrest and social upheaval as a result of the major technological changes produced by a surging industrialism. The economic panics of the 1880s and 1890s produced unemployment and unrest such as the Haymarket Riot of 1886 and the Pullman Strike of 1894. The influx of immigrants into the growing but unplanned cities produced a sprawl of tenements. Inadequate sanitation facilities, water supplies, and health care services led to the typhoid epidemic of 1895.

Addams's experiences at Hull House convinced her that the settlement house could not be isolated from the political and economic crosscurrents of the day.

---

[13] Jane Addams, *Twenty Years at Hull House* (New York: Macmillan, 1911), p. 7.

[14] James W. Linn, *Jane Addams: A Biography* (New York: Appleton-Century, 1935), p. 65.

Like other progressive reformers, she believed that general reform required the removal of corrupt politicians from office. Organizing the Nineteenth Ward Improvement Association to put pressure on local politicians to improve service, Addams was appointed "garbage inspector" of her ward. Active in the pursuit of educational reform, she served as a member of the Chicago Board of Education from 1905 to 1909.

Hull House

Under Jane Addams's leadership, Hull House offered a variety of educational programs, social activities, and recreational experiences, ranging from a public kitchen and coffee house to art exhibits and musical and dramatic performances.

The first organized activity at Hull House, a weekly reading group conducted by Ellen Starr, was an effort to bring people together for literary appreciation and socialization. It developed into a number of social clubs designed to meet the differing needs of the settlement house's clients.

As Hull House attracted more people, other facilities were added, such as an art gallery, a music hall and music school, and a theater. Classes in arts and crafts, Sunday concerts and recitals, lectures and exhibitions became regular features of the Hull House program.

Addams was particularly interested in the educational and social needs of children and youth in the improverished tenement area that Hull House served. Because of their parents' long working hours, many youngsters were either locked in their tenement rooms or allowed to roam the noisy, dirty, and dangerous streets. To alleviate their conditions, a nursery school and kindergarten became part of the Hull House complex.

Addams's Social and Educational Philosophy

While Jane Addams was foremost a practitioner of social reform, she also developed a social and educational philosophy that had evolved from her actual experiences as a self-educated social worker. Her philosophy of *socialized education* shows her to be a progressive who thought about reform in broad and general terms.

For Jane Addams, education was not restricted to schooling but encompassed a range of institutions, agencies, and processes. Addams's views of formal education (schooling) and informal education (the total learning environment) were reciprocal rather than exclusionary. The city was a comprehensive but undifferentiated environment of immense learning potentiality; the school was therefore not to be isolated by its four walls but was to be involved in the city's social, economic, and political life. As inhabitants of a rapidly changing society, children and youth—Addams believed—needed to understand the complexity and pervasiveness of the industrial order. For Addams, socialized education should include:

1. practical experiences and activities related to industrial training and home economics;

2. an historical examination of the development of industry and the role that labor played in that development; and
3. the development and exercise of aesthetic values in the creating of industrial products.

Jane Addams as Author

Throughout her life, Jane Addams, a prolific author, described the socio-political conditions in Chicago during the early progressive era. She lectured extensively to raise money for Hull House. Possessing the progressive inclination for journalism, she wrote articles for such popular magazines as *The Atlantic Monthly* and *The Ladies' Home Journal.*

In *Democracy and Social Ethics* (1902), Addams asserted her general social and educational philosophy. Stressing human interdependency, she argued for an education that emphasized both the essential worth of every individual and the need to develop strategies of associated group effort to achieve societal reform. In discussing educational methods, Addams asserted that every person had the right to have his or her full powers "freed" by education, and that society would lose if any citizen was not educated to the degree that his or her moral power was available for progressive social change.

In 1907, Jane Addams's *Newer Ideals of Peace* examined the deleterious effects of militarism on social life by contrasting the industriousness of the modern city with the fortresslike isolation of a military camp's feudal town. *Newer Ideals of Peace* presented her views on child welfare and women's rights as well as on militarism. In contrast to the military training imposed on youth in the old society, an "enlightened state" would provide "training in relation to industry" and would facilitate it by "uniform compulsory education laws in connection with uniform child labor legislation."[15] In the same volume, Addams also argued for suffrage and increased opportunities for women's participation in political life.

In calling the city an extended family with "enlarged housekeeping," she argued that "city housekeeping," or governance, had failed because women, "the traditional housekeepers, have not been consulted as to its multiform activities." She continued:

> Logically, the electorate should be made up of those who have at least tried to care for children, to clean houses, to prepare foods, to isolate the family from moral dangers, those who have traditionally taken care of that side of life which inevitably becomes the subject of municipal consideration and control.[16]

In *The Spirit of Youth and the City Streets* (1909), a collection of case histories, Addams dealt with the problem of juvenile delinquency in a large industrial city.[17]

---

[15] Jane Addams, *Newer Ideals of Peace* (New York: Macmillan, 1907), pp. 156-57.

[16] Ibid., p. 114.

[17] New York: Macmillan, 1909.

Her basic premise was that the problems of juvenile crime, alcoholism, and drug addiction that were so common in large cities such as Chicago were caused not only by a lack of educational opportunity, but also by a lack of organized recreational opportunities for youth. As a result, young people, suffering from constant drudgery, take to the city streets to find their amusement, which often leads to delinquency. They do not have either the maturity or the education to make sound judgments, and therefore they are easily led into criminal activity.

In *The Long Road of Woman's Memory*, published in 1916, Jane Addams sought to show that all women, whether rich or poor, native-born or immigrant, were sisters-in-spirit. Using historical examples, Addams sought to show that the changing roles of women in society, both in the United States and worldwide, are universal and that the immigrant women in Chicago's tenements have much in common with women everywhere. Outlining the duties of women toward their families, society, and themselves, she argued that women best fulfill themselves by becoming active in the democratic process.

In a complex industrial society, it is insufficient for a woman to devote herself only to caring for her immediate family; to care properly for a family in the city, women had to become involved with civic responsibilities as well. As society became more complicated, it was necessary for women to extend their "sense of responsibility to many things outside her own home."[18]

Believing educational reform to be closely related to social reform, Addams developed a broad conception of social work. Her concept of socialized education stressed the progressive impulse in education. Like John Dewey, Addams believed that all group learning had a social impact on its participants. Wishing to ameliorate the depersonalizing effects of industrial society, she argued that children and youth should study industrial society and industrial processes in order to develop a more humane outlook.

THE CONSERVATION MOVEMENT, AGRICULTURAL EDUCATION, AND NATURE STUDY

As indicated earlier, the conservation of natural resources such as minerals, forests, and soils was an important aspect of the progressive era. Related to conservation of natural resources was a desire to regenerate American rural life by revitalizing country schools and community institutions. Once again, the progressives believed that the application of scientific principles, expressed in a science of agriculture, would make agricultural life and production efficient and effective.

The progressive proclivity for conservation of natural resources and the regeneration of rural life was demonstrated in President Theodore Roosevelt's public pronouncements and policies. Harboring a romanticized view of the American West, Roosevelt wanted to both conserve and preserve the nation's

---

[18] *The Long Road of Woman's Memory* (New York: Macmillan, 1916), pp. 101-4.

resources. In actual policy formulation, these views were not always complementary and stirred up considerable tension and debate. For example, Gifford
Pinchot, Roosevelt's chief conservation adviser and head of the Division of
Forestry, believed that the timber resources of national forests could be conserved
by applying scientific management principles; these involved selective planting and
harvesting—often under the aegis of a corps of forestry experts. In contrast, John
Muir, acclaimed as America's leading naturalist, saw the national forests as a
national legacy to be preserved in their pristine and primitive condition.

Not only did Theodore Roosevelt encourage conservation, he also supported
the study and regeneration of America's farms and rural communities. While the
large cities grew in an unplanned and chaotic manner, the nation's rural sections
were experiencing decay as rural youth left in increasing numbers for the promise
of the city. Roosevelt demonstrated his desire to reform and regenerate rural life
by appointing the National Commission on Country Life.[19]

Liberty Hyde Bailey

In education, the various impulses of resource conservation, rural renewal,
and the application of scientific principles to agriculture were best expressed in the
career and work of Liberty Hyde Bailey (1858-1954).[20]

Bailey, a professor of horticulture and dean of the College of Agriculture at
Cornell University, was a pioneer in the emerging field of scientific agriculture. At
Cornell, where he organized the Agricultural College, he engaged in research on
hybridization and developed a terminology for horticulture. Not only concerned
with developing an agricultural science for application to farming, Bailey also
wanted to generate an educated awareness among the general population about the
relationships between nature, science, and agriculture.[21] Like other progressives,
he was concerned about rural decline and the exodus to the large cities. To achieve
these educational goals, Bailey encouraged the Nature Study Movement, which
involved the preparation of teachers and the design of curricular materials on nature
and agriculture.[22]

Bailey reflected the progressive attitude that scientific research could serve
broad social and economic as well as political reform. He believed that he could

[19] For the work of the National Commission on Country Life, see the *Report of the Country Life Commission,* Senate Document No. 705, 60th Congress, 2nd session, Washington, D.C., 1909.

[20] For biographies of Bailey, see Andrew D. Rodgers, *Liberty Hyde Bailey* (Princeton, N.J.: Princeton University Press, 1949); and Philip Dorf, *Liberty Hyde Bailey* (Ithaca, N. Y.: Cornell University Press, 1956).

[21] For Bailey's ideas on agricultural science, nature study, and related areas, see Liberty Hyde Bailey, *The State and the Farmer* (New York: Macmillan, 1909); *The Holy Earth* (New York: Scribners, 1915); *Wind and Weather* (New York: Macmillan, 1916); *What Is Democracy?* (Ithaca, N.Y.: Comstock, 1918); *Universal Service: The Hope of Humanity* (New York: Sturgis and Walton, 1918).

[22] Liberty H. Bailey, *The Nature-Study Idea: Being an Interpretation of the New School Movement to Put the Child in Sympathy with Nature* (New York: Macmillan, 1903).

develop a theoretical framework in agriculture and horticulture that could be applied to scientific farming, to popular education, and to the regeneration of America's rural life. An energetic researcher, Bailey led horticultural expeditions to the Amazon rain forests and to the Caribbean islands, while also remaining active in progressive political causes. As a recognized national authority in agriculture, President Theodore Roosevelt named Bailey to chair the Country Life Commission, which sought to improve rural life.

In its report, the Country Life Commission included the following recommendations for education:

1. Schooling should relate as directly as possible to the actual conditions of agricultural life and work.
2. Agricultural education should be based on the immediate needs of the farm, the farm family, and the rural community.
3. The development of agricultural education, extension courses, and programs was a national need.

These recommendations lent credibility to the efforts of farm leaders and agricultural interest groups lobbying for the passage of the Smith-Lever Act in 1914 that would give federal support to agricultural extension and home economics programs.

Bailey's efforts had a direct impact on rural education and an indirect impact on education generally. For example: agriculture entered the secondary curriculum of rural schools; teachers in rural areas received pre- and in-service preparation in agriculture; nature study entered the general curriculum in many schools; and textbooks incorporated materials on nature study. Bailey's advocacy of nature study was part of a continuum of pedagogical progressivism that had existed since the late eighteenth and early nineteenth centuries. Rousseau's *Emile* had idealized nature and peasant life as the basis of natural education; Pestalozzi and Fellenberg—in their educational experiments in Switzerland—stressed nature studies and farming; Francis Parker included nature studies and field trips as part of an activity-based curriculum.

ROBERT LAFOLLETTE AND THE WISCONSIN IDEA

One of the striking characteristics of the progressive era, especially in its early phase, was the close working relationship that developed between progressive political leaders and progressive educators. One of the most noteworthy examples, the *Wisconsin Idea*, which took place during Governor Robert M. LaFollette's administration, involved cooperation between the state executive and the president and faculty of the University of Wisconsin. The next section examines the assumptions of the Wisconsin Idea, identifies its key participants, and comments on its results and impact.

The Key Participants

Robert Marion LaFollette (1855-1925) had a long and distinguished career as a progressive political reformer both in Wisconsin and in national politics. He was governor of Wisconsin from 1901 to 1906, U.S. senator from 1905 to 1925, and the Progressive party candidate for president in 1924. To secure reform, LaFollette devised what became the standard progressive reformist political strategy: (1) identifying problems, particularly those involving collusion between business interests and politicians, and exposing them to the public; (2) after being elected on a reform platform, introducing legislation designed to remedy such problems; (3) using experts, often university professors, to research issues and to assist in establishing regulatory commissions to prevent the reoccurrence of the problem.

LaFollette's own career illustrates the temperament and reformist orientation of a political reformer who used educators as allies in the reform process.[23] In campaigning for governor in 1900, LaFollette's platform for political reform included: (1) ending the caucus system, which allowed political bosses to handpick candidates, and establishing the direct primary; (2) inaugurating tax reform to eliminate loopholes for special interests and create a more equitable system of assessment and a state income tax; (3) advancing legislation to control unfair pricing practices by railroads. To win election, LaFollette had to raise the consciousness of the voters and gain their support for reform. Because of the complexity of the issues, he also needed to enlist the support of experts. In the process, LaFollette established a unique set of relationships that bridged the gap between the general populace and the expert, frequently the university professor.

Charles R. Van Hise

In part, the success of the Wisconsin Idea depended upon the cooperation of the University of Wisconsin and its president, Charles R. Van Hise (1857-1918). A professor of metallurgy and geology, Van Hise was president of his alma mater from 1903 until 1918. Van Hise's major publications, *The Conservation of Natural Resources in the United States* (1910), *Concentration and Control: A Solution of the Trust Problem in the United States* (1912), and *Conservation and Regulation in the United States during the World War* (1917-1918), reveal the progressive concern for conservation of natural resources and the regulation of big business.[24] His presidency at the University of Wisconsin revealed two tendencies common to progressive educators: a commitment to extend educational services to larger segments of the population, and a willingness to enlist academic experts to study and to solve significant social, political, and economic problems. These two tendencies worked

---

[23] For a biography of LaFollette, see Belle Case and Fola LaFollette, *Robert M. LaFollette,* 2 vols. (New York: Macmillan, 1953).

[24] Charles Van Hise, *The Conservation of Natural Resources in the United States* (New York: Macmillan, 1910); *Concentration and Control: A Solution of the Trust Problem in the United States* (New York: Macmillan, (1912); *Conservation and Regulation in the United States during the World War,* 2 parts (Washington, D.C.: GPO, 1917-18).

to remove higher education from its ivory tower isolation and relocate it in the community, the marketplace, and legislative chamber.

As president of the University of Wisconsin, Van Hise identified the primary institutional mission as that of serving both students and citizens of the state. He developed and enlarged the basic research mission of the university so that expert knowledge could be applied to social and economic problems. He also pioneered in the university extension concept in which professors traveled to offer courses and serve as consultants throughout the state.

Richard Ely

The Wisconsin Idea's success depended not only on cooperation between the state's governor and university president, it also required faculty members who possessed recognized credentials in their field of expertise. Such a person was Richard Ely (1854-1943), director of the School of Economics, Political Science, and History at the University of Wisconsin. In his career as university professor, Ely became committed to reform causes during the progressive era.

Like many other professors, Ely, who received his bachelor of arts degree from Columbia University, also did advanced study at German research universities. He received his doctorate in economics from the University of Heidelberg and also studied at the universities of Halk, Geneva, and Berlin. He was a product of the German research concept that involved graduate students in original and specialized research under the direction of a professor who was a recognized authority. Upon returning to the United States, Ely was appointed in 1881 to the faculty of the newly-created Johns Hopkins University.

As a professor of political economy, Ely—like other academics who used their expertise for progressive reform—relied on two vehicles to establish his credentials: a record of scholarly publication that identified him as an expert, and participation in professional organizations in the emerging academic disciplines that contributed to policy formulation. For example, Ely's major works, *The Past and Present of Political Economy* (1884), *Outlines of Economics* (1893), *Studies in the Evolution of an Industrial Society* (1903), and *Property and Contract in Their Relation to the Distribution of Wealth* (1914), pointed to the uses of economics—as an academic discipline—to policy formulation. In addition to his publications, Ely was an active organizer of professional groups and associations that were vehicles of reformist attitudes and that served as agencies of expert opinion for reform causes. He was an important force in organizing the American Economic Association, which gave academic legitimacy to the new field of study; he helped to organize the Episcopal Church's Christian Social Union; he was the first president of the American Association for Labor Legislation and was a leading member of the American Association for Agricultural Legislation.

Although he would later break with LaFollette over the senator's isolationism and opposition to the entry of the United States into World War I, Ely was a firm ally of the governor in launching and sustaining the Wisconsin Idea. As an academic supporter of reform initiatives and regulation, Ely believed that: (1) the laissez-faire assumptions of Herbert Spencer's Social Darwinism should be rejected in economics; (2) government had a positive role to play as a regulator of the economy and as a conservator of natural resources; (3) economists should use the modern methods of science rather than rely on inherited philosophical conceptions; (4) economic principles were relative to time, place, and circumstance and were not grounded in metaphysical preconceptions.

JOHN DEWEY'S LABORATORY SCHOOL

Historians have identified John Dewey (1859-1952), one of America's leading pragmatist philosophers and educators, with progressivism in education. While friendly to progressivism both as a broad social and political movement and to the Progressive Education Association, Dewey, in *Experience and Education*, criticized progressives who were straying into a romantic cult of childhood and departing from education grounded in social experience. No friend of traditional schooling's routine, rote, and regimentation, Dewey advocated progressive schooling as a laboratory for testing new educational theories. Here we shall examine Dewey's Laboratory School at the University of Chicago as a pioneer example of the progressive school as a laboratory setting.

John Dewey came to Chicago in 1894, when he was offered a position by William R. Harper, president of the University of Chicago, as head of the Department of Philosophy, Psychology, and Pedagogy. Prior to accepting this position, Dewey, a graduate of the University of Vermont, had taught school in Oil City, Pennsylvania. He had received a doctorate in political science and philosophy from Johns Hopkins University in 1884. From 1884 to 1888 he had been an assistant professor of philosophy at the University of Minnesota, and a professor of philosophy at the University of Michigan from 1889 to 1894. When he left the University of Chicago in 1904, Dewey was appointed professor of philosophy at Columbia University.

Dewey's years in Chicago were significant for both his own development as a philosopher and for the impetus that he gave to progressivism in education. Philosophically, Dewey had rejected Hegelian idealism and was developing his own version of pragmatism, known as instrumentalism or experimentalism. Pedagogically, Dewey's work at the Laboratory School represented a major exploratory venture into the new version of schooling that progressives would proclaim in the twentieth century's early decades.[25]

From 1893 to 1903, Dewey sought to operationalize his educational ideas by putting them into actual school practice. To this end, the Laboratory School was to be (as its name indicates) a laboratory—a place to implement, test, verify, or reject

---

[25] Robert L. McCaul, "Dewey's Chicago," *The School Review,* 47 (Summer 1959): 269; and Harold B. Dunkel and Robert L. McCaul, "Dewey: 1859-1959," *The School Review,* 47 (Summer 1959): 123.

innovative practices. Dewey presented his conception of the progressive school in *The School and Society* (1899), writing that schools should be "embryonic" communities, active with the "occupations that reflect the life of the larger society and permeated throughout with the spirit of art, history, and science." Such schools were to be among the agencies that would create a "worthy, lovely, and harmonious" larger society; they were little communities that saturated children with the "spirit of science" and provided them the "instruments of effective self-direction."[26]

When it began operations in 1896, Dewey's school consisted of sixteen pupils and two teachers; by 1902, 140 children were attending, instructed by a staff of twenty-three teachers. Following Dewey's promise, instruction was viewed as the challenge of "bringing a child into intimate relations with concrete objects, positive facts, definitive ideas, and specific symbols" in a school environment that was an "embryonic society" and "miniature community."

Basing his curriculum for the Laboratory School on conceptions drawn from experimentalist philosophy and "organismic psychology," Dewey related instruction to stages of child growth and development. Further, instruction was centered in the group and in activities. The human group was, he believed, a rich source of social interaction and learning. Unlike the passivity of the conventional school, activities were rooted directly in children's instructive need for making and doing.

In Dewey's first stage, children of ages four to eight followed their personal and social interests in play, games, occupations, industrial arts, stories, and discussion. During the second stage, children from eight to eleven or twelve years were involved in explorations of American history, metallurgy, physics, natural and physical science, and in the symbolic learning of reading, calculating, and composing. The third stage, which involved children from ages twelve through fourteen, emphasized the various arts and sciences as human instruments for achieving human progress.[27]

Since instruction in Dewey's Laboratory School emphasized the social nature of learning, the school's basic unit of organization was the small group. The four- and five-year-olds were organized into groups for field trips, nature study excursions, and construction activities. The six-year-olds studied the relationship of climate, soil, and topography to food production by activities that ranged from studying the climatic regions of the earth to preparing meals in the school's kitchen. The seven-year-old group learned about technology by applying the scientific method to the smelting of ores. They also extended their horizons in space (geography) and time (history) by studying the development of human occupations.

The group of eight-year-old children moved into the more disciplinary study of history and science as they examined the trading and maritime pursuits of the Mediterranean peoples. The nine-year-olds were involved as a group in the inte-

[26] John Dewey, *The School and Society* (Chicago: University of Chicago Press, 1974), p. 16.

[27] John Dewey, *School and Society,* pp. 105-15. Also, see Katherine Camp Mayhew and Anna Camp Edwards, *The Dewey School* (New York: Atherton, 1966), for an account written by two members of the Laboratory School staff.

grated study of history, geography, literature, and foreign languages. Beginning with their own state of Illinois, they extended their investigations to the United States. The ten-year-old group compared life in the New England and Southern colonies. In relationship to the colonial period, they examined the development of human activities and industries for the production of food and clothing.

The eleven-year-olds studied different approaches to history and science. They examined English village life and then studied the effects of European colonialism on India's social, political, and economic life. They were introduced to elements of physics, physiology, and mathematics.

Twelve-year-olds continued their work in science, geography, and history. Members of this group were active in school assemblies, the newspaper, and club activities. Thirteen-year-olds studied the process by which social and political life was conditioned by, and organized around, industrial life. Students aged fourteen and fifteen were engaged in a more structured disciplinary study of history, physics, algebra, geometry, and foreign languages.

The various subjects were pursued in an integrated rather than discrete fashion. More specific disciplinary study was pursued by the older students. The entire curriculum emphasized concomitant learning, in which a student learns other matters in addition to the primary focus of the problem or activity.

CHILD-CENTERED PROGRESSIVISM

The second phase of the progressive movement in education took place from 1919 to 1930, when the United States moved from World War I, through the prosperity of the 1920s, to the Great Depression of the 1930s. During this decade, progressive education became detached from the earlier mood of generalized social reform and focused on the child-centered school. Progressivism in education at this time emphasized children's freedom, the expressive arts, and Freudian psychoanalytical theory.

In 1919 the Progressive Education Association was organized under the leadership of Stanwood Cobb. During the 1920s, the major voices in the association were those of educators who were involved in private experimental schools. Although the Progressive Education Association never formally adopted a comprehensive philosophy of education, it did assert that "the aim of Progressive Education is the freest and fullest development of the individual, based upon the scientific study of his mental, physical, and social characteristics and needs."[28] The association also stated seven guiding principles: (1) Children should be left free to develop naturally. (2) Interest is the motive of all work. (3) The teacher is a guide to learning and not a taskmaster. (4) Pupil development should be studied scientifi-

---

[28] The statement of the aims and principles of the Progressive Education Association appeared on the inside cover of *Progressive Education,* 1 (1924), and reappeared on subsequent issues until 1929.

cally. (5) Greater attention should be given to everything that affects the child's physical development. (6) There should be greater cooperation between the school and the home. And (7), the progressive school should be an educational laboratory. The Progressive Education Association also sponsored the publication of a journal, *Progressive Education*, which carried its ideology throughout the country.

Progressive Education

Progressive Education, published from 1924 to 1955, represented the climate of opinion within the association and the educational attitudes of its more articulate members. It provided information on new schools that were bringing about curricular innovations. For example, the 1925 anniversary issue was a veritable catalogue of the major experimental schools of the day. Among the schools described were Margaret Naumberg's Walden School in New York, Abigail Eliot's Ruggles Street Nursery School in Boston, the nursery schools of the Bureau of Experiments in New York, the Merrill-Palmer School in Detroit, and the Lincoln School at Teachers College.

Since the Progressive Education Association was an umbrella organization for like-minded educators, it never developed a systematic or coherent philosophy. While *Progressive Education* reflected the association's philosophical ambiguity, it did publicize developments that were at the cutting edge of educational thought and practice. For example, during the early 1930s, articles, especially by Lois Meek, examined parent education as a part of early childhood education. Meek described strategies for preparing parents on early child education. Meek described a number of ways of advising parents about how to raise and educate their children, suggesting nursery school study and observation groups, family clinics, and family consultation bureaus.[29]

After the early 1930s, *Progressive Education* revealed the growing ideological and pedagogical tensions between the child-centered and the social reconstructionist wings of the association. In particular, George S. Counts's address "Dare Progressive Education Be Progressive?" set the stage for the wide-ranging controversy between the child-centered and social reconstructionist camps that raged during the Depression era of the 1930s.

During the 1940s, World War II stimulated the journal's contributors to examine the theme of "education for democracy." However, the association's Committee on Philosophy provided what came closest to being a philosophical statement for the association when it stated that "the child is at all times a unity" and "a unique, dynamic living organism," that each individual grows "through functional activity," and that "feeling or emotion accompanies all conscious human experience."[30]

[29] For example, see Lois Meek, "The Pre-School Movement," *Progressive Education*, 6 (1929); and "Individual Guidance for Parents," *Progressive Education*, 10 (1933).

[30] "A Brief Report of the Committee on Philosophy," *Progressive Education,* 18, no. 5 (1941).

Kilpatrick and the Project Method

The career of William Heard Kilpatrick (1871-1965) illustrates the development of progressive education in several ways: It reveals the development of a practitioner who first rebelled against traditional schooling's bookishness and rote methods and then developed a theoretical rationale for that rebellion. It illustrates a concerted effort to translate Dewey's pragmatic instrumentalist philosophy into an instructional methodology. Finally, it shows the transition of progressivism from child-centered schooling into a body of doctrine that found its way into teacher education programs.

Kilpatrick, son of a Southern Baptist minister, was born in White Plains, Georgia. He had an orthodox religious upbringing, which he would later abandon for pragmatism's promise of an open rather than closed universe. A product of rural America, Kilpatrick would seek to reconstruct small-town community values and adapt them to a society that was becoming increasingly urban and technological.

Kilpatrick, who attended Mercer University, a Baptist institution, received his bachelor of arts degree in 1891 and then studied for a year at Johns Hopkins University. Returning to Georgia, he taught algebra and geometry in the town of Blakely for three years; he later taught school in Savannah and Columbus.[31]

Francis W. Parker, pioneer progressive educator. *(From frontispiece of Francis W. Parker, Notes of Talks on Teaching. New York: E.L. Kellogg & Co., 1891.)*

[31] For a biographical study, see Samuel Tenenbaum, *William Heard Kilpatrick: Trail Blazer in Education* (New York: Harper & Row, Pub., 1951.)

As a classroom teacher and part-time principal, Kilpatrick revealed his anti-traditional propensities. Although he had not yet formulated a philsophical rationale, he inaugurated a series of innovations. He rejected report cards and grades as external rewards that were disconnected from internal motivation and the natural consequences of learning. Such external rewards, he felt, encouraged a sense of superiority in some students and inferiority in others. He also advocated group projects to cultivate a sense of cooperation and community in students.

Eager to supplement his own educational background, Kilpatrick attended teacher's institutes. At one institute, he heard a presentation by Francis W. Parker, the pioneer progressive, which confirmed his child-centered inclination. In 1898, he attended John Dewey's lectures at the University of Chicago, which introduced him to instrumentalism. In 1907 he went to Teachers College, Columbia University, where he again studied with Dewey. Remaining at Teachers College, he received his doctorate and was then appointed to its faculty as a professor of philosophy of education. His popular lectures, which attracted thousands of students, enabled him to render Dewey's instrumentalism into a set of pedagogical and methodological principles known as the *project method.*[32]

Kilpatrick's elaboration of the project method followed the typical progressive pattern in that it: (1) rejected traditional school practices; (2) introduced methodological innovations emphasizing the child's interests and needs, group activities, and concomitant learning; (3) evolved into a social theory for revitalizing a sense of community through educational reforms carried out by the schools.

Like other educational innovators and "reformers" before him, such as Rousseau, Pestalozzi, and Parker, Kilpatrick challenged the historical conception of education that saw learning structured around books. Kilpatrick, in particular, rejected the bookish practices of teachers who slavishly organized instruction around the indirect and second-hand information found in textbooks. Too often, Kilpatrick argued, students who succeeded in school did so not out of comprehension but rather out of their ability to memorize and give back information to teachers. When schooling was based on textbooks, it degenerated into a set of mindless routines in which teachers assigned lessons from textbooks, drilled their students on the assignments, heard recitations of memorized responses, and then tested their ability to follow predigested formulas. Such bookish routines not only left untapped the child's creativity but militated against using the scientific method in problem solving.

As a methodological innovation, Kilpatrick's project method united Dewey's "complete act of thought," or problem solving according to the scientific method, with the learners' purposeful efforts in planning, directing, and executing their work by solving problems arising in their own individual and group experience. In uniting thought and action, the project method would provide teachers with a usable way to instill the scientific method and cultivate a sense of community in their students.

---

[32]William Heard Kilpatrick, *The Project Method* (New York: Teachers College Press, Columbia University, 1921).

Kilpatrick identified four types of projects that enlisted the purposeful activities of learners. Type I involved rendering a concept, idea, or plan into external concrete form. For example, students might design and build a boat or write a script for a play and then present it. In Type II, the purpose was to enjoy an aesthetic experience such as listening to music or viewing a painting. Type III involved solving an intellectual problem. Type IV involved acquiring a specific skill such as typing, writing, or swimming. In carrying out the projects, particularly those of Types I and IV, students were to: (1) identify and develop their purposes, (2) plan the steps or actions needed to achieve their purposes, (3) execute or implement their plans by acting on them, and (4) judge or appraise the results of their action.

Kilpatrick's project method was not only a reaction against traditional schooling and a methodology of instruction, it was also the educational embodiment of a social theory designed to foster a democratic sense of community.

Harold Ordway Rugg

Harold Rugg's career illustrates the transition that some progressive educators experienced as they moved from a child-centered perspective to a social reconstructionist orientation.[33] The transformation in Rugg's progressivism is revealed by his career and major publications.

Harold Rugg (1886-1960) was awarded his doctorate from the University of Illinois in 1915, where he had specialized in education and sociology under the direction of William C. Bagley. In 1917, his *Statistical Methods Applied to Education* argued for the use of statistical and empirical research as the basis for the scientific study of schooling.[34] In 1919, Rugg joined the faculty of Columbia University's Teachers College. Here, he wrote his social science pamphlet series that initially was widely used in the schools but was dropped when it became controversial because of its ideological orientation. Rugg's *The Child-Centered School,* published with Ann Schumaker in 1928, was a clear statement of his child-centered progressivism.[35]

The Philosophy of the Child-Centered School.   The concept of the child-centered school was not unique to Rugg; it had been evolving through the earlier efforts of the great European educational reformers, Rousseau, Pestalozzi, Owen, and Froebel. In the United States, the child-centered concept gained renewed impetus through the work of Francis Parker, G. Stanley Hall, and John Dewey. Rugg's endorsement of the child-centered philosophy of education was part of a continuum that reached a high point among the progressive educators during the 1920s.

[33] A very useful work on Rugg is Peter Carbone, Jr., *The Social and Educational Thought of Harold Rugg* (Durham, N.C.: Duke University Press, 1977).

[34] Ibid., pp. 8-10.

[35] Harold Rugg and Ann Schumaker, *The Child-Centered School* (New York: World Book Co., 1928), p. 23.

Rugg's metamorphasis from child-centered to social reconstructionist progressive was demonstrated in his *Culture and Education in America* (1931), which argued that the school could be a conscious agency of social reform.[36] In *The Great Technology* (1933), Rugg examined industrial civilization, arguing that human creativity could be liberated as the scientific method was applied to social organization as well as industrial production.[37] He projected a new education in which community agencies such as the family, neighborhood, press, church, government, and industry would be part of a new school of living. Rugg developed an orientation to social reform that emphasized art and aesthetic experience as integrative components of an emerging "great society" or "technocracy."

In contrast to the conventional subject matter presented in teacher-centered schools, the child-centered school would liberate children's creativity in a new educational environment; learning would be based on children's interests, needs, and activities.

The child-centered philosophy held that schooling should be based on the child's freedom to learn. For example, the first step toward liberating children's minds was to free them from the physical constraints of lock-step conventional school architecture and organization. Fixed seats, nailed to the floor, were replaced by movable tables and chairs that could be arranged according to children's projects and activities. The formal recitation was replaced by individual and group projects and activities. The child-centered philosophy stimulated by a permissiveness that reoriented the school around the child. While instruction in conventional schools was teacher initiated, in child-centered schools it was based on children's immediate interests. In a learning environment in which initiative is emphasized, activities have a dominant instructional focus. Active, rather than passive, learning was prized.

While the conventional school curriculum was organized around discrete subjects such as reading, spelling, mathematics, history, science, and geography, the new child-centered school emphasized activity-oriented projects based on each child's own interests and the group's shared interest. In this informal learning atmosphere children came to literacy, mathematical, scientific, and historical skills and knowledge as a result of their interests, activities, and projects.

The life of the school was to be active, not passive; children were to work, not merely listen. School subjects such as reading, writing, and arithmetic were to develop out of children's activities and methods of learning, not out of the memorization of distinct studies. The curriculum was to be organized around four chief impulses: social, constructive, expressive, and inquisitive.

While traditional schooling valued social efficiency and defined growth as an increasing desire to conform to social conventions, Rugg wrote that child-centered schools encouraged the release of interior creativity. Revealing his emphasis on aesthetic values, Rugg saw child-centered schools eliciting self-expression in the arts. Their philosophy assumed that every child is endowed with the capacity for self-expression through language, dance, painting, music, drama, and other art forms

[36] New York: Harcourt, Brace, 1931, pp. 35-38.
[37] New York: John Day, 1933, p. 79.

and media. The emphasis was not upon finished work but upon the ongoing release of the child's creative capacities.

The Organization of the Child-Centered School

For the philosophy of the child-centered school to be implemented, Rugg observed the necessity of altering the organization of the convention school. While the organization of the formal school was rigid, that of the child-centered school was flexible and tentative. While a day in a conventional school day was organized into prescribed time-frames (such as spelling from 9:00 to 9:30, penmanship from 9:30 to 10:00, composition from 10:00 to 10:30, and so on, a day in a child-centered school was more flexibly arranged to provide for maximum individualization and group projects and activities. The child's interest, not the master schedule, was the governing principle. The schedules were tentative in order to develop educative units through the cooperation of students and teachers.[38]

The Curriculum of the Child-Centered School

For Rugg, the curriculum of the child-centered school was broadly conceived. Its scope encompassed contemporary life in a continuum of activities ranging from immediate experience in the local community to the international dimension of human life and society. In order to reduce the gap between the child's experience in the school and the problems of contemporary civilization, curricular objectives encouraged creative self-expression, developed a sympathetic understanding of others, and cultivated cultural open-mindedness. To achieve these broad objectives, the curriculum of the child-centered schools consisted of activities which encompassed the entire range of students' and teachers' activities, such as field trips, nature study, research projects, construction projects, group discussions, and creative, expressive, and appreciative activities.

Because of his affinity for cultivating aesthetic experience, Rugg recommended a substantial plan for the creative and fine arts in the curriculum. The arts, he believed, held great potentiality for stimulating creativity and self-expression. In a technological society, the arts contained the possibility for personal and social integration.

Counts and Social Reconstructionism

During the Depression-ridden decade of the 1930s, a dramatic controversy developed between child-centered progressives and those who argued that the schools should be used for social reconstruction. The 1930s saw massive unemployment, retrenchment of educational spending, school closings, dismissals of teachers, and the radicalization of many American intellectuals. Within the Progressive Education Association, a number of professors of education began to argue that progressive educators should direct their energies to the major social, economic, and

---

[38] Rugg and Schumaker, *Child-Centered School,* pp. 70-87.

political issues of the day. At the Progressive Education Association Convention of 1932, Professor George S. Counts, of Teachers College, Columbia University, delivered an address entitled "Dare Progressive Education Be Progressive?" His remarks were later expanded into a book, *Dare the School Build a New Social Order?*

Counts's address charged that progressives had romanticized the child's nature and had ignored the social reality in which children lived. In attacking the middle-class orientation of progressive education, he stated that "These people have shown themselves entirely incapable of dealing with any of the great crises of our time—war, poverty, or depression." Arguing that progressive education should neither reflect the established order nor remain neutral, Counts stated, "Any concrete school program will contribute to the struggle for survival that is ever going on among institutions, ideas, and values; it cannot remain neutral in any firm and complete sense. Partiality is the very essence of education, as it is of life itself."[39] In urging progressives to point the way to the creation of a new society—a co-operative democracy—Counts, commenting on the modernizing trends of science and technology, asserted that humankind had entered a new age in which "ignorance must be replaced by technology, competition by cooperation, trust in providence by careful planning, and private capitalism by some form of social-ized economy."

While Counts's polemic struck an enthusiastic and responsive chord in many members of the association, his child-centered critics charged him with neglecting the interests of children and of seeking to use the schools for ideological indoctrina-tion. The child-centered progressives continued to argue as in the preceding years that the educational process should remain open-ended and with no other goal than the continuing growth of the child.

THE DECLINE OF PROGRESSIVE EDUCATION

The last phase of the progressive education movement came after World War II, when the nation as well as the schools were readjusting to a peacetime society. In the early 1950s, an educational movement called life adjustment education began. Receiving support from the U.S. Office of Education and from various state depart-ments of education, life adjustment emphasized the need to provide youth with functional experiences in practical arts, home and family life, health, physical fit-ness, recreation, and civic competency. Although its direct connections with progressive education were tenuous, the critics of life adjustment saw it as an out-growth of progressivism. A number of critics charged that life-adjustment education was anti-intellectual and tended to lower the academic standards of American

[39] George S. Counts, "Dare Progressive Education Be Progressive?" *Progressive Educa-tion,* 9 (April 1932): 257-63; *Dare the School Build a New Social Order?* (New York: John Day 1932); See also Gerald L. Gutek, *George S. Counts and American Civilization: The Educator as Social Critic* (Macon, Ga.: Mercer University Press, 1983).

public schools. A leading critic of life-adjustment education was Arthur E. Bestor, Jr., a professor of history at the University of Illinois, who wrote *Educational Waste-lands* and *The Restoration of Learning.* According to Bestor, the purpose of educa-tion was to develop intellectual competency. Bestor asserted that intellectual discipline was cultivated by the systematic study of such fundamental academic subjects as mathematics, science, English and foreign languages, and history. The criticisms of such individuals as Bestor, Admiral Hyman Rickover, and Max Rafferty sparked a reexamination of the purposes of American education. The Soviet space success with *Sputnik* in 1957 provoked a general reemphasis on academic subjects and disciplines in American education.

While the national debate was taking place, an internal debate was being waged in the thinning ranks of the Progressive Education Association. The basic split between the child-centered progressives and the social reconstructionists had never really been healed. After World War II, the association was dominated by college professors of education; and there was a turning away from specific pedagogical concerns to wider social, political, and philosophical issues. Issues such as international and intercultural education and the reconstruction of the economy preoccupied those who remained in the association. Finally, in 1955 the Progressive Education Association voted itself out of existence.

CONCLUSION

Although the formal life of the Progressive Education Association ended in 1955, progressivism as a movement in American education had a significant impact. During its various historical phases, progressivism developed a broad view of educa-tion that was greater than schooling and that related education to social, political, and economic reform. Many innovative progressive ideas became part of the Ameri-can educational mainstream. Greater recognition was given to children's interests and needs. Educational experimentation and innovation were encouraged. The scientific examination of pupil progress became part of conventional education. Progressive education, as a movement, succeeded in bringing reform and change to American education. The names of John Dewey, Harold Rugg, William Heard Kilpatrick, and George Counts won a major place in the annals of American educa-tional history. Like any movement, progressive education was partially successful in achieving its broad goals. In the end, American education became a synthesis of traditional and progressive impulses.

DISCUSSION QUESTIONS

1. Define progressivism as a movement in American life.
2. Identify and examine the problems facing American education at the onset of the progressive era.

3. Analyze the progressive concern for conservation of natural resources. What parallels exist between the conservation movement of the progressive era and the contemporary ecology movement?
4. Analyze the progressive impulse to bring about reform by regulatory activity.
5. What was the role of the academic expert in progressive reform efforts?
6. How was progressive education a diverse, rather than a single, movement?
7. Analyze Rice's findings on the condition of American education.
8. Did Jane Addams's social and educational philosophy and practice contribute to social reform or to social control?
9. Analyze the Wisconsin Idea as a working relationship between political and educational leaders.
10. What long-range effects did the guiding principles of the Progressive Education Association have on American education?
11. Was Kilpatrick's project method a product of child-centered or social reformist progressivism?

RESEARCH TOPICS

1. Read a carefully selected general history of the progressive era; in a short sketch, identify the major trends of the era.
2. Read several books by John Dewey. Using Dewey's concept of community, write an interpretive essay that deals with the problem of community and society during the progressive era.
3. Read and review Cremin's definitive book on progressive education, *The Transformation of the School.*
4. Select a book written by a prominent "muckraker" of the progressive era. Review the book as an example of informal education.
5. Read Jane Addams's *Twenty Years at Hull House* and comment on her educational activities.
6. Prepare a short paper that discusses Liberty Hyde Bailey's views on conservation and nature study.
7. Prepare a short paper that analyzes John Dewey's critique of progressive education as presented in *Experience and Education.*
8. Prepare a short paper that describes Dewey's work at the University of Chicago Laboratory School.
9. Analyze Harold Rugg's transition from a child-centered to a social reformist position by a selective reading of his published works.

REFERENCES AND READINGS

Addams, Jane. *Newer Ideals of Peace.* New York: Macmillan, 1907.
____. *The Long Road of Women's Memory.* New York: Macmillan, 1916.
____. *The Spirit of Youth and the City Streets.* New York: Macmillan, 1909.

____. *Twenty Years at Hull House.* New York: Macmillan, 1911.
Bailey, Liberty Hyde. *Universal Service: The Hope of Humanity.* New York: Sturgis and Walton, 1918.
____. *What Is Democracy?* Ithaca, N.Y.: Comstock, 1918.
____. *The Nature-Study Idea.* New York: Macmillan, 1903.
____. *The State and the Farmer.* New York: Macmillan, 1909.
Bates, J. Leonard. *The United States, 1898-1928: Progressivism and a Society in Transition.* New York: McGraw-Hill, 1976.
Black, C. E. *The Dynamics of Modernization: A Study in Comparative History.* New York: Harper & Row, Pub., 1966.
Bestor, Arthur E., Jr. *Educational Wastelands.* Urbana: University of Illinois Press, 1953.
____. *The Restoration of Learning.* New York: Knopf, 1955.
Carbone, Peter, Jr. *The Social and Educational Thought of Harold Rugg.* Durham, N.C.: Duke University Press, 1977.
Case, Belle, and LaFollette, Fola. *Robert M. LaFollette.* New York: Macmillan, 1953.
Counts, George S. *Dare the School Build a New Social Order?* New York: John Day, 1932.
Cremin, Lawrence A. *The Transformation of the School: Progressivism in American Education, 1876-1957.* New York: Knopf, 1962.
Dewey, John. *The School and Society.* Chicago: University of Chicago Press, 1974.
Dorf, Philip. *Liberty Hyde Bailey.* Ithaca, N.Y.: Cornell University Press, 1956.
Gould, Lewis L., ed. *The Progressive Era.* Syracuse, N.Y.: Syracuse University Press, 1974.
Graham, Patricia Albjerg. *Progressive Education: From Arcady to Academe—A History of the Progressive Education Association, 1919-1955.* New York: Teachers College Press, Columbia University, 1967.
Gutek, Gerald L. *George S. Counts and American Civilization: The Educator as Social Theorist.* Macon, Ga.: Mercer University Press, 1983.
Hofstadter, Richard. *The Progressive Historians.* New York: Knopf, 1968.
Katz, Michael B. *Class, Bureaucracy, and Schools: The Illusion of Educational Change in America.* New York: Praeger, 1971.
____. *School Reform: Past and Present.* Boston: Little, Brown, 1971.
Kilpatrick, William H. *The Project Method.* New York: Teachers College Press, Columbia University, 1921.
Linn, James W. *Jane Addams: A Biography.* New York: Appleton-Century, 1935.
Mann, Arthur. *The Progressive Era.* Hinsdale, Ill.: Dryden Press, 1975.
Mayhew, Katherine C., and Edwards, Anna C. *The Dewey School.* New York: Atherton Press, 1966.
Page, Walter Hines. *The Rebuilding of Old Commonwealths.* New York: Doubleday, 1902.
Rice, Joseph M. *The People's Government.* Philadelphia: John C. Winston, 1915.
____. *The Public School System of the United States.* New York: Century, 1893.
Rodgers, Andrew D. *Liberty Hyde Bailey.* Princeton, N.J.: Princeton University Press, 1949.
Rugg, Harold O. *Culture and Education in America.* New York: Harcourt, Brace, 1931.
____. *Great Technology: Social Class and Public Mind.* New York: John Day, 1933.
____, and Schumaker, Ann. *The Child-Centered School.* New York: World Book Co., 1928.
Tenenbaum, Samuel. *William Heard Kilpatrick: Trail Blazer in Education.* New York: Harper & Row, Pub., 1951.
Van Hise, Charles. *The Conservation of Natural Resources in the United States.* New York: Macmillan, 1910.

10
NORMALCY AND DEPRESSION: AMERICAN SOCIETY AND EDUCATION, 1920–1940

As it entered the 1920s, the United States was a nation that had been changed by its brief but bloody ordeal in Europe's trenches and battlefields. An examination of the politics, society, economics, and intellectual life of the 1920s sets the stage for viewing educational developments both in that decade and during the crisis-ridden 1930s.

ENDING THE WAR

The wartime leader of the United States, President Woodrow Wilson (1856-1924), a Democrat, had championed political progressivism from his election in 1912 to American's entry into the war on the side of the Allies in 1917. Wilson, who attended Princeton University, received his bachelor's degree in 1879. He then earned a law degree from the University of Virginia in 1881. Deciding to embark on a career as a political scientist in higher education, Wilson entered Johns Hopkins University in 1883. In 1885, Wilson's well-received and influential book. *Congressional Government*, was published and established him as an authority in the field.[1] In 1886, Johns Hopkins awarded Wilson the doctorate of philosophy.

[1] *Congressional Government: A Study in American Politics* (Boston: Houghton Mifflin, 1900).

After teaching at various colleges, Wilson joined the faculty of Princeton University, his alma mater, in 1890. Twelve years later, in 1902, he became president of Princeton. As Princeton's president, Wilson has been characterized as a "conservative reformer."[2] Reacting against the specialization of the German research model, Wilson sought to revitalize the humanistic aspects of collegiate education. Seeking to intellectualize undergraduate education, he introduced the preceptorial system in which professors worked closely with students in tutorial arrangements.

In 1910, Wilson was elected governor of New Jersey and quickly became a leading candidate for the Democratic nomination for president, which he received in 1912; in the three-way election of 1912, Wilson defeated William Howard Taft, the Republican candidate, and Theodore Roosevelt, the Progressive party candidate.[3]

When the hostilities on Europe's battleground had ended, Wilson hoped to secure peace on the basis of his Fourteen Points. He hoped that World War I would be the last war and that the nations of the earth would join in a new era of international cooperation in the League of Nations. Wilson, however, failed to convince the Senate to ratify the Treaty of Versailles, with its covenant for American participation in the League of Nations. Vigorously campaigning to sway public opinion in favor of American participation, Wilson suffered a stroke that incapacitated him.

In the election of 1920, Warren G. Harding, a Republican senator from Ohio, defeated the Democratic candidate, James Cox, governor of Ohio. Harding, who had campaigned on a platform of "normalcy not nostrums," was elected. Harding's victory reflected the national mood to avoid the intrigue of Old World affairs and to return to isolation.

The years 1919 and 1920, which saw the end of Wilson's administration and the inauguration of Harding's administration, were portentous ones for American politics, society, and education. Two key elements in this period that had educational significance need to be examined: internationalism versus isolationism, and the Red Scare.

Wilson believed that the United States had entered a new era in its national life as a result of its participation in the First World War. America could no longer be isolated from events occurring elsewhere in the world. The League of Nations, he believed, would protect humanity from future wars. The United States must join the league and champion the cause of adjudicating disputes between nations through legal and nonviolent means. During his presidency, Wilson used that office to educate Americans about the world and their future role in it. He strongly

---

[2] For Wilson's academic career, see Henry W. Bragdon, *Woodrow Wilson: The Academic Years* (Cambridge, Mass.: Harvard University Press, 1967).

[3] A well-done and interesting analysis of the "progressive" rivals, Theodore Roosevelt and Woodrow Wilson, is John Milton Cooper, *The Warrior and the Priest: Woodrow Wilson and Theodore Roosevelt* (Cambridge, Mass.: Harvard University Press, 1983).

believed that the presidency carried with it an educational responsibility in the broad sense.

Although Wilson could not persuade two-thirds of the members of the Senate to ratify the Versailles Treaty, which he had worked to negotiate, he did kindle the spirit of internationalism in some sections of American political and educational life. Several members of the Wilson administration such as Franklin D. Roosevelt would re-emerge as leaders at a later time. Wilsonian idealism also captured the minds of many educators, especially those who taught political science, history, and social sciences in colleges and universities in the 1920s and 1930s. Although the United States might retreat into isolationism, Wilsonian internationalism succeeded in winning large sectors of academic support. When international studies emerged after World War II as an important part of American education, certain of its origins could be traced to Wilson's efforts.

As Wilson sought to develop a larger international role for the United States, his opponents—Senators Henry Cabot Lodge, William Borah, Robert LaFollette, and others—expressed isolationist sentiments. The United States, the isolationists reasoned, should avoid tangling alliances with Europe, as George Washington had recommended in his Farewell Address. It should pursue its own national interests, protected by what seemed at the time to be the formidable barriers of the two great oceans. Isolationism would continue to be a strong political and social force in the United States until well after the end of World War II. In educational terms, isolationists believed that citizenship education should concentrate on the study of American history and government and cultivate a "pro-American" rather than internationalist attitude.

Coincidental, but related to, the debate between internationalists and isolationists, was the Red Scare of 1919-1920. With the collapse of the Tsarist regime and the fall of the short-lived provisional government of Prince Lvov and Alexander Kerensky, the Bolshevik Revolution brought Lenin to power in Russia. "Bolshevism," as Soviet communism was then called, struck terror into the governments of many Western nations, which feared a worldwide communist revolution. In the United States, this fear became known as the Red Scare. Individuals and groups with leftist political views were suspected of plotting to overthrow the government of the United States. Attorney General A. Mitchell Palmer conducted a number of raids on anarchist, socialist, and communist organizations, especially the Industrial Workers of the World. His actions led to arrests and deportations.

The Red Scare reactivated strong nativist sentiments in sections of the country, not only against leftist political organizations but also against the foreign born and recent immigrants, who were suspected of importing the virus of Bolshevism and anarchism to the United States. Indeed, the spirit of the Red Scare rekindled a sense of political fundamentalism, especially in rural America, that sought to revitalize old values.

The Red Scare held significant implications for education in both the informmal and formal sense. Committees of citizens were formed to examine school textbooks and libraries to eliminate anti-Americanism, as they defined the term. Textbooks in history and the social studies were scrutinized for "unpatriotic" and "un-American" passages.[4] Patriotic organizations wanted more military history. Fundamentalist religious groups sought to prevent discussions of evolution in biology textbooks.

Teachers, too, were scrutinized to make sure that they did not deviate from "true patriotism." Although the tactics of the Red Scare would diminish as the 1920s wore on, they were to resurface in a more pervasive form of longer duration during the McCarthy era of the 1950s.

During the 1920s, when nativist sentiments and antiforeign prejudices were strong in many sections of the country, American public schools were often dominated by a climate of opinion that considered the true national character to be white, Protestant, and Anglo-Saxon. The tone of the country's schools, although there were rare exceptions, was assimilationist and sought to educate American youngsters to fit into a homogenized society. It was not until the 1960s, four decades later, that bilingualism, ethnicity, and multiculturalism appeared in American education.

Throughout the 1920s, a tension existed between what could be regarded as two Americas: that of small-town and rural society and that of the big cities. Small-town America (referred to as "Main Street" by Sinclair Lewis) defined American ethical life in terms that still resembled the McGuffey reader frame of reference. Fundamentalist religious values, patriotism, isolationism, and a fear of foreigners were manifested in this ethic.

Small-town Americans feared that the direction of national life was passing to the teeming masses of the big cities with their ethnic populations and political machines. While these value conflicts simmered below the surface of American society, they took overt form in issues such as the prohibition of alcoholic beverages, an intensely debated issue in American life during the 1920s.

The clash in values took dramatic form in the Scopes "monkey" trial of 1924 in Dayton, Tennessee, which drew national attention. In this case, John Scopes, a high school biology teacher, was charged with violating the Tennessee law prohibiting the teaching of evolution or denying the theory of Divine Creation. Assisting the prosecution was the three-time presidential candidate and "great commoner," William Jennings Bryan, who sought to convict Scopes of violating the literal teaching of creation according to the Book of Genesis. Scopes was defended by the articulate, astute, and often vitriolic criminal lawyer, Clarence Darrow. The trial drew national attention and focused on fundamental belief systems.[5] Scopes was convicted but fined only a minimal amount. Some sixty years later, in the 1980s, many of the same issues reappeared in legal battles over curriculum content that were waged between creationists and evolutionists.

[4] Frances FitzGerald, *America Revised: History Schoolbooks in the Twentieth Century* (New York: Random House, 1979), pp. 35-36.

[5] Ray Ginger, *Six Days or Forever? Tennessee v. John Thomas Scopes* (New York: Oxford University Press, 1958).

THE ECONOMY AND SOCIETY OF THE 1920s

Although this clash of values affected educational policies and curricula during the 1920s, its impact was overshadowed by the unprecedented prosperity that occurred between 1920 and 1929. The presidencies of Warren Harding (1921-1923) and Calvin Coolidge (1923-1929) personified the new prosperity.

For many Americans during the 1920s, the goal was to make a fortune and make it quickly through speculation on the stock market. Wealth would come to those who acted quickly and invested boldly. In many ways, President Coolidge's statement, "The business of America is business," summed up the dominant national values during the 1920s.

Although some leaders of the earlier progressive era were still politically active such as Senator Borah, Senator LaFollette, and Newton D. Baker, progressivism had been eclipsed by the politics of normalcy and prosperity. Certain segments of the population did not share in the Harding-Coolidge prosperity, however. The 1920s experienced a series of agricultural recessions; minority groups, particularly blacks and Hispanic Americans, were largely forgotten. The ethics of prosperity that affected education could be summed up as individualism and competition.

According to the ethical code dominant in the 1920s, prosperity would come to those who acted for and in their own self-interest; the community would also benefit from individual initiative. Government, education, and society in general should encourage individual initiative and action. Material inventions—automobiles, airplanes, electric lights, motion pictures, and radio—were the signs of a new, modern, and better world. Such inventions were the products of individuals like Thomas A. Edison and Henry Ford, who through their own efforts had efficiently and effectively invented, created, and developed the tangible things of prosperity that made progress possible.

Following the ethical guidelines of prosperity, the role of government was to encourage invention, discovery, investment, and expansion rather than regulate it. Indeed, regulation such as that of the earlier progressive decade was likely to retard humankind's—especially America's —advancement into the new age.

The role of education was to prepare the agents of the new prosperity: the inventors, investors, entrepreneurs, and corporate leaders of the new economic order. Indeed, during the 1920s, the high school reached the point of consolidation. More and more American adolescents were entering high school, and many were completing secondary education. To be sure, the number of minority students was still much smaller than that of older stock.

Educational administration, in particular, modeled itself along business and corporate lines. For many school administrators, schools were to run as effectively and efficiently as businesses. At the same time that administrative circles were imitating business models in school operations and encouraging the morality of the business world, curricular progressivism reached its high point in many private schools and in some public schools.

The Prosperity of the 1920s

During the 1920s, the United States, stimulated by the technology of the assembly line and the increasing production of consumer goods such as automobiles, washing machines, refrigerators, vacuum cleaners, radios, and a range of new electric appliances, became one of the world's most highly developed industrial nations. The decade of 1920s was one of prosperity for many—but not all— Americans. The decade saw industrial production doubling, the gross national product rising by 40 percent, and per capita income increasing by 30 percent.

The business corporation, with its stockholders, trustees, directors, and managers, became the nation's dominant economic unit. In many areas, the large corporation replaced the small entrepreneur and family-owned business. The manager, in particular, trained in the techniques of business administration, became a new entity on the American economic and educational scene.

While the United States experienced economic prosperity in the 1920s, there was strong evidence of weakness and imbalance. Through the 1920s, farmers suffered from a chronic agricultural depression. Despite gains for factory workers, significant disparities in income existed. Due to the purchase of stock on margin, the prosperity of the middle classes was often more an illusion than a reality. These economic weaknesses would become acute in the Wall Street crash of 1929 and the ensuing Great Depression of the 1930s.

Industrialism and the Assembly Line

The United States, beginning with the turn of the century onward, experienced a complete industrial and technological transformation. This industrial transformation was part of the great change that had begun in the Western world with the Industrial Revolution of the early nineteenth century. The industrial transformation was best illustrated by the rise of assembly-line production, which not only had great economic consequences but social and educational ones as well.

As the United States was emerging as a world power at the time of World War I, it was also becoming one of the world's industrial giants. America's rise was facilitated by the development of the assembly line, on which machines, tended by their human operators, transformed raw materials into finished products as they moved through a sequence of carefully structured manufacturing operations. Although the assembly line was found in virtually every large American industry, it reached its zenith in the automobile industry. The characteristics of assembly-line production were the reduction of the manufacturing process into carefully synchronized stages, the use of interchangeable parts, and having each worker function in a methodical way on one routine part of the manufacturing process.

While the assembly-line process raised industrial productivity and efficiency, it also had consequences that were educational in the broad sense. The assembly line required that those who worked on it be efficient in their use of time and motion. Products ranging from automobiles to hairpins needed to be made quickly, efficiently, and as cheaply as possible.

The industrialism of the 1920s was more complex than that of the pre-Civil War nineteenth century; it was really technological in substance and scope. Technology, the interrelating of science with industry to increase productivity, ushered in an era characterized by an engineering frame of mind. Indeed, President Herbert Hoover, elected in 1928, was known as the "great engineer" since he had been a mining engineer in his youth and had recognized the new industrial trends.

In the 1920s, the engineering frame of reference was expressed by the rise of scientific management and the efficiency expert. Scientific managers tried to keep all the interrelated parts, processes, and units of the assembly line and the corporation functioning in an integrated and efficient manner. Efficiency experts studied the time and motion spent on a task in order to find ways of reducing effort, time, and cost.

During the 1920s, professional educators, especially school administrators and curriculum specialists, sought to apply the new industrial technology to educational institutions. If industries could be managed efficiently, so could schools and school systems. The 1920s became the period of the school survey, in which teams of educational experts, usually professors of educational administration, studied school systems, especially large urban ones, with an eye to improving their educational efficiency and instructional delivery. Professors such as Franklin Bobbitt and W. W. Charters designed curricula according to their analysis of human activities. Charters analyzed the time spent in performing the tasks associated with various occupations in order to make performance more efficient and cost effective. For example, he analyzed the tasks performed by secretaries and applied his findings to improving their performance and to reshaping secretarial training.[6]

In addition to the movements for scientific management and efficiency that had an impact on education in the 1920s, there were also those educators, especially George S. Counts, who recognized that the rise of a technological society was exerting an effect that was so pervasive and profound on American society and education that it was in actuality a "great transformation." In *Secondary Education and Industrialism*, Counts identified themes that would preoccupy educators during the ensuing decades: Educators, Counts claimed, had failed to analyze the social impact of industrialism on modern society. Instead, they either persisted in educating for a rural-agrarian society that had already slipped away into the past or were concerned with techniques rather than issues of substance. Counts called upon educators "to make the school function in the building of a new civilization."[7]

As Counts studied technology's social impact, he concluded that technology had produced the rise of interrelated, complex, specialized, but impersonal human relationships; and that the decline of older values, associated with the frontier, had created a need for new values that would integrate the viable elements of America's

---

[6] See W. W. Charters, *Analysis of Secretarial Duties and Traits* (Baltimore: Williams and Wilkins, 1924).

[7] George S. Counts, *Secondary Education and Industrialism* (Cambridge, Mass.: Harvard University Press, 1929), pp. 1-12.

democratic heritage with the emerging ones of technological society. The challenge for educators was, then, to formulate a broader conception of community in which the impersonalism of technological society would be recast into democratic and shared values. Although Counts's argument calling for educators to come to grips with a technological society would surface again during the Depression years of the 1930s, educators during the boom years of the 1920s tried to introduce social and educational efficiency into the schools.

Cultural Change

During the 1920s, modern mass entertainment originated and developed rapidly. Broadcasts of dramas, "soap operas," athletic events, newscasts, and concerts were programed by independent radio stations and national networks. Radio broadcasting introduced a powerful new informal educational force into American life, as Americans turned the dials of their radio sets to be entertained and informed. The motion picture industry, based in Hollywood, continued to create stars and screen personalities. The advent of the "talkie" in 1929 brought both sight and sound to an audience of millions.

Both radio and the motion picture worked to create an homogenized mass culture. Local and regional differences remained but were beginning to erode before the standardized language of the radio announcer and the mass-produced values of the Hollywood screen. Radio and motion pictures brought about cultural change, reduced social isolation, and educated Americans in an informal way. They also brought with them a dramatic new way of providing information, but it was brief and lacked the larger perspective of the printed page. As the 1920s unfolded, the mass media revealed its potency as an instrument of marketing both products and values. Educators, however, were slow to realize the power of this new force of informal education.

Social Change

The 1920s, following World War I, brought significant social change to American life. The war, which had broadened the industrial workforce to include larger numbers of women, had generated continuing alterations that redefined the role of women in American society. Although more women were employed outside of home, their career options did not broaden significantly. Most women continued to be employed as teachers, nurses, or secretaries. Significantly, however, women discovered a new freedom in many areas of the country, especially in the larger cities, that was made possible by their entry into economic life. In political life, the Nineteenth Amendment, ratified in 1919, gave the right to vote to women. Politics still remained largely the domain of males, but a few women were elected to office and participated in political organizations.

The 1920s, as most postwar eras, experienced significant social changes that had a direct impact on the family and an indirect one on American education. The era saw a pronounced break with the residual social restraints lingering from the

Victorian era. For many young women, the less restrictive 1920s made it possible to achieve greater personal self-expression.

Two significant trends that reshaped education were the development of a more permissive attitude toward children, and the social prolonging of adolescence. Earlier the educators, such as the European Rousseau, Pestalozzi, and Froebel, and the Americans Francis Parker and G. Stanley Hall, had argued that childhood should be recognized as an intrinsically valuable period of human growth and development. Taking up the theme of permissiveness, many educators during the 1920s urged greater freedom for children. Child-centered progressive educators such as Margaret Naumberg and Marietta Johnson proclaimed that education during the child's early years should be based on learning that arose from the child's own interest and needs. Through activities and projects, children were encouraged to express themselves freely and creatively, without fear of adult prescription or censorship. A more permissive attitude toward childrearing and early childhood education was also encouraged by the disciples of Sigmund Freud, the originator of psychoanalysis. Neo-Freudian educators saw teaching and learning as a therapeutic exercise for both teachers and children.

While younger children were experiencing more permissive education modes, young people—especially of high school age—were living through the first stages of an evolving American "youth culture." The enactment of compulsory attendance laws and restrictions on child labor saw more adolescents entering and completing high school. With the high school population becoming more varied in terms of socioeconomic background and career interests, some educators wanted to redefine the high school from a college preparatory to a multipurpose institution. The lengthened period of adolescence also saw the origins of what would become the teen-age culture of the later decades of the twentieth century. Youth, entering the workforce at a later age, developed its own vernacular, mores, and entertainment styles and began to form a separate subculture. Although the social patterns of the teen-age subculture were apparent in the 1920s, the full impact of this new social trend would directly affect American education in the decades after World War II, beginning with the 1950s.

For the United States, the prosperity of the 1920s was a brief interlude between World War I and the onset of a staggering economic crisis that began with the Wall Street crash of 1929. Ushering in the Great Depression, the crash brought America and many of its schools to a virtual standstill. We shall now examine education and society during the depression-ridden decade of the 1930s.

THE GREAT DEPRESSION OF THE 1930s

From 1929 to 1939, the United States and much of the world was gripped by a great economic catastrophe, the Great Depression. The prosperity of the 1920s evaporated abruptly on October 29, 1929, when a panic swept the New York Stock

Exchange, as thousands of investors rushed to unload their stocks.[8] The Great Depression that followed the Wall Street crash was the most devastating economic crisis to ever occur in the United States. Although statistics varied, it is generally estimated that the ranks of unemployed wage earners reached 12,000,000 by 1932. The Great Depression profoundly altered American political and social attitudes. Its psychological shock waves eroded the heady optimism of the 1920s. In particular, the psychological effects of the Depression had profound consequences on the American character.[9]

The Impact on Education

The impact of the Great Depression on education was manifested in several ways: (1) Fiscal retrenchment due to a shrinking tax base caused a reduction in the teaching force and educational programs. (2) Many began to seriously question traditional American values, particularly those associated with business ethics and the free enterprise system. (3) The alliance between businessmen and school administrators weakened. Of these three areas of impact, the fiscal pressures upon the schools were most direct. Business closings and the resultant massive unemployment reduced the revenues generated by local taxes, which had traditionally supported public schooling. The reduced revenue collections produced demands for fiscal retrenchment that fell heavily on local school boards. It should be remembered that the state contribution to school funding was very low in the 1930s and that state governments were also experiencing the same fiscal stringencies as local governments.

The fiscal crisis that the public schools faced became acute in 1931 and 1932. The immediate response of local school boards in many states, especially in the hard-pressed South and Southwest, was to reduce the length of the school year and to close schools. In the spring of 1932, for example, one-third of a million elementary and secondary school students were out of school due to school closings. Among the examples of school closings or greatly reduced school years were the following: Georgia had closed 1,318 schools with an enrollment of 170,790 students; 81 percent of the children in rural Alabama were no longer attending school because of school closings; in Arkansas, more than 300 schools had reduced their school year to sixty days; and 1,000 West Virginia schools had been forced to close.[10]

Schools in the more prosperous Northern industrial states also were forced to shorten the school year. In many states, schools remained in session but local school boards were unable to pay teachers their salaries. Teachers were issued promissory notes that promised to pay when additional revenues had been col-

---

[8] For analysis of the weaknesses of the prosperity of the 1920s, see William E. Leuchtenburg, *The Perils of Prosperity, 1914-1932* (Chicago: University of Chicago Press, 1958).

[9] The anxieties of the Depression era are recounted in Studs Terkel, *Hard Times: An Oral History of the Great Depression* (New York: Pantheon, 1970).

[10] Avis D. Carlson, "Deflating the Schools," *Harper's,* 147 (November 1933): 705-13.

lected. The general tendency throughout the country during the Depression was for school districts to reduce the number of teachers, increase class size, and reduce the number of courses in the high school curriculum.

While schools experienced the consequences of severely reduced revenues, the Depression also had serious effects on children. The Depression resulted in increased malnutrition among children. For example, New York City's health department reported that 20.5 percent of the school children it examined in 1932 showed evidence of malnutrition. In Chicago, 11,000 children were being fed by teachers, who themselves were not being paid.[11] In addition, families suffered psychological anxieties that resulted from the heads of households being unemployed or the fear of impending economic disaster.

In the early stages of the Depression, many adolescents became tramps and traveled from city to city by hopping railroad freightcars. They were not alone in this phenomenon but joined a large number of unemployed adults who were "on the bum" looking for jobs, hand outs, or escape from depressed home conditions.

HOOVER, ROOSEVELT, AND THE NEW DEAL

President Herbert Hoover, who was elected in 1928 on a platform that promised more and greater prosperity, committed his administration to policies of economic individualism. He asserted that local and state governments had the responsibility for relieving the plight of the victims of the Depression rather than the federal government. Hoover and his associates predicted that the Depression was a temporary malaise that would soon disappear and be followed by a return to prosperity.

Hoover responded to the economic depression by reasserting his faith in the free enterprise system. Rejecting arguments for federal intervention, Hoover believed that such interference would not only jeopardize economic recovery but would constitute an unwarranted invasion by government into the private sector. An advocate of individualism and volunteerism, Hoover called upon private charities and local governments to provide relief to the unemployed.

In the election of 1932, Hoover's challenger was Franklin D. Roosevelt, New York's Democratic governor, who campaigned on the promise of a "New Deal" for Americans. Roosevelt, who had won 22,809,638 popular votes and 472 electoral votes, defeated Hoover, who had won 15,758,901 popular votes and 59 electoral votes.

Roosevelt, who had promised relief, recovery, and reform, had been swept into the presidency, which he would win again in 1936, 1940, and 1944.[12]

---

[11] David A. Shannon, ed., *The Great Depression* (Englewood Cliffs, N.J.: Prentice-Hall, 1960), pp. 51-52.

[12] Recommended treatments of Roosevelt and his New Deal are: James MacGregor Burns, *Roosevelt: The Soldier of Freedom* (New York: Harcourt Brace Jovanovich, 1970); Frank B. Freidel, *Franklin D. Roosevelt* (Boston: Little, Brown, 1973); William E. Leuchtenburg, *Franklin Roosevelt: A Profile* (New York: Hill and Wang, 1967).

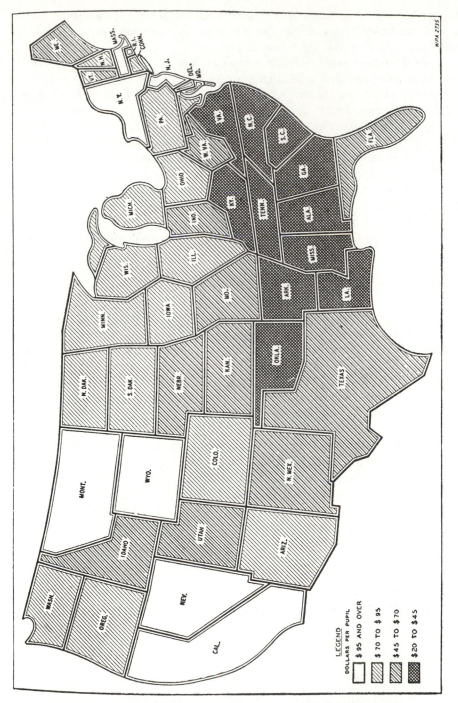

The map illustrates current expenditure per pupil in average daily attendance in the various states, 1935-36, the mid-years of the Great Depression. *(From The Advisory Committee on Education, Report of the Committee. Washington, D.C.: G.P.O., 1938, p. 23.)*

Roosevelt, assistant secretary of Navy during World War I, was well versed in progressivism's politics, philosophy, and programs, which he had seen functioning during the administration of Woodrow Wilson. Roosevelt's New Deal policies were designed to maintain the essential features of the American political system by responding to the pressing economic problems with both regulation, as the earlier progressives had done, and by action for economic recovery through the intervention of the federal government, which was the bold and new feature.

Franklin D. Roosevelt was inaugurated on March 4, 1933, in the midst of a severe economic crisis. Nearly 13,000,000 persons, or 25 percent of the nation's workforce, were unemployed. Banks had been closed in thirty-eight states. In the midst of this severe economic crisis, the new president sought to reassure many Americans who were gripped by a kind of psychological paralysis by proclaiming that "the only thing we have to fear is fear itself—nameless, unreasoning, unjustified terror."

During his first hundred days in office, from March 9 to June 16, 1933, the outline of Roosevelt's New Deal emerged. A series of laws designed to speed relief, recovery, and reform was proposed by the president and enacted by Congress. Among them were the following: the Emergency Banking Relief Act, which provided federal assistance and supervision to banks; the Federal Deposit Insurance Corporaton (FDIC), which gave federal protection to bank deposits; the Unemployment Relief Act, which assisted those who were out of work; and the Tennessee Valley Authority Act (TVA), which controlled flooding and provided electrical power to the proverty-stricken rural areas of the upper South; the Agricultural Adjustment Act (AAA), which took land out of production and subsidized farmers; and the National Recovery Administration (NRA), which stimulated economic recovery by planning and cooperation between government, business, and labor.

While much of the New Deal's emergency relief and reform legislation had only an indirect impact on education and schools, several other laws and the agencies that they created had a more direct impact: The Civilian Conservation Corps (CCC), the Public Works Administration (PWA), and the Works Progress Administration (WPA). The administration had a range of objectives in relationship to the CCC, PWA, and WPA such as: providing relief for the unemployed by creating federally funded jobs, stimulating the economy, restoring hope that the possibility of work existed, and setting up many projects, ranging from construction to the arts.

In the second phase of the New Deal, several major pieces of legislation were enacted. The Social Security Act, enacted in 1935, provided old-age pensions, financed equally by a tax on employers and employees. The National Labor Relations Act, introduced by Senator Robert Wagner, a New York Democrat, was passed. The Wagner Act: (1) established the National Labor Relations Board (NLRB) to adjudicate management-labor disputes; (2) guaranteed labor's right to organize unions and to engage in collective bargaining; and (3) outlawed unfair labor practices.

Although the New Deal legislation touched all sectors of American society, much of Roosevelt's program indirectly rather than directly affected American education. Like the earlier progressive movement, the Roosevelt administration used experts, often from academic institutions, as resource people to gather evidence and to draft the rationales for reform legislation. Roosevelt's cadre of experts was referred to as the "Brain Trust."[13] At the same time that he used academic experts, Roosevelt, a thorough-going political pragmatist, rejected notions of abstract social planning that were current among many American intellectuals, such as George Counts and the educators associated with *The Social Frontier.*

Several agencies such as the CCC, the WPA, and the National Youth Administration (NYA) did have a direct impact on education. The educational efforts of these agencies is examined in the following sections. It should be noted that the New Deal did not attempt to alter the basic structure of public schooling in the United States, however. The principles of state responsibility and local control remained intact.

The Civilian Conservation Corps (CCC)

In accepting the Democratic nomination for president in 1932, Roosevelt stated that "relief, both for the unemployed and for agriculture, will come from . . . the converting of many million acres of marginal and unused land into timber land through reforestation."[14] Roosevelt's idea of stimulating employment through reforestation and reclamation projects was motivated by: (1) a resurgence of the old progressive theme, nurtured in the 1900s by Theodore Roosevelt and Gifford Pinchot, that the federal government should actively encourage the conservation of natural forest, water, and soil resources; (2) a desire to alleviate and remedy the conditions that had led to the dust bowl, by the reforestation of lands that were being stripped of their topsoil; (3) the immediate need to employ the vast army of unemployed youth in useful work. From these motives came the Civilian Conservation Corps, a federally financed and organized program that had immense educational implications.

The CCC originated as a component of the Federal Emergency Relief Act, passed in 1933, designed to alleviate unemployment through "the performance of useful public works." Those eligible to admission to the CCC were unemployed, unmarried males between the ages of seventeen and twenty-three. The minimum term of service was six months and the maximum two years. Enlistees would receive housing, clothing, food, and a wage of one dollar per day.

The objectives of the legislation were to relieve unemployment, and to conserve and restore the nation's natural resources. The legislation providing the CCC was extended for two years in 1935 and then for three more years in 1937. The enactment of compulsory military service, as part of the preparedness program immediately before World War II, ended the CCC.

[13] Arthur S. Link and William B. Catton, *American Epoch: A History of the United States Since 1900,* 2, *The Age of Franklin D. Roosevelt, 1921-1945* (New York: Knopf, 1973) p. 132.

[14] F. A. Silcox, "Our Adventure in Conservation: The CCC," *The Atlantic Monthly,* 140 (1973): 718.

The CCC was controversial and drew criticism from representatives of organized labor, especially from William Green, president of the American Federation of Labor, the nation's largest labor union, who, objecting to the "proposed regimentation of labor," said it smacked "of Fascism, Hitlerism, and . . . Sovietism."[15] The Roosevelt administration defended the CCC by explaining that the corps' role would be merely to provide housing arrangements and clothing distribution and some preliminary training.

Roosevelt appointed Robert Fechner, a labor leader, as head of the emergency Conservation Work Organization, which had jurisdiction over the CCC. The organizing, staffing, and implementing of the project was shared by the Departments of Labor, War, Agriculture, and Interior. In its first year, the CCC employed 550,000 men, with the usual number of six-month enlistees being 300,000.

The efforts of the CCC were directed to conservation, and the following specific projects were undertaken: forest fire prevention measures, the establishment of trails, the construction of lookout towers and buildings, the planting of trees, and insect control measures. In addition to measures related directly to the conservation of natural resources, the CCC had two related efforts: (1) a portion of each CCC worker's pay was sent home to dependents to provide some relief through employment; (2) food and other supplies needed by CCC members were often purchased from local businesses to stimulate the local economy.

Not only was the CCC to be an instrument for the conservation of natural resources, it was also to perform an educational function. Each CCC camp was to have an educational adviser.[16] The U.S. Office of Education published the following objectives to guide the CCC's educational programs:

1. development of powers of self-expression, self-entertainment, and self-culture;
2. development of pride and satisfaction in cooperative work;
3. development of an understanding of social and economic conditions;
4. preservation and strengthening of good habits of health and mind;
5. improvement of employment opportunities by vocational training and counseling; and
6. development of an appreciation of nature and rural life.

The national education program director of the CCC was Howard Oxley. While the camp commander was in charge of both the education and conservation programs, the education adviser and education staff carried on the instructional program. Although no uniform curriculum was followed throughout the country, courses were offered in such subjects as citizenship, botany, English, forestry, first aid, hygiene, surveying, zoology, algebra, astronomy, bookkeeping, entomology, geology, history, music, and painting. In addition to these subjects, the CCC also offered instruction in reading and writing to the small number of illiterates who

[15] "Job Bill 'Fascism' Alleged by Green," *The New York Times* (March 2, 1933), p. 4.

[16] C. S. Marsh, "The Educational Program of the Civilian Conservation Corps," *School and Society,* 39 (March 31, 1934): 400-5.

were identified as a result of initial screening. Life in the CCC camp, often a tent city, also included organized recreational, athletic, and physical fitness activities.

The Works Progress Administration (WPA)

The Works Progress Administration (WPA) was involved in construction projects such as the building of post offices, armories, and dams and in conservation projects for flood control, reforestation, and recreation. In addition, the WPA also undertook projects of a broadly educational and artistic nature.[17] The Federal Theater Project, under WPA auspices, produced plays, musicals, circuses, and other entertainment projects that provided employment to actors, writers, and others. Artists were employed to create murals, mosaics, and sculptures for federal buildings. Historians and other writers were put to work organizing archives, directories, local histories, bibliographies, and guidebooks.

The Federal Art Project was the means by which the federal government employed artists by subsidizing art classes and projects. Teachers employed by the project supervised children from ages six to sixteen in free classes that were held in settlement houses, schools, clubs, libraries, and community centers. The interests of the federal government in art education revived the "artist-teacher" concept that had been pioneered among progressive educators. The federal government's involvement was based on the need to provide work for unemployed artists and to create artistic opportunities for the children and young people.

The National Youth Administration

The National Youth Administration (NYA) was established to assist youth in completing their education, especially at the college level. With the Depression, many students were forced to support themselves due to the economic distress faced by their families; at the same time, the number of jobs that would have enabled them to do so decreased sharply. The NYA made federal funds available to students so that they could complete their college education. The guidelines of the program were:

1. In return for work, the federal government, through the NYA, paid students who qualified for aid a maximum of twenty dollars per month during the academic year.
2. Nonprofit colleges and universities were eligible to receive payments.
3. The colleges and universities selected eligible students, who were required to meet scholastic requirements and carry three-fourths of the usual academic program.
4. The institutions arranged and supervised the students' work assignments.[18]

---

[17] For treatments of artistic programs supported by New Deal agencies, see William McDonald, *Federal Relief Administration and the Arts* (Columbus: Ohio State University Press, 1969); and June D. Matthews, *The Federal Theater, 1935-1939* (Princeton, N.J.: Princeton University Press, 1967).

[18] Betty and Ernest K. Lindley, *A New Deal for Youth: The Story of the National Youth Administration* (New York: Viking, 1938), pp. 156-63.

THE DEPRESSION AND EDUCATIONAL IDEOLOGY

The Depression also had a profound impact upon educational ideology. The philosophical and ideological debates stimulated a polarization among educators that surfaced in several educational organizations. Much of the ideological polarization came from divisions over the relationship between educators and schools, on the one hand, and larger political, social, and economic issues on the other. Some educators, such as the essentialists, argued that the school's primary function was the transmission of skills and knowledge from adults to children. In contrast, social reformist progressive and social reconstructionist educators wanted the educational profession and schools to be agencies of deliberate social change. While these larger issues were being debated, ideological conflicts developed within educational organizations such as the Progressive Education Association, where child-centered progressives argued with social reconstructionist progressives over socioeconomic and educational policies. Within some teacher organizations, especially the American Federation of Teachers, it was debated whether teachers should pursue "bread and butter" issues (as had been recommended by the pioneer American labor leader, Samuel Gompers), or more definite agendas for broader sociopolitical and economic change.

Critics of the Status Quo

As indicated earlier, during the 1920s, the dominant forces in American education had allied themselves with the business ethic and had appropriated the corporate model for imitation in school organization. The onset of the Great Depression, however, weakened the alliance between business and educational leaders. Merle Curti, in *The Social Ideas of American Educators*, reinterpreted the educational contributions of such revered educators as Horace Mann, Henry Barnard, Booker T. Washington, and William James, in terms that were broadly social, political, and economic as well as pedagogical. Curti wrote that "It was common for educators to show sympathy with the position of industry and finance in its struggles with labor. . . . ." He then raised the question whether "the dillusionment with business leaders had truly severed the ancient alliance between educators and businessmen."[19]

During the late 1920s, and in particular during the 1930s, an intellectual climate of opinion developed that questioned this alliance, especially as manifested in the allegiance to the ethic of economic individualism. In the social sciences, particularly in the "new history" of Charles Beard, both the historical origins and the contemporary relevance of economic individualism were questioned, criticized, and abandoned in favor of the coming age of "collectivism." Beard's interpretation of American history had a decided impact on the American Historical Association's Commission on the Social Studies in the Schools, of which he was a member and of which George S. Counts was director of research.

[19]Merle Curti, *The Social Ideas of American Educators* (Paterson, N.J.: Littlefield, Adams, 1959), pp. 218, 580.

Beard, who would influence Counts and other social reconstructionist educators, based his interpretation of history on the conditioning role played by economic forces. In his monumental book, *An Economic Interpretation of the United States Constitution*, Beard asserted that "economic elements are the chief factor in the development of political institutions" and that U.S. history could be examined as "controlling interests" either favored or opposed to change.[20]

In his educational thinking, Beard believed that education, especially schooling, was based on a social frame of reference. Schools should not be divorced from social issues but should examine them from a frame of reference that included historically dominant and emergent social trends. Educational programs should, Beard believed, examine the impact of industrialism and encourage progressive social change. These themes, developed by Beard, found their way into the emergent social reconstructionist education ideology of the 1930s.

The Commission on the Social Studies in the Schools

In 1926, the American Historical Association established the Commission on the Social Studies in the Schools, composed of prominent historians, social scientists, and educators. Although the ideological range of the commission's members varied, those inclined to a greater social role for education such as Beard, Counts, and Jesse Newlon, were influential in shaping its conclusions. As it began its work, the commission decided to engage in broad socioeconomic and educational analysis rather than limited "surveys of textbooks, curricula, or methods." It further assumed that the United Sates was "undergoing a period of profound change" and that social services needed to direct this change.[21]

While Beard's economic interpretation of history was part of the intellectual milieu that challenged the status quo, the social philosophy of John Dewey formed another element in the emerging social reformist frame of reference. By the time of the Great Depression of the 1930s, Dewey, who had developed the instrumentalist version of pragmatism, was renowned as one of America's leading philosophers. Not only was Dewey a voice to be reckoned with in philosophy, he also was a commanding authority in educational theory. His works on education were standard reading in educational philosophy.[22] Dewey's Laboratory School at the University of Chicago was regarded as the prototype of many progressive schools. His books on social philosophy, especially *Individualsm: Old and New* (1929) and *Liberalism and Social Action* (1935), gave credence to the view that a new social order was in the making and that educators should contribute to the creating of the new society.

[20] Charles A. Beard, *An Economic Interpretation of the United States Constitution* (New York: Macmillan, 1913), p. 6.

[21] Report of the Commission on the Social Studies, *Conclusions and Recommendations* (New York: Scribners, 1934), pp. 1-4.

[22] Among Dewey's works on education that established his reputation are: *Democracy and Education* (New York: Macmillan, 1916); *The Quest for Certainty* (New York: Minton, Balch, 1929); *Experience and Education* (New York: Macmillan, 1938). Useful works on Dewey are: George R. Geiger, *John Dewey in Perspective* (New York: Oxford University Press, 1958); and Sidney Hook, *John Dewey:An Intellectual Portrait* (New York: John Day, 1939).

In *Individualism: Old and New*, Dewey challenged the ethics of the "pecuniary culture" of economic individualism and urged its replacement by a "service-oriented" set of values arising from a new intellectual and political consensus.[23] Arguing that the inherited conceptions of economic individualism had been rendered obsolete by the emergence of an industrial order, Dewey discerned a tendency to "corporateness" and "association" in all areas of life. Attributing the current state of "economic insecurity" and intellectual drift to the remnants of individualistic thinking, Dewey recommended the control of industry and government for constructive social ends.

In *Liberalism and Social Action*, Dewey continued to elaborate on themes similar to those expressed in *Individualism: Old and New*.[24] Recognizing the rise of antiliberal Fascist and Nazi totalitarianism in Europe, Dewey proposed to rescue liberalism by examining and reconstructing it as a vital social philosophy. The doctrines of "laissez-faire liberalism," holding that progress could come only from "private economic enterprise" that was "socially undirected" and free "from social control" were inadequate to meet the challenges of a technological society. What was needed, Dewey argued, was a renascent liberalism that:

1. possessed a "conception of intelligence" that would integrate and give direction to social movements;
2. would use the emergent social sciences as instruments for creating new forms of social and educational organization;
3. would conquer "material insecurity" and enable the multitudes of people to participate "in the vast cultural resources that are at hand."[25]

Counts and a New Social Order

Although educational theorists such as John Dewey, William H. Kilpatrick, and Harold Rugg expressed the sentiments of socially oriented progressives on designing directions for socioeducational change during the Depression era, George S. Counts epitomized the progressive educators who were urging American educators to assume the ideological commitment to create a "new social order."[26]

For Counts, the Depression was a period of profound social transition. He feared that big business monopolists, the "economic aristocracy," would dominate American life as the ownership of productive property came to rest in fewer and fewer hands. The result was that most of the population was becoming wage earners who were dependent upon the economic aristocracy. With severe class antagonisms between the haves and the have-nots, profound and prolonged economic crises could destroy the political moderation of American democracy.

---

[23] John Dewey, *Individualism: Old and New* (New York: Capricorn, 1962). Originally published in 1929.

[24] (New York: Capricorn, 1963). Originally the Page-Barbour Lectures of 1935.

[25] Ibid., pp. 45-48.

[26] Gerald L. Gutek, *George S. Counts and American Civilization: The Educator as Social Theorist* (Macon, Ga.: Mercer University Press, 1984), pp. 15-41.

To Counts, American society was moving from the agrarian society of the past into the emerging industrial society of the future. An education based on an earlier age of small businesses and farms was ill-equipped to meet the challenges raised by an industrial and technological society.[27] According to Counts's analysis, Americans had persisted in ignoring serious weaknesses in the economic system until the collapse of the stock market in 1929 sent the entire economic structure into chaos. The Great Depression of the 1930s was symptomatic of the crisis that arises when an interdependent economic mechanism breaks down in one of its related areas. When dislocation occurs in one sector, it spreads through the entire apparatus. The unresolved crisis of the Depression manifested all the contradictions of American society. Like other social reformist progressive educators, Counts found an underlying cause of America's economic dislocation to be derived from:

> An ideal of rugged individualism, evolved in a simple pioneering and agrarian order at a time when free land existed in abundance, is urged to justify a system which exploits pitilessly and without thought of the morrow the natural and human resources of the nation and the world.[28]

In indicting economic individualism, Counts claimed the economic artistocracy used outworn symbols of the past such as "free enterprise," "the American system," "rugged individualism," and "individual initiative" to block needed efforts at economic and social reform. Counts, like Dewey, reasoned that great historic forces produced by technology had eroded the reality of economic individualism.

In 1932, Counts addressed the annual convention of the Progressive Education Association with the challenge of "Dare Progressive Education Be Progressive?" He attacked those progressive educators who believed that the educational program could be based simply on the interests of children, as romantics who refused to recognize that all education takes place in a social context. An education that was genuinely progressive had to deal with the great issues of the day; it could not remain isolated from social, economic, and political conflict. Later in 1932, Counts broadened his argument to include the members of America's educational profession in his *Dare the School Build a New Social Order?*

As indicated earlier, both Counts and Charles A. Beard had been members of the American Historical Association's Commission on the Social Studies in the Schools. He accepted much of Beard's economic interpretation of history, which he applied to education. In the early 1930s, following upon his interest-generating *Dare the School Build a New School Order?*, Counts joined with other reform-minded educators in establishing a reconstructionist journal called *The Social Frontier*. As editor of *The Social Frontier*, which carried articles by such influential theorists as Dewey, Kilpatrick, Rugg, Curti, Beard, and others, Counts advocated the ill-defined concept of *democratic collectivism*. The choice of the

---

[27] George S. Counts, *Dare the School Build a New Social Order?* (New York: John Day, 1932), p. 33.

[28] Ibid., pp. 34-35.

term was unfortunate since the critics of *The Social Frontier* associated it with the collectivist policies of the Soviet Union.

As editor of *The Social Frontier*, Counts and his associates agreed that "the age of individualism and *laissez faire* in economy and government" was ending and that a new collectivist age was emerging.[29] Claiming that a complex economic mechanism embraced the entire nation, *The Social Frontier's* editorialists argued that more coordination under unified planning and direction was needed.

During the 1930s, Counts and other "frontier" educators, claiming that schools could not be neutral in the social crisis, argued that "all education contains a large element of imposition."[30] For Counts, the real issue in educational philosophy was not whether imposition should take place but rather what was to be the source of that imposition. Historically, he reasoned, such imposition had come from the upper economic classes. Instead of accepting the status quo, Counts challenged teachers to "deliberately reach for power" and "to fashion the curriculum and the procedures of the school" so that they could shape the "social attitudes, ideals, and behavior of the coming generation."[31]

Counts believed that American teachers were well suited to create a new social order. He urged them to unite with scientists and scholars to seek and to use power fully in the public interest.

Essentialism

While Counts was urging American educators to commit themselves to creating a new social order, the essentialists, a more educationally conservative group, were challenging the progressive tendency in American education. Urging a return to basic skills and subjects, the essentialists recommended that educators concentrate their efforts on schooling rather than on reforming society.

Rejecting much of progressivism, a committee of professional educators—consisting of Michael Demiashkevich, Walter H. Ryle, M. L. Shane, Louis Shores, and Guy M. Whipple—met in Atlantic City in 1938 to prepare the essentialist platform, which was a remonstrance against declining scholastic standards. Essentialism, a term coined by Demiashkevich, defined the school's primary function as that of preserving the basic elements of the cultural heritage by deliberately transmitting it to the young. In stating their case, the essentialists raised the question:

> Should not our public schools prepare boys and girls for adult responsibility through systematic training in such subjects as reading, writing, arithmetic, history, and English, requiring mastery of such subjects, and, when necessary, stressing discipline and obedience?[32]

[29] "Collectivism and Collectivism," *The Social Frontier,* 1 (November 1934): 3.

[30] Counts, *Dare the School?,* p. 12.

[31] Ibid., pp. 12, 28-29.

[32] Adolph E. Meyer, *The Development of Education in the Twentieth Century* (Englewood Cliffs, N.J.: Prentice-Hall, 1949), p. 149.

William C. Bagley (1872-1946), a professor of education at Columbia University's Teachers College and editor of *School and Society*, elaborated the essentialist rationale and recommendations for improving the academic quality of American education. (It is interesting to note that Bagley and Counts were colleagues at Teachers College.)

In his 1930s version of basic education, Bagley contended that despite "its vast extent and heavy cost to society, public education in the United States is in many ways appalling, weak, and ineffective." As Arthur Bestor and Admiral Rickover would do in the 1950s and as critics would do in the 1980s, Bagley compared American and European educational systems and found American schools to be academically inferior. At the elementary level, Bagley argued that "Age for age, the average pupil of our elementary schools does not meet the standards of achievement in the fundamentals of education that are attained in the elementary schools of many other countries."[33] Bagley also found that American high school graduates were scholastically behind those of western European nations. Like many advocates of basic education in the 1970s and 1980s, essentialist educators condemned the large number of functional illiterates who were awarded high school diplomas.

In a way that was similar to the various national reports on education that appeared in 1983-84, Bagley, writing in 1938, commented that an increase in the crime rate had occurred at the same time that public school attendance had also increased. If American public schooling had been intellectually and morally effective, increased school attendance should have reduced the crime rate. Bagley's comments on the failure of compulsory school attendance to reduce the crime rate again resembled the charges of basic education critics in the 1970s and 1980s that public schools were becoming centers for drug abuse, violence, and vandalism rather than agencies for cultivating respect for law and order. Condemning the policy of automatic promotion, Bagley said that the practice led to "the complete abandonment in many schools of rigorous standards of scholastic achievement as a condition of promotion from grade to grade, and the passing of all pupils 'on schedule.' "[34]

Believing that the curriculum should be organized systematically and sequentially and that instruction should stress logical, chronological, and causal relationships, Bagley denounced the "incidental learning" theory of progressives such as William Heard Kilpatrick, who had claimed that students would learn skills and knowledge concomitantly or incidentally by solving problems, participating in group activities, and working on projects. The essentialist attack on incidental learning resembles latter-day criticism of 1960s curricular innovations such as the "New Mathematics," the "New Social Studies," and various process-oriented approaches to science education.

During the late 1930s, when the essentialist platform appeared, the United States was still gripped by economic depression. As indicated earlier, George S.

[33] William C. Bagley, "An Essentialist Platform for the Advancement of American Education," *Educational Administration and Supervision,* 24 (April 1938): 241-56.

[34] Ibid., p. 245.

Counts had asked *Dare the School Build a New Social Order*? Counts's query stimulated the growth of social reconstructionism. This educational movement enlisted professional educators to join other progressive individuals and groups to create a new society based on an ideology of "democratic collectivism." Adamantly rejecting the philosophy that educators should use the schools as agencies of social engineering, Bagley contended that the social reconstructionist philosophy would commit schools to a particular political ideology and would lead to the indoctrination of students. Instead of indoctrinating children and youth, Bagley argued that democracy would be served best by schools that stressed fundamental skills and permanent subjects. According to Bagley's rationale, a democratic society required literate citizens; in a literate society, knowledge of fundamental intellectual skills and subjects was the "basis for intelligent understanding and for the collective thought and judgment which are the essence of democratic institutions."[35] Bagley's judgment that citizenship for a democratic society required an education based on intellectual disciplines anticipated Arthur E. Bestor's *The Restoration of Learning*, published in 1956.[36]

The Essentialist Rationale for Education.   Bagley identified the key concepts of essentialist educational philosophy. In contrast to the rather vague outlines of Counts's New Social Order and the open-ended objectives of child-centered progressives, Bagley was precise and specific in his essentialist approach to education. For Bagley, as well as other essentialists, American schools should:

1. *Emphasize effort*, since learning is difficult and requires effort and time spent on specific tasks; while the child's interest should not be ignored, all learning should not be based on the child's limited range of experience.
2. *Emphasize discipline*, since giving a person absolute freedom without regard to personal and social consequences leads to moral and social anarchy; genuine freedom comes only by the systematic discipline of learning the skills and subjects needed to live in a civilized society.
3. *Emphasize the accumulated knowledge* created by sustained inquiry, scientific investigation, and literary and artistic achievement; schools must transmit the cultural systematically and deliberately rather than accidentally, since deliberate transmission protects the human race from degenerating into barbarism.
4. *Emphasize teacher-initiated instruction* from teachers who, as intellectually and socially mature individuals, recognize and appreciate the value of basic skills and knowledge.
5. *Emphasize the logical organization of subject matter*, which is essential for learning organized bodies of knowledge; since the cultural heritage is vast and complex, it is best presented as subject matter disciplines arranged either logically or chronologically.

[35] Ibid., p. 251.

[36] Arthur E. Bestor, Jr., *The Restoration of Learning: A Program for Redeeming the Unfulfilled Promise of American Education* (New York: Knopf, 1955).

6. *Emphasize long-range goals,* since the human race has abiding interests and concerns of a perennial nature; the school's educational program should not be based on the immediately and momentarily relevant and popular, since the essentials of a good education are permanent.

Based upon the essentialist rationale, Bagley's curriculum for elementary education included:

Basic social arts, such as communicating, recording, computing, and measuring, which reflected fundamental skills such as reading, writing, speaking, and arithmetic.

Space and time to widen the spatial horizon and broaden the time perspective. Space and time can be equated with geography and history.

Health education to inculcate the principles of health instruction and health practices.

Natural science, which included basic concepts, principles, and methods of such natural sciences as biology, botany, zoology, and chemistry.

Fine arts, such as art, music, and other creative expressive skills and activities.

CONCLUSION

The years between World War I and World War II were significant in bringing momentous social and educational problems and issues before the American people. The 1920s, in particular, saw the United States becoming an industrial and technological society characterized by great interdependence. The 1930s saw the national economic prosperity end in a severe depression. During the Depression era, with its New Deal legislation, American educational institutions attempted to cope with severe fiscal retrenchment. The Depression decade witnessed significant educational debates between educational progressives, social reconstructionists, and essentialists.

DISCUSSION QUESTIONS

1. Examine Wilson's efforts to have the United States join the League of Nations. How do Wilson's ideas on international order relate to current proposals for international education?

2. Compare the Red Scare of the 1920s and the McCarthy witch-hunts of the 1950s. What implications did these events have for intellectual and educational freedom?

3. Analyze the tensions between urban and rural America during the 1920s. What consequences did these tensions generally have on education?

4. Examine the educational implications of mass production techniques and the assembly line.

5. Examine the origins and impact of such informal educational forces as radio broadcasting and motion pictures on American society.
6. Identify and analyze the significant educational trends of the 1920s.
7. Analyze the impact of the Depression of the 1930s on education and school- · ing in the United States.
8. Review the chapter on progressivism. Was Franklin D. Roosevelt a progressive?
9. Identify and describe the New Deal agencies that related most directly to education, schools, youth, and children.
10. Compare and contrast the education critics of the 1930s, 1950s, and 1980s.

RESEARCH TOPICS

1. Read a biography of Woodrow Wilson. In a biographical sketch, comment on his education and on his social and educational philosophy.
2. Using oral history techniques, interview and record the impressions of individuals who experienced the Depression of the 1930s. Focus your questions on the Depression's effects on society and education.
3. Read biographies of Herbert Hoover and Franklin Roosevelt. In a paper, compare and contrast their socioeconomic backgrounds and their political and social philosophies.
4. Investigate the role played by academic experts in the early stages of the New Deal.
5. Investigate and write a short paper that describes the educational efforts and programs of the Civilian Conservation Corps.
6. Research and write a paper that identifies and analyzes the major educational objectives of the essentialists.
7. Read and review a book written by an historian who was identified with the "new history."
8. Read George S. Counts's *Dare the School Build a New Social Order?* Are Counts's arguments relevant to contemporary education and society?
9. Read John Dewey's *Individualism: Old and New.* Determine if Dewey's social philosophy, as expressed in this book, is relevant to contemporary American society.

REFERENCES AND READINGS

Burns, James M. *Roosevelt: The Soldier of Freedom.* New York: Harcourt Brace Jovanovich, 1970.
Cooper, John M. *The Warrior and the Priest.* Cambridge, Mass.: Harvard University Press, 1983.
Counts, George S. *Dare the School Build a New Social Order?* New York: John Day, 1932.
____. *Secondary Education and Industrialism.* Cambridge, Mass.: Harvard University Press, 1929.

Curti, Merle. *The Social Ideas of American Educators.* Paterson, N.J.: Littlefied, Adams, 1959.
Dewey, John. *Individualism: Old and New.* New York: Capricorn, 1962.
___. *Liberalism and Social Action.* New York: Capricorn, 1963.
Freidel, Frank B. *Franklin D. Roosevelt.* Boston: Little, Brown, 1973.
Geiger, George R. *John Dewey in Perspective.* New York: Oxford University Press, 1958.
Ginger, Ray. *Six Days or Forever? Tennessee v. John Thomas Scopes.* New York: Oxford University Press, 1958.
Gutek, Gerald L. *George S. Counts and American Civilization: The Educator as Social Theorist.* Macon, Ga.: Mercer University Press, 1984.
Hook, Sidney. *John Dewey: An Intellectual Portrait.* New York: John Day, 1939.
Leuchtenburg, William E. *Franklin Roosevelt: A Profile.* New York: Hill and Wang, 1967.
___. *The Perils of Prosperity, 1914-1932.* Chicago: University of Chicago Press, 1958.
Link, Arthur S. and Catton, William B. *American Epoch: A History of the United States since 1900,* 2, *The Age of Franklin D. Roosevelt 1921-1945.* New York: Knopf, 1973.
Matthews, June D. *The Federal Theater, 1935-1939.* Princeton, N.J.: Princeton University Press, 1967.
McDonald, William. *Federal Relief Administration and the Arts.* Columbus: Ohio State University Press, 1969.
Shannon, David A. *The Great Depression.* Englewood Cliffs, N.J.: Prentice-Hall, 1960.
Terkel, Studs. *Hard Times: An Oral History of the Great Depression.* New York: Pantheon, 1970.
Tyack, David, Lowe, Robert, and Hansot, Elisabeth. *Public Schools in Hard Times: The Great Depression and Recent Years.* Cambridge, Mass.: Harvard University Press, 1984.

11
SOCIETY
AND EDUCATION
AFTER WORLD WAR II:
1945–1960

The years after World War II, from 1945 to 1960, marked a fifteen-year span during which the United States readjusted from wartime mobilization to peace. Like every postwar period, this era brought momentous social and economic changes to American life and society. In this chapter we shall examine the social changes that reshaped the patterns of American life and education.

THE CULTURAL TRANSFORMATION
OF AMERICAN LIFE

The most apparent alteration in the foundations of American life in the postwar era was the broadening of the economic base. More people than ever before were now included in the "great American middle class." The mass conscription of World War II and the socioeconomic mobility created by the burgeoning wartime industries had eroded many of the ethnic enclaves that had characterized American life in earlier years. The pattern of assimilation was particularly apparent in the growth of suburban communities that surrounded the large American cities.

Socioeconomic Changes

The postwar years, especially from 1945 to 1960, witnessed important socio-economic, demographic, and political changes that had pronounced effects on

American education. In particular, the rapid increase in population, called the "baby boom," and the relocation of many Americans from large cities to the suburbs had serious implications for America's schools.

When the war ended, there was a strong demand for housing. The construction of private residences had ceased during the war years so that construction of defense plants would have first priority. New housing starts were located in suburban areas. In some metropolitan areas, such as Los Angeles, Chicago, and New York, the suburban population doubled during the 1950s. At the same time that the suburbs, usually located in concentric rings around the large cities, grew, the cities' population remained the same or increased slightly. By 1960, 60 million people, or one-third of the national population, were located in suburbs. The movement to the suburbs of the 1950s was essentially a migration of white families. Blacks and members of other minority groups lived in the large cities, especially their inner-core areas. When former city dwellers relocated in the suburbs, they generally did not recreate the ethnic enclaves that had existed in the larger cities. Southern black migration to Northern cities increased dring World War II and continued to grow afterward, as did Puerto Rican and Mexican-American migration. The immediate impact of the white migration to the suburbs was a greatly increased demand for new schools, classrooms, and teachers in areas that hitherto had been rural or small town.

During the 1950s, there also was a rapid increase in the American population. The large family was the pattern among the young married couples. By 1960 the nation's population had grown by 19 percent. The movement to the suburbs and the increasing population of school-age children had some obvious consequences for American education. First, the suburban system became an educational reality that took its place beside urban and rural school districts. Since they generally had populations comprised of affluent upper-middle-class business and professional persons, the suburbs had the financial resources to build new schools and support extensive and varied educational programs. In addition, the professional and business classes, who saw education as a means of social and economic mobility, were heavily committed to schools that would move their children upward in American society.

The suburban school districts, with their rapidly growing population of school-age children, built many new schools in what some have called "the brick-and-mortar decade" of American education. In these newly constructed schools, new architectural designs replaced the conventional multistory rectangular school building. During the 1950s and early 1960s, many of the large sprawling high schools that resembled shopping malls were built.

While the tax base in suburban school districts was climbing upward, the large urban school districts were beginning to see industries and business moving out, causing a corresponding decrease in the financial support available for schools. Inner-city schools began to deteriorate physically. With fewer new schools being built in the large cities, existing facilities became overcrowded.

Second, the white movement to suburbs and the black concentration in the large cities accelerated de facto racial segregation. The majority of suburban schools had predominantly white populations, while inner-city schools were predominantly black. In addition to racial segregation, there was segregation on economic class lines. The more affluent groups were attending suburban public schools, while economically disadvantaged children and youth were attending city schools. Theoretically, segregation based on residence was reducing the "commonness" and comprehensiveness of the public school system. The educational resources available to suburban and urban students were so uneven that equality of educational opportunity was becoming a myth.

The expansion of the middle class unleashed rising tides of consumerism, as the demand accelerated for goods and services that had been restricted during wartime. The gap between the life-styles of rich and poor also narrowed dramatically, most families possessed an automobile, with many owning more than one.

The political legacy of the Great Depression and the national mobilization required by World War II was a massive growth in the power and services of the federal government. While the national government was involved in many areas of life such as housing, agriculture, and transportation, it still held back from entering directly into elementary and secondary education. The reluctance of the federal government to involve itself directly in education was due to such factors as: (1) the long tradition that held education to be a local and state prerogative; (2) the fear of Southern white conservative politicians that the entry of the federal government into school affairs would bring about the end of racial segregation; and (3) a strong feeling that private and religious schools would demand federal aid, which would breach the traditional wall of separation between church and state. While many Americans had grown comfortable with an increased federal involvement in many areas of life, many remained strongly opposed to a greater federal role in education.

The Ascendency of the Corporate Ideal

One of the characteristics of American life after World War II was the rise of the corporate ideal, which some commentators personified as the "man in the gray flannel suit." While the "rugged individual" had expressed the business ethos in earlier periods, the 1950s and 1960s saw the corporation executive, often the middle manager, emerge as the model. The corporate executive was a product of an educational system that continually stressed cooperative teamwork as the most effective, if not democratic, way to get things done. He had also learned the lessons of war time mobilization, which saw groups and committees working to achieve increased productivity to win the war. Commentators such as the sociologist C. Wright Mills wrote about the emergence of a "power elite" of political, business, and military leaders as the real holders of power in postwar America.[1]

[1] C. Wright Mills, *The Power Elite* (New York: Oxford University Press, 1959).

The corporate style of life, at least in the early 1950s, had strong implications for education in the United States. Educationally, its members were drawn from prestigious Ivy League eastern colleges. The corporate elite had a strong impact as an educational model. It stimulated educational administrators to think of themselves as officers in educational corporations who occupied positions similar to their more highly salaried counterparts in business and industry.

President Truman and the Fair Deal

Harry S. Truman, who succeeded to the presidency upon Franklin Roosevelt's death in 1945, sought to continue New Deal social and economic policies, and to develop a bipartisan foreign policy.[2] Truman's efforts touched upon education indirectly but the major issues and crises of his administration had large educational implications and were prophetic of things to come in the 1960s.

In September 1945, Truman presented a twenty-one-point program to Congress that identified his major social welfare and economic goals. He proposed full employment legislation, expanded unemployment legislation, a permanent Fair Employment Practices Commission, an increased minimum wage, comprehensive housing legislation, the creation of a National Science Foundation, grants for hospital construction, farm price supports, a comprehensive health program, an atomic energy program, the inauguration of the St. Lawrence Seaway Project, and assistance to the states to assure equal educational opportunities.

Several items in Truman's program had significance for education. His advocacy of fair employment practices anticipated the affirmative action legislation of the 1960s. His proposal for a National Science Foundation anticipated the establishment of such an agency in later years, which would stimulate not only basic scientific research but also science education. Although his plan for financial assistance to the states to achieve greater equality of educational opportunities failed, Truman's proposal inaugurated the debates over federal aid to education in the postwar decade.

Truman's Re-election in 1948.   The election of 1948 was a bitter struggle in which the incumbent president Harry S. Truman, as the Democratic nominee, waged an uphill but successful campaign against Thomas E. Dewey, the Republican candidate, and two third-party candidates, J. Strom Thurmond of the States' Rights Democrats and Henry Wallace, the Progressive party candidate, both of whom led significant defections from Democratic ranks. Truman was re-elected on a platform that called for an expansion of Social Security, the repeal of the Taft-Hartley labor relations act, an increase in the minimum wage, slum clearance, federal housing,

[2] For accounts of the Truman administration, see Alonzo L. Hamby, *Beyond the New Deal: Harry S. Truman and American Liberalism* (New York: Columbia University Press, 1973); Susan M. Hartman, *Truman and the 80th Congress* (Columbia: University of Missouri Press, 1971); J. Joseph Huthmacher, *The Truman Years* (Hinsdale, Ill.: Dryden Press, 1972).

federal aid to education, and the containment of Soviet expansionism. At the national level, Truman's advocacy of federal aid to education and containment of the Soviet Union held the greatest implications for education. The debates over federal aid to education would be waged throughout the late 1940s and 1950s, with proponents and opponents of diverse motivations arguing the merits and threats that federal aid to education posed for the republic. Although Truman's containment policy did not appear to relate directly to education, the Cold War era was to have a great impact on education in the United States.

Among the implications of the Cold War for education were the following: (1) There was a growing concern about the internal security of the United States and a mounting fear of internal subversion. (2) The general mood of apprehension about the threat of Soviet communism helped to stimulate the rise of Senator Joseph McCarthy and what became known as McCarthyism, a series of investigations searching to identify risks to American security. As the antisubversive hunt proceeded, a number of educators and intellectuals were investigated. (3) Finally, the era of the Cold War ushered in an attitude that American students, especially at the junior high, high school, and college levels, needed to be educated about the dangers of communism. We shall examine these trends in greater detail later in the chapter.

In his inaugural address on January 5, 1949, Truman called upon Congress to enact a series of "Fair Deal" proposals, which included federal aid to education. The president's efforts in this area failed because Congress was sharply divided on the issue. Southern white states' rights Democrats, often cooperating in an effective coalition with conservative Northern Republicans, would support aid to education only if there were no antidiscrimination criteria in the legislation. Black congressmen supported aid only if it provided for racially integrated schools. In addition to the controversies centering on racial integration in the schools, Roman Catholic spokesmen lobbied for federal aid to parochial schools. Conservative members of Congress opposed federal aid as an invasion of state and local prerogatives. The education lobby, especially the National Education Association (NEA) and the National Congress of Parents and Teachers energetically lobbied for federal aid for public schools but opposed aid for nonpublic schools. Because of these various contending viewpoints, Congress failed to pass any federal aid to education legislation during Truman's administration. While aid proposals were introduced in subsequent years, it was not until the National Defense Education Act of 1958 during the Eisenhower administration and the Elementary and Secondary Education Act of the Johnson administration that significant federal assistance to education occurred.

While the Truman administration produced an initiative, albeit an unsuccessful one, for federal aid, efforts for equal employment opportunities and civil rights legislation were successful. As these initiatives developed throughout the 1950s, 1960s, and 1970s, civil rights legislation and federal court decisions brought about major social, economic, and racial change in the United States.

FEDERAL AID TO EDUCATION

Prospects for federal aid to education improved when Senator Robert A. Taft, the Republican senator from Ohio and the leader of the conservative wing of the Republican party, dropped his long-standing opposition and came out in support of aid. Senator Taft in 1946 introduced a bill in the Senate that incorporated a range of compromises and satisfied the demands of various groups that had been in contention on the issue. Taft's bill provided a flat grant to all states, allowed states to determine if funds were to be provided to nonpublic schools, distributed federal funds equally among black and white schools in states with racially segregated schools, and pledged noninterference by the federal government in matters relating to school segregation.[3] Although Taft's bill passed the Senate, it failed in the House of Representatives.

Although both Truman and Taft supported federal aid to education, the prospects for Congressional enactment became mired in sectarian controversey.[4] In 1949, the Senate passed an aid measure but the House Committee on Education and Labor disagreed on an acceptable version of federal aid. A bill sponsored by North Carolina congressman Graham A. Barden, a conservative Democrat, that limited federal funds exclusively to public schools and prohibited federal support for auxiliary services such as transportation and health, was attacked by many leaders of the Roman Catholic hierarchy. After bitter debate, the Barden bill died in committee.

The result of these efforts to secure federal aid to education was acrimonious controversy, often along sectional and sectarian lines. While federal aid was a fiercely debated issue, proposals made little headway until the late 1950s, when Cold War tensions worked to produce legislation that tied aid to schools to the national defense.

The sectarian controversies that proposals for federal assistance to education provoked were also felt at the state and local levels. In particular, the Everson case in 1947 and the McCollum case in 1948 revealed the tensions that support for religious schools engendered.

In 1947, Everson, a taxpayer of Ewing Township, New Jersey, brought suit, claiming that the board of education's reimbursement for school bus transportation paid to parents of both public and Catholic parochial schools, violated the First Amendment of the Constitution.[5] The Supreme Court by a five-to-four majority ruled that the reimbursement was a form of providing a general government service, such as providing public highways, rather than direct aid to religious institutions. In its decision, however, the Court reaffirmed the separation of church and state.

[3] For an excellent analysis of the federal aid issue, see Diane Ravitch, *The Troubled Crusade: American Education, 1945-1980* (New York: Basic Books, 1983), pp. 26-42. Senator Taft's changing views on federal aid are examined in James T. Patterson, *Mr. Republican: A Biography of Robert A. Taft* (Boston: Houghton Mifflin, 1972), pp. 261-62, 320-26.

[4] Ravitch, *Troubled Crusade*, pp. 33-39.

[5] *Everson* v. *Board of Education*, 330 U.S. 1 (1947); also see Ravitch, *Troubled Crusade*, pp. 29-31.

Roman Catholics, using the "child benefit" theory, contended that the Everson decision sustained their claim that children attending Catholic schools were entitled to auxiliary services such as nonreligious textbooks and health services that benefited the child directly. Protestant spokesmen, especially members of Protestants and Other Americans United for Separation of Church and State (POAU), saw the Everson decision as a breach of separation of church and state. During the late 1940s, the controversy over aid to religious schools remained divisive and unresolved.

In 1948, the Supreme Court ruled in the *McCollum* case that an Illinois law that permitted released time for religious instruction in public schools during regular school hours was unconstitutional. The Court's eight-to-one decision found that the law violated the First Amendment since it used the public schools to disseminate denominational religious doctrines.[6]

CIVIL RIGHTS

The postwar years were a time when black Americans began a concerted effort to end racial segregation and to achieve equality of opportunity both in employment and in education. The administrations of President Truman (1945-1952) and President Eisenhower (1952-1960) were concerned with civil rights issues. Characteristic of his willingness to face difficult issues, President Truman sought to break the long-standing legacy of racial discrimination in the United States.

The Committee on Civil Rights

In 1946, President Truman appointed the Presidential Committee on Civil Rights. With the president's encouragement, the committee defined its mission to both educate the American people and to make legislative recommendations. The committee's report, *To Secure These Rights*, which described racial discrimination in employment, health care, voting practices, and education, also condemned racially segregated schooling as unfair to black children.[7] According to the committee, segregated black schools had a lower per pupil expenditure and lower teachers' salaries than schools attended by whites; black schools also had inadequate facilities and curricula in comparison to all white schools.

The Committee on Civil Rights recommended:

1. The reestablishment of the Fair Employment Practices Committee (FEPC).
2. The establishment of a permanent national civil rights commission.
3. The denial of federal aid to states that segregated schools and public facilities.
4. A federal antilynching law.

[6]*McCollum* v. *Board of Education*, 333 U.S. 203 (1948); also see Ravitch, *Troubled Crusade*, p. 32.

[7]Committee on Civil Rights, *To Secure These Rights: The Report of the President's Committee on Civil Rights* (New York: Simon & Schuster, 1947).

5. Federal protection of the right to vote and the abolishing of the poll tax.
6. Ending racial discrimination in the armed forces, health care facilities, housing, and interstate transportation.

President Truman agreed with the recommendations of his committee but could not muster enough support for their enactment. Frustrated by Congress, he ended, by executive order, racial segregation in the armed forces and prohibited discrimination in federal agencies in 1948.

In 1949, President Truman sought to secure passage of civil rights legislation, but again his program was blocked by a coalition of states' rights Southern Democrats and conservative Republicans. His achievement in the area of civil rights lay more in creating a sense of readiness for such legislation than in its actual enactment.

In the 1950s, the thrust of the civil rights movement focused on the nation's schools, colleges, and universities. Leading the struggle for civil rights was the National Association for the Advancement of Colored People (NAACP), which began an intensive and meticulously researched battle in the courts to challenge and end de jure racial segregation, which had been given legal sanction in the *Plessy* v. *Ferguson* case in 1896.

At the end of the nineteenth century, segregationist attitudes had resurfaced in the South with the enactment of "Jim Crow" laws that disenfranchised black voters through such tactics as the white primary, the grandfather clause, literacy tests, and the poll tax. In 1896, the Supreme Court, in *Plessy* v. *Ferguson,* gave what amounted to legal sanction to the segregation process that had been developing throughout the 1880s and 1890s.[8] This decision upheld a Louisiana law that segregated railroad passengers according to race on the basis of the separate-but-equal doctrine. If the facilities were equal, the justices reasoned, then they could be segregated. The separate-but-equal doctrine was extended to cover a range of facilities, including schools.

Legal Action Against Segregation

The initiative against the separate-but-equal doctrine was taken by the NAACP, which began a long fifty-year struggle to overturn the *Plessy* verdict. The NAACP strategy was to concentrate on segregation in professional and graduate schools in order to establish the groundwork for an attack on segregation in the public schools.

In 1938, the Supreme Court heard the *Gaines* case.[9] Lloyd L. Gaines, a black applicant, sought admission to the University of Missouri law school, which was attended solely by whites. Since Missouri did not have a separate-but-equal law school, the Court ruled that Gaines was being denied equality of the privileges provided for "separated groups" within the state and that he should be admitted to the law school.

[8]*Plessy v. Ferguson,* 163 U.S. 537 (1896).
[9]*Missouri Ex Rel Gaines v. Canada,* 305 U.S. 337 (1938).

Ten years later, the Supreme Court heard the *Sipuel* case, which was similar to the *Gaines* case.[10] In 1948, Ada L. Sipuel, a black applicant, sought admission to the University of Oklahoma law school, an all-white institution. Sipuel was advised to defer her application until Oklahoma created a separate law school for blacks. The Court, finding that Oklahoma was denying Sipuel's rights under the equal protection clause of the Fourteenth Amendment, ruled that she was entitled to a legal education within the same time frame that applicants from other groups were provided with such an education.

The *Sweatt* v. *Painter* case in 1950 was brought by Herman M. Sweatt, a black applicant seeking admission to the all-white University of Texas law school. Sweatt's application had been rejected. The university quickly established a small segregated law school that admitted Sweatt, the only student. Deciding in favor of Sweatt, the Supreme Court ruled that the alternative law school did not match the facilities, faculty, and academic quality of the University of Texas law school and did not provide an equal education.[11]

***Brown* v. *Board of Education*.**   After laying the legal groundwork in cases dealing with the admission of blacks to racially segregated graduate and professional schools, the NAACP took on the broader and more emotional issue of segregation in the public schools. In *Brown* v. *Board of Education of Topeka*, the NAACP attorneys, led by Thurgood Marshall, challenged the separate-but-equal precedent established in *Plessy* v. *Ferguson* in 1896. Using sociological and psychological findings as well as legal precedents, Marshall argued that racially segregated schools violated the due process clause of the Fourteenth Amendment, denied black children equality of educational opportunity, and caused them psychological damage.

Agreeing with the NAACP's arguments, the Supreme Court, in *Brown* v. *Board of Education*, overturned the separate-but-equal doctrine. The Court ruled that segregated schools were "inherently unequal" and violated the Fourteenth Amendment. Chief Justice Earl Warren stated:

> Segregation of white and colored children in public schools has a detrimental effect upon the colored children. The impact is greater when it has the sanction of the law; for the policy of separating the races is usually interpreted as denoting the inferiority of the Negro group. A sense of inferiority affects the motivation of a child to learn. Segregation with the sanction of law, therefore, has a tendency to retard the education and mental development of Negro children and to deprive them of some of the benefits they would receive in a racially integrated school system.[12]

One year after its *Brown* decision, the Supreme Court ordered that implementation should proceed "with all deliberate speed." Between 1954 and 1957, the path

[10] *Sipuel* v. *Oklahoma Board of Regents*, 332 U.S. 631 (1948).

[11] *Sweatt* v. *Painter*, 339 U.S. 629 (1950).

[12] *Brown* v. *Board of Education*, 347 U.S. 483 (1954).

that school desegregation would take remained unclear, and the process was slow and uneven. In some border states, local school authorities began gradual desegregation. In the deep South, some politicians pledged massive resistance to the desegregation ruling, and legislatures enacted laws to evade compliance. The old states' rights arguments from the days of John C. Calhoun were resurrected as some Southern politicans claimed the right of "interposition" to block compliance with the Court's ruling. The Eisenhower administration, while determined to uphold the Court's decision in the *Brown* case, was equally determined to move cautiously. Events, however, were to cause Eisenhower and his administration to move dramatically and decisively.

Little Rock.   At Little Rock, Arkansas, Governor Orval Faubus attempted to block the local school board's initiative to desegregate. In 1957, the Little Rock board of education developed a plan to begin school desegregation by admitting nine black students to Central High School. Governor Faubus, claiming that public order was threatened, ordered the Arkansas National Guard to duty to prevent the black students' admission. Federal Judge Ronald Davies ordered the board of education to implement the desegregation plan. Faced with a federal injunction, Governor Faubus withdrew the National Guard. In late September when school reopened, a large mob threatened the black students, who were sent home by school authorities. At this point, President Eisenhower, on September 24, 1957, federalized the Arkansas National Guard and sent the 101st Airborne Division to Little Rock to ensure that the decisions of the federal courts were carried out. Protected by armed paratroopers, the black students were admitted to Central High School.

The Montgomery Alabama Bus Boycott.   While the NAACP advanced the civil rights cause through the courts, blacks—especially in the South—embarked on an action-oriented course. In December 1955, a black boycott of the Montgomery, Alabama, public bus system began when Rosa Parks was arrested for failing to give up her seat to a white man on one of the city buses. The black community, led by the Reverend Martin Luther King, Jr., began a year-long boycott that ended when the Supreme Court declared segregated public transportation unconstitutional.

The social action stage of the civil rights movement continued to accelerate throughout the late 1950s and early 1960s. A number of black civil rights organizations were formed that worked alongside of the older NAACP and the Urban League to secure full civil rights for black Americans. Martin Luther King, Jr. organized the Southern Christian Leadership Conference, which, following Gandhian tactics, used nonviolent resistance against racial segregation. College students organized the Student Nonviolent Coordinating Committee (SNCC), which sent black and white students to lead voter registration drives in the South's black communities.

From 1945 to 1960, the cause of civil rights and black equality moved steadily ahead. President Truman had set the stage, and President Eisenhower had responded in the face of crisis to carry civil rights forward. It was the patient legal efforts of the NAACP that secured a momentous victory in the *Brown* case. In the mid- and late 1960s and early 1970s, black activism would continue to assert itself.

INTERNATIONALISM, COLD WAR, AND McCARTHYISM

During and after World War II, American society and education were influenced by twin forces: those that were internal to and arose within American society and those that were external, or international, in impact. By the mid-twentieth century, it was increasingly difficult to disentangle the two sets of forces. In particular, international developments came to exert a growing influence on domestic policy. While the American public schools remained primarily a state responsibility that was delegated to local units, international events exerted an increasingly greater influence on schooling. The increasing sophistication of the mass media, particularly television, came to have a greater impact on the informal education of Americans, especially in shaping the way in which they saw their own country in relationship to the world. This section examines how a series of events related to foreign policy came to have at first an indirect and then direct impact on American education.

The years of the Truman administration marked the beginning of the Cold War between the United States and the Soviet Union.[13] As the Cold War developed through a series of international crises in which the United States and the Soviet Union tried to check other's world influence, a pervasive attitude of anticommunism arose in the United States. At times, the American response was anti-Soviet and directed against the expansionist designs of the Soviet Union; at other times, it was a highly ideological one in which the United States, as leader of the "free world," was regarded as the bastion of democracy against Soviet totalitarianism. To understand the evolving American world view, it should be recalled that: (1) American society, including its children and youth, were well aware that they were living in a precarious age of nuclear weapons capable of wreaking worldwide destruction; (2) despite a few calls for a return to isolationism, most Americans supported a wider international role for their country; (3) concerted efforts were being made in the schools to educate American children and youth about the threat of communism; (4) in American domestic life and politics, there was a growing fear of internal subversion by Soviet agents in the United States.

It was in this general climate of opinion that American life and institutions, including educational ones, responded to the bipolar world of the Cold War. Although President Truman was a strong proponent of civil rights legislation, some

[13] For the origins of the Cold War, see Lloyd C. Gardner, *Architects of Illusion: Men and Ideas in American Foreign Policy, 1941-1949* (Quadrangle Books, New York: 1972); Walter La Faber, *America, Russia, and the Cold War, 1945-1971* (New York: John Wiley, 1972); Lawrence Whittner, *Cold War America: From Hiroshima to Watergate* (New York: Praeger, 1974).

interpreters see his administration as laying the groundwork for what became the intense antisubversive investigations of the 1950s, many of which the president, himself, opposed.[14] In 1947, President Truman established the Loyalty Review Board by which the federal government could discharge employees for suspected disloyalty. In 1950, legislation introduced by Senator Pat McCarran established the Subversive Activities Control Board, which could identify an organization as subversive and require it to register with the board, and submit its membership lists and financial accounts for review. Although President Truman vetoed the McCarran bill, it was passed by Congress over his veto. The McCarren-Walter immigration act, which continued a quota system for immigration and forbade immigration of those identified as subversive, also passed.

These initial antisubversive laws had several effects. Intended to identify and remove Soviet spies and agents from federal employment, they also intensified a climate of suspicion. Reminiscent of the Red Scare of the 1920s, the 1950s saw state legislatures and occasional school districts requiring professors, teachers, and educational personnel to sign oaths attesting to their loyalty to federal and state governments. They also had about them an ex post facto effect, in that they held individuals accountable for past associations. Finally, they encouraged a mood of censorship, in which textbooks and other educational materials were examined for allegedly un-American or subversive views.

The anticommunist mood was accelerated by a series of dramatic and controversial court cases that attracted national and international attention. The arrest and conviction of Dr. Klaus Fuchs, an atomic scientist in England, for espionage led to information that implicated several Americans. David Gold, a research scientist, and David Greenglass, an army sergeant, were convicted of espionage and imprisoned. Accused of spying, Ethel and Julius Rosenberg were sentenced to death. The Rosenberg case drew widespread attention and generated international protests against the death sentence, which was executed on June 10, 1953. An investigation by the House Un-American Activities Committee identified Whittaker Chambers as a key witness. Chambers, who admitted membership in the Communist party from 1924 to 1938, claimed that since 1939 he had been providing information about communist subversion to the federal government. Chambers accused Alger Hiss, a well-known expert on international relations, of membership in the Communist party. Hiss, a graduate of the Harvard Law School, had headed the Carnegie Endowment for World Peace and had also served in the departments of agriculture and state. After a series of sensational charges and counter charges between Chambers and Hiss, Hiss was convicted of perjury in 1950 and sentenced to five years in prison. Although still being studied by historians, the Hiss-Chambers episode in the 1950s further stimulated the mood of anticommunism in the United States. Hiss was an intellectual, a graduate of a leading university, and an academic expert. The episode stimulated suspicion about the loyalty of many intellectuals,

---

[14] For the revisionist interpretation that McCarthyism was a product of the Truman administration, see Athan Theoharis, *Seeds of Repression* (New York: Quadrangle Books, 1971).

writers, and teachers to the United States. This mood was quickly translated into politics and became a campaign issue throughout the 1950s.

McCarthyism

The anticommunist and antisubversive mood of the 1950s generated a movement in the United States known as McCarthyism, named for its principal protagonist, Joseph McCarthy, Republican senator from Wisconsin.[15] Although McCarthy raised the issue of communist subversion in schools and colleges, his major investigations were directed against employees in the federal government, especially in the state department and the army. McCarthy capitalized on what was regarded as a "sell-out" of the Chinese Nationalist government of Chiang Kai-shek to the communists. In particular, he accused academic experts on China of engineering the "betrayal" of Chiang's government.

CONTAINMENT, INTERNATIONAL RELATIONS, AND INTERNATIONAL EDUCATION

While the Cold War was having its effects on American domestic society, politics, and education during the late 1940s and 1950s, it was also shaping foreign policy and the way in which Americans viewed the world. The notable trend in policy during the Truman administration was designed to contain Soviet influence and expansion.[16] The Eisenhower administration, although using the rhetoric of liberating the Soviet satellite nations, adhered to a modified version of containment. Beginning with the Truman administration and continuing through the Eisenhower years (1952-1960) and the Kennedy-Johnson administrations (1961-1968), the United States made concerted efforts to internationalize the education of its people.

Seeking to prepare Americans for a larger international role, American education reflected an enlarged international dimension. For example, the school curriculum, particularly social studies, took on a greater international focus.[17] In social studies textbooks, sections appeared on the United Nations and on various

[15] For treatments of McCarthy and McCarthyism, see David M. Oshinsky, *A Conspiracy So Immense: The World of Joe McCarthy* (New York: Free Press, 1983); Lately Thomas, *When Even Angels Wept: The Senator Joseph McCarthy Affair—A Story Without a Hero* (New York: Morrow, 1973).

[16] The doctrine of containment is attributed to the diplomat-scholar George F. Kennan. See George F. Kennan, *American Diplomacy, 1900-1950* (Chicago: University of Chicago Press, 1951). A useful analysis of containment can be found in Norman A. Graebner, *Cold War Diplomacy, 1945-1960* (New York: Van Nostrand, 1962).

[17] For efforts to internationalize education, see Harold Taylor, *The World and the American Teacher* (Washington, D.C.: American Association of Colleges for Teacher Education, 1968); Edith W. King, *The World: Context for Teaching in the Elementary School* (Dubuque, Iowa: William C. Brown, 1971); James M. Becker and Howard D. Mehlinger, eds., *International Dimensions in the Social Studies* (Washington, D.C.: National Council for The Social Studies, 1968).

regional security pacts. In colleges and universities, regional area studies focusing on the Soviet Union and eastern Europe, southeast Asia, and Latin America were established to prepare specialists in the history, languages, politics, and economics of these areas. Courses in world history, at both the secondary and higher levels, broadened their focus to include Asia and Africa in addition to the conventional focus on Europe.

Teacher education programs, too, took on an international focus as a renewed emphasis was given to comparative and international education. Many colleges of education also developed overseas components that focused on the role of education as an instrument of development and modernization. While this increased emphasis on international relations and international education continued during the period from the early 1950s to the mid-1970s, at least a part of this emphasis originated with the national policies that sought to contain Soviet and communist expansion.[18]

The United States developed the regional security pact as a major foreign policy concept. To implement this concept, the United States would unite with nations in a particular region to protect that region from threats to its security. The concept of the regional security pact grew out of an interpretation of history which asserted that if the nations of Europe had united against Hitler in the 1930s rather than appeasing him, World War II could have been averted. The first major regional security pact was the North Atlantic Treaty Organization (NATO), organized in 1949, with Belgium, Canada, Denmark, France, Great Britain, Ireland, Italy, Luxembourg, the Netherlands, Norway, Portugal, and the United States as the original signatories. Later participants in NATO were Greece, Turkey, and West Germany. The principle underlying NATO was that the signatory nations would plan a joint defense against an aggressor nation and would enter into other areas of mutual cooperation and support as well.

It was this mixture of motives—anticommunism, a desire to contain the Soviet Union, and a genuine wish to aid underdeveloped nations—that prompted the United States to support a wide range of foreign assistance programs. The initial thrust was the Point Four program of aid to developing nations. This effort was followed by the creation of the Agency for International Development (AID) designed to provide financial aid and technical resources from the United States to developing countries. As a part of these programs, teams of American experts were sent to foreign countries to advise and aid in their internal economic development. Often these experts included teams of educational experts who advised their counterparts in developing nations on ways to modernize their educational systems.[19] Often an area of concentration was in developing agricultural institutes and schools to improve the production of food and other commodities.

---

[18] One of the most penetrating analyses of the relationship of international education to foreign policy and world views is Kenneth Melvin, *Education in World Affairs: A Realistic Approach to International Education* (Lexington, Mass.: 1970).

[19] A thorough treatment on international and development education is provided in Harold G. Shane, ed., *The United States and International Education: The Sixty-Eight Yearbook of the National Society for the Study of Education* (Chicago: University of Chicago Press, 1968).

Throughout the 1950s, 1960s, and 1970s, the American policy was to contribute to the military defense of friendly countries and to create economic conditions that promoted their internal security. By the late 1960s and early 1970s, critics alleged that this policy was simplistic and at times counterproductive. When carried to extremes, these critics charged, the United States policy supported undemocratic regimes as long as they were strongly anticommunist.

SCHOOLING IN POSTWAR AMERICA: 1945-1960

So far we have examined those large national issues—postwar readjustment, foreign policy, and civil rights—that reshaped American society, politics, and education during the Truman and Eisenhower administrations. We now turn to developments in American schooling. In the following sections we shall discuss the emergence of life-adjustment education, the critics of the 1950s, and the curricular revisions that resulted from these educational debates.

Curricular Debates

When World War II ended, the perennial debates over the nature of the school curriculum resurfaced, especially at the secondary level. In the 1880s and 1890s, the debate had centered on whether the high school should become a multipurpose "people's college" or remain a college preparatory institution. The Committee of Ten had pushed the high school strongly in the college preparatory direction; this tendency was reversed by the Commission on the Reorganization of Secondary Education, which moved the institution in the multipurpose direction.

After World War II, the debate rejoined as "professional" educators—namely, professors of education, school administrators, members of state departments of education, and others—called for a high school program that recognized the diverse needs of a larger and more varied high school population. Using the earlier arguments that the high school should be a multipurpose institution, the educators of the late 1940s and early 1950s called for an institution that would meet the varied needs of adolescents, ranging from social adjustment to vocational training to citizenship, recreation, and a range of curricular alternatives. The arguments of the proponents of multipurposism were strengthened by what seemed to be a need to provide educational correctives to increasing social dislocation and juvenile delinquency. By the late 1940s, multipurpose secondary education would take the guise of "life-adjustment education."

The academic opponents of the high school as a multipurpose institution argued that the genuine function of secondary education was college preparation. In the late 1940s and early 1950s, the academic philosophy won support mainly from college professors, especially in the liberal arts and sciences. In the mid-1950s, this perspective attracted a broader range of support.

Life-Adjustment Education

From 1945 through 1954, a movement called life-adjustment education attracted significant support among some professional educators in colleges of education and secondary schools. By the mid-1950s, life adjustment would unleash a torrent of criticism.[20] Life-adjustment education originated on June 1, 1945, at an invitational meeting of vocational educators sponsored by the Division of Vocational Education of the Office of Education in Washington, D. C. At this meeting, Charles A. Prosser, the veteran vocational educator, introduced a resolution which stated that while vocational schools were suited "to prepare 20 percent of the youth of secondary school age" for "skilled occupations" and that high schools would "continue to prepare another 20 percent" for college entry:

> We do not believe that the remaining 60 percent of our youth of secondary school age will receive the life-adjustment training they need and to which they are entitled as American citizens—unless and until administrators of public education, with the assistance of the vocational education leaders, formulate a similar program for the group.[21]

In the wake of the Prosser Revolution, U.S. Commissioner of Education John W. Studebaker called a series of regional meetings in 1946 that was then climaxed by a national meeting in 1947 in Chicago. The purpose of the meetings was to give curricular substance to life-adjustment education and to recommend strategies for implementing it in the nation's schools.

The National Commission on Life-Adjustment Education for Secondary School Youth, established in 1947, sought to devise a secondary education program for the estimated 60 percent of American youth who were being trained for neither skilled occupations nor college.[22] Life-adjustment education suggested the following directions for American education, especially for secondary schooling:

1. Schooling should be redefined in terms that were broader than the conventional academic programs. Schools should deal with a wide range of issues and problems that had personal, social, emotional, economic, vocational, and other implications.
2. The American public high school was an institution for all adolescents regardless of their academic and vocational talent and destination. Since all American adolescents were in attendance, the high school should diversify its instructional program to meet their personal and social needs.

As life-adjustment education was shaped and implemented, it took a variety of forms ranging from a life-adjustment core curriculum in some schools to a few nonacademic functional electives in other schools. While definitions of life-adjustment education were elusive, it came to resemble a "functional" alternative to the academic curriculum. Life-adjustment programs had multiple objectives such as:

[20] Ravitch, *Troubled Crusade*, pp. 64-69.

[21] U.S. Office of Education, *Life-Adjustment Education for Every Youth* (Washington, D. C.: GPO, n.d.), p. 15.

[22] U.S. Office of Education, *Vitalizing Secondary Education*, in Franklin R. Zeran, *Life-Adjustment Education in Action* (New York: Chartwell House, 1953), p. 43.

effective citizenship, social adjustment, guidance, worthy use of leisure, positive mental and physical health, successful family life, and personal development.

As an educational movement, life adjustment enjoyed a brief but dramatic life. Although it had an impact on many schools throughout the country, its effects were few in other school systems. By the mid-1950s, it was bitterly attacked and condemned by conservative academic critics such as Arthur E. Bestor, Jr., and Admiral Hyman Rickover as well as some progressives who regarded it as a distortion of genuine progressive education. Life-adjustment education was important as an educational movement in its own right as well as for the reaction that it provoked.

In some ways, life-adjustment education can be viewed as a response to the social and psychological uneasiness produced by the cultural changes that followed immediately after World War II. Foremost were those that were altering family life. Commentators called attention to rising divorce rates and the increasing incidence of juvenile delinquency. The migration to the suburbs saw many families living in increasingly more affluent but still evolving communities. For children and adolescents, the new patterns of postwar life were unstable and unsettling. Life-adjustment education promised a degree of social stability by providing youth with coping and adjusting skills that would serve them in changing situations.

Life-adjustment education was also an educational response to the prolongation of adolescence that had been occurring in American society since the early twentieth century. Most American youngsters no longer went immediately from childhood to adult occupations and responsibilities. The great majority of American youth were attending school until age 17 or 18. The life-adjustment advocates recognized that the increased secondary enrollments, especially in many public high schools, numbered many who did not intend to seek admission to college. The response of the life-adjustment educators was to devise a widely varied functional curriculum that would be of interest and be immediately useful to these noncollege preparatory students. Among the educators who were attracted to life adjustment's banners were vocational educators, guidance counselors, and a variety of student-centered progressives who believed that school should be an introduction to the activities of life.

Since it was a broad and ill-defined movement, life-adjustment education varied from school district to school district. It might be an introduction to careers, on-the-job training, a course in correct social manners, or learning how to baby-sit, decorate a room, or develop a pleasing and popular personality. Indeed, it ranged from a serious inquiry into adolescent problems to determining the correct shade of lipstick and nail polish. When the attack began, life adjustment's detractors began to snipe at its trivial and outrageously nonacademic aspects and then at its vague but genuine core assumptions.

The most vociferous critics of life adjustment education were academicians associated with colleges of liberal arts and sciences, such as Arthur E. Bestor, Jr., a University of Illinois history professor, who condemned the anti-intellectual aspects of life-adjustment education in his books, *Educational Wastelands* and *The*

Restoration of Learning. Bestor and a group of like-minded associates went on to found the Council on Basic Education as an organization dedicated to restoring solid academic subject matter to American education, especially to the secondary schools. Bestor's attack was joined by other critics such as Admiral Hyman Rickover, a U.S. naval officer who deplored the academic slothfulness of many American schools, and Max Rafferty, a California school administrator turned conservative politician, who condemned progressive election for weakening the sense of patriotic values as well as academic standards in American public education.

It is important to note that the attacks on life-adjustment education were broadened to encompass a wide range of educational programs associated with progressivism. John Dewey, experimentalism, Progressive Education, the project method, and other innovations that appeared to be derived from progressive theories as well as life-adjustment education were given a wholesale condemnation by the educational critics of the 1950s.

Educators inclined to progressivism, especially in schools or education, found themselves on the defensive as they parried the critics' thrusts. At times, they found themselves having to defend the educational efficacy of progressive innovations and also their commitment to American civic values. The battle lines were drawn in acrimonious skirmishing and contentious frontal assaults, with neither side showing a willingness to compromise or to create an educational synthesis.

In many respects, the mid-1950s were twilight years for progressive education as a distinct movement. Progressivism became intertwined with life-adjustment in the public mind. Educators associated with progressivism, such as Archibald W. Anderson, an historian of education at the University of Illinois, and others, sought to distinguish between life adjustment and progressivism, but to little avail. Anderson and others asserted that progressivism, based on Dewey's experimentalism, called for more than an adjustment to existing conditions. It called on learners to transform their environment by interacting with it and solving social problems. These subtle distinctions between progressivism and life adjustment neither resolved the debate nor separated the two educational approaches from each other.

The Legacy of Life Adjustment

The decade from 1945 to 1955, when life-adjustment education enjoyed a short-lived popularity and then a demise fraught with controversy, was a dramatic prelude to the educational changes that would come in the late 1950s. In retrospect, the impact of the life-adjustment movement was as varied as its curricular designs had been during its peak of popularity. The movement did polarize its defenders and its critics. This polarization was to continue into the 1960s, 70s, and 80s. Life-adjustment education also had an influence on other movements that followed in its wake. The emphasis on values clarification resembled, to an extent, the concept expressed by life-adjustment education that adolescents should examine and seek to define their values. The argument that high school education should equip graduates with saleable skills was not unlike the arguments advanced by vocational educators associated with life adjustment who urged adoption of a functional curriculum. Finally, many of the curricular designs associated with life adjustment were readapted for incorporation into the middle schools that were established around the country during the late 1960s and early 1970s.

CRITICS OF THE 1950s

During the 1950s, a number of educational critics appeared. Their books and articles, usually attacking progressive and life-adjustment education, generally asserted that academic standards had been eroded in American public schools, especially high schools, due to the influence of the educational philosophy of John Dewey, progressive education, and the nonintellectual stress on methodologies practiced in departments and schools of education. For many of these critics, educational reforms were needed to restore conventional academic subject matter to the center of education. Among this type of critic were Arthur E. Bestor, Jr., Robert Hutchins, and Admiral Hyman Rickover. These critics, often political and social liberals, saw the liberal arts and the sciences as the basis of a genuine education. For them, elementary education was to provide training in basic literacy and in mathematical skills; secondary schooling was to provide a common academic curriculum. Generally, the critics of the 1950s sought to redirect public education by charging that: (1) American public schooling had grown pedagogically weak due to life-adjustment education; (2) American public schools were academically inferior to European schools; (3) an overly permissive attitude in American schools had lowered civic and moral standards.

Bestor and Intellectual Disciplines

Arthur E. Bestor, Jr., an historian at the University of Illinois, wrote *Educational Wastelands* (1953) and *The Restoration of Learning* (1955), which provoked a significant debate over the purposes of American education. Bestor's critique was divided into two parts: an attack on professional educators for devitalizing the academic quality of American education by advocating life-adjustment programs; and advocacy of a curriculum of intellectual disciplines for American secondary education.

Bestor charged that education professors, members of state departments of education, and school administrators had formed an interlocking directorate that had "undermined public confidence in the schools." Professional educationists had, he contended, divorced "schools from the disciplines of science and scholarship, which citizens trust and value."[23]

At the heart of Bestor's critique was his philosophical conviction that certain intellectual disciplines represented "fundamental ways of thinking." When translated into a curriculum, such indispensable intellectual disciplines were history,

[23] Arthur E. Bestor, Jr., *The Restoration of Learning* (New York: Knopf, 1955), p. 4.

mathematics, science, languages, and literature, which had developed as a result of "mankind's long quest for usable knowledge, cultural understanding, and intellec-tual power."[24]

For Bestor, these intellectual disciplines were orderly ways of thinking with organized structures and methods of their own. The curriculum that he recommended was to stress the ordered relationships and methods of inquiry appropriate to each basic field of knowledge. Teacher competency should be based on the skilled teaching of subject matter in each intellectual discipline.

Bestor saw the school's primary purpose as that of transmitting the Western cultural heritage by means of well-defined intellectual disciplines. Intellectual power, a product of disciplined learning, would enable succeeding generations to master the challenges of a changing environment.

After identifying reading, writing, and arithmetic as fundamental in the elementary school, Bestor specified that the secondary school curriculum should consist of five great learned disciplines:

1. The study of the English language involved first learning the fundamental skills of reading and writing and then proceeding to the systematic study of grammar. As they progressed, students were to read and analyze increasingly complex examples of literature and to practice writing under competent criticism.
2. Beginning with the simple practice of counting, mathematical instruction would then lead systematically through arithmetic to the more abstract and sophisticated mathematical reasoning of algebra, geometry, and calculus.
3. Science instruction was to begin diffusely with the natural sciences and then become organized into the systematic branches of biology, chemistry, and physics.
4. History was to be studied continuously, beginning with diffuse narratives and then continuing into the methodical study of great chronological and geographical divisions, with special emphasis on political and constitutional aspects.
5. Students were to study systematically at least one foreign language, beginning early enough to ensure mastery by the completion of high school.

Hyman G. Rickover

Hyman G. Rickover, known as the father of the nuclear submarine, was another leading educational critic of the 1950s. Admiral Rickover had become increasingly apprehensive about the declining academic quality of American education. In testimony before Congressional committees and in articles, books, and speeches, Rickover unfavorably compared the academic quality of American students to their European counterparts. In his *Report on Russia, Education and Freedom, Swiss Schools and Ours: Why Theirs Are Better,* and *American Education: A National Failure,* Rickover claimed that the quality of American education had been eroded under the influence of Dewey's experimentalist philosophy.

[24] Ibid., p. 4.

Rickover's arguments, resembling those of the essentialists some twenty years earlier, suggested that: (1) American schools had neglected academically talented students; (2) public schools had contributed to an educational lag that was adversely affecting American science, technology and culture; and (3) Americans could learn from European education that respected and encouraged human intelligence by rigorous academic study and discipline. Although especially interested in science, like Bestor, Rickover also believed that a "foundation of a liberal arts education" was needed so that educated persons could use their "specialized training wisely."[25] Rickover outlined the core of a liberal education as history, anthropology, economics, foreign languages and literatures, mathematics, science, and English.[26]

Rickover believed that European multiple-track system of secondary education was superior to America's comprehensive high schools. European educators, the Admiral reasoned, had consciously related a student's academic aptitude to an appropriate type of schooling. In contrast, American educators had wrongly refused to develop curricula based on students' academic aptitudes on the grounds that such a practice was elitist and undemocratic.

Rickover's testimony and report before the House Committee on Appropriations in 1959 took place in a time of educational crisis and controversy. He claimed that Soviet graduates of the ten-year school were at least two years ahead of their American counterparts in mastering "sound, basic education," which he defined as "mathematics, the sciences, mastery of the mother tongue, knowledge of their own classical literature and that of major foreign nations, foreign languages, and —though their history study is colored by Marxist doctrine."[27] Further, Rickover commented that the Soviet identified their talented youth, particularly those in the upper 30 percent, who were sent on to universities for work in selected areas such as science and engineering.

Based upon his comparisons of American and European educational systems, Rickover—like Bestor—proposed a general reform program. His program made the following recommendations:

1. American educators should commit themselves to liberal education, that "marvelous pedagogical invention" which would provide the knowledge base for specialized and professional training.
2. American educators should revise their commitment to the comprehensive high school as an agency of adolescent socialization and create a secondary system of multiple tracks appropriate to students' academic abilities.
3. A National Standards Committee should be established to keep the public informed about the condition of American education and to formulate national scholastic standards to make the United States competitive internationally.

---

[25] Hyman G. Rickover, *Education and Freedom* (New York: Dutton, 1959), p. 146.

[26] Idem, *Report on Russia: Hearings Before the House Committee on Appropriations— 86th Congress* (Washington, D.C.: GPO, 1959), p. 3.

[27] Ibid., p. 2.

4. Elementary and secondary education should provide a sufficiently broad terminal education for average and below-average students to prepare them for a modern technological society and a solid academic foundation for scholastically talented students to prepare them for subsequent professional education.

Max Rafferty

In retrospect, the critics of the 1950s could be placed on a continuum ranging from the scholar-historian Bestor to the more popular grassroots educator-politician, Max Rafferty. A professional educator and school administrator, Rafferty was elected California's superintendent of public instruction in 1962 and reelected in 1966. His last attempt at public office was an unsuccessful bid for the U.S. Senate in 1968.

In the late 1950s and early 1960s, Rafferty represented a basic education position based on a conservative political ideology. Although Bestor, Rickover, and Rafferty might concur on certain weaknesses in American education and on some remedies for reforming them, they differed philosophically.

Rafferty's book *Suffer, Little Children* revealed a pedagogical position resting on a conservative political ideology.[28] For Rafferty, the American cultural and educational heritage was conceived in the patriotic nationalism of the Revolutionary era and nurtured in the nineteenth-century common school's devotion to literacy, civic order, discipline, and hard work. According to his view of America's educational past, the sound development of public schooling had been distorted by John Dewey, experimentalist philosophers, and progressive education. The experimentalist's cultural and ethical relativism had eroded the belief in unchanging moral values. Progressivism had degenerated into socialization and life-adjustment education that negated the school's function as an academic institution.

Rafferty developed a critique of the conditions plaguing the public schools that noted: (1) a decline of academic standards, (2) a decline of respect for the authority of the teacher, (3) a lowering of moral and ethical standards in the schools that led to delinquency and violence and to the "Cult of the Slob," and (4) a general decline of civic and moral values and responsibilities.

Although there were other critics of American education in the 1950s and early 1960s such as James D. Koerner, Mortimer Smith, and others, Bestor, Rickover, and Rafferty were national figures who expressed the basic philosophy of the movement. While there were variations in the viewpoints of the critics, certain themes emerged. Among them were:

1. Academic standards and levels of achievement had declined in American public schools because of curricular tampering.
2. Progressive educators, experimentalist philosophers, life adjusters, and social experimenters had confused and distorted the purpose of the school. Whereas the school's primary function is academic, anti-intellectual forces had made it a confused multipurpose agency. As a result, the public, parents, students,

[28] New York: Signet, 1962).

teachers, and administrators no longer had a clear concept of the school's purpose and function.

3. When compared with the school systems of other countries, especially those of western Europe, American schools and students were academically inferior. This unfortunate result was due to the fact that many European systems had national standards and institutional tracks based on the students' academic abilities.

4. The school curriculum should consist of academic skills and subjects that are organized systematically and sequentially and taught deliberately and planfully by competent teachers, who are subject matter specialists.

5. The entry of ethically and culturally relative values into the schools as a result of pragmatism, progressivism, and experimentalism weakened inherited and traditional civic, patriotic, and moral values.

SPUTNIK

In October 1957, the Soviet Union launched a space satellite, *Sputnik*, into orbit around the earth. The initial American reaction to *Sputnik* was a skeptical disbelief that the supposedly technologically backward Soviets could have beat the United States in the race into space. This initial reaction led to a public search for the internal weaknesses that had caused the United States to lose its hitherto unquestioned scientific and technological superiority over the Soviet Union. Although critics such as Bestor, Rafferty, and Rickover had been condemning the U.S. public school's academic softness since the early 1950s, *Sputnik* stimulated widespread demands for more rigorous academic standards and programs, especially in mathematics and science.

Sputnik broadened the debate over the quality and condition of American public education that had been going on since the early 1950s. The following series of events made *Sputnik's* launching a watershed in American educational history:

1. Two years earlier, in 1955, the Progressive Education Association formally disbanded.

2. Life-adjustment education had undergone sustained attack and had been discredited.

3. The continuing Cold War between the United States and the Soviet Union had made education an important element in national security.

In the broadened context of *Sputnik*, the discussion of American education, in professional as well as public circles, turned to priorities. If the United States were to meet the Soviet challenge, then it had to improve its scientific, engineering, and technological capabilities. This required a curricular shift to basic sciences such as chemistry and physics and to mathematics in the schools. In addition, the United States' world role required attention to foreign language instruction. As well as requiring a return to more rigorous academic subject matter, the emerging priorities also had a quantitative dimension in that more funds were to be expended to prepare more teachers for more classrooms. As the 1950s passed their halfway mark, the arguments used by the essentialists of the late 1930s were finally getting a positive response. The *Sputnik* era also anticipated the educational criticisms and reforms of the 1980s.

The National Defense Education Act

As the 1950s neared their end, the long-standing debate over federal aid to education was interrupted by fears that the United States was losing its scientific, technological, and educational superiority to the Soviet Union. The Soviet success in orbiting *Sputnik* and well-publicized American space failures at that time produced a mood of national crisis that "something was wrong with American schools." Although grossly exaggerated by Cold War fears, this climate of opinion brought contentious factions together in Congress to enact the National Defense Education Act (NDEA) in 1958. The NDEA rested on two premises: first, national security required the "fullest development of the mental resources and technical skills" of American youth. And second, the national interest required federal "assistance to education for programs which are important to our national defense."[29]

Following the rubric that federal aid to education should be for a specific purpose rather than a general one, the legislation was designed to assist those areas related to national defense. To avoid the controversies that had blocked the passage of other proposals for federal aid, the NDEA provided categorical aid to specific programs.

The NDEA gave federal assistance to programs designed to improve instruction in mathematics, science, and foreign languages—three curricular areas related to national defense. Mathematics and science were related to basic research and the development of space-age technologies. Critics of foreign language instruction in the United States had charged that Americans were generally unprepared to cope with a multilingual international reality. The NDEA also provided matching grants to the states to improve secondary school guidance and counseling programs.

THE CONANT REPORTS

As the 1950s came to an end, a series of reports by James B. Conant took a dispassionate and searching look at American education. Scholarly but practical, Conant's reports and recommendations lacked the acrimony of the critics of the mid-1950s and the urgency of the *Sputnik*-induced reforms. Conant identified the large issues that would face American education in the 1960s and 1970s.

Conant, a former president of Harvard University, was recognized for his leadership in science, diplomacy, and education. Beginning his academic career as a

---

[29] Advisory Commission on Intergovernmental Relations, *The Federal Role in the Federal System: The Dynamics of Growth; Intergovernmentalizing the Classroom: Federal Involvement in Elementary and Secondary Education* (Washington, D.C.: GPO, 1981), p. 25.

professor of chemistry, he became chief executive of Harvard. During World War II, he advised the federal government on science policy. Following the war, he was U.S. commissioner to Germany. In the late 1950s and early 1960s, Conant's reports on the condition of American secondary education had a pronounced impact on educational policy formulation. Essentially, the Conant strategy was to investigate the condition of schooling through a comprehensive survey procedure that involved both qualitative and quantitative research. For example, data was collected from selected high schools that were visited by Conant's research team. As a result of the field survey, Conant developed a number of generalizations regarding the condition of American secondary schools. From these generalizations came recommendations to improve American high schools. Conant's recommendations were then widely disseminated to educational administrators, government leaders, school board members, and the general public. Those political and educational leaders who made educational policies were often influenced by Conant's recommendations.

Conant, in *The American High School Today*, recognized that public high schools served students of differing academic abilities and career interests. He also believed that the comprehensive high school performed a unifying social and political mission by providing a common, general secondary and civic education to all students.[30] As a comprehensive institution, the high school had the responsibility of socially integrating students from different socioeconomic, ethnic, and racial backgrounds.

Conant designed a series of recommendations to improve the quality of American secondary education. His most general recommendation advocated establishing a core curriculum of four years of English, three or four of social science, and at least one year of mathematics and science. These core requirements would occupy one-half of all students' programs; the remaining courses would consist of electives based on students' interests and career goals. Conant also recommended: (1) improved counseling services to aid students in selecting elective courses based on their interests, aptitudes, and career goals; (2) more individualized instruction based on students' interests and needs; (3) school organization according to homogeneous subject matter ability groupings; (4) diversified career and vocational programs to provide students with saleable skills. For example, high schools were to reflect the job market in their communities by offering programs in distributive education, vocational education, agriculture, clerical skills, industrial training, and other areas that prepared students with marketable skills.

Conant's recommendations sought to revitalize the high school curriculum. He sought to instill academic rigor and standards by recommending that half of every student's program be based on academic disciplines such as mathematics, English, science, and social science. However, he did not neglect the high school's role regarding students' general development. For example, Conant's recommendations included more counseling services, individualized instruction, and elective courses to meet differing interests and career goals.

[30] New York: McGraw-Hill, 1959, pp. 7-8.

Conant's *Slums and Suburbs* (1961), revealed his concerns about the possibility of maintaining high schools as comprehensive educational institutions.[31] He feared that profound social and demographic changes in American society were eroding the high school's comprehensive mission. In particular, Conant determined that severe and potentially dangerous inequalities existed in the quality of life and education in the nation's large metropolitan areas. While affluent suburban high schools offered college preparatory programs of high academic quality, ill-equipped schools in impoverished urban ghettoes offered, at best, poorly designed vocational training programs.

In many large cities, poverty caused by de facto racial segregation further aggravated inequalities suffered by blacks, Hispanics, and other minority groups. Only in moderately sized cities and in some consolidated rural school districts was the comprehensive high school a reality, with all students sharing a common facility.

Conant's *Slums and Suburbs* warned Americans that the deterioration of the comprehensive high school in large metropolitan areas jeopardized the long-standing principle of equality of educational opportunity. Unless reversed, American secondary education could become a dual system, with one track for upper socioeconomic groups and the other for lower ones. *Slums and Suburbs* predicted the problems that American secondary schools would face in the coming decades.

THE POSTWAR GROWTH OF HIGHER EDUCATION

After World War II, American higher education experienced an unprecedented expansion in enrollment, facilities, and faculty. While institutions of higher education in most Western nations remained highly selective and admitted only an elite minority of their college-age populations, American state colleges and universities in the post-war decades became increasingly popular mass institutions. In 1946, 2 million students, taught by 165,000 faculty members, were attending America's colleges and universities. By 1970, some 8 million students were being taught by 500,000 faculty members. While only 5 percent of youth aged 18 to 21 were enrolled in college-degree programs in 1910, this proportion had reached 60 percent by 1970.[32]

The G.I. Bill

The first sign of the coming transformation of higher education in postwar America occurred with the enactment of the G.I. Bill. Known officially as the Servicemen's Readjustment Act of 1944, the G.I. Bill, designed to give greater career opportunities to the returning war veterans, was signed by President

---

[31] New York: McGraw-Hill.

[32] Ben J. Wattenberg, ed., *The Statistical History of the United States: From Colonial Times to the Present* (New York: Basic Books, 1976), pp. 382-83; Idem, *Projections of Educational Statistics to 1983-84* (Washington, D.C.: GPO, 1974), pp. 17-18.

Roosevelt on June 22, 1944, sixteen days after the allies had invaded Normandy. Although the legislation provided federal aid to veterans to help them readjust to civilian life in the areas of hospitalization, education, and the purchase of homes, farms, and businesses, the law's major thrust was educational. The Servicemen's Readjustment Act included the following provisions:

1. The federal government would subsidize tuition, fees, books, and educational materials for veterans and contribute to living expenses incurred while attending college or other approved institutions.
2. Veterans were free to attend the educational institution of their choice.
3. Colleges were free to admit those veterans who met their admission requirements.

From 1944 through 1951, 7,800,000 veterans received educational benefits. Of that number, 2,232,000 attended colleges or universities.[33] The effects of the increased enrollments caused by the G.I. Bill were significant for American society and its institutions of higher learning.[34] For example: (1) Higher educational opportunities were made available to a larger and more varied socioeconomic group than ever before. (2) Engineers, technicians, and managers needed by the steadily evolving technological economy were prepared from the ranks of returning veterans. (3) Education served as a social and psychological safety valve that eased the traumas and tensions of adjustment from wartime to peace.

For America's colleges and universities, the army of former G.I.s that joined the student bodies of their institutions had transforming effects. Colleges and universities required more classrooms, laboratories, larger libraries, and greatly increased faculties. The increased enrollments began a cycle of growth for colleges and universities that would not end until the mid-1970s. College and university administrators and faculty had to learn to educate a student population that was no longer limited to those aged 18 to 23 or so. The veterans, who ranged considerably in age, brought with them a discipline, eagerness to learn, and sense of maturity that differed from the usual student stereotype. Finally, the idea that higher education was the privilege of a well-born elite was finally shattered.

Community College Growth

Recognizing that higher education was a national concern, Harry S. Truman appointed the President's Commission on Higher Education in 1946. Its report, *Higher Education for American Democracy*, issued in 1948, called for a general expansion of enrollments and facilities in America's colleges and universities. The commission's recommendations were prophetic of the trends of the 1950s and

---

[33] Ravitch, *Troubled Crusade,* p. 14.

[34] For the early commentaries, see *Hearings before the House Select Committee to Investigate Educational and Training Programs under the G.I. Bill* (Washington: GPO, 1944); see also Robert Havighurst, Walter Easton, John Baughman, and Ernest Burgess, *The American Veteran Back Home* (New York: Longmans, 1951).

1960s. For example, the commission's call for a greatly expanded network of two-year community colleges took place in most of the states. Its recommendation that each state establish a board or commission to coordinate and plan the growth of higher education also occurred in many states.

After World War II, junior colleges experienced a major transformation as they developed into community colleges. The earlier term "junior college" implied that the institution's major goal was to provide academic coursework that students could transfer to four-year colleges. While specific, this goal limited the junior college to performing the limited academic function of providing a general education as an upward extension of the high school. During the early 1950s, many existing junior colleges were redefined as community colleges, and hundreds of new two-year colleges were created. These community colleges, each with its own board of directors or trustees, served independent districts. Continuing to perform their original function of providing the first two years of undergraduate education, they also assumed myriad other educational functions in the communities they served. For example, community colleges came to:

1. provide continuing education for medical technicians, for industrial training, and for technical skills;
2. serve as educational, recreational, and social centers for adult learners; and
3. provide educational and cultural activities and programs for community residents.

In many states, community colleges became an integral component of the state educational system, providing the first two years of collegiate education to students who later transferred to four-year institutions. This ceased some of the pressures of massive student enrollment that were straining the resources of four-year colleges. For example, California was a leader in establishing community colleges as part of a statewide system of higher education.

A brief recital of events related to the community college in California illustrates what occurred later in other states. The first enabling legislation in California for the establishment of junior colleges was enacted in 1907, when high school districts were authorized to offer postgraduate courses. In 1917, the first state aid legislation for junior colleges was passed. In 1921, the California legislature authorized the formation of junior college districts. The Master Plan for Higher Education in California (1960-1975) diverted part of the enrollment from state colleges and universities to the public community colleges.[35] The presence of an extensive community college system facilitated selective state college and university admission policies without denying the opportunity for higher education to the majority of the college-age population.

Like California, Florida also developed an extensive community college system. In 1955, the Flordida legislature provided funds for existing junior colleges

---

[35] Leland L. Medsker, *The Junior College: Progress and Prospect* (New York: McGraw-Hill, 1960), p. 210.

and authorized appointment of a community college council for planning future growth. In addition to pioneering efforts in California and Florida, many other states developed extensive community college systems.

Master Plans for Higher Education

Following the recommendation of the President's Commission on Higher Education and in response to their own desire for orderly growth in higher education, several states began to establish higher education boards or commissions to coordinate the expansion of their colleges and universities. The trend to coordinated planning ran counter to the historic decentralization of American higher education that produced wide diversity in institutional size, organization, faculties, curricula, and academic standards. While decentralization encouraged healthy diversity, it also produced an inefficient use of financial and human resources in higher education.[36]

In several states in the late 1950s, public colleges and universities cooperated on devising master plans for future development. In 1959, California's legislature established the Coordinating Council for Higher Education. The council—composed of three representatives each from the University of California, the state colleges, the public junior colleges, the private institutions, and the general public—was to advise the governing boards of institutions and state officials on: budgetary review and requests for capital outlays; interpretation of functional differentiation in the publicly supported institutions; recommendations for changes in higher education programs; planning for the growth of higher education; and recommendaions concerning the needs and locations of new facilities and programs.

Through planning and coordination, California developed a state system of public higher education composed of community colleges, four-year state colleges, and the University of California. The community colleges were to offer courses through, but not beyond, the fourteenth grade that would be transferable to higher institutions; they were also to offer courses in vocational and technical fields and in general education. The four-year state colleges were to provide undergraduate and graduate instruction through the master's degree in the liberal arts and the sciences, in applied fields, in education, and in the professions. The University of California, the primary state-supported academic research institution, was to provide undergraduate and graduate instruction in the liberal arts and sciences, education, and the professions. The university had sole jurisdiction in law, medicine, dentistry, veterinary medicine, and architecture. It also had sole authority to award the doctorate, with the exception of some areas where it awarded joint doctorates with the state colleges.[37]

Like California, other states developed mechanisms and agencies for planning their development in higher education in the 1950s and 1960s. The concept of co-

[36] T. R. McConnell, *A General Pattern for American Public Higher Education* (New York: McGraw-Hill, 1962), p. 136.

[37] Ibid., pp. 152-56.

ordinated planning was new to higher educational institutions, however, and was sometimes subverted by their executive officers. While efforts at coordination were initiated in many states, the 1950s and 1960s saw a great deal of unplanned expansion in American higher education.

The rapid growth of higher education generated both optimisim and confusion on the nation's college and university campuses. The optimistic tone of the 1950s and 1960s was a product of several tendencies. Growth and development was measured in quantitative terms such as expanding facilities, constructing new buildings, and establishing new programs. With the quantitative growth of enrollments, facilities, and programs, administrative and teaching ranks increased. Although some states made efforts at planning, the general direction was one of expansion rather than coordination and systematization. In such an expansionist period, an optimistic excitement prevailed on the country's campuses as college and university presidents earned their reputations by achieving quantitative institutional growth. The era of brick-and-mortar expansion would contribute to such problems of the 1980s as underutilized facilities, large and immobile faculties, and declining enrollments. However, the problems of the 1980s were not those of the 1950s.

Not only were colleges and universities expanding quantitatively, they were also becoming centers of national power, prestige, and policy-making. In postwar America, the military-industrial complex was also expanding. The nation's industries had become sophisticated, complicated corporations, that needed a large force of technicians, planners, marketing experts, engineers, and managers. No longer did young men and women advance in the business world by "on-the-job" initiative and accumulated practical experience. America's new corporate leaders and managers of the 1950s and 1960s needed credentials earned in higher education as a necessary condition for career advancement.

While corporate industry was reshaping higher education's purposes and curricula, the United States' emergence as the world's leading industrial and military power also had an impact. Scientific research, occurring in university laboratories, was a key element in military innovations. Professors, who were experts on the various nations and regions of the world, were used as consultants to advise government agencies on international and strategic policies. The demand for the expert knowledge that the universities could supply to industry and government brought power and prestige to higher education.

As centers of recognized expert authority, universities and their faculties were characterized by optimism during the growth period of the 1950s and 1960s. The role of the professor was altered by the events of the era. No longer primarily researchers and teachers, professors became national policymakers, consultants to industry and government, and occasionally enterprising academic entrepreneurs.

If the 1950s and 1960s were decades of quantitative growth and power for higher education, they also were a time of confusion about fundamental purposes and directions. The multipurpose "multiversity" moved simultaneously in several directions. Under the impetus of specialization, undergraduate education, curricula, and students were often neglected. Some professors, attracted by the exciting sirens of off-campus consulting, neglected basic teaching responsibilities. Expansion required funding grants from government or private sources. In seeking funding, university administrators and professors developed "grantsmanship" strategies that often forfeited decision-making to those outside of academe.

CONCLUSION

The United States in the post-World War II era was a transitional society. Americans enjoyed a new affluence but also experienced psychic and social tensions. The 1950s witnessed accelerated efforts to achieve civil rights by black Americans. The first years of peace gave way to the international and national tensions that were generated by the Cold War. For American schools and colleges, the era was one of expansion and confidence. By the end of the 1950s, serious debates over the purposes and nature of education surfaced. The Soviet success with *Sputnik* caused Americans to rethink their national priorities and give education increased support. The 1950s and early 1960s unleashed the tendencies that would transform the United States from an industrial into a complex corporate society.

DISCUSSION QUESTIONS

1. Identify and analyze the major changes that reshaped American life and society after World War II.
2. Explore the impact of suburbia on American education.
3. Examine the social and educational policies of the Truman administration.
4. Examine the civil rights issues in postwar America.
5. Analyze the strategy used by the NAACP to end racial segregation in public education.
6. Examine the impact of the Cold War on American politics, society, and education.
7. In what ways did American education assume a broader International focus in the 1950s and 1960s?
8. What was the rationale for life-adjustment education? What was the nature of the critique of life-adjustment education?
9. What were the major criticisms of the leading educational critics of the 1950s?
10. What was the educational impact of *Sputnik*?
11. Analyze the changes taking place in higher education in the postwar era.

RESEARCH TOPICS

1. Collect and analyze data regarding demographic trends in your locality during the post-World War II era. Do these trends agree with or differ from the generalizations made in the chapter?
2. Read C. Wright Mills's *The Power Elite.* Identify the trends that had a relationship to education in the broad sense.
3. Research the federal aid to education issue after World War II. Who were the leaders on both sides of the debate? What were the issues?
4. Examine newspapers or popular magazines published at the time of the *Brown* v. *Board of Education* case. Analyze and comment on these press reactions.
5. Examine the publications of your state office or department of education during the 1950s. Identify and analyze publications dealing with the Cold War, internationalism, and the threat of communism.
6. Consult and read newspaper and popular magazine articles relating to the McCarthy era and its controversies. Attempt to capture the mood of the era in an interpretive essay.
7. Examine the concept of international education as presented in books on that topic. Prepare a short paper that defines the concept.
8. Identify and examine publications of your state department or office of education on life-adjustment education.
9. Read and review a book written by one of the educational critics of the 1950s.
10. Read Conant's *The American High School Today.* Compare and contrast Conant's recommendations with those of recent reports on secondary education.

REFERENCES AND READINGS

Becker, James M., and Mehlinger, Howard D., eds. *International Dimensions in the Social Studies.* Washington, D.C.: National Council for the Social Studies, 1968.
Bestor, Arthur E., Jr. *The Restoration of Learning.* New York: Knopf, 1955.
Conant, James B. *Slums and Suburbs.* New York: McGraw-Hill, 1961.
___. *The American High School Today.* New York: McGraw-Hill, 1959.
Graebner, Norman A. *Cold War Diplomacy, 1945-1960.* New York: Van Nostrand, 1962.
Hamby, Alonzo, I. *Beyond the New Deal: Harry S. Truman and American Liberalism.* New York: Columbia University Press, 1973.
Hartman, Susan M. *Truman and the 80th Congress.* Columbia: University of Missouri Press, 1971.
Hutchmacher, J. Joseph. *The Truman Years.* Hinsdale, Ill.: Dryden Press, 1972.
Kennan, George F. *American Diplomacy, 1900-1950.* Chicago: University of Chicago Press, 1951.
King, Edith W. *The World: Context for Teaching in the Elementary School.* Dubuque, Iowa: William C. Brown, 1971.
McConnell, T. R. *A General Pattern for American Public Higher Education.* New York: McGraw-Hill, 1962.

Medsker, Leland L. *The Junior College: Progress and Prospect.* New York: McGraw-Hill, 1960.

Melvin, Kenneth. *Education in World Affairs: A Realistic Approach to International Education.* Lexington, Mass.: H. Heath, 1970.

Mills, C. Wright. *The Power Elite.* New York: Oxford University Press, 1959.

Oshinsky, David M. *A Conspiracy So Immense: The World of Joe McCarthy.* New York: Free Press, 1983.

Patterson, James T. *Mr. Republican: A Biography of Robert A. Taft.* Boston: Houghton Mifflin, 1972.

Rafferty, Max. *Suffer, Little Children.* New York: Signet, 1962.

Ravitch, Diane. *The Troubled Crusade: American Education, 1945-1980.* New York: Basic Books, 1983.

Rickover, Hyman G. *Education and Freedom.* New York: Dutton, 1959.

Shane, Harold G., ed. *The United States and International Education, The Sixty-Eight Yearbook of the National Society for the Study of Education.* Chicago: University of Chicago Press, 1968.

Taylor, Harold. *The World and the American Teacher.* Washington, D.C.: American Association of Colleges for Teacher Education, 1968.

Theoharis, Athan. *Seeds of Repression.* New York: Quadrangle, 1971.

Thomas, Lately. *When Even Angels Wept: The Senator Joseph McCarthy Affair—A Story Without a Hero.* New York: Morrow, 1973.

Whittner, Lawrence. *Cold War America: From Hiroshima to Watergate.* New York: Praeger, 1974.

Zeran, Franklin R. *Life-Adjustment Education in Action.* New York: Chartwell House, 1953.

12
SOCIETY AND EDUCATION DURING THE NEW FRONTIER AND GREAT SOCIETY: 1960–1970

The decade of the 1960s spanned the presidencies of John F. Kennedy (1961-1963) and Lyndon Baines Johnson (1963-1968). Both Kennedy, with his New Frontier, and Johnson, with his Great Society, sought to redirect American society at home and abroad. Kennedy inherited the legacies of a continuing Cold War between the Soviet Union and the United States and a growing momentum for civil rights. Johnson, who shared this legacy, attempted to rekindle the spirit of New Deal social reformism and welfare programs by building a Great Society, in which education was a key element.

Both the Kennedy and Johnson administrations had to grapple with the growing involvement of the United States in Vietnam. It was the Vietnamese entrapment that led not only to the undoing of the Great Society but to a decade of turmoil and pervasive social change.[1]

KENNEDY AND THE NEW FRONTIER

John F. Kennedy was elected president in 1960, a year when Cold War tensions remained high.[2] Kennedy, who consistently gave foreign policy a high priority, faced a series of international crises during his administration. Among them were

[1] For a treatment of the Kennedy and Johnson era, see Jim F. Heath, *Decade of Disillusionment: The Kennedy-Johnson Years* (Bloomington: Indiana University Press, 1975).

[2] For treatments of Kennedy, see Arthur M. Schlesinger, Jr., *A Thousand Days: John F. Kennedy in the White House* (Boston: Houghton Mifflin, 1965); James MacGregor Burns, *John*

the Berlin crisis during the summer of 1961, when the Soviets sealed off East Berlin with a fortress-like wall; the abortive Bay of Pigs invasion by U.S.-backed Cuban exiles in April 1961; and the Cuban missile crisis of October 1962, which saw the Soviet Union and the United States come to the brink of war. Along with these dramatic crises, the Kennedy administration embarked on increasing the American presence and intervention in Vietnam, where Viet Cong insurgents, supported by communist North Vietnam, were seeking to overthrow the noncommunist regime in South Vietnam.

Kennedy's administration, called the New Frontier, moved in several directions in foreign policy; these directions were to have an impact on national security and on what was termed international education during the 1960s. One direction was to build up America's military capability so that the United States could deal with the Soviet Union from a position of strength. To this end, the Kennedy administration constructed an arsenal of nuclear weapons and built up the country's conventional military forces. The other direction in foreign policy was to erase the picture of the heavy-handed "ugly American," who was often ignorant of other nations.

The Peace Corps

The Peace Corps, headed by R. Sargent Shriver, was established in 1961 to help developing nations meet their educational and training needs. Prior to overseas assignment, Peace Corps volunteers received intensive instruction in the language, geography, history, and culture of the host country. Volunteers were expected to live in the socioeconomic level of the host country to which they were assigned. At the height of the Peace Corps program in 1966, more than 12,000 volunteers were working in fifty-six countries, primarily on projects designed to improve agriculture, health, education, and community development.

Throughout the 1960s, American universities, through the Agency for International Development (AID), worked in a number of Third World nations on a variety of projects to improve education, health, welfare, agriculture, and the general economy.

Kennedy's Educational Programs

In his State-of-the-Union Address on January 30, 1961, Kennedy called for legislation to provide federal funding for public schools, higher education, basic research, and medical training. This was followed by his "Special Message to Congress on Education" in February, which outlined specific proposals for education, such as:

1. federal assistance for elementary and secondary school construction and raising teachers' salaries;

Kennedy: A Political Profile (New York: Harcourt, Brace, 1960); William R. Manchester, *Portrait of a President: John F. Kennedy in Profile* (Boston: Little, Brown, 1962); for Kennedy on education, see John F. O'Hara, ed., *John F. Kennedy on Education* (New York: Teachers College Press, Columbia University, 1966).

2. federal loans to colleges and universities to construct student housing;
3. a program to encourage scholarships for talented and needy college students;
4. appointment of a commission to recommend improvements in vocational education.[3]

Kennedy's general school-aid proposals encountered opposition from the same line-up of contending factions that had blocked federal assistance to education in previous administrations. The exclusion of aid to private schools raised Roman Catholic opposition. Conservatives who feared the entry of the federal government into education were also opposed.

In his educational message of 1962, President Kennedy advised Congress that significant advances in the discovery and transmission of knowledge needed to be translated into the school curriculum. While the institutes of the National Science Foundation and the Office of Education had helped to keep teachers up-to-date, Kennedy believed that the opportunities for attending these institutes were too limited. He also urged efforts to raise standards in teacher education programs. The president stated that:

> ... the key to educational quality is the teaching profession. About one out of every five of the nearly 1,600,000 teachers in our elementary and secondary schools fails to meet full certification standards for teaching or has not completed four years of college work. Our immediate concern should be to afford them every possible opportunity to improve their professional skills and their command of the subjects they teach.[4]

On January 23, 1963, Kennedy expressed his commitment to aid higher education when he said:

> Now a veritable tidal wave of students is advancing inexorably on our institutions of higher education, where the annual costs per student are several times as high as the cost of a high school education, and where these costs must be borne in large part by the student or his parents. Five years ago the graduating class of the secondary schools was 1.5 million; five years from now it will be 2.5 million. The future of these young people and the nation rests in large part on their access to college and graduate education. For this country reserves its highest honors for only one kind of aristocracy—that which the Founding Fathers called "an aristocracy of achievement arising out of a democracy of opportunity."[5]

---

[3] *Public Papers of the Presidents of the United States* (Washington, D.C.: Office of the Federal Registrar, 1962-1964), pp. 107-11.

[4] John F. Kennedy, *Message from the President of the United States Relative to an Educational Program,* H.R. Document No. 330 (Washington, D.C.: GPO, 1962), pp. 4-5.

[5] Idem, *Message from the President of the United States Relative to a Proposed Program for Education,* H.R. Document No. 54 (Washington, D.C.: GPO, 1963), p. 5.

The phrase "a democracy of opportunity" demonstrated Kennedy's determination to provide greater access to higher education for more students. His use of the term "an aristocracy of intellect" reflected his resolution that, although enrollments were increasing, American higher education would maintain its standards of excellence. Under the auspices of the Kennedy administration, the Higher Education Facilities Act of 1963 was passed. In focusing attention on the need for expanded facilities, President Kennedy stated:

> The long-predicted crisis in higher education facilities is now at hand. For the next fifteen years, even without additional student aid, enrollment increases in colleges will average 340,000 each year. If we are to accommodate the projected enrollment of more than 7 million college students by 1970–a doubling during the decade–$23 billion of new facilities will be needed, more than three times the quantity built during the preceding decade. This means that unless we are to deny higher education opportunities to our youth, American colleges and universities must expand their academic facilities at a rate much faster than their present resources will permit.[6]

The Higher Education Facilities Act of 1963 provided grants to colleges and universities to construct buildings, laboratories, libraries, and other facilities. The act made private and church-related as well as public institutions eligible for federal aid. However, facilities constructed in church-related institutions were limited to those being used for instruction or research in the natural or physical sciences, mathematics, modern foreign languages, engineering, library use, or other secular areas.

The Higher Education Act of 1965, enacted during the Johnson administration, provided federal funding for community service and continuing education programs, college libraries and library training and research, developing institutions, and student assistance. It offered grants to qualified high school graduates of exceptional financial need who could not afford to attend a college or university.

Kennedy and Civil Rights

During his administration, Kennedy continued to pursue expanded federal initiatives for civil rights. Several dramatic events illustrated the expanded federal role. In 1962, James Meredith sought admission to the all-white University of Mississippi. The Justice Department, headed by the president's brother, Robert Kennedy, dispatched federal marshalls to protect Meredith and to secure his entrance to the university. The ensuing riots left two dead and many injured. However, Meredith was admitted to classes and graduated from the institution. In 1963, Governor George Wallace, who had vowed to block the integration of the University of Alabama, was forced to yield to federal pressures. Although major legislative breakthroughs for civil rights were not forthcoming during the Kennedy years, it was clear that the president and his administration were prepared to use federal power when the occasion required it.

[6] Ibid., p. 7.

THE JOHNSON ADMINISTRATION

On November 22, 1963, President Kennedy was assassinated in Dallas, Texas, and Vice-President Lyndon Baines Johnson became president.[7] Johnson, who had begun his career as a teacher and school principal in Texas, launched a program that he called the Great Society, which included large-scale federal aid to education. Johnson, who began his political career during Roosevelt's New Deal, was a consummate politican who was able to move much of his proposed legislation through Congress.

Johnson and Education

After his landslide victory over Senator Barry Goldwater, the Republican candidate, in the election of 1964, Johnson, who wanted to be known as the "education president," moved to get federal aid to education legislation enacted by Congress. Since 1945, efforts at general federal aid to education had failed in Congress. Conservatives in both parties had opposed federal intrusion into education, an area that they reserved to local and state governments. Many Southern white senators and representatives opposed legislation that would break down racially segregated schooling. Catholics had opposed aid bills that did not provide assistance to parochial schools. With the exception of the National Defense Education Act of 1958, federal aid to education had been mired in the quicksands of contending congressional factions.

Johnson was successful in getting Congress to enact the Elementary and Secondary Education Act of 1965 (ESEA), an aid bill that provided more than $1 billion in federal funds to assist schools. Although still categorical, ESEA was broad in scope. As part of Johnson's War on Poverty, the major thrust of the ESEA sought to equalize educational opportunities, especially in inner-city and rural poverty areas. Local educational agencies that wished to participate in the ESEA had to prepare proposals within the guidelines of the act's titles.

To avoid the religious controversies that had impeded federal aid programs in the past, the ESEA legislation, following the child-benefit theory, made federal aid available to educationally disadvantaged children in both public and parochial schools. It assisted children rather than schools. Among the major categories, or titles, of aid provided by ESEA were:

1. grants to the states to improve school libraries and to purchase textbooks and other instructional materials;
2. funds to establish educational centers to provide services and encourage innovative programs;

[7]For treatments of Johnson, see Eric F. Goldman, *The Tragedy of Lyndon Johnson* (New York: Knopf, 1969); Hugh Sidney, *A Very Personal Presidency : Lyndon Johnson in the White House* (New York: Atheneum, 1968); Doris Kearns, *Lyndon Johnson and the American Dream* (New York: Harper & Row, Pub., 1976); James MacGregor Burns, *To Heal and to Build: The Programs of President Lyndon B. Johnson* (New York: McGraw-Hill, 1968).

3. educational research and training grants for universities to carry on and disseminate educational research; and
4. grants to state educational agencies to improve planning, information gathering, and training of personnel.

The enactment of the ESEA set the basic directions in education that the federal government was to follow for the remainder of the decade. Its major focus was on educational innovation, with a special emphasis on the education of the disadvantaged. The federal government was to encourage programs to improve the education of the handicapped, those in poor areas, and bilingual education.

The passage of the Johnson legislation revealed a shift in the congressional attitude toward school assistance. In the past, Congress had enacted legislation to aid a specific area, such as vocational education with the Smith-Hughes Act, or mathematics and science education with the National Defense Education Act. The Elementary and Secondary Education Act of 1965 represented a more general assistance package than previous enactments. For example, Title I, Federal Assistance for Local Educational Agencies for the Education of Children of Low-Income Families, supported school construction and developed special programs for educationally deprived children. Title II, a five-year program to make books and other printed materials available to schoolchildren, funded the purchase of library books, textbooks, periodicals, magnetic tapes, phonograph records, and other instructional materials. Title III provided for the establishment of model schools, pilot programs, and community centers to supplement the offerings of local school systems in continuing adult education, guidance and counseling, remedial instruction, special educational services, enriched academic programs, and health services. Title IV stressed improvement of educational research, the dissemination of information to teachers and teacher education institutions, and the establishment of regional educational laboratories. Title V was intended to assist state departments of education in administering the new programs.

For President Johnson, federal aid to education was an important element in the War on Poverty. To break the cycle of poverty, federal encouragement and funding were given to programs to improve inner-city schools and to provide job retraining.

Johnson's administration, emphasizing educational programs for minority groups and for poverty areas, won passage of the Economic Opportunity Act of 1965, which created a number of early childhood educational programs, known collectively as Operation Head Start. These programs were designed to give economically and culturally disadvantaged children a concerted early educational opportunity before they entered school.

Head Start programs were intended to give lower-income children cultural and educational experiences that were generally available to middle-class youngsters. They provided story-telling, field trips, group games, songs, play, and other activities that stimulated learning readiness. Dental and physical examinations were included. Head Start programs also enlisted parents in the educational program in order for learning activities to be continued and reinforced at home.

The Job Corps was another Johnson administration initiative in the War on Poverty. It was designed for high school dropouts who needed special vocational training to learn saleable skills that would prepare them for employment. Job Corps training programs included consumer education courses, remedial reading programs, and other more specialized training.

Johnson and Civil Rights

One of Johnson's early legislative achievements was securing enactment of the Civil Rights Act of 1964, the hitherto most far-reaching law of its kind. It not only gave federal protection to voting rights but guaranteed civil rights in employment and education. It guaranteed equal access to public accommodations and sought to prevent hiring discrimination by employers who held government contracts. It established a community relations service to assist communities in resolving racial tensions. Significant for education, the act empowered the federal government to file school desegregation suits and to withhold federal funds from school districts involved in racial discrimination.

The Civil Rights Act of 1968 continued federal efforts to prohibit racial discrimination. The act protected civil rights workers and provided severe penalties for interfering with voting rights.

Along with the Civil Rights acts, a series of Supreme Court decisions also advanced racial integration in the schools. A key decision was *Griffin* v. *the School Board of Prince Edward County* in 1964.[8] In Prince Edward County, Virginia, the refusal of the board of supervisors to levy taxes for the 1959-60 school year forced the public schools to close. The Prince Edward School Foundation, a private association, was organized to operate nonpublic schools for white children. In the 1960-61 school year, the foundation's major funding came from state and county tuition grants. The Supreme Court ruled that the closing of the Prince Edward County public schools had denied black students the equal protection of the laws guaranteed by the Fourteenth Amendment. The county supervisors' action had forced children to attend racially segregated schools, which, although designated as private schools, received county and state funds.

Since the late 1950s, the Supreme Court had attempted to implement its decision that school desegregation should proceed "with all deliberate speed." In 1968, in the *Green* v. *County School Board* and *Monroe* v. *Board of Commissioners* decisions, the Supreme Court ruled unconstitutional local plans that permitted students the option to transfer to avoid desegregation. In 1969, the Supreme Court, in *Alexander* v. *Holmes County Board of Education* discarded the all-deliberate-speed doctrine for school desegregation. Reversing lower court decisions that granted a time extension to some Mississippi school districts for desegregation, the Court ruled that every school district in the land was to end dual school systems "at

---

[8] *Griffin* v. *School Board of Prince Edward County,* 377 U.S. 218 (1964).

once." In its 1971 decision in *Swann* v. *Charlotte-Mecklenburg*, the Supreme Court upheld the use of citywide busing to achieve integration.[9]

Johnson and Vietnam

Like his predecessor, Johnson was plagued by the continuing conflict in Vietnam. As the military situation escalated, Johnson asked Congress in 1964 to pass the Gulf of Tonkin Resolution, authorizing the president to take the "necessary measures to repel any armed attack against the forces of the United States." From 1965 onward, full-scale American involvement in Vietnam increased until 500,000 American troops had been committed. The war dragged on without a decisive victory for either the South Vietnamese and the Americans or for the North Vietnamese and the Viet Cong insurgents. Mounting frustration in the United States over the war stimulated dissent, social unrest, and demonstrations, especially by young people, against the Johnson policy. In the years from 1965 to 1968, Johnson remained steadfast in pursuing the war, while his opponents remained equally determined to end America's involvement. While continued participation in the war was the focal point, the later 1960s brought a profound social revolution that had significant implications for education. Let us now examine some aspects of the "cultural revolution" of the late 1960s.

CULTURAL CHANGE

The 1960s has been referred to as a "troubled decade," a time of social protest and discontent, and as a period of cultural revolution. It was an era of intense debate and activism, especially by many young people who wanted to bring about dramatic social, political, economic, and educational changes in the United States. While the war in Vietnam was a catalyst for change, the issues that generated debate, controversy, and activism were diffuse and varied. Minority groups such as blacks, Hispanics, and women tried to win greater equality in American society; and student activism erupted on the nation's college and university campuses.

Black Consciousness

By the mid-1950s, blacks, impatient with the slow process of legal desegregation, embarked on a more activist course. Several incidents led to a full-scale civil rights movement; among them was the dramatic Montgomery, Alabama, bus boycott. On December 1, 1955, Rosa Parks, a black woman, refused to yield her seat on a local bus to a white person, in violation of a city ordinance. Montgomery's black population, led by the Reverend Martin Luther King, Jr., boycotted the city's

---

[9]*Green* v. *County School Board,* 391 U.S. 430 (1968); *Monroe* v. *Board of Commissioners,* 391 U.S. 377 (1968); *Alexander* v. *Holmes City Board of Education,* 396 U.S. 19 (1969); *Swann* v. *Charlotte-Mecklenburg,* 407 U.S. 1 (1971).

public transportation system. The boycott ended when the Supreme Court ruled Alabama's segregated seating law unconstitutional.

Based upon the Gandhian strategy of nonviolent resistance, King founded the Southern Christian Leadership Conference (SCLC) to lead an organized opposition to racial segregation.[10] The SCLC, along with the Student Nonviolent Coordinating Committee (SNCC), began a series of actions such as the restaurant "sit-in" to protest racial discrimination.

The late 1960s saw the refocusing of civil rights efforts. While de jure segregation was being slowly dismantled and blacks were registering to vote in the Southern states, de facto racial segregation in the large cities of the Northern industrial states, where half of the nation's black population lived, remained largely impervious to change. The legal success of the civil rights movement in the early 1960s and Johnson's War on Poverty had raised black expectations but had not brought dramatic economic gains for many blacks.

In the inner-city ghettos, the conditions of urban blight, unemployment, and poverty were most severe. In the mid- and late 1960s, a series of riots and civil disorders gripped the large cities of the United States. In August 1965, residents of the Watts district of Los Angeles rioted after allegations of police brutality had been made. The National Guard was mobilized to restore order. The toll of the Watts riots was 34 dead, 1,000 injured, and $40 million lost in damage to property. During the summer of 1967, especially violent riots erupted in Newark, New Jersey, and in Detroit, Michigan. After the assassination of Martin Luther King on April 4, 1968, in Memphis, Tennessee, severe rioting occurred in several cities, including Chicago and the nation's capital, Washington, D.C.

On July 28, 1967, President Johnson established the National Advisory Commission on Civil Disorders, headed by Governor Otto Kerner of Illinois as chairman and Mayor John Lindsay of New York City as vice-chairman. The commission examined the historical, sociological, economic, legal, and educational causes of racial disorders. Relating the urban school to its context, the commission found that the quality of education in the inner-city schools of the black ghetto was unequal to that provided for most white children. In its report, the commission stated:

> . . . for many minorities, and particularly for the children of the racial ghetto, the schools have failed to provide the educational experience which could help overcome the effects of discrimination and deprivation.
>
> This failure is one of the persistent sources of grievance and resentment within the Negro community. The hostility of Negro parents and students toward the school system is generating increasing conflict and causing disruption within many city school districts.[11]

[10] For a well-written biographical sketch of King, see Roderick Nash, *From These Beginnings . . .: A Biographical Approach to American History* (New York: Harper & Row, Pub., (1978), II: 195-239.

[11] *Report of the National Advisory Commission on Civil Disorders* (New York: Bantam Books 1968), pp. 424-25.

In the mid-1960s, the older civil rights movement, which had been led by such bi-racial organizations as the NAACP and the Urban League, began to differ on strategies. For example, the NAACP continued to work for civil rights through the legal and political systems. The SCLC used large-scale nonviolent resistance to racial discrimination. SNCC, led by H. Rap Brown, urged "black power" and the creation of separate black institutions. Despite the splintering of civil rights organizations, Martin Luther King, Jr., emerged as the moral leader of black Americans, a position that he maintained until he was assassinated.

School desegregation, increased employment opportunities, and full political participation were obvious goals of blacks throughout the 1960s. In addition to these tangible goals, a raising of black consciousness occurred, which manifested itself in black nationalism and social identity.[12] A general search for the roots of black culture led to an interest in Afro-American history. Black studies programs were established in many colleges and universities. At the elementary and secondary school level, units were developed, particularly in the social studies, that dealt with the black contribution to American culture.

Hispanic Consciousness

During the 1960s and throughout the 1970s, Hispanic Americans, especially those of Cuban, Mexican, and Puerto Rican ancestry, organized to improve their social, political, and economic situation in the United States.[13] Recognizing that education was a key element, Hispanics worked to establish bilingual programs. Following the model of the black studies programs, they also sought to establish Hispanic studies programs and special counseling services in colleges and universities.

The Bilingual Education Act of 1968 provided federal funds to local school districts to help them meet the needs of students of limited English-speaking ability. It was estimated that some three million children between the ages of three and eighteen were members of non-English-speaking families. Although the act encouraged bilingual programs, it did not require districts to establish them. However, in 1970 the Office of Civil Rights of the Department of Health, Education, and Welfare issued guidelines requiring districts enrolling more than 5 percent non-English-speakers to take "affirmative steps to rectify the language deficiency" so that such students could participate effectively in the educational program.[14]

Bilingual education, defined as instruction in two languages for part or all of the school day, included the study of the history and culture associated with a

---

[12] The following books express the black consciousness of the 1960s: James Baldwin, *The Fire Next Time* (New York: Dell, 1964); Stokely Carmichael and Charles V. Hamilton, *Black Power* (New York: Vintage, 1967); Malcom X, *The Autobiography of Malcom X* (New York: Grove Press, 1964).

[13] For books dealing with Hispanics and education, see Manuel T. Herschel, *Spanish-speaking Children of the Southwest* (Austin: University of Texas Press, 1965); Julian Samora, *La Raza: Forgotten Americans* (Notre Dame, Ind.: University of Notre Dame Press, 1966); Francesco Cordasco and Eugene Bucchioni, *Puerto Rican Children in Mainland Schools* (New York: Scarecrow Press, 1968).

[14] Diane Ravitch, *The Troubled Crusade: American Education, 1945-1980* (New York: Basic Books, 1983), pp. 273-74.

student's mother tongue. Bilingual education has generated considerable public and professional controversy between advocates of transitional and maintenance programs. Proponents of transitional programs hold that instruction in the student's mother tongue should be carried on until the student can use English effectively. Proponents of maintenance programs want instruction that will maintain biculturalism. While bilingual education programs exist in many languages, depending upon the language composition of the school population, and range from American Indian languages to Chinese, Japanese, and Greek, the largest group participating in bilingual programs is Hispanic students. California and the Southwestern states have traditionally had large Spanish-speaking populations, primarily Mexican-American. The big cities also have large Hispanic communities, particularly Puerto Rican, Cuban, and Mexican.

Women's Liberation

In the 1960s, the women's liberation movement began to demand equal educational, employment, and political opportunities for women. Although the feminist movement was not new to American life, it developed new strategies in the 1960s.[15] While the women's movement included diverse groups with varied objectives, it sought in particular to end discriminatory employment practices that had relegated women to second-class citizenship and to stereotypic occupations such as nursing, elementary school teaching, and secretarial and clerical positions. Feminist spokespersons such as Betty Friedan and Gloria Steinem challenged the traditional attitude that a woman's appropriate career was that of housekeeping, cooking, and childrearing.

The women's drive for equality in employment accelerated as law suits were filed to end discrimination in hiring. The Civil Rights Act of 1964 had made it illegal to discriminate in employment on the basis of sex. In 1972, the Equal Rights Amendment (ERA) was sent by Congress to the states for ratification but failed to secure sufficient approval in the various state legislatures.

The women's liberation movement had momentous implications for education. It destroyed the long-standing traditional concept that there was an appropriate education for men and for women. For example, the doctrine of appropriateness had curricular implications in that manual training programs, technical courses, and medical, engineering, and legal studies had been considered appropriate undertakings for males. Home economics, domestic science courses, nursing, elementary school teaching, and secretarial programs had been considered appropriate studies for women. With these conventional sanctions eroding, women began to enroll in large numbers in professional programs in medicine, law, engineering, journalism, and other areas.

---

[15] For the women's movement, see Vivian Gornick and Barbara K. Moran, eds., *Woman in Sexist Society: Studies in Power and Powerlessness* (New York: Basic Books, 1971); Aileen S. Kraditor, ed., *Up from the Pedestal: Selected Documents from the History of American Feminism* (New York: Quadrangle, 1968); William O'Neill, *The Woman Movement: Feminism in the United States and England* (New York: Barnes and Noble, 1969).

As had been true of blacks, Hispanics, and other minorities, women also sought to have their contributions to American life and culture reexamined. The roles played by women in science, law, education, politics, and other areas were now being treated in textbooks and in academic courses. Using the black studies model, colleges and universities established women's studies programs.

CHANGING STUDENT ATTITUDES IN HIGHER EDUCATION

The expanding enrollments of the 1950s and 1960s brought a greater diversity of students to college and university campuses. Although it is simplistic to stereotype whole generations of students, some generalizations about student attitudes can illuminate the changes that took place in American higher education in the 1960s. The 1950s, characterized as the "Eisenhower years," were a time when growth, "bigness," and increasing affluence were regarded as unquestioned and desirable social norms. The students of the 1950s, often oriented to the specific career goals of the corporate world, followed the structured curricula that prepared them to be executives, managers, scientists, teachers, and engineers. Social and political activism did not have a high priority for the college students of the 1950s.

The 1960s brought new students with differing attitudes to the nation's campuses. Some students experienced a sense of social and political activism that has been characterized as the new radicalism.[16]

Organized student activism began in 1962, when the Students for a Democratic Society (SDS) met in Port Huron, Michigan, and issued a manifesto that called for the radical restructuring of American society. Essentially, the SDS advocated broad social welfare programs, a more equitable redistribution of wealth, and an end to the war in Vietnam. Beyond specifics, however, the SDS was antagonistic to what it regarded as the American political-social-economic establishment. It called for an ill-defined "Participatory Democracy" that would bring hitherto underrepresented minority groups into political power. At its height, SDS could muster nearly 100,000 followers, most of them upper-middle-class students. In 1970, SDS split into contending ideological factions: the anarchistic Weathermen, who espoused violence as an instrument of change; and the Progressive Labor group, a neo-Marxist cadre. In the early 1970s, SDS splintered and its membership fell dramatically. Quite contrary to those who had predicted the end of ideology in the 1950s, the 1960s—at least on many college campuses—promised to be intensely ideological.

---

[16] For treatments of the new radicals of the 1960s, see Paul Jacobs and Saul Landau, *The New Radicals: A Report with Documents* (New York: Random House, 1966); Priscilla Long, ed., *The New Left: A Collection of Essays* (Boston: Porter Sargent, 1969); Kirkpatrick Sale, *S.D.S.* (New York: Random House, 1973); Mitchell Cohen and Dennis Hale, *The New Student Left* (Boston: Beacon Press, 1966); Clayborne Carson, *In Struggle: SNCC and the Black Awakening of the 1960s* (Cambridge, Mass.: Harvard University Press, 1981); Seymour M. Lipset and Gerald M. Schaflander, *Passion and Politics: Student Activism in America* (Boston: Little, Brown, 1971).

Leftist student organizations, such as SDS and other groups, developed a wide-ranging ideological platform for creating a new social order in the United States. They believed that colleges and universitites should become vanguard centers in bringing about their preferred view of social change. To do this, they pursued activist tactics ranging from issuing manifestos, to holding rallies, to organizing demonstrations, to occupying offices and classrooms in sit-ins. These tactics were designed to identify, expose, and purge colleges and universities of establishment ideology and the influence of the military-industrial complex; these would be replaced with a new ideology of their own creation that combined elements of humanism, neo-Marxism, anarchism, and social democracy. Essentially, the radical left students embraced a varied program for social change that included:

1. transforming educational institutions, particularly colleges and universities, into agencies of deliberate social, political, and economic change;
2. restructuring American economic life to achieve a more equitable redistribution of wealth, especially for blacks, Hispanics, migrant workers, and other economically disadvantaged minority groups;
3. achieving full civil rights for black and other minority groups;
4. ending the United States' involvement in the Vietnam War and eliminating American support for regimes judged to be exploitative on behalf of vested interests; and
5. securing an end to the arms race, instituting nuclear disarmament, and promoting peaceful coexistence with the Soviet Union.

In addition to this agenda for political and economic change, the student activist groups also wanted to achieve educational and social alterations as well. In this aspect, their specific programs were not as clearly stated nor agreed to by the various factions of students. In an obvious way, they wanted education to be overtly ideological in character and exemplify their version of social democracy. Aside from their ideological stance, some students were alienated by the impersonal character of the large university, in which students became numbers in the bureaucratic machinery of institutionalized instruction. They also objected to a highly structured curriculum that emphasized mastery of knowledge. Rebelling against structured disciplines, some students sought to replace lectures with free-form discussions, or "dialogues," that centered on political, social, economic, or personal issues rather than on "irrelevant" learned disciplines.

Student protests of the 1960s were also directed against the conventional social mores of middle-class America. At times, they advocated breaking down conventional sexual mores and patterns that they regarded to be coercive of personal expression and freedom. They were also influenced by the growing drug culture that considered LSD and other substances to be mind-expanding agents that would induce a higher consciousness.

While the range of student activist organizations and objectives was large and varied, certain organizations and events were especially significant during the mid- and late 1960s and early 1970s, the era of protest activities.

In early 1960s, the Student Nonviolent Coordinating Committee (SNCC) had been a focal organization for students, both black and white, who had dedicated themselves to working for civil rights for blacks. SNCC's activities brought students to the South, where they joined local black organizations in voter registration drives, sit-ins, and demonstrations to combat racism, segregation, and discrimination. Many white students learned the tactics of social protest that they would use later from their participation in SNCC. However, when SNCC took a black nationalist position, white students were often unwelcome in the organization.

In 1964, a small group of activist students at the University of California at Berkeley organized the Free Speech Movement (FSM). The FSM, led by Mario Savio, had as its initial objective forcing the university administration to grant them space to solicit members and funds for off-campus political causes. The FSM used tactics that were to be imitated on other college campuses, such as confrontations with police and the occupation of campus buildings. While it achieved its initial objective, the FSM soon broadened its goals and attracted students who were alienated by the impersonality of the large university with its bureaucratic structures.

The Rise of the Multiversity

While the FSM and other activist student organizations were motivated to action by conditions that were external to the university, there was a sense in which they were reacting to and against changes that had taken place within higher educational institutions, particularly the large universities. This transformation of the university had been epitomized by the term "multiversity," coined by Clark Kerr in the early 1960s. Kerr, then president of the University of California, claimed that the concept of the university as an institution guided by a single unifying mission had been altered by the rise of the multiversity, a multiple-purpose institution that served myriad publics. According to Kerr, the American university had experienced two great transformations: (1) the first in the late nineteenth century, when the land-grant movement and the German research ideal combined to reshape inherited patterns; (2) the second after World War II, when universities began to educate masses of students and engage in federally funded research.[17]

Kerr's concept of the multiversity arose from his experience at the University of California, which had a total operating budget of nearly half a billion dollars. The university was spending nearly $100 million for building construction, employing over 40,000 persons, maintaining operations in more than 100 locations, conducting projects in more than 50 foreign nations, offering 10,000 courses, and projecting an enrollment of 100,000 students. No longer a unified community of students and professors, the multiversity, a collection of interest groups and specialists that merely shared a common name, was at best "an inconsistent institution."[18]

[17] Clark Kerr, *The Uses of the University* (Cambridge, Mass.: Harvard University Press, 1963), pp. 86-87.

[18] Ibid., pp. 18-19.

Kerr's description of the multiversity was significant because it summed up both the historical development of American higher education and predicted its future. His description also pointed to the large modern university as the locus of contending groups pursuing their own special interests. For example, there were the students, who through their registrations, determined program development. The faculty had gained control over admissions, course approval, examinations, degree-granting, appointments, and academic freedom. State political authorities, such as the board of trustees, the state department of finance, the governor, and the legislature controlled funding. External organizations such as agriculture and business associations, unions, public school groups, and the mass media promoted their own interests. The university administration attempted to implement policies and manage the resources and personnel of the institution. [19] In describing student life, Kerr observed that the "multiversity is a confusing place for the student. He has problems establishing his identity and a sense of security within it."[20]

In the wake of the Free Speech Movement, the University of California's Academic Senate established a Select Committee to identify causes and recommend solutions to the problem of student alienation. In its report, *Education at Berkeley*, the Select Committee concluded that the students perceived themselves to be victims of a great national and international situation that had reached a crisis in higher education.[21] The major reasons for this crisis were identified as the changing role of the university, the proliferation of knowledge, the growth of population, the change in social and economic expectations, and the emergence of a new generation of students. All of the major constitutents of the muitiversity—teachers, students, areas of knowledge, and society—were affected by the unprecedented changes that had occurred. The great task of the modern university, stated the report, was the complex challenge of preserving academic integrity while accepting change.

To combat feelings of alienation on the large campus, the Select Committee recommended the increased use of seminars, tutorials, and student representation on academic policymaking committees. In place of the traditional survey courses, it suggested problem-centered courses. Seeing no necessary contradiction between teaching and research, the Select Committee believed that the interpenetration of the two pursuits would contribute to a sense of integration and coherence. The recommendations of the Select Committee embraced the general response to student unrest that would take place throughout the country in the 1960s.

Antiwar Protests

By the mid-1960s, student activism was galvanized against the continuing acceleration of the United States' involvement in the war in Vietnam. Student

[19] Ibid., pp. 20-28.

[20] Ibid., p. 42.

[21] Charles Muscatine, et al., *Education at Berkeley: Report of the Select Committee on Education* (Berkeley: University of California Printing Department, 1966), pp. 3-7.

protests were directed in particular against President Johnson, who, while committed to civil rights and the ending of poverty, was also determined to arrest what he regarded as communist aggression in Southeast Asia. Johnson, who persistently defended the American military presence in Vietnam, committed American ground troops to combat areas in the spring of 1965. Student protests were directed against the Selective Service System (the draft), and university cooperation in research and recruitment efforts for aiding the military.

From 1965 onward, antiwar activitists, often attracting students who were unaffiliated with any particular radical organization, protested the American policy in Vietnam. The scale of protest activities ranged from "teach-ins," to demonstrations, to the seizure of campus buildings. The teach-in was a series of lectures, discussions, and dialogues, sometimes extending for several days, in which students and sympathetic faculty members discussed the Vietnam War and general issues of war and peace, poverty, and racism. Demonstrations generally took the form of the protest rally, which involved antiwar speeches and the singing of protest ballads. The protest rallies attracted prominent writers and entertainers such as Joan Baez, Jane Fonda, and Dr. Benjamin Spock.

In some situations, protesting students became increasingly intolerant of those who did not accept their views and disrupted classes. The most dramatic event, widely covered by the television media, occurred at Columbia University, where militant students occupied several campus buildings.[22] After eight days of tension, police cleared the buildings, with injuries and arrests resulting. Antiwar protests and demonstrations occurred on university and college campuses throughout the nation durng the late 1960s, reaching a peak in 1968-1969.

Nineteen sixty-eight was a climactic year for the student activist movement as thousands of college students worked for the candidacy of Senator Eugene McCarthy in the presidential primaries. Some observers have commented that the so-called children's crusade contributed to President Johnson's decision not to seek reelection. At the Democratic National Convention in Chicago in the summer of 1968, violent confrontations occurred between the Chicago police and antiwar demonstrators. With Senator McCarthy's failure to win the Democratic presidential nomination, many disappointed students returned to their campuses to pursue politics of polarization or dropped out of higher education altogether. From 1968 to 1971, student unrest spread throughout the nation, culminating in the Kent State University tragedy in the spring of 1970.

The response of university administrators varied from acquiescence to student demands and long drawn-out negotiations, to the use of police to clear buildings of demonstrators. The response of faculty members also varied. Some supported the students' demands; others resisted them as violating academic freedom. At several institutions, faculty committees sought a middle course and tried to mediate between protesters and besieged administrators.

---

[22] A Proactivist treatment is Roger Kahn, *The Battle for Morningside Heights: Why Students Rebel* (New York: Morrow, 1970); a thoughtful commentary is provided in Charles Frankel, *Education and the Barricades* (New York: W. W. Norton & Co., Inc., 1968).

A result of the much-televised student protests, demonstrations, and sit-ins was a growing public antagonism to the student activists. Violence, such as the "days of rage" in Chicago by the Weathermen faction, alienated many students as well as the public. Leftist students failed to enlist the support of organized labor and minority groups and became increasingly isolated. State legislators began to question and reduce funding for universities.

The student activist episode that shocked America most was the Kent State University tragedy of May 4, 1970. Some students at Kent State had joined in a national student strike to protest the entry of American troops into Cambodia. A group of protesters had set fire to the campus ROTC building and prevented firemen from putting out the fire. The governor of Ohio ordered National Guard troops to the campus. During a confrontation with rock-throwing students, guardsmen fired on the crowd and killed four. A week later, two black students were killed at Jackson State College in Mississippi.

The tragedies at Kent State and Jackson State sent shock waves through the nation. After some sympathy demonstrations and counteractions, the mood on campuses grew increasingly reflective.[23] Student activism diminished slowly and ended in the early 1970s. There were several reasons for the change of attitude. Among them were the following:

1. The SDS, which sought to polarize American society, itself became polarized. The most radical anarchistic faction, the Weathermen, became increasingly isolated from the student community because of its use of violence. The Marxist line of the Progressive Labor faction did not appeal to many students.
2. The Nixon adminstration had decided to abandon the war in Vietnam. As American forces left the area, the antiwar issue dissipated.
3. Student activists had alienated potential allies both in the larger society and on the campus. Labor union members, often the allies of students in other countries, were alienated by the counterculture, with its rejection of traditional values and lack of patriotism. Student violence, the disruption of classes, and the disregard for the orderly adjudication of disputes made most liberals disenchanted with the student movement. In fact, some liberals saw the student movement as a threat to academic freedom.
4. Although there was some initial cooperation between black and white students in the civil rights movement in the late 1960s and early 1970s, the two groups grew increasingly suspicious of each other. Black students tended to pursue their own objectives such as the establishment of black studies programs, the admission of more black students, or the hiring of more black faculty members. White students, in contrast, pursued more general goals such as ending the war, reducing military spending, and changing the society.
5. Even at its height, the student protest movement had enlisted only a small minority of students. It had attracted mostly humanities and social science students rather than those in science and professional programs.

[23] The changing student attitude is revealed in Steven Kelman, *Push Comes to Shove: The Escalation of Student Protest* (Boston: Houghton Mifflin, 1970). The Kent School tragedy is discussed in I. F. Stone, *The Killing at Kent State* (New York: New York Review-Vintage Books, 1971); and Alexander Kendrick, *The Wound Within* (Boston: Little, Bown, 1974).

6. Finally, the student movement lost its momentum. Economic changes in the larger society such as the high inflation rates of the mid-1970s and the recession of the early 1980s caused the new generation of students to look to their own careers and future economic security rather than to social issues. Increasingly, the activists who argued for more relevant education in the late 1960s and early 1970s had themselves become irrelevent by the late 1970s and early 1980s.

Although student activism had subsided by the mid-1980s, many issues that had surfaced during the movement continued to remain unresolved. For example, what was the appropriate role of students in the governance of colleges and universities? What was the appropriate social, political, and economic role of colleges and universities in the American social order?

The Counterculture

Student activism had been part of a larger and more pervasive shift in cultural mores and values termed the counterculture. A broad, diffuse movement, the counterculture influenced many young people, especially white upper-middle-class youth, who rejected the work ethic and the traditional family, social, and religious values of their paremts. It also polarized American society, as many people such as working-class men and women, religious fundamentalists, and large numbers of the middle-class resisted what they saw to be a threat to the American social order. The counterculture brought changes to American society and education; while some of these effects were momentary, others had a longer and more formative impact. The counterculture had its greatest impact on many of the nation's college campuses, but it spilled over into American society at large as it reshaped the life-style and values of many young people.

Although the term counterculture has resisted definition, various intellectuals and academics—usually identified with the movement—sought to describe it. Theodore Roszak, in his widely read book, *The Making of a Counter Culture* (1969), predicted the emergence of a new culture in which scientific and technological bureaucracies would be replaced by a more personalist culture.[24] For Charles Reich, author of *The Greening of America* (1970), the new culture, with its heightened "consciousness," would be one of utopian peace and harmony.[25] Timothy Leary, a psychologist, recommended the use of what he regarded as consciousness-raising drugs.

The counterculture manifested itself in many diverse ways. Rock music replaced the ballad and folk song. Long hair was worn by both men and women, and sandals and blue jeans bcame the universal style of dress. Communal living arrangements were experimented with by the 1960s flower children.

After its more dramatic and exotic aspects had diminished, perhaps the greatest impact of the counterculture was its rejection of the Protestant work ethic

[24] New York: Doubleday.

[25] *The Greening of America: How the Youth Revolution Is Trying to Make America Livable* (New York: Random House, 1970).

that had influenced so much of American life and education. The work ethic, which placed a premium on material wealth as a sign of progress and values, was rejected. Also discarded was the concept that education, especially in the form of schooling, should prepare a person for productive, wealth-generating work. For many adherents of the counterculture, education was to be existentially relevant to personal interests. Schooling itself was at times rejected as a conditioning process that made persons the objects of the establishment.

SCHOOLING IN THE 1960s

Such social changes, engendered by the rising consciousness of minority groups and by student activism, had some effects on educational curriculum and instruction. The major developments in schooling can be examined in terms of curriculum changes in the early 1960s that grew out of the National Defense Education Act of 1958 and to organizational and instructional innovations that were part of an "educational revolution." As the 1960s entered their second half, the impact of the Elementary and Secondary Education Act was to redirect schooling to programs of compensatory education designed to equalize the educational opportunities of minority students.

During the early 1960s, many speeches, articles, and books announced that the United States was on the verge of an educational revolution.[26] In retrospect, the claims of an impending revolution in education were overstated. Nevertheless, the 1960s witnessed significant innovations in curriculum, organization, and instructional designs. Let us examine the impact on those educational innovations.

Curriculum Revisions of the 1960s

The early 1960s saw concerted efforts at curricular revision that had been prompted primarily by the post-*Sputnik* fears that American capabilities in science, mathematics, and engineering had deteriorated in comparison to those in the Soviet Union. Federal funding through the National Defense Education Act of 1958 stimulated curriculum revision, as university professors turned their attention to reshaping the elementary and secondary school curriculum. The mood of curriculum restructuring was also stimulated by the continuing debates that had begun in the early 1950s over the quality of American education. In these debates, critics such as Bestor, Rafferty, and Rickover had attacked American public schooling for its weak intellectual rigor and academic standards. While these critics had prepared the soil for curricular change, it was the incentive of federal funding that planted the seeds.

---

[26] For an example, see Francis Keppel, *The Necessary Revolution in American Education* (New York: Harper & Row, Pub., 1966); and Ronald Gross and Judith Murphy, eds., *The Revolution in the Schools* (New York: Harcourt, Brace, 1964).

The general strategy for curricular change in the early 1960s took the following form:

1. Teams of mathematicians, chemists, physicists, and biologists examined the existing curriculum in these subjects and recommended revisions. Although including occasional elementary and secondary school educators and professors of education, these academic teams were dominated by university professors of mathematics or the scientific disciplines.
2. The various teams of experts devised new curricula which generally stressed that: (a) instruction in a subject such as chemistry should be organized around its necessary structures, and (b) students should try to replicate the subject by the inquiry processes that scientists originally followed.
3. The new curricula, often called the New Mathematics, New Physics, or New Chemistry, were to be introduced to small groups of selected teachers who were to pioneer teaching them in their particular schools. These teachers usually attended special NDEA institutes at sponsoring colleges and universities.

Underlying the various curricular reforms was the learning theory of Jerome Bruner, which emphasized the structure of disciplines and the use of the inquiry, or discovery, method.[27] As committees of scholars and scientists attempted to identify the structures of the academic disciplines, they generally replaced the conventional stress on description and factual information with key concepts. The inquiry method, for example, sought to approximate the processes used by scientists and scholars in their research.

Rather than having teachers or textbooks directly present basic principles to them, students were to investigate problems and reach their own conclusions. The curricular innovations of the 1960s were supported by federal funds. Philanthropic organizations such as the Carnegie and Ford foundations also supported the new curricula. Commercial publishers promoted the movement by designing and marketing "learning packages" that featured the new curricular designs.

Organizational and Methodological Innovations of the 1960s

While teams of mathematics and science professors were revising the elementary and secondary school curricula, the 1960s also experienced what was boldly proclaimed to be a revolution in education. Educational administrators and curriculum specialists, usually identified with professional education, introduced a series of innovations in school architecture and design, curriculum organization, scheduling, staffing, and the use of television and other instructional technologies. For example, school architects designed new schools that abandoned the four-walled, self-contained classroom in favor of large open spaces and interest centers that

---

[27] Jerome Bruner, *The Process of Education* (Cambridge, Mass.: Harvard University Press, 1960).

radiated outward from a central "learning resource center." The learning resource center was usually the former library, but it now contained film-strip viewers, tape recorders, television monitors, and other instruments of the new technology.

As schools were redesigned, so were the staffing patterns of the teachers and the schedules of the students within them. The innovation that attracted the most attention was team teaching, which involved having teachers share responsibilities for planning, organizing, and delivering instruction.

The early experiments with team teaching were conducted by the School and University Program for Research and Development at Harvard University, the Claremont Graduate School Team Teaching Program in California, and the Wisconsin School Improvement Program. J. Lloyd Trump, who headed the Committee on Staff Utilization of the National Association of Secondary School Principals, was a forceful proponent of team teaching.[28] Trump's concept of team teaching required careful planning and implementation. He recommended that 40 percent of instruction occur in large group sections, 40 percent in individualized learning experiences, and 20 percent in small group seminars. Despite the publicity that it received, team teaching did not have the profound impact that Trump and others predicted. The bandwagon effect generated for team teaching in the early 1960s often caused it to be introduced in haphazard fashion in some school districts. In some situations, a crude version of team teaching merely brought two teachers together to share the same classroom.

During the early 1960s, attacks were made on the "lock-step" scheduling that saw students moving in groups from one fifty-minute class to another. Flexible scheduling, organized into modules, allowed students to pursue subjects in varying time blocks. The "nongraded school" was designed to remove the inflexibility of the graded system by eliminating the conventional grade labels attached to children. According to the proponents of the nongraded school, it was an organizational pattern in which students could progress at their own individual rate of learning. In a nongraded school, for example, academically talented students could progress at a faster rate, while those who needed special or remedial attention could move at a rate that was appropriate for them.

The 1960s also saw the development of new instructional technologies such as educational television, programmed learning, and computer-based instruction. Since the early 1950s, educators had been experimenting with educational television. In 1957, Alexander J. Stoddard initiated the National Program in the Use of Television in the Schools, which was financed by the Ford Foundation's Fund for the Advancement of Education. In 1961, the six-state Midwest Program on Airborne Television Instruction, located at Purdue University, began to telecast lessons to schools and colleges from high-flying airplanes. A significant open-circuit effort was the Chicago College of the Air, which televized credit courses over WTTW, the public television channel in Chicago. In 1965, the National Center for School and College Television at Indiana University was established as a central

[28] J. Lloyd Trump and Dorsey Baynham, *Focus on Change: Guide to Better Schools* (Chicago: Rand McNally, 1961).

clearinghouse on educational television. As the 1960s ended, more than 10,000,000 students were receiving part of their instruction by television.

What Happened to the Educational Revolution?

As the 1960s came to a close, it was apparent that the predicted revolution in education had not achieved its prophesized effects. To be sure, American schooling had been changed by the new curricula and other educational innovations, but the effects of the change were limited. Although more assessment of the innovations is needed, the following hypotheses suggest why the schools may have resisted major transformation:

1. By the late 1960s, large urban school systems were facing urgent problems of pronounced racial and social change and declining fiscal resources that sidetracked costly innovations.
2. Many of the new mathematics and science curricula had not been tested adequately in the field before being introduced in the schools. University professors in the mathematics and science disciplines, with little experience in instruction in elementary or secondary schools, tried to bring about change from the top downward. This tendency often caused confusion and ultimate rejection by teachers and parents.
3. School administrators eager to jump on the bandwagon of educational innovation failed to set the stage by preparing their communities, schools, and staffs for the change in curriculum or organization that was necessary. As a result, the new curriculum or innovation quickly became formalized and soon resembled what had been taking place in the schools prior to the introduction of the reform. For example, open-space learning centers designed for a range of large and small groups, as well as individualized learning activities, were cordoned off and divided by partitions into the old self-contained classrooms that they had been designed to replace.
4. The very decentralization of the American system of education into thousands of local school districts made sweeping national reforms difficult if not virtually impossible. Many school districts were virtually untouched by innovations of the 1960s.

THE RADICAL AND ROMANTIC CRITICS

By the mid-1960s, a new breed of educational critic had appeared. Unlike the essentialists of the 1930s or Bestor, Rafferty, and Rickover during the 1950s, who had urged a return to rigorous intellectual disciplines and the raising of academic standards, the critics of the late 1960s resembled Rousseauean romantics or child-centered progressives.

The new critics argued that schools were overly centralized, bureaucratic, formalized, routine, mindless, and stifling of children's freedom and teachers' creativity. They urged a flexibility that would permit learners and teachers to shape their own educational environments along more humanistic contours.

The books written by the new critics resembled a twentieth-century version of Rousseau's *Emile*. They emphasized permissive classroom styles and arrangements that were to be free of interference by coercive administrators. For example, the best-selling novel, *Up the Down Staircase*, portrayed a novice high school English teacher who was able to reach her students by thwarting a bureaucratic administration.[29] A series of books came from the pens of angry critics of American schooling such as Herbert Kohl, Jonathan Kozol, George Dennison, and John Holt.[30] The romantic critics were anti-institutional and urged that children should be free to follow their own curiosity, interests, and inclinations. Teachers, in turn, were to be enthusiastic, exciting, and creative.

The cause of informal and open learning received national attention when Charles E. Silberman's *Crisis in the Classroom* appeared in 1970.[31] Silberman, director of the Carnegie Corporation's Study of the Education of Educators, criticized public schools for being overly formal. Excessive routine and formality had created devitalized and often inhumane schools governed by mindless bureaucracy. For Silberman, the remedy was to create more open, informal, and humanistic schools. He argued that the British primary school, or integrated day school, presented a model that could be adapted to American elementary education. Informal open classrooms would encourage teachers to follow and guide learners' interests. At the secondary level, American high schools were to be reformed by eliminating unnecessary rules and regulations, by allowing more student alternatives, and by a substantial curriculum revision that stressed the structure of academic disciplines as suggested by Bruner.

Silberman and other advocates of open learning and humanistic education stimulated an American interest in the British primary school,[32] which rested on the premise that children learned most effectively through a direct involvement with their immediate environment, in which they were free to pursue their own interests with the guidance of teachers. Rather than following the scheduled time sequences of the more formal school, the British primary school stressed longer blocks of time where the children worked individually or in small groups at a wide range of activities. The British primary school quickly gained a following among enthusiastic American educators, who began to implement it as open-space education.

---

[29] Bel Kaufman, *Up the Down Staircase* (Englewood Cliffs, N.J.: Prentice-Hall, 1964).

[30] Among the new critics were: George Dennison, *The Lives of Children* (New York: Random House, 1969); James Herndon, *The Way It Spozed to Be* (New York: Simon & Schuster, 1968); John Holt, *How Children Learn* (New York: Pitman, 1967); Jonathan Kozol, *Death at an Early Age* (Boston: Houghton Mifflin, 1967).

[31] *Crisis in the Classroom: The Remaking of American Education* (New York: Random Hose, 1970).

[32] The major source on the British primary school is Lady Bridget Plowden, et al., *Children and Their Primary Schools: A Report of the Central Advisory Council in Education* (London: Her Majesty's Stationery Office, 1966). Other works on open education are: John Blackie, *Inside the Primary School* (London: Her Majesty's Stationery Office, 1967); Mary Brown and Norman Precious, *The Integrated Day in the Primary School* (New York: Agathon Press, 1970); Lillian S. Stephens, *The Teacher's Guide to Open Education* (New York: Holt, Reinhart & Winston, 1974).

During the late 1960s and early 1970s, the open education movement steadily gained ground in the United States. A noteworthy example of such implementation occurred in North Dakota, where a number of small schools were converted into informal or open schools. Throughout the country, school districts inaugurated open classrooms, or open-space, schools. In some cases, the open school theory was applied correctly and produced the desired educational consequences. In other situations, it was introduced hastily by educators who failed to understand its full pedagogical requirements. As a result, certain open-space situations merely consisted of a large room or open area in which several teachers taught in a conventional manner.

CONCLUSION

The 1960s were a period of promise and protest. Important achievements were registered in advancing civil rights and in providing educational opportunities for previously neglected disadvantaged minority groups. At the same time, the protracted conflict in Vietnam brought discontent to the surface of American society. Student protests in higher education ran to the very nerve centers of society. Many of the well-publicized reforms, both of a social and educational nature, turned out to be exaggerated. The 1970s and 1980s were to see these reform efforts give way to attempts to stabilize the society.

DISCUSSION QUESTIONS

1. Discuss the educational policies of the Kennedy administration from both a domestic and an international perspective.
2. Compare and contrast the social and educational policies of Kennedy's New Frontier and Johnson's Great Society.
3. Examine the context that led to the enactment of the Elementary and Secondary Education Act of 1965, and explore the consequences of this act on American education.
4. Trace the development of civil rights and racial desegregation efforts during the Kennedy and Johnson administrations.
5. Identify and analyze the various elements of social change during the 1960s.
6. How were the bilingual educational programs of the 1960s and 1970s a reversal of earlier educational policies that stressed the assimilation of immigrant children?
7. Examine the educational implications of the women's liberation movement of the 1960s and 1970s.
8. Using Kerr's concept of the multiversity, identify and describe the major changes that occurred in American higher educational institutions in the 1960s.

9. Analyze the concept of the counterculture. What are its implications for educational change?

10. Analyze the criticisms of the romantic critics of the late 1960s and contrast them with those of critics of the 1950s and 1980s.

RESEARCH TOPICS

1. Read a carefully selected biography of John F. Kennedy. In a short paper, examine his educational background and the formative experiences that shaped his style of leadership.

2. Read a carefully selected biography of Lyndon B. Johnson. In a short paper, examine his education and the formative experiences that shaped his political and educational philosophy.

3. If there is a black studies or Hispanic studies program in your college or university, research its origins and write a short paper that describes the program in historical perspective.

4. Read a biography of Martin Luther King, Jr. In a short paper, examine his education and his social and educational philosophy.

5. Examine the development of bilingual education by reviewing guidelines and other documents prepared by your state office or department of education. Write a short paper that establishes an historical context for your state's policy regarding bilingual education.

6. Read several accounts of the student radicalism of the 1960s. From your reading, prepare a short paper that identifies and examines the goals and expectations of the activist students of that decade.

7. Using oral history techniques, interview administrators, professors, and students who were involved in the activism of the 1960s. Record their impressions and prepare a paper that summarizes the climate of opinion of the era.

8. Read Roszak's *The Making of a Counterculture* and Reich's *The Greening of America.* Write a critical review assessing their social and educational relevance in historical perspective.

9. Using oral history techniques, interview several elementary and secondary school teachers who were involved in implementing the educational innovations of the 1960s. Record their impressions and prepare a paper that focuses on the educational practitioners' interpretation of change in an historical perspective.

10. Read Kaufman's *Up the Down Staircase.* Write a review that compares and contrasts her impressions with those of contemporary educational critics.

REFERENCES AND READINGS

Altbach, Philip. *Student Politics in America: An Historical Analysis.* New York: McGraw-Hill, 1974.
Baldwin, James. *The Fire Next Time.* New York: Dell, 1964.

Bruner, Jerome. *The Process of Education.* Cambridge, Mass.: Harvard University Press, 1960.

Burns, James MacGregor. *John Kennedy: A Political Profile.* New York: Harcourt, Brace, 1960.

___. *To Heal and to Build: The Programs of President Lyndon B. Johnson.* New York: McGraw-Hill, 1968.

Carmichael, Stokely, and Hamilton, Charles V. *Black Power.* New York: Vintage Press, 1967.

Carson, Clayborne. *In Struggle: SNCC and the Black Awakening of the 1960s.* Cambridge, Mass.: Harvard University Press, 1981.

Cohen, Mitchell, and Hale, Dennis. *The New Student Left.* Boston: Beacon Press, 1966.

Cordasco, Francesco, and Bucchioni, Eugene. *Puerto Rican Children in Mainland Schools.* New York: Scarecrow Press, 1968.

Dennison, George. *The Lives of Children.* New York: Random House, 1969.

Feuer, Lewis S. *The Conflict of Generations: The Character and Significance of Student Movements.* New York: Basic Books, 1969.

Frankel, Charles. *Education and the Barricades.* New York: W. W. Norton & Co., Inc., 1968.

Goldman, Eric F. *The Tragedy of Lyndon Johnson.* New York: Knopf, 1969.

Gornick, Vivian, and Moran, Barbara K., eds. *Woman in Sexist Society: Studies in Power and Powerlessness.* New York: Basic Books, 1971.

Graham, Hugh Davis. *The Uncertain Triumph: Federal Education Policy in the Kennedy and Johnson Years.* Chapel Hill: University of North Carolina Press, 1984.

Gross, Ronald, and Murphy, Judith, eds. *The Revolution in the Schools.* New York: Harcourt, Brace, 1964.

Heath, Jim F. *Decade of Disillusionment: The Kennedy-Johnson Years.* Bloomington: Indiana University Press, 1975.

Herndon, James. *The Way It Spozed to Be.* New York: Simon & Schuster, 1968.

Herschel, Manuel T. *Spanish-speaking Children of the Southwest.* Austin: University of Texas Press, 1965.

Holt, John. *How Children Learn.* New York: Pitman, 1967.

Hook, Sidney, ed. *In Defense of Academic Freedom.* New York: Pegasus, 1971.

Jacobs, Paul, and Landau, Saul. *The New Radicals: A Report with Documents.* New York: Random House, 1966.

Kahn, Roger. *The Battle of Morningside Heights: Why Students Rebel.* New York: Morrow, 1970.

Kaufman, Bel. *Up the Down Staircase.* Englewood Cliffs, N.J.: Prentice-Hall, 1964.

Kearns, Doris. *Lyndon Johnson and the American Dream.* New York: Harper & Row, Pub., 1976.

Kelman, Steven. *Push Comes to Shove: The Escalation of Student Protest.* Boston: Houghton Mifflin, 1970.

Keppel, Francis. *The Necessary Revolution in American Education.* New York: Harper & Row, 1966.

Kerr, Clark. *The Uses of the University.* Cambridge, Mass.: Havard University Press, 1963.

Kozol, Jonathan. *Death at an Early Age.* Boston: Houghton Mifflin, 1967.

Kraditor, Aileeen S., ed. *Up from the Pedestal: Selected Documents from the History of American Feminism.* New York: Quadrangle, 1968.

Lipset, Seymour M., and Schaflander, Gerald M. *Passion and Politics: Student Activism in America.* Boston: Little, Brown, 1971.

Long, Priscilla, ed. *The New Left: A Collection of Essays.* Boston: Porter Sargent, 1969.

Malcom X. *The Autobiography of Malcom X.* New York: Grove Press, 1964.

Manchester, William R. *Portrait of a President: John F. Kennedy in Profile.* Boston: Little, Brown, 1962.

Muscatine, Charles, et al. *Education at Berkeley: Report of the Select Committee on Education.* Berkeley: University of California Printing Department, 1966.

National Advisory Commission on Civil Disorders. *Report of the National Advisory Commission on Civil Disorders.* New York: Bantam Books, 1968.

O'Hara, John F., ed. *John F. Kennedy on Education.* New York: Teachers College Press, Columbia University, 1966.

O'Neill, William. *The Woman Movement: Feminism in the United States and England.* New York: Barnes and Noble, 1969.

Ravitch, Diane. *The Troubled Crusade: American Education, 1945-1980.* New York: Basic Books, 1983.

Reich, Charles A. *The Greening of America: How the Youth Revolution Is Trying to Make America Livable.* New York: Random House, 1970.

Roszak, Theodore. *The Making of a Counterculture.* New York: Doubleday, 1968.

Sale, Kirkpatrick. *S.D.S.* New York: Random House, 1973.

Samora, Julian. *La Raza: Forgotten Americans.* Notre Dame, Ind.: University of Notre Dame Press, 1966.

Schlesigner, Arthur M., Jr. *A Thousand Days: John F. Kennedy in the White House.* Boston: Houghton Mifflin, 1965.

Sidney, Hugh. *A Very Personal Presidency: Lyndon Johnson in the White House.* New York: Atheneum, 1968.

Silberman, Charles E. *Crisis in the Classroom: The Remaking of American Education.* New York: Random House, 1970.

Stephens, Lillian S. *The Teacher's Guide to Open Education.* New York: Holt, Rinehart & Winston, 1974.

Stone, I. F. *The Killings at Kent State.* New York: New York Review—Vintage Books, 1971.

Trump, J. Lloyd, and Baynham, Dorsey. *Focus on Change: A Guide to Better Schools.* Chicago: Rand McNally, 1961.

13
SOCIETY
AND EDUCATION
IN THE 1970s

The 1970s, following the turbulent 1960s, appeared deceptively calm. The economic changes of the 1970s triggered by the energy crisis, inflation, and recession were so pervasive that their social and educational consequences are likely to have a more enduring impact on American society than the more dramatic 1960s. The events of the 1970s saw three presidents, Nixon, Ford, and Carter, grapple with the problems of a changing nation in a changing world.

RICHARD NIXON'S PRESIDENCY

In the election of 1968, Richard M. Nixon, the Republican nominee, defeated Hubert H. Humphrey, the Democratic candidate, and George C. Wallace, running as the candidate of the American Independent party.[1] A feature of Wallace's campaign was his vitriolic attacks on interference by federal agencies and officials in the lives of ordinary citizens. Wallace, claiming to have grassroots populist support, waged a campaign that touched on several educational issues, particularly his

[1] For treatments of Nixon and his administration, see Fawn Brodie, *Richard Nixon* (New York: W. W. Norton & Co., Inc., 1981); Earl Mazo and Stephen Hess, *Nixon* (New York: Harper & Row, Pub., 1968); Rowland Evans and Robert Novak, *Nixon in the White House* (New York: Random House, 1971). For his own account, see Richard Nixon, *RN* (New York: Grosset and Dunlap, 1978).

317

opposition to "forced busing." His campaign speeches, criticizing fuzzy-thinking intellectuals, condemned forced busing to achieve racially integrated schools. The election of 1968, revealing a neoconservative trend, marked a shift from the social protest and dissent of the late 1960s. Nixon, claiming to represent a "silent majority" of Americans, promised a return to law and order.

Nixon's Domestic Policies

From Franklin Roosevelt's New Deal of the 1930s onward, the general trend in American domestic politics has been to have the federal government assume a larger role and responsibility in dealing with economic and social problems. The Johnson administration's Great Society, with its War on Poverty and support of civil rights, encouraged a larger federal role in education. Nixon's first administration, from 1969 to 1973, reversed the trend and transferred more responsibility to state and local governments. The emphasis on greater local control was a persistent policy of the Republican administrations of Nixon, Ford, and Reagan in the 1970s and 1980s. Greater state and local control had significant implications for the direction and support of education during the 1970s and 1980s.

A key feature in Nixon's domestic policy was revenue sharing, which distributed federal funds to state and local governments to meet local needs.[2] In 1972, Congress approved a revenue-sharing plan that made $30.1 billion available to local and state governments. Revenue sharing was based on a philosophy that local government units, being closer to the people, could assess their needs better than the more remote and more bureaucratic federal government. This view, expressed by both Nixon and Wallace in their campaigns in 1968, was that direct federal funding would bring the interference of federal bureaucrats into local affairs. The reaffirmation of the role of local government, a theme that would be used during the Reagan administration of the 1980s, revealed a growing distrust of big government.

In the United States, public schools, organized and governed through local school districts, have been supported primarily by local property taxes and state aid. The federal government historically did not provide general aid to education. However, the Elementary and Secondary Education Act of 1965, sponsored by the Johnson administration, signalled a departure from this historic pattern. During the 1970s and 1980s, the pattern of a more restricted federal role in education resurfaced. Although schools might receive federal funds distributed to state and local governments through revenue sharing, the general tendency was to decrease such educational funding.

Nixon's Economic Policies

In the early 1970s, national attention began to shift from the Vietnam conflict, domestic social protest, and civil rights to the ailing economy. The economic

[2] For an analysis of revenue sharing, see F. T. Juster, ed., *The Economic and Political Impact of General Revenue Sharing: A Report to the National Science Foundation* (Washington, D.C.: GPO, 1976).

problems of the 1970s and 1980s, such as worsening inflation, spiraling federal deficits, and periodic recession, had a national impact that touched schools, students, and teachers as well as the general public.

Upon assuming the presidency, Nixon inherited a seriously growing inflation that had been aggravated by Johnson's policy of increasing military expenditures for the Vietnam War without raising taxes. By 1970, the inflation rate had climbed to 6 percent, unemployment was at 6 percent, the federal budget deficit had reached $25 billion, and business failures were increasing. In August 1971, a worsening economy caused President Nixon to impose a price and wage freeze for ninety days. Nixon's action stemmed the inflationary tide, albeit temporarily, and checked the recession. The economic uncertainty of the early 1970s would remain a feature of national life in that decade and into the 1980s.

The Economy and Education

The economic problems of the 1970s and 1980s had a profound impact on American society and on its educational structures as well. The most pervasive general consequence was a change in mood. No longer absorbed with issues of social and political change, students now sought career paths leading to economic security and status. A shift in enrollment patterns occurred as college students deserted the humanities and social sciences for professional programs in business, law, medicine, and dentistry.

A more pessimistic and uncertain mood characterized the national climate of opinion; hard fiscal realities were having an impact on educational institutions ranging from elementary and secondary schools to universities. The most striking demographic change was that the United States was approaching zero population growth. The number of school-age children, especially those of elementary school age, was declining. The result was that the 1970s saw markedly declining elementary and secondary enrollments.

The phenomenon of declining enrollments had fiscal and educational consequences. State aid, in most states, rested on funding formulas in which the amount of aid received by a local school district was based on the average daily attendance of pupils enrolled in that district. As the numbers of students declined, the amount of funding received decreased correspondingly. At the same time that state aid either decreased or remained constant, voters in many local school districts—motivated by their own economic fears—resisted efforts of school officials to raise property tax rates. Adding to the schools' economic woes was the ideology of the Republican administrations in Washington that called for a diminished role in education and an increase in local initiatives.

Local school districts, especially in Northern industrial states where school enrollments experienced their sharpest decline, responded by reducing expenditures and trimming budgets. For a generation of school administrators whose professional careers had been launched in the quantitative expansion of the 1950s and 1960s, budget trimming, fiscal retrenchment, and program cutting presented a new and especially formidable challenge. The challenge was made even more onerous by the fact that the nation's spiraling inflation rate was severely impacting schools. Operations costs for textbooks, supplies, heating and lighting, and maintenance were steadily rising. Equally serious were teachers' demands for increased salaries and medical benefits. Teachers' unions grew more militant as their members suffered from the economic pressures of an inflationary tide that was reducing their real income and purchasing power.[3] The result was that while school revenues decreased or remained fixed, expenditures increased.

The fiscal constraints felt in many school districts brought about the new phenomenon of the school closing. Many school districts, in often protracted and emotionally charged decisions, closed some of their schools to reduce the costs of operating underused facilities. School closings, caused by declining enrollments and reduced revenues, forced school boards in many districts to reduce the number of full-time teachers on their professional staffs. Thus, the quantitative educational expansion of the 1950s and 1960s yielded to declining enrollments, school closings, and reductions in force (RIF) in the 1970s and early 1980s.

Nixon and Civil Rights

The Johnson administration had pursued a vigorous program of civil rights, which included school desegregation. In contrast, the general strategy of the Nixon administration shifted the responsibility for school desegregation from the Justice Department to the courts.

Despite the appointment of more conservative justices to the Supreme Court such as Warren Burger, Harry Blackmun, Lewis Powell, and William Rehnquist, the Court, with Burger as Chief Justice, upheld the previous Warren Court's desegregation decisions. For example, the Court in 1971 upheld busing as an instrument for achieving racially integrated schools.

Foreign Policy under Nixon and Kissinger

In foreign affairs, the Nixon administration proved especially adept in pursuing what it regarded as a realistic policy; its objectives were to end the United States' involvement in the Vietnamese conflict, establish diplomatic and trade relations with the People's Republic of China, and negotiate an arms control agreement and detente with the Soviet Union. Nixon and Henry Kissinger, his chief foreign policy advisor, succeeded in achieving these objectives. The next section examines foreign affairs in the 1970s and comments on their educational implications.

Nixon's foreign policy rested on a realistic and pragmatic world view that was shared by Kissinger. Nixon had begun his political career by winning elections in California first as a congressman and then as a senator in campaigns marked by

---

[3] For teachers' organizations and the use of collective bargaining, see Charles R. Perry and Wesley A. Wildman, *The Impact of Negotiations in Public Education: The Evidence from the Schools* (Worthington, Ohio: Charles A. Jones, 1970); Marshall O. Donley, *Power to the Teacher: How America's Educators Became Militant* (Bloomington: Indiana University Press, 1976).

strong anticommunist rhetoric. While not identified directly with McCarthyism, Nixon was a caustic critic of what he labelled the Truman "sell-out" of Chiang Kai-shek's Nationalist China to communism. By the time of his presidency, Nixon viewed world relations in terms of great-power politics rather than in terms of the moral issues of good and evil.

Nixon's chief advisor on foreign affairs, Henry A. Kissinger, a Harvard professor and recognized expert on foreign policy, like the president, saw international relations in realistic rather than idealistic terms.[4] International relations, for Kissinger, represented the efforts of nations to maintain their vital interests through diplomacy and stratagem. For Kissinger, the goal of American foreign policy was to manage and control the rivalries between nations for the advantage of the United States rather than to pursue an ideological struggle against world communism.

Ending the Vietnam War

For Nixon and Kissinger, the key to achieving their foreign policy objectives as well as to ending the intense domestic conflicts that had wracked the previous Johnson administration was to find a way out of Vietnam. The administration's strategy was to step up the bombing of North Vietnam while gradually reducing the number of American ground troops in South Vietnam. To alleviate pressure on the faltering South Vietnamese army, Nixon, in April 1970, ordered the bombing of communist supply lines in Cambodia, which was accompanied by an invasion of United States army units. The American incursion into Camboida dramatically revived the antiwar demonstrations that had shown signs of subsiding. Once again, large antiwar demonstrations erupted on college and university campuses (see pp. 304-307.)

After protracted negotiations with North Vietnamese representatives, Kissinger succeeded in negotiating the American disengagement from Vietnam in 1973. The withdrawal of American forces after eight years of combat left South Vietnam to the North Vietnamese, who occupied and forcefully united that country under communist rule. With the United States finally free of its long ordeal in Southeast Asia, the student antiwar protests ended.

Watergate

In the election of 1972, Nixon scored an impressive landslide victory over Senator George S. McGovern, the Democratic candidate; garnering over 60 percent of the popular vote, Nixon carried every state except Massachusetts. Despite Nixon's overwhelming victory, certain individuals associated with the Committee to Reelect the President maneuvered to harass and spy on opposition candidates. Their efforts involved breaking into the Democratic national headquarters, located in the Watergate apartment complex in Washington, D.C. The arrest of those who

[4] For a commentary on Kissinger, see Marvin Kalb and Bernard Kalb, *Kissinger* (Boston: Little, Brown, 1974.

perpetrated this illegal entry precipitated a national crisis of constitutional proportions that led eventually to Nixon's resignation as president.

Senate investigations of the Watergate affair, led by North Carolina's Senator Sam Erwin, revealed that the president and key members of his staff were implicated in obstructing justice by attempting to cover-up the investigation of the break-in. The House Judiciary Committee, charging Nixon with obstruction of justice, abuse of power, and contempt of Congress, voted to impeach the president, who resigned on August 9, 1974.[5]

The hearings of the Erwin committee, televised nationally, produced shock waves that reverberated across the nation. In an indirect way, they stimulated a searching inquiry into the condition of the American polity and of the ethics of those entrusted to positions of leadership. Several members of Nixon's staff who were implicated in the Watergate scandal were well-trained and skilled administrators and managers but appeared to be lacking in ethical sensibilities. Watergate stimulated not only a national examination of the nation's political conscience but a revival of civic education. While the revival of civic education was not as dramatic as the Cold War response to *Sputnik*, it did focus attention on the schools' role in preparing citizens for life and participation in a democratic society.[6]

SOCIETY AND EDUCATION IN ECONOMIC TRANSITION

The 1970s, a decade of social and economic transition, worked to change the character of American life and the expectations of the American people. The causes of this transition had been produced by international forces so complex and interrelated that it appeared that the national destiny was subject to forces beyond the control of domestic planning and policies. Let us look more closely at this profound transition.

The Energy Crisis and Inflation

On October 6, 1973, Syria and Egypt launched a military attack against Israel. After initial Egyptian and Syrian successes, the Israelis were able to stem the tide and push their adversaries back into their own territories. Henry Kissinger, now secretary of state, sought to play a Bismarckian role as an "honest broker," in arranging a diplomatic settlement of the Near Eastern conflict. Although the fighting ended in late October, Arab members of the Organizaion of Petroleum Exporting Countries (OPEC) cut off oil shipments to the United States in retalia-

[5] For accounts of Watergate, see Leon Jaworski, *The Right and the Power* (New York: Reader's Digest Press, 1976); and John W. Dean, *Blind Ambition* (New York: Simon & Schuster, 1976).

[6] A thorough treatment of civic education can be found in R. Freeman Butts, *The Revival of Civic Learning: A Rationale for Citizenship Education in American Schools* (Bloomington, Ind.: Phi Delta Kappa Educational Foundation, 1980); also, see James P. Shaver, ed., *Building Rationales for Citizenship Education* (Arlington, Va.: National Council for the Social Studies, 1976).

tion for American support of Israel. The embargo had a direct effect on the American economy and became known as the "energy crisis."

The oil embargo produced dramatic and immediate effects on the American economy as well as long-term social and psychological consequences for the nation. The oil embargo and the resulting energy crisis revealed the growing interdependenccy of the world economy. A series of events in the Middle East had immediate consequences for American motorists and long-range significance for the American economy.[7]

In 1973, at the time of the oil embargo, the United States was importing one-third of its needed petroleum consumption requirements. Gasoline shortages developed, and long lines formed at service stations as motorists sought to keep the tanks of their automobiles full. As the United States and other petroleum-importing nations purchased crude oil from other sources, the cost of oil rose dramatically. Within a few weeks of the Arab oil embargo, gasoline and home heating fuel prices more than doubled. March 1973 brought the end of the Arab oil embargo, but the energy crisis and its effects on the U.S. economy remained.

The energy crisis had several educational consequences: (1) Federal policies were developed to both educate Americans about the crisis and to reduce America's reliance on imported oil. (2) Educators began to talk about "energy education" and "energy conservation programs" designed to inform young people of the realities of the energy scarcity. (3) In a very practical way, educational administrators sought to make teachers and students "energy conscious" and to effect energy savings in heating and insulating school buildings.

Throughout the 1970s, the energy crisis and the increasing costs of oil and other petroleum products, especially gasoline, had a significant impact on the nation's economy. Dramatically increasing energy costs aggravated a rampant inflation that was marked by high interest rates and a slowing of economic growth. Simultaneously with inflation, a series of recessions produced rising unemployment. The administrations of Gerald Ford, who succeeded Nixon as president, and Jimmy Carter, who was elected in 1976, were unable to deal effectively with the two-pronged economic problems of inflation and recession.

Inflation.   The inflationary decade of the 1970s was marked by rapidly escalating living costs and larger federal budget deficits. In particular, increased energy costs had an interlocking effect on other areas such as transportation, manufacturing, and farming. Between 1970 and 1980, prices rose at an unprecedented rate. For example, the price of automobiles increased 70 percent, home construction by 60 percent, and many food items doubled in cost. Although they were increasing, wages fell behind the rising cost of living; the real income of wage earners—measured in purchasing power—actually declined. The Federal Reserve Board, chaired by Paul Volcker, struggled to curb inflation by reducing the supply

[7]Treatments of the energy crisis are Richard Barnet, *The Lean Years* (New York: Simon & Schuster, 1980); and Robert Stobaugh and Daniel Yergin, eds., *Energy Future* (New York: Ballantine Books, 1980).

of money in circulation. The result was a prime interest rate that reached 20 percent by 1980.

The Consequences for Education.   The rising cost of energy and incessant inflation slowed the rate of economic growth during the decade, with the GNP for the 1970s registering only 3.2 percent, as contrasted to 3.7 percent for the 1960s. American corporations lost their supremacy in world trade to Japanese, West German, and other competitors. *The Nation at Risk*, a major national report on the condition of American education, partly attributed the decline of American economic productivity to an erosion in the quality of American education. Claiming that the world economic preeminence of the United States was no longer secure, *The Nation at Risk* stated:

> The risk is not only that the Japanese make automobiles more efficiently than Americans and have government subsidies for development and export. It is not just that the South Koreans recently built the world's most efficient steel mill, or that American machine tools, once the pride of the world, are being displaced by German products. It is also that these developments signify a redistribution of trained capability throughout the globe. Knowledge, learning, information, and skilled intelligence are the new raw materials of international commerce and are today spreading throughout the world as vigorously as miracle drugs, synthetic fertilizers, and blue jeans did earlier. If only to keep and improve on the slim competitive edge we still retain in world markets, we must dedicate ourselves to the reform of our educational system for the benefit of all—old and young alike, affluent and poor, majority and minority. Learning is the indispensable investment required for success in the "information age" we are entering.[8]

Specifically, the economic changes of the 1970s were most severe for heavy industries such as iron and steel, mining, and automobile manufacturing. In particular, the steel mills of the Northeast and Middle West, once the world's most productive industries, now grown obsolete, succumbed to the more efficient international competitors, idling thousands of American workers, many of whom were permanently displaced. As the 1970s ended, imported automobiles had captured almost one-fifth of the American domestic market. While older traditional industries were suffering from foreign competition, some corporations, by concentrating on the research, development, and sale of high-technology products such as computers, electronic items, and robotics, gained new markets in what was called the "information age."

The emergence of the information age of the 1970s, with its emphasis on high technology, computers, and electronics, signalled momentous changes for American society and education. First, it raised concerns that the curricula of American schools were suffering from an obsolescence similar to that which beset many traditional older industries. This obsolescence was espcially pronounced in two

---

[8] The National Commission on Excellence in Education, *A Nation at Risk: The Imperative for Educational Reform* (Washington, D.C.: GPO, 1983), pp. 6-7.

areas: (1) a weakness in basic intellectual skills that prevented many students from learning the new skills for computer-assisted information systems, and (2) ineffective vocational, clerical, and service-oriented educational programs. Several of the national reports on education appearing in the 1980s called for more rigorous standards in basic intellectual skill building. For example, *Action for Excellence,* by the Task Force on Education for Economic Growth of the Education Commission of the States, argued for an expansion and redefinition of basic skills beyond minimal competency in "reading, writing, mathematics, science, reasoning," and the use of computers to meet the demands of the "technologically sophisticated workplace" of the future.[9] The same report also urged "educational partnerships between businesses and schools" to improve the "skills and employability for millions of American young people."[10]

The economic and technological changes of the 1970s and 1980s focused attention on the basic sciences, mathematics, and technology. Most of the national commissions of the 1980s and their reports found that the general competencies of American students in science and mathematics had declined. *Educating for the 21st Century*, the report of the Commission on Precollege Education in Mathematics, Science, and Technology, appointed by the National Science Board and the National Science Foundation, warned that ". . . the quality of our manufactured products, the viability of our trade, our leadership in research and development, and our standards of living are being challenged."[11] According to the authors of the report:

> Prepared citizens (especially in science, mathematics, and technology as well as other basic academic and technical subjects) are required for the operation of the nation's essential industries and services, the ability of those industries to compete internationally and for military security.[12]

The Commission on Precollege Education called for raising state-mandated requirements in mathematics and science and requiring computer science. It also recommended federal assistance to improve the quality of mathematics and science education at all levels.

In addition to the economic changes that threatened America's position internationally, economically-caused demographic changes also altered population patterns in the United States during the 1970s. Many industries that had been located in the Northeastern and Midwestern states relocated to the Southern and Western Sunbelt states. The relocation of industries produced a migration of population to the Sunbelt, which in turn had serious consequences for schools. Northern

[9] Task Force on Education for Economic Growth, Education Commission of the States, *Action for Excellence* (Denver, Colo.: Education Commission of the States–A. B. Hirschfeld Press, 1983), p. 17.

[10] Ibid., p. 30.

[11] National Science Board, *Educating Americans for the 21st Century* (Washington, D.C.: National Science Foundation, 1983), p. v.

[12] Ibid., p. 65.

industrial states suffered a decline in tax revenues for public schools and a declining school-age population. Certain Southern and Western states experienced a need to expand their school facilities and to hire additional teachers.

As indicated, the population of the Northeastern and Midwestern states did not increase during the 1970s; in contrast, the Sunbelt states added population. For example, California, Texas, and Florida registered very large population gains. Other Southern and Western states such as Colorado, North Carolina, Arizona, and Georgia also experienced large population increases.

Especially hard hit by the migration to the Sunbelt were the large Northern cities whose central areas, the inner cities, were increasingly populated by low-income minority groups. Experiencing a declining tax base, the school systems of large cities faced severe financial pressures and deteriorating educational facilities and services.

THE FORD AND CARTER ADMINISTRATIONS

It was in the context of these major economic and demographic changes of the 1970s that Nixon's successors to the presidency, Gerald Ford and Jimmy Carter, attempted to chart the nation's course. When Nixon resigned as president due to his impeachment by Congress, he was succeeded in August by Gerald R. Ford, who had been appointed earlier to the vice-presidency. Ford faced myriad problems such as restoring confidence in the federal government, an incessant inflation, and continuing unemployment.[13] Generally conservative, Ford looked to free enterprise to remedy the country's economic problems. He sought to restore confidence in government and in the nation's faltering economy.

In the election of 1976, Ford, the Republican nominee, narrowly lost to Jimmy Carter, a former Georgia governor who was the Democratic candidate. Carter, enjoying the support of liberal, minority, and Southern voters, promised to heal the wounds caused by Watergate and to restore honesty to government. Carter's campaign theme emphasized "a government as good and as honest and as decent and as competent and as compassionate and as filled with love as are the American people."[14]

Although generally regarded as an intelligent and industrious president, Carter's administration appeared to lack a well-defined philosophy and sense of direction. Carter followed a moderate, middle-of-the-road course, avoiding extreme liberalism and conservatism.[15] Like Nixon and Ford, he grappled unsuccessfully with the nation's economic problems, especially inflation and federal budget deficits, the rates of which both continued their upward climb.

[13] Ford's own account of his efforts to restore confidence in the wake of Watergate is *A Time to Heal* (New York: Harper & Row, Pub., 1979).

[14] Michael G. Krokones, "The Campaign Promises of Jimmy Carter: Accomplishments and Failures," *Presidential Studies Quarterly*, 15, no. 1. (Winter 1985): 137.

[15] For Carter as president, see Haynes Johnson, *In the Absence of Power* (New York: Viking, 1980); and Jimmy Carter, *Keeping Faith* (New York: Bantam Books, 1982).

Carter enjoyed some limited successes in achieving his domestic goals. To deal with the energy problem, he established the Department of Energy in 1977. He also won approval of several initiatives aimed at improving the quality of the environment such as the Clean Air Act of 1977, control of strip mining, and efforts at land preservation.

An important success of the Carter administration was the creation of the Department of Education. Campaigning for president in 1976, Carter promised to create a department of education that would: coordinate federal educational initiatives by bringing the various programs under the direction of one agency, and raise educational issues to national prominence.[16] Carter's pledge to create a federal department of education had won him the endorsement of the National Education Association in 1976. Opponents of the new department charged that it would not only add to federal interference and bureaucracy but involve the national government in an area that properly belonged to state and local governments. Although introduced in 1978, the legislation to create the Department of Education was not enacted by Congress until 1979, when it passed after much debate by a narrow margin.

President Carter appointed Shirley Hufstedler, a judge of the U.S. Court of Appeals, as the first secretary of education. She served from May 1980 until

Shirley Hufstedler, Secretary of the Department of Education, 1980-1981. *(U.S. Department of Education Collection.)*

[16] Karen S. Gallagher, "The Department of Education: The Politics of Education under Carter and Reagan," unpublished manuscript.

January 1981 and was followed in office by Terrel H. Bell, who was appointed by President Reagan. Among Secretary Hufstedler's priorities for the new department were: (1) ensuring equal educational opportunities for all, (2) supporting state and local efforts for educational improvement, (3) promoting educational research and evaluation, (4) disseminating information about education, and (5) coordinating, managing, and accounting for federally supported education programs.[17] Much of Hufstedler's efforts were devoted to organizing and staffing the new department. President Carter's failure to win reelection in 1980 cut short Secretary Hufstedler's long-range goals.

In the area of racial integration and civil rights, Carter continued the efforts begun by earlier administrations. During his campaign in 1976, Carter had endorsed voluntary rather than mandatory busing to achieve racially integrated schools. Nevertheless, once in offfice, he supported federal efforts to achieve greater racial integration, vetoing a bill that would have prohibited the Justice Department from initiating lawsuits to require school districts to use busing for this purpose.[18]

In foreign affairs, Carter, rejecting the political "realism" of Nixon and Kissinger, pursued a policy that resembled Wilsonian idealism in its emphasis on humanitarian goals. Following moralistic guidelines, Carter reduced American assistance to authoritarian regimes and spoke out against foreign governments that violated human rights. For example, Carter ordered a U.S. boycott of the 1980 Olympic Games in Moscow because the Soviet Union had invaded Afghanistan. Under Carter's good offices, Prime Minister Begin of Israel and President Sadat of Egypt reached agreements at Camp David in 1978 that led to a peace treaty between the two nations.

U.S. Department of Education.

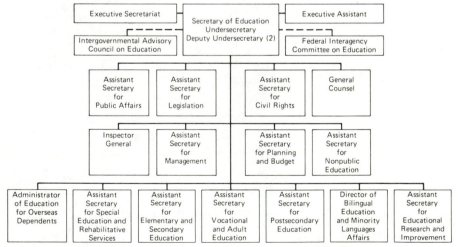

Published by the Office of Public Affairs, National Institute of Education, U.S. Department of Education

[17] Ibid.

[18] Krokones, "Campaign Promises," p. 140.

Continuing the policy of improving relations with mainland China that had begun with the Nixon administration, the Carter administration established full diplomatic relations with the People's Republic in 1979. Recognition of communist China not only increased trade between the two nations but also stimulated educational exchange. At first, only college and university presidents and heads of educational organizations were invited to tour schools, colleges, and universities in China. Later educational tours and traveling seminars involved larger numbers of American educators. Chinese educators also came to the United States to study the American educational system, particularly its scientific and technological components.

For both the Chinese and American governments, education as well as trade became important elements in improved relations. China, recovering from its diplomatic isolation and the disruptive consequences of Mao Tse-tung's Cultural Revolution, was seeking to modernize its industry and agriculture. American science and technology, as well as the education that sustained and developed them, would be important to China's modernization policy. As well as providing markets needed by the United States, a China no longer hostile to American interests would help improve the U.S. position in Asia. China, wary of Soviet intentions on her long northern border, also needed a United States that was no longer antagonistic to the Peking regime.

One of the most dramatic and severe tests of the Carter administration's foreign policy came in November 1979, when militant students in Iran, in the throes of a fundamentalist Islamic revolution led by Ayatollah Khomeini, seized the American embassy, holding fifty-eight Americans hostage. Despite diplomatic efforts and an abortive rescue attempt, Carter was unable to resolve the hostage crisis, which dragged on until late fall of 1980, when the hostages were released in the first days of the incoming Reagan administration.

Carter, who in the summer of 1979, talked about "a crisis of confidence" and a "national malaise" slowly lost the confidence of many voters. In the election of 1980, he was defeated by Ronald Reagan, the Republican candidate, who promised the electorate a "new beginning."

DEVELOPMENTS IN SPECIAL EDUCATION

While many of the major changes of the 1970s discussed earlier showed the United States and its educational institutions to be increasingly affected by alterations in the world economy and political structure, one important educational development—the national recognition of the educational rights of special learners—was unique to the American domestic situation. In some respects, developments in special education grew out of the larger civil rights movement of the 1960s. In other respects, however, the nation's attention to special education resulted from the efforts of parents' groups and special educators.

In the 1970s, the general public and political leaders, as well as professional educators, gave increased attention to special education. The civil rights movement and judicial decisions in the 1960s that fostered racial integration brought attention to the rights of people in other categories such as the handicapped, who had been denied equal educational opportunities. In schools, the segregation of children on the basis of race and handicap was sometimes interrelated.

While equal educational opportunities were a factor in raising national consciousness regarding the handicapped, the medical and psychological professions had developed new concepts relating to physiological and behavioral problems, which were translated into educational practice. Persons especially interested in the educational problems of the handicapped, such as parents, had organized strong advocacy groups to promote educational opportunities for handicapped children.

It was in this milieu of greater public awareness to the rights of handicapped persons that a District Court decision in 1971 ordered Pennsylvania school districts to educate all retarded learners between the ages of four and twenty-one. The concept of a "right to education" was expanded to include mentally and emotionally handicapped youngsters.

Congress enacted the Vocational Rehabilitation Act of 1973 and the Education of All Handicapped Children Act of 1975, which had far-reaching implications for America's schools. The federal legislation was designed to remove restrictions that had denied handicapped persons access to educational opportunities. The Vocational Rehabilitation Act provided for vocational training in mainstream settings, the promotion and expansion of employment opportunities, and the removal of architectural and transportation barriers. The act sought to encourage more handicapped individuals to enter the nation's workforce and to remove unnecessary obstacles to their hiring and in their working conditions.

By enacting the Education of All Handicapped Children Act (P.L. 94-142), Congress established a national policy that the nation's handicapped children between the ages of three and twenty-one would be assured an "appropriate public education," designed to meet their unique needs. P.L. 94-142 had far-reaching implications in that it directly affected the approximately eight million handicapped children in the United States. According to the law, handicapped children were identified as:

> mentally retarded, hard of hearing, seriously disturbed, orthopedically impaired, or children with specific learning disabilities, who by reason thereof require special education and related services.[19]

P.L. 94-142's mainstreaming provisions touched virtually every child, teacher, and school in the United States. Among its provisions were the following:

1. Each state was to identify and locate its handicapped children and provide a curriculum responsive to the needs of each child.

---

[19] The Education for All Handicapped Children Act of 1975 (P.L. 94-142), *Federal Register,* 42 (163), August 22, 1977.

2. Each state was to establish an advisory board—composed of handicapped individuals, teachers, and parents of handicapped children—to advise and comment on needs, regulations, and evaluative procedures.

3. Handicapped children were to be "mainstreamed," or educated whenever possible in the least restrictive environment, preferably a regular classroom, with nonhandicapped children. Handicapped children were to be placed in separate classes only when their exceptionality made it impossible to educate them in regular classrooms.

4. Due process provisions were to be observed to protect handicapped children against improper placement and to provide their parents or guardians with the right of access to pertinent records.

5. School personnel were to prepare an individualized educational plan (IEP) for each handicapped child. Each plan was to be developed by a team that included a school representative (usually the building principal), the teacher, and the child's parent or guardian. Whenever appropriate, the child was to be involved in designing her or his IEP.

6. Instruments and methods for testing and evaluating handicapped children were to be racially and culturally nondiscriminatory and in the child's primary language or "mode of communication."

7. Related transportation and developmental, corrective, and supportive services were to be provided to handicapped children. This included speech pathology, audiology, psychological seminars, physical and occupational therapy, recreation, counseling, and medical services needed for diagnosis and evaluative purposes.

8. If handicapped children could not be educated with other children, then they were to be educated in their homes, hospitals, or other institutions. Placement of children in private institutions was to occur without expense to parents or guardians.

9. If states failed to comply with the law, federal funds could be withheld after a reasonable notice and hearing.

10. If local school districts were unable or unwilling to comply with the law, the state was authorized to suspend payments to them. The state was then to use the funds to provide direct service to the children.

P.L. 94-142 brought momentous change to American public education. While most educators, as well as the public, agreed that handicapped persons should no longer be denied access to educational opportunities, the mainstreaming provisions required by the legislation caused apprehension among teachers who lacked skill in educating handicapped children. Much of this fear was alleviated by the efforts of the American Association of Colleges of Teacher Education (AACTE), which developed special teacher education programs that included "mainstreaming" awareness and procedures.[20]

Other concerns about P.L. 94-142 came from school boards and officials who, while they might agree with the law's intent, lacked sufficient funds to pro-

---

[20] Dean C. Corrigan and Kenneth R. Howey, eds., *Special Education in Transition: Concepts to Guide the Education of Experienced Teachers* (Reston, Va.: Council for Exceptional Children, 1980); see also *A Common Body of Practice for Teachers: The Challenge of Public Law 94-142 to Teacher Education* (Washington, D.C.: American Association of Colleges of Teacher Education, 1980).

vide required services. To avoid costly duplications of staff and services, local school districts joined in special education cooperatives that affiliated several districts into larger units. Another area of concern that remains unresolved was the fear of some educators that the detailed provisions of the law regarding the curricular programs for the handicapped child would bring the courts into the area of curriculum making and evaluation.

CONCLUSION

In many respects, the 1970s was a crucial decade, a transitional era that bridged the liberalism and social activism of the 1960s and the revived conservatism of the 1980s. The 1970s saw changing demographic patterns—a reaching of zero population growth and a population movement to the Sun belt—that had serious consequences for education, especially public schools. Declining enrollments and shrinking revenues caused a reduction in the teaching force in many school districts. A series of crises in foreign policy, energy, politics, and the economy worked to weaken the optimism that had marked the nation's entry into the 1960s.

DISCUSSION QUESTIONS

1. Describe the concept of revenue sharing and analyze its implications for educational funding.
2. Examine the impact of the economic inflation and recession of the 1970s on public schools and other educational agencies.
3. Analyze the impact of the demographic changes of the 1970s on schools.
4. What were the implications of Watergate for American civic education?
5. Analyze the energy crisis, and examine the rise of energy education.
6. Examine the concern about environmental quality and the rise of environmental and ecological education.
7. Compare and contrast the foreign policies of the Nixon and Carter administrations. Deduce and analyze the implications for international education.
8. Identify the key events related to education for the handicapped in the 1970s. Place these events in an historical perspective.

RESEARCH TOPICS

1. Read a biography of Richard Nixon. In a sketch, describe his education, the formative stages in his career, and his social and educational philosophy.
2. Analyze and describe the enrollment patterns in a local school district over the past twenty years.

3. Using oral history techniques, interview a local school administrator on the enrollment and revenue trends of the 1970s. Prepare a paper based on your research.

4. Using oral history techniques, interview a member of a teachers' organization or union (such as the American Federation of Teachers or the National Education Association) on issues, negotiations, and other related matters. Prepare a summary paper based on your research.

5. Read accounts of the Carter administration. Prepare a paper describing his social and political philosophy and its implications for education.

6. Research and describe the issues surrounding the establishment of the Department of Education in a short paper.

7. Using oral history techniques, interview an educator who has visited the People's Republic of China. Write a paper describing his or her impressions.

REFERENCES AND READINGS

Barnet, Richard. *The Lean Years.* New York: Simon & Schuster, 1980.

Brodie, Fawn. *Richard Nixon.* New York: W. W. Norton & Co., Inc., 1981.

Butts, R. Freeman. *The Revival of Civic Learning: A Rationale for Citizenship Education in American Schools.* Bloomington, Ind.,: Phi Delta Kappa Educational Foundations, 1980.

Carter, Jimmy. *Keeping Faith.* New York: Bantam Books, 1982.

Corrigan, Dean C., and Howey, Kenneth R., eds. *Special Education in Transition: Concepts to Guide the Education of Experienced Teachers.* Reston, Va.: Council for Exceptional Children, 1980.

Dean, John W. *Blind Ambition.* New York: Simon & Schuster, 1976.

Donley, Marshall O. *Power to the Teacher: How America's Educators Became Militant.* Bloomington: Indiana University Press, 1976.

Evans, Rowland, and Novak, Robert. *Nixon in the White House.* New York: Random House, 1971.

Ford, Gerald. *A Time to Heal.* New York: Harper & Row, Pub., 1979.

Jaworski, Leon. *The Right and the Power.* New York: Reader's Digest Press, 1976.

Johnson, Haynes. *In the Absence of Power.* New York: Viking, 1980.

Kalb, Marvin, and Kalb, Bernard. *Kissinger.* Boston: Little, Brown, 1974.

Kendrick, Alexander. *The Wound Within.* Boston: Little, Brown, 1974.

Mazo, Earl, and Hess, Stephen. *Nixon.* New York: Harper & Row, Pub., 1968.

National Science Board. *Educating Americans for the 21st Century.* Washington, D.C.: National Science Foundation, 1983.

Nixon, Richard. *RN.* New York: Grosset & Dunlap, 1978.

Perry, Charles R., and Wildman, Wesley A. *The Impact of Negotiations in Public Education: The Evidence from the Schools.* Worthington, Ohio: Charles A. Jones, 1970.

Shaver, James P., ed. *Building Rationales for Citizenship Education.* Arlington, Va.: National Council for the Social Studies, 1976.

Stobaugh, Robert, and Yergin, Daniel, eds. *Energy Future.* New York: Ballantine, 1980.

14
SOCIETY
AND EDUCATION
IN THE 1980s

The 1980s did not mark a radical change from the problems that American society and education had faced in the 1970s. Inflation, unemployment, and massive federal budget deficits continued to gnaw at the national psyche. The decade witnessed a resurgence of conservatism both in politics and in education. The conservative political ideology of the Reagan administration was applied to the nation's economy, social outlook, foreign policy, and educational philosophy. The back-to-the-basics theme, which had gathered momentum at the local and state levels of education throughout the 1970s, found national expression in the educational policies and politics of the Reagan administration. A feature of the 1980s was the myriad reports on education that expressed alarm over the declining quality of American education and urged reforms to restore rigorous academic standards.

THE REAGAN ADMINISTRATION

Ronald Reagan's victory over Jimmy Carter in 1980 and his reelection in 1984 over Walter Mondale, the Democratic nominee, signalled national triumphs for a resurgent political conservatism. A former sportscaster, movie actor, and television host, and two-term governor of California, Reagan proved to be an excellent campaigner and communicator. He won his victories by promising to restore old-fashioned values, reduce the role of government, and regain America's preeminence as a major world power.

During his first term in office, Reagan sought to reduce the inflation rates that had spiraled upward during the previous Carter administration. "Reaganomics," as the administration's economic policy was called, involved severe reductions in federal spending for social and educational programs, and lowering taxes to stimulate private investment and to increase industrial productivity. Following the president's prodding to reduce spending, Congress cut $35 billion in 1981 from federal programs, primarily in social welfare and education programs. While cutting spending for social programs, Reagan was determined to increase military appropriations. Military spending increased from $165 billion to $200 billion.

Reagan's economic policy led to huge federal deficits. In 1982 a major recession occurred, with unemployment rates reaching 10 percent. Reagan, however, adhered to his economic policy, and the rate of inflation slowly fell to less than 7 percent in 1982. By late 1983, the rate of unemployment was also decreasing. However, it remained high in heavy-industry sectors in some Northern states and among minorities, especially young blacks.

Although Reagan had promised in 1980 to end the existence of the newly created Department of Education, he did not take that expected action. Terrel H. Bell, secretary of education in the Reagan cabinet, astutely made education a major priority of the Reagan administration. At the same time that the Reagan adminis-

Terrell H. Bell, Secretary of the Departent of Education, 1981-1985. *(U.S. Department of Education Collection.)*

tration reduced federal spending for education, Bell succeeded in focusing national attention on the quality of American elementary and secondary schools, primarily through *The Nation at Risk*, the report of the National Commission on Excellence in Educaion, which he had appointed.

Unlike the liberal Kennedy-Johnson administrations of the 1960s, the Reagan administration developed a conservative strategy and policy on education. Along with other social programs, federal spending on education was also reduced. Under Bell, the federal role became that of stimulating educational reform in the various states and of disseminating information about successful state and local programs. Taking a basic education posture, the Reagan administration endorsed the Commission on Excellence's call for a return to the basic subjects. Reagan himself urged a return to old-fashioned discipline and values and prayer in the schools. As with his economic, defense, and foreign policies, Reagan remained consistent to his conservative ideological principles on education. When Bell resigned as secretary of education in 1984 to become a professor of school administration at the University of Utah, Reagan nominated William J. Bennett, the chairman of the National Endowment for Humanities, as Bell's successor as the third secretary of education. Bennett, a conservative, was expected to pursue a basic education posture.

THE EDUCATION REPORTS OF THE 1980s

The early 1980s saw the issuing of many reports that examined "the crisis in American education." The various reports analyzed what was wrong with American education and then made a series of broad recommendations to remediate the deficiencies. Although it is difficult to assess what long-term impact the reports will have on education, it is possible to provide a background context for them and to analyze their salient features.

The Background of the Reports

Throughout the 1970s there had been a concerted movement for "basic education" that had originated with citizen's groups, politicians, and other non-professional sources. In some regions of the country, professional educators had endorsed and implemented a basic education approach. For example, Samuel A. Owen, superintendent of the Greensville County schools in Virginia, had inaugurated a program that rejected age-based social promotion and required that students demonstrate mastery of basic academic skills before being assigned to the next higher grade. The Greensville program had attracted national attention as had similar efforts in scattered school districts around the nation.[1] For the most part, however, professional educators had ignored or been opposed to the basic education movement.

[1] Samuel A. Owen and Deborah L. Ranick, "The Greensville Program: A Commonsense Approach to Basics," *Phi Delta Kappan* (March 1977), pp. 531-33; also see "Goodbye to the Rubber Diploma," *Time* (Sept. 26, 1977), pp. 46-47.

In analyzing the rise of the basic education movement in the 1970s, the educational historian Diane Ravitch noted the presence of a generalized public apprehension that the quality and standards of American education had deteriorated because of a deemphasis of basic skills and academic subject matter in the curriculum, and the use of social promotion to advance students rather than demonstrated mastery of academic skills and subjects. Ravitch herself recommended a basic education orientation resting on a foundation of the liberal arts and science.[2]

Although the basic education movement of the 1970s had been amorphous and lacked a clearly articulated philosophy, its various spokespersons had compiled a list of criticisms about the condition of American education that anticipated the reports of the 1980s. Among the criticisms were the following:

1. An overemphasis on educational experimentation, the use of social promotion, and the neglect of rigorous academic standards had caused a deterioration in the quality of American education.
2. Schools had done little to correct the general decline in the fundamental moral, ethical, and civic values that was taking place in the United States.
3. The quality of instruction had deteriorated because of the introduction of innovative practices and the employment of poorly prepared teachers.
4. American schools had become overly bureaucratic and expensive; noninstructional costs were to be reduced by concentrating on basic academic needs rather than nonacademic frills.
5. Student achievement had been measured imprecisely; achievement tests that measured academic mastery of basic skills and subjects were to be used for promotion.[3]

A Reexamination of American Secondary Education

In addition to basic education, another educational element was present in the early 1980s: a reexamination of the purposes, structure, organization, curriculum, and outcomes of American secondary education. Periodically, the American high schools have experienced such national scrutiny. For example, the Committee of Ten in 1873, the Commission on the Reorganization of Secondary Education in 1918, and the Conant report of 1959 were national examinations of secondary education that led to significant reshaping of the high school curriculum. Among the reports of the 1980s that scrutinized the condition of American secondary education were:

High School: A Report on Secondary Education in America, sponsored by the Carnegie Foundation for the Advancement of Teaching.

Horace's Compromise: The Dilemma of the American High School, cosponsored by the National Association of Secondary School Principals and

[2] Diane Ravitch, "Why Basic Education?" paper presented at the Conference on Basic Education, Council of Basic Education (Portland, Oregon, April 27, 1978).

[3] Gerald L. Gutek, *Basic Education: A Historical Perspective* (Bloomington, Ind.: Phi Delta Kappa Educational Foundation, 1981), pp. 9-13.

the Commission on Educational Issues on the National Association of Independent Schools.

Academic Preparation for College: What Students Need to Know and Be Able to Do, sponsored by the College Board.[4]

Socioeconomic Changes

The educational reports of the early 1980s were issued within a climate of opinion that was comprised of various social, economic, and cultural strands. Often for varied reasons, certain segments of the American people were critical of the conditions of American education and wanted reforms in the nation's schools. Since World War II, especially in the 1960s, some fundamental alterations had occurred in the social institutions and values of American society. Some Americans, primarily young people, had questioned—and rejected—traditional civic and ethical values and sexual mores. Family structures were changing as divorce rates and the number of single-parent families increased. The 1960s and 1970s saw the rise of the drug culture and increasing violence and vandalism not only in schools but in the general society. These momentous social changes and problems were anxiety producing for many Americans. Some critics blamed public schools for being overly permissive. For such critics, the answer to a disquieting and anxiety-producing social change was a restoration of rigorous discipline, teacher-centered authority, and the teaching of clearly defined civic and ethical standards, often patriotic and religious in nature, to reverse the tide and restore traditional values.

More specific than the pervasive social change but still grossly generalized was the attitude that schools were responsible, at least in part, for the economic problems plaguing the United States since the 1970s. Critics from the business community charged that many graduates of American schools lacked the fundamental skills needed for efficiency in the workplace of the 1980s. The success of foreign competitors, especially the West Germans and Japanese, was attributed to the superiority of the educational systems in those countries, while declining American productivity was attributed to the failure of American schools to develop competently trained individuals who possessed the creativity and sense of discipline demanded in a highly competitive world economy.

The Educational Politics and Policies
of the Reagan Administration

Still another key element in the climate of opinion of the early 1980s were the educational politics and policies of Ronald Reagan and Terrel Bell. The Reagan-Bell educational policies were designed to: (1) focus national attention on the need

[4] For the reports on secondary education, see Ernest L. Boyer, *High School: A Report on Secondary Education in America* (New York: Harper & Row, Pub., 1983); Theodore R. Sizer, *Horace's Compromise: The Dilemma of the American High School* (Boston: Houghton Mifflin, 1984); College Board, *Academic Preparation for College: What Students Need to Know and Be Able to Do* (New York: College Board, 1983); "The High School at the Crossroads," *Educational Leadership,* 41, no. 6 (March 1984).

for educational reform, (2) reduce federal spending for education, (3) encourage state and local educational reforms and initiatives, and (4) use the presidency and the Department of Education as a bully pulpit to emphasize basic education, merit pay for teachers, and the restoration of traditional values in the schools.

President Reagan's educational assumptions rested on the premise that American schools "need a few fundamental reforms" rather than "vast new sums of money. . . ." Among the needed reforms were:

1. restoration of "good old-fashioned discipline";
2. ending drug and alcohol abuse by children and youth;
3. raising academic standards and expectations;
4. encouraging good teaching by paying and promoting teachers on "the basis of their competence and merit";
5. revitalizing the educational role of parents and local and state governments; and
6. emphasizing basic academic skills and subjects.[5]

A key event in initiating the debates over educational reform in the early 1980s was the issuance of *A Nation at Risk* by the National Commission on Excellence in Education, which was appointed by Secretary Bell. The sections that follow examine several of the national reports on education that appeared in the early 1980s.

A NATION AT RISK

In April 1983, *A Nation at Risk: The Imperative for Educational Reform*, the report of the National Commission on Excellence, chaired by Daniel P. Gardner, president of the University of California, appeared. Finding the United States to be "at risk," the report stated:

> . . . the educational foundations of our society are presently being eroded by a rising tide of mediocrity that threatens our very future as a nation and a people.
>
> If an unfriendly foreign power had attempted to impose on America the mediocre educational performance that exists today, we might well have viewed it as an act of war. As it stands, we have allowed this to happen to ourselves. We have even squandered the gains in student achievement made in the wake of the *Sputnik* challenge. Moreover, we have dismantled essential support systems which helped make those gains possible. We have, in effect, been committing an act of unthinking, unilateral disarmament.[6]

[5] Ronald Reagan, "Excellence and Opportunity: A Program of Support for American Education," *Phi Delta Kappan,* 66, no. 1 (September 1984): 13-15.

[6] Washington, D.C.: GPO, 1983, p. 5.

The dramatic and direct prose of *A Nation at Risk* attracted national attention and stirred national debate over the condition of American schools. Like the essentialists of the 1930s and the critics of the 1950s, the authors of the report, in comparing American educational achievement to that of other nations, particularly West Germany and Japan, found American performance to be inferior. Among the indicators of risk identified by the commission were:

1. A high rate of functional illiteracy among young people and adults: 13 percent of all 17-year-olds, 23 million adults, and 40 percent of minority youth.
2. An "unbroken" decline in performance of American students from 1963 to 1980 on the College Board's Scholastic Aptitude Tests (SATs) and consistent declines in English, mathematics, and science.
3. The need of colleges to establish remedial mathematics courses and complaints by business and military leaders "that they are required to spend millions of dollars on costly remedial education and training programs in such basic skills as reading, writing, spelling and computation."[7]

The commission issued a series of recommendations on curriculum reform, the use of institutional time, and teacher effectiveness. Among its recommendations were:

... that state and local high school graduation requirements be strengthened and that, at a minimum, all students seeking a diploma be required to lay the foundations in the Five New Basics by taking the following curriculum during their four years of high school: (1) 4 years of English; (2) 3 years of mathe-

Members of the National Commission on Excellence in Education. *(U.S. Department of Education Collection.)*

[7]Ibid., pp. 8-9.

matics; (3) 3 years of science; (4) 3 years of social studies; and (5) one-half year of computer science. For the college bound, 2 years of foreign language in high school are strongly recommended in addition to those taken earlier.

. . . that schools, colleges, and universities adopt more rigorous and measurable standards, and higher expectations, for academic performance and student conduct, and that 4-year colleges and universities raise their requirements for admission. This will help students do their best educationally with challenging materials in an environment that supports learning and authentic accomplishment.

. . . that significantly more time be devoted to learning the New Basics. This will require more effective use of the existing school day, a longer school day, or a lengthened school year.

. . . that citizens across the nation hold educators and elected officials responsible for providing the leadership necessary to achieve these reforms, and that citizens provide the fiscal support and stability required to bring about the reforms we propose.[8]

The commission's recommendation for improving teacher effectiveness was more extensive than its other recommendations. It recommended: (1) that standards for admission to teacher education programs be raised and that prospective teachers demonstrate aptitude for teaching and competence in an academic discipline; (2) that teachers' salaries be raised but that increases be based on effective evaluation of performance; (3) that school boards adopt an eleven-month contract for teachers; (4) that career ladders be established for teachers that distinguish between beginning, experienced, and master teachers; (5) that efforts be made to solve teacher shortages in mathematics and science by using nonschool personnel; (6) that financial incentives such as loans and grants be used to attract students to teaching; and (7) that master teachers have a role in designing teacher education programs and in supervising teachers during probationary service.

A Nation at Risk attracted national attention, especially in the media. Secretary Bell devised a strategy that kept the report before the public. A series of twelve regional meetings, followed by a national forum, was conducted under the auspices of the Department of Education. These regional forums, attended by 10,000 public and private school educators, school board members, and political leaders, were designed to: (1) keep the report of the commission in the news, (2) stimulate implementation efforts at the state and local levels, (3) identify and disseminate models of operative reform efforts, and (4) define the role of the federal government as a stimulator and encourager of educational reform and as a disseminator of information but not as a source of federal funding.[9]

As the regional forums met throughout 1983, certain key issues emerged. As reported by Secretary Bell, these were:

---

[8] Ibid., pp. 23-31.

[9] T. H. Bell, *Report by the Secretary on the Regional Forums on Excellence in Education* (Washington, D.C.: U.S. Department of Education, 1983), p. 4.

1. improving the teaching profession by increasing teachers' salaries and status by merit pay and career ladders as alternatives to single salary schedules;
2. improving teacher preparation programs by modifying the contentional programs used by schools of education;
3. improving standards by raising high school graduation and college admission requirements and increasing the length of the school day and school year; and
4. encouraging new partnerships between business and schools to improve the quality of education.[10]

An important element in Bell's strategy to use the federal government as a pulpit for educational change but not as a funding source was the effort to publicize "model programs" that were compatible with the administration's general direction.[11]

Critics of *A Nation at Risk*

The direction and context of the national commission's reform efforts drew fire from teachers' organizations and some educational groups who believed that teachers were being made scapegoats for national problems, the solutions of which were beyond the capability of schools to resolve, and that severe reductions in and the elimination of programs by the Reagan administration had imperiled American education, especially the efforts at equality of educational opportunity for women, minority groups, and the handicapped.

The National Education Association cited a number of achievements that had advanced equality of educational opportunity. For example:

1. As of 1979, 85 percent of white students and 75 percent of black students were earning high school diplomas—three times the percentage of 1949.
2. The median educational level of blacks had increased "from eighth grade in 1960 to twelfth grade in 1980."
3. Black students had improved "reading, writing, and arithmetic skills" and "the gap between blacks and whites on standardized test scores" had been reduced.

In addition, the NEA pointed out that disadvantaged children in federally aided programs had made significant gains in reading and mathematics achievement and that bilingual education had given "millions of youngsters an equal chance to learn and participate in American society." Further, Title IX, prohibiting sex discrimination in education, had dramatically increased women's educational opportunities. The NEA, then, charged that these gains were being jeopardized by the "serious erosion" of the national commitment "to quality and equality."[12] Specifically, the

---

[10] Ibid., pp. 9-19.

[11] Staff of the National Commission on Excellence in Education, *Meeting the Challenge: Recent Efforts to Improve Education Across the Nation* (Washington, D.C.: U.S. Department of Education, 1983).

[12] National Education Association, *Teachers' Views on Equity and Excellence* (Washington, D,C.: National Education Association, 1983), pp. 3-4.

NEA pointed to policies of the Reagan administration "to relax requirements that schools receiving federal funds must comply with antidiscrimination statutes" and to drop "750,000 children" from Chapter 1 programs designed to improve the education of disadvantaged children. Condemning efforts to cut bilingual programs, programs for the handicapped, and to eliminate the Women's Educational Equity Act Program, the NEA warned against a misguided desire to "return to the McGuffey's Reader or to the curricula we used 20 years ago. . . ."[13]

Generally suspicious of the proposals for merit pay and career ladders, the NEA countered by proposing its own recommendations for improving teaching, which included:

1. improving the conditions of learning by reducing class size and improving the quality of educational materials;
2. attracting and retaining talented teachers by "competitive entry-level salaries" and "rewards for competence" that did not "selectively raise the pay for a few teachers at the expense of many";
3. transforming the traditional role of teachers by including them "in decision— making about teaching and learning" and reducing their noninstructional tasks;
4. establishing constructive and comprehensive teacher evaluation systems;
5. creating more opportunities for professional growth and development designed by professional educators and supported by school districts; and
6. improving teacher education programs according to standards that teachers "believe are basic to success in the classroom."[14]

The American Federation of Teachers (AFT) responded to the issues generated by *A Nation at Risk* with a series of papers that defined the specific issues, identified the controversies, and then stated its own position.[15] Although not rejecting proposals to lengthen the school day and school year, the AFT emphasized more effective use of the time currently allotted. It suggested that increased homework assignments and curricular and institutional improvements were more cost-effective means of instructional improvement than lengthening the school day or year.

Again, while expressing willingness to discuss merit pay for teachers and career ladders, the AFT emphasized a broader set of recommendations on the issue of quality teacher recruitment and retention: (1) general across-the-board salary increases for teachers, (2) more rigorous teacher certification requirements, (3) improved objective methods of teacher evaluation, (4) improved school discipline procedures, (5) greater teacher input and collegiality in designing approaches to staff development and, (6) improved teaching-learning conditions and smaller class

[13] Ibid., pp. 4-6.

[14] National Education Association, *The Teaching Profession* (Washington, D.C.: National Education Association, 1983), pp. 2-6.

[15] "Length of School Day and School Year," "Incentive Schemes and Pay Compensation Plans," "Teacher Recruitment and Early Career Incentives," "Teacher Preparation and Certification," "Standards, Curriculum, and Testing," "Elementary and Secondary Teacher Evaluation," "School Improvement" (Washington, D.C.: American Federation of Teachers, 1983).

size. The AFT also endorsed a reform of teacher education and certification that emphasized higher admission standards and rigorous inquiry-based professional curricula, with greater attention to liberal arts and sciences, written entry examinations, and an extended internship prior to certification.

In terms of curriculum change, the AFT policy on educational reform that was adopted at its 1983 convention called for "stricter high school graduation requirements in academic subjects including math, science, English, history, and foreign languages, though not at the expense of other essentials like music, art, and vocational education."[16]

ACTION FOR EXCELLENCE

Action for Excellence, the report of the Task Force on Education for Economic Growth, was issued in 1983.[17] Sponsored by the Education Commission of the States, the task force, chaired by James B. Hunt, Jr., governor of North Carolina, was a prestigious panel that included thirteen governors, fourteen business leaders from major corporations, as well as educators and other organizational leaders. Motivated by concerns like those of the Commission on Excellence in Education, the task force was particularly concerned with declining U.S. economic growth and productivity in the face of growing international competition. Part of its agenda was to encourage a "partnership" between businesses and schools to make American schooling more effective and responsive to economic needs. In defining the challenge facing American education, the task force stated that "technological change and global competition make it imperative to equip students in public schools with skills that go beyond the basics."[18]

For the authors of *Action for Excellence*, the American educational system had been weakened by lowering standards, educational deficits, and "blurred goals," with the result that other nations, especially Japan and West Germany, were challenging America's position as a scientific and technological leader. A consequence   the declining economic role of the United States was structural unemployment stemming from industrial obsolescence. To regain America's threatened technological supremacy, the task force identified two imperatives: expanding and upgrading the definition of basic skills beyond reading, writing, and arithmetic; and mobilizing the educational system to teach the required new skills effectively.

In analyzing the causes of America's educational crisis, the task force, like the Commission on Excellence, catalogued a list of problem areas, such as:

1. problems in student achievement, such as inadequate reading, writing, comprehension, and mathematics skills;

[16] "Length of School Day and School Year," p. 2.

[17] Denver: Education Commission of the States, 1983.

[18] Ibid., p. 9.

2. serious educational deficits in mathematics and science, the specific areas most closely related to technological progress, manifested by "a lack of general scientific and mathematical literacy" and by projected shortages of skilled scientists and engineers; this educational deficit was aggravated by a science curriculum suffering from obsolescence;

3. a "teacher gap," resulting in a shortage of "qualified teachers in critical subjects" such as mathematics and science; and

4. a low salary scale, in which teachers were paid according to "rigid salary schedules" rather than a "system for rewarding exceptional teachers for their superior performance."[19]

After identifying the problems facing American education, the task force developed an action plan to improve the nation's educational quality.[20] Its chief recommendation was that the state governors, working with their legislators, boards of education, and business leaders, develop and implement an action plan to improve schools from kindergarten through grade twelve. Each state plan was to incorporate the objectives of preparing a "well-educated workforce" with the "changing skills" needed for economic growth. It was also "to establish alliances among community, business, labor, government, and education leaders to improve education" for "economic growth." The task force recommendation paralleled the strategies of the Commission on Excellence and Secretary Bell in that the state governor was to act as the chief agent of educational reform. Influenced by business interests, the task force related educational reform to economic growth.

The task force's second recommendation urged the creation of broad and effective partnerships, especially with business leaders, to improve schools. Such projected "partnerships between businesses and schools" were to: (1) encourage business leaders to share "their expertise in planning, budgeting, and management" with school administrators; (2) customize job-training efforts between businesses and schools; (3) train students and teachers in the skills, techniques, and equipment actually used in businesses. The *Action for Excellence* agenda revealed a major trend of the 1980s—that the nation's businesses were becoming involved in shaping educational policies. The theme of business-school partnership was stressed by the Reagan administration and by the various forums, conferences, and state plans for educational reform stimulated by *A Nation at Risk*.

The task force's third recommendation, the marshalling of resources essential for improving public schools, called upon local communities and states "to assign higher budget priority" to educational improvement and to make certain that existing resources were used more effectively and efficiently, or, in the task force's terminology, "selectively invested" to promote educational quality. Like *A Nation at Risk, Action for Excellence* failed to propose new revenue sources for the nation's public schools, especially those in economically hard-pressed urban areas.

In recommendation four, the task force dealt, as did other national reports, with the need to improve teacher recruitment, preparation, status, and salaries. It

[19] Ibid., pp. 22-30.
[20] Ibid., pp. 34-41.

endorsed the career ladder concept, by which responsibility, pay, and status would change as teachers advanced through various career stages.

The task force's fifth recommendation would make students' academic experience more intense and productive. Local school systems were advised to establish "firm, explicit, and demanding requirements concerning discipline, attendance, homework, grades, and other essentials of effective schooling." The academic rigor of the curriculum was to be strengthened and nonessential, academically "soft" courses eliminated. While the existing school day and year were to be used more effectively, efforts were encouraged to increase learning time by eliminating nonessential dimensions and lengthening the school year.

In its recommendation, the task force urged state boards of education to provide "quality assurance in education" by establishing objective systems to measure and reward teacher effectiveness and performance. While quality assurance evaluation would reward effective teachers, it was also to lead to the dismissal of those judged ineffective. Public school systems were advised to institute the "periodic testing of general achievement and specific skills" and colleges and universities were to "upgrade their entrance requirements."

Recommendation seven, improving leadership and management in the schools, repeated a much-emphasized theme of the 1980s that the school principal, as the chief instructional leader, was a key person in school reform.

The eighth recommendation called for the improved service of students who were now "unserved or underserved." Specifically, increased participation by women and minority students in mathematics and science courses and careers was stressed. Returning to a theme of the late 1950s, the task force called for the identification of academically gifted students and for the development of curricula sufficiently rigorous and enriching to challenge and develop their talents.

SECONDARY EDUCATION REPORTS

While the various national reports of the 1980s addressed the general condition of American education, particular attention was focused on secondary education. Ernest Boyer's *High School: A Report on Secondary Education in America* and Theodore Sizer's *Horace's Compromise* examined the high school.

High School: The Carnegie Foundation Report

In *High School: A Report on Secondary Education in America,* Ernest L. Boyer analyzed the condition of the high schools in the 1980s in a fashion resembling James B. Conant's monumental study of American secondary education in the 1950s.[21] Boyer, president of the Carnegie Foundation for the Advancement of

[21] The Carnegie Foundation for the Advancement of Teaching (New York: Harper & Row, Pub., 1983).

Teaching and former U.S. commissioner of education, in this study sponsored by the Carnegie Foundation, based his report on the findings of educators who visited and closely observed the administration, curriculum, instruction, teachers, and students of fifteen public high schools, regarded as representing a cross-section of American secondary education. Geographically dispersed, the schools varied in size, location, and socioeconomic mix.[22] The educators who conducted the field research for Boyer's study identified the following key issues for their inquiry and subsequent report: goals, curriculum, teachers, teaching and learning, technology, structure, leadership, relationships of schools to other institutions, and community support.[23]

Boyer found, like the Commission on Excellence in *A Nation at Risk* and the task force in *Action for Excellence*, that high schools, lacking a "clear and vital" vision of their mission, were unable to formulate "widely shared common purposes" or "educational priorities." To create a unifying sense of purpose, Boyer and his associates proposed four essential goals for American high schools designed to assist students to:

1. develop critical thinking and effective communication skills by mastering language;
2. "learn about themselves, the human heritage," and their "interdependent world" by means of a core curriculum resting on "consequential" and "common" human experiences;
3. prepare "for work and further education" through an elective program that develops "individual aptitudes and interests"; and
4. fulfill "social and civic obligations through school and community service."[24]

Core of Common Learning. Boyer proposed a secondary curriculum, referred to as the "core of common learning," consisting of 14½ academic units that were to be distributed as follows:

Language	5 units
(English composition, speech, literature, foreign languages, and the arts)	
History	2½ units
(American history, Western civilization, and non-Western studies)	
Civics	1 unit
(classical political ideas and the structure and functions of contemporary government)	
Science	2 units
(physical and biological)	
Mathematics	2 units
Technology and health	2 units
Seminar on work and independent projects	½ unit each

[22] Ibid., p. 111.

[23] Ibid., p. 7.

[24] Ibid., pp. 66-77.

Although his proposed curriculum was divided into separate courses, Boyer emphasized the need for commonly shared, interdisciplinary outcomes. Many of the interrelationships from the various courses were to be made by students in their senior independent research project dealing with a significant contemporary issue.[25] Critics of Boyer's proposed core curriculum contended that it reduced the comprehensive high school to a single-purpose college preparatory function and that it dismissed vocational preparation.[26]

Horace's Compromise: The Sizer Report

Like Boyer's *High School, Horace's Compromise*, the report of a study group on high schools headed by Theodore R. Sizer, focused on the condition of American secondary education.[27] Sizer, former headmaster of Phillips Academy and former dean of Harvard's Graduate School of Education, created a synthesis that encompassed the liberating tendencies of the 1960s with the emphasis on academic competency of the early 1980s. *Horace's Compromise* did not share the basic opinions of other national reports of the 1980s. Like Boyer's study, however, Sizer's investigation did employ intensive field study and observation of selected representative high schools. Sizer's team of educational researchers focused on a "triangle" of students, teachers, and curricula.[28] From the case studies of the high schools visited, Sizer developed the following general recommendations to improve American secondary education:

1. Too many high schools underestimated their students' potential by overemphasizing adolescent vulnerability and inexperience; they needed to respect their students by raising their expectations and standards of accountability.[29]
2. The awarding of the high school diploma should be based on the exhibition of an "agreed-on level of mastery" rather than on accumulated credits earned by covering a long list of unrelated subjects.[30]
3. Following the premise that "less is more," high school curricula and instruction should stress important concepts and modes of inquiry rather than extensively covering detailed information of isolated subjects.[31]

[25] Ibid., p. 117.

[26] Daniel Tanner, "The American High School at the Crossroads, *"Educational Leadership,* 41, no. 6 (March 1984): 11.

[27] Theodore R. Sizer, *Horace's Compromise: The Dilemma of the American High School* (Boston: Houghton Mifflin, 1984), is the first report from a study of high schools cosponsored by the National Asssociation of Secondary School Principals and the Commission on Educational Issues of the National Association of Independent Schools.

[28] Ibid., p. 5.

[29] Ibid., pp. 33-34.

[30] Ibid., pp. 33-34.

[31] Ibid., p. 89.

In contrast to many of the national reports of the 1980s, Sizer did not recommend a prescribed curriculum of mandated subjects to be studied for specific periods of time. Instead, Sizer rather asked three basic questions that high schools were to answer in terms of their graduates:

1. Are they capable of self-instruction that will enable them to "observe and analyze a situation or problem" by understanding, criticizing, rejecting, or accepting it?[32]
2. Are they decent persons?
3. Can they effectively use the principal modes of inquiry and observation represented by the major academic disciplines?

Instead of advocating the one best secondary school curriculum, Sizer relied on these focusing questions to suggest a model for organizing high schools into four large departments of inquiry and expression, mathematics and science, literature and the arts, and philosophy and history.

Sizer's model also identified spheres of learning designed to advance students' achievement. As a first sphere of learning, he recommended development of the intellectual skills of reading, writing, speaking, listening, measuring, estimating, calculating, and seeing as the "staples of all schooling," including that of high schools. These intellectual skills, according to Sizer, were to be taught by coaching, in which teachers constructively criticized students' work to improve their performance.[33]

In the acquisition of knowledge, the second sphere of learning, the chief pedagogical strategy was to be telling, or explaining by lecture, textbooks, films, and other means of transmitting knowledge. Students who lacked the essential "standards of literacy, numeracy, and civic understanding" should continue to work exclusively on these necessary intellectual skills. Using the premise that curricular choices depend on priorities, students, teachers, families, and communities were to follow their preferences. Subject matter should relate to, support, and develop skill learning. Furthermore, it should be connected to students' interests, lead to a destination, and be integrated with other learning, subjects, and experiences.

The development of understanding, or the stimulation of the powers of discrimination and judgment by provocative questioning, was Sizer's third sphere of learning. For effective questioning, small seminar discussions were identified as the appropriate pedagogical method and situation.[34]

Of all the reports of the 1980s, *Horace's Compromise* marked the greatest departure from the tendency to mandate more prescribed subjects in the curriculum. Sizer's recommendations were directed at raising expectations and achievement outcomes, but in a more flexible atmosphere.

[32] Ibid., p. 131.
[33] Ibid., p. 99.
[34] Ibid., pp. 109-19.

CONCLUSION

It is still too early to place *The Nation at Risk, Action for Excellence*, and the other national reports on education into a broad historical perspective. To do so requires sufficient time and perspective to determine the degree to which their recommendations have been implemented and to assess their impact upon the nation's schools. It is possible, however, to identify several trends that have appeared in the 1980s.

The roles of the federal, state, and local governments appear to be shifting. While basic alterations of a constitutional nature are unlikely in the educational responsibilities of these units of government, the state governors, legislatures, and offices of education are likely to become catalysts for educational reform in general and curricular change and funding increases in particular. The federal government, especially under the Reagan administration, is likely to continue to stimulate reform efforts, especially those reflecting a basic education philosophy, and to disseminate information about model programs at the local level. However, it is unlikely that federal funding will increase. There is a possibility that some additional funding, spurred by congressional initiatives, will be available for science and mathematics education.

The arena of educational reform efforts in the 1980s is likely to be at the state level. Governors will become the educational change agents as the issues of the 1980s are debated and acted upon. The following will receive attention: improvement of teachers' salaries either by general increments, career ladders, or merit pay; revised certification requirements for teachers, with more coursework required in the liberal arts and sciences, and subject area specialization a strong possibility; teacher examinations, both at entry and after the probationary period; and stronger curricular requirements in mathematics, science, English, history, and other academic subjects at the secondary level.

The American high school will also experience change, particularly in the area of curriculum, as a result of the reform efforts of the 1980s. Vocational programs and elective courses are likely to decrease; a greater emphasis on basic academic subjects such as mathematics, science, and English will occur in many states and will be reflected in college admission requirements.

In addition, the decades ahead will see the continuing impact of computers and other forms of educational technology upon the educational system. Computer literacy will take its place alongside the traditional skills of reading, writing, and arithmetic.

DISCUSSION QUESTIONS

1. Analyze the social and educational implications of the resurgent conservative ideology of the 1980s.
2. Identify the key elements in the social, political, and economic contexts of the various national reports of the early 1980s.

3. Identify and analyze the educational policies of President Reagan and Secretary of Education Bell.

4. Examine the response of the American Federation of Teachers and the National Education Association to the proposed educational reforms in the 1980s.

5. Analyze the criticisms of the business community regarding the quality of American public education in relationship to economic growth.

6. Identify the common features of 1980s proposals for secondary school reform.

RESEARCH TOPICS

1. Read *The Nation at Risk* and write a paper that analyzes its underlying educational philosophy.

2. Read and then compare and contrast the critiques and recommendations made by Ernest L. Boyer in *High School: A Report on Secondary Education in America* and by Theodore Sizer in *Horace's Compromise: The Dilemma of the American High School.*

3. Using comparative education books or articles, prepare a comparative paper on Japanese and American education, with special attention directed to the issues raised by the national reports of the 1980s.

4. After reviewing articles about educational reform in the popular press, write a summary article that describes the general tone of the media on that subject.

5. Research and analyze the positions of the National Education Association and the American Federation of Teachers on educational reform. In an essay, compare and contrast their positions.

6. Read and write a commentary that analyzes *Action for Excellence*, the report of the Task Force for Economic Growth.

REFERENCES AND READINGS

Bell, T. H. *Report by the Secretary on the Regional Forums on Excellence in Education.* Washington, D.C.: U.S. Department of Education, 1983.

Boyer, Ernest L. *High School: A Report on Secondary Education in America.* New York: Harper & Row, Pub., 1983.

College Board. *Academic Preparation for College: What Students Need to Know and Be Able to Do.* New York: College Board, 1983.

Coombs, Philip H. *The World Crisis in Education: The View from the Eighties.* New York: Oxford University Press, 1985.

Goodlad, John I. *A Place Called School: Propspects for the Future.* New York: McGraw-Hill, 1983.

Gutek, Gerald L. *Basic Education: A Historical Perspective.* Bloomington, Ind.: Phi Delta Kappa Educational Foundation, 1981.

National Commission on Excellence in Education. *A Nation at Risk: The Imperative for Educational Reform.* Washington, D.C.: GPO, 1983.

National Education Association. *The Teaching Profession.* Washington, D.C.: National Education Association, 1983.

____. *Teachers' Views on Equity and Excellence.* Washington, D.C.: National Education Association, 1983.

Roberts, Arthur D., and Cawelti, Gordan. *Redefining General Education in the American High School.* Alexandria, Va.: Association for Supervision and Curriculum Development, 1984.

Sizer, Theodore R. *Horace's Compromise: The Dilemma of the American High School.* Boston: Houghton Mifflin, 1984.

Staff of the National Commission on Excellence in Education. *Meeting the Challenge: Recent Efforts to Improve Education Across the Nation.* Washington, D.C.: U.S. Department of Education, 1983.

Task Force on Education for Economic Growth. *Action for Excellence.* Denver, Colo.: Education Commission of the States, 1983.

INDEX